S0-ARX-471

"THE SYSTEM"

PATTERSON SMITH REPRINT SERIES IN
CRIMINOLOGY, LAW ENFORCEMENT, AND SOCIAL PROBLEMS

1. Lewis: *The Development of American Prisons and Prison Customs, 1776-1845*
2. Carpenter: *Reformatory Prison Discipline*
3. Brace: *The Dangerous Classes of New York*
4. Dix: *Remarks on Prisons and Prison Discipline in the United States*
5. Bruce *et al: The Workings of the Indeterminate-Sentence Law and the Parole System in Illinois*
6. Wickersham Commission: *Complete Reports, Including the Mooney-Billings Report.* 14 Vols.
7. Livingston: *Complete Works on Criminal Jurisprudence.* 2 Vols.
8. Cleveland Foundation: *Criminal Justice in Cleveland*
9. Illinois Association for Criminal Justice: *The Illinois Crime Survey*
10. Missouri Association for Criminal Justice: *The Missouri Crime Survey*
11. Aschaffenburg: *Crime and Its Repression*
12. Garofalo: *Criminology*
13. Gross: *Criminal Psychology*
14. Lombroso: *Crime, Its Causes and Remedies*
15. Saleilles: *The Individualization of Punishment*
16. Tarde: *Penal Philosophy*
17. McKelvey: *American Prisons*
18. Sanders: *Negro Child Welfare in North Carolina*
19. Pike: *A History of Crime in England.* 2 Vols.
20. Herring: *Welfare Work in Mill Villages*
21. Barnes: *The Evolution of Penology in Pennsylvania*
22. Puckett: *Folk Beliefs of the Southern Negro*
23. Fernald *et al: A Study of Women Delinquents in New York State*
24. Wines: *The State of the Prisons and of Child-Saving Institutions*
25. Raper: *The Tragedy of Lynching*
26. Thomas: *The Unadjusted Girl*
27. Jorns: *The Quakers as Pioneers in Social Work*
28. Owings: *Women Police*
29. Woolston: *Prostitution in the United States*
30. Flexner: *Prostitution in Europe*
31. Kelso: *The History of Public Poor Relief in Massachusetts: 1820-1920*
32. Spivak: *Georgia Nigger*
33. Earle: *Curious Punishments of Bygone Days*
34. Bonger: *Race and Crime*
35. Fishman: *Crucibles of Crime*
36. Brearley: *Homicide in the United States*
37. Graper: *American Police Administration*
38. Hichborn: *"The System"*
39. Steiner & Brown: *The North Carolina Chain Gang*
40. Cherrington: *The Evolution of Prohibition in the United States of America*
41. Colquhoun: *A Treatise on the Commerce and Police of the River Thames*
42. Colquhoun: *A Treatise on the Police of the Metropolis*
43. Abrahamsen: *Crime and the Human Mind*
44. Schneider: *The History of Public Welfare in New York State: 1609-1866*
45. Schneider & Deutsch: *The History of Public Welfare in New York State: 1867-1940*
46. Crapsey: *The Nether Side of New York*
47. Young: *Social Treatment in Probation and Delinquency*
48. Quinn: *Gambling and Gambling Devices*
49. McCord & McCord: *Origins of Crime*
50. Worthington & Topping: *Specialized Courts Dealing with Sex Delinquency*

PUBLICATION NO. 38: PATTERSON SMITH REPRINT SERIES IN CRIMINOLOGY, LAW ENFORCEMENT, AND SOCIAL PROBLEMS

"THE SYSTEM"

AS UNCOVERED BY

The San Francisco Graft Prosecution

BY

FRANKLIN HICHBORN

(Author of "The Story of the California Legislature of 1909";
"The Story of the California Legislature of 1911"; and "The
Story of the California Legislature of 1913.")

Montclair, New Jersey

PATTERSON SMITH

1969

Originally published 1915
Reprinted 1969 by
Patterson Smith Publishing Corporation
Montclair, New Jersey

SBN 87585-038-3

Library of Congress Catalog Card Number: 69-14933

CONTENTS

Chapter		Page
I.	The Union Labor Party Movement...	11
II.	The Ruef Board of Supervisors.......	22
III.	The San Francisco Ruef Ruled.......	30
IV.	San Francisco After the Fire of 1906..	49
V.	Graft Prosecution Opens.............	73
VI.	Ruef's Fight to Take the District Attorney's Office	87
VII.	Oliver Grand Jury Impaneled.........	96
VIII.	Ruef Loses Fight for District Attorney's Office	107
IX.	Ruef and Schmitz Indicted...........	110
X.	Fight to Evade Trial................	121
XI.	Ruef a Fugitive....................	130
XII.	The Trapping of the Supervisors.....	139
XIII.	Confessions of the Bribe-taking Supervisors	154
XIV.	The Source of the Bribe Money.......	168
XV.	Ruef Pleads Guilty to Extortion......	186
XVI.	Schmitz Convicted of Extortion.......	208
XVII.	Schmitz Ousted from Office..........	215
XVIII.	The Real Fight Begins...............	240
XIX.	The Glass Trials and Conviction......	269
XX.	The Ford Trials and Acquittals.......	279
XXI.	The San Francisco Election of 1907...300	
XXII.	Higher Courts Free Schmitz and Ruef.320	
XXIII.	The Defense Becomes Arrogant......	335
XXIV.	Jury Fixing Uncovered.............	357

Chapter   Page

XXV. The Shooting of Heney..............370
XXVI. The Calhoun Trial...................388
XXVII. The San Francisco Election of 1909...405
XXVIII. Dismissal of the Graft Cases.........425
XXIX. Ruef's Last Refuge Fails.............440
XXX. Conclusion 455

APPENDIX.

Judge Lawlor's Ruling in Motion to Dismiss
    Graft Cases i
How the Supervisors Were Bribed............ vii
Gallagher's Order Removing Langdon from
    Office of District Attorney............... xii
The Ruef "Immunity Contract"............... xix
"Immunity Contract" Given Supervisors....... xxi
District Attorney Langdon's Plan for Reorgan-
    izing the Municipal Government.......... xxii
Roosevelt's Letter to Spreckels on the Graft
    Situation xxv
Governor Johnson's Statement Regarding Ruef's
    Imprisonment xxviii
Schmitz's Attempt to Control San Francisco's
    Relief Funds xxxiii
Receipts and Disbursements of the Graft Prose-
    cution xxxiv

PREFACE.

A tethered bull does not know that he is tied until he attempts to go beyond the rope's limits.

A community does not feel the grip of the "System" until it attempts resistance. Then it knows.

San Francisco during the Ruef-Schmitz regime was no more under the heel of the "System" than when other "bosses" dominated; no more so than to-day; no more so than other communities have been and are.

The political "boss" is merely the visible sign of the "System's" existence. However powerful he may appear, he is, after all, but agent for the "System." The "boss" develops power, does the "System's" work until he is repudiated by the people, when another "boss," usually in the name of "reform," takes his place.

But the second "boss" serves the same "System." Ruef entered San Francisco politics as a "reformer." He supplanted other "bosses." But Ruef in his turn served the "System" they had served.

San Francisco, when Ruef had reached his point of greatest possible power, rose against him. The "System" was not immediately concerned. Ruef had lived his day; the hour for another "boss" to succeed him had come. But San Francisco proposed to get at those back of the "boss"; to get at the "System." And then San Francisco found the "System" more powerful than herself; more powerful than the State of California.

And San Francisco was beaten down, humiliated, made to understand that within her borders the laws could not be enforced against those to whom the "System" granted immunity from punishment.

To secure evidence against bribe-givers, the State granted immunity to bribe-takers who confessed their crimes and joined with the State to bring larger criminals to justice. And the "System's" agents cried outrage that bribe-takers should go free of punishment.

But the "System" granted immunity from punishment to those who had bribed. And the apologists for the "System" will tolerate no criticism of this sort of immunity.

Other communities have risen against the "System's" agents, the "bosses," and the "bosses" have given place to other agents. But few communities, if any, have attacked the "System" as did San Francisco. Had they done so, unquestionably they would have found themselves as ineffective against corruption as San Francisco has been shown to be.

The "System" is confined to no particular State or locality; it permeates our entire public life. Judge Lindsey in Colorado calls it "The Beast." In California we call it "The Southern Pacific Machine," for in California the Southern Pacific Company was its chief beneficiary. Other communities call it the "Organization." The bull does not discover his rope until he strains at it; the community knows little or nothing of the overpowering "System" until it resists. San Francisco resisted and discovered.

The mere bribing of a board of supervisors was not extraordinary. Our newspapers furnish us daily with sorry recital of bribe-taking public officials discovered in other communities. But the effective, searching. resistance to bribe-giving which San Francisco offered was extraordinary. It was a new thing in American politics. It compelled the "System" to show its real strength, and that, too, was new in American politics, and extraordinary, also.

The "System" at San Francisco had taken the usual precautions which ordinarily ensure it against successful opposition, or even question. It had, through its agents, selected the candidates for public office, including the District Attorney. With the District Attorney loyal to the "System" the "System" was secure against attack. And even were the District Attorney to resist the "System," still was the "System" secure, for the "System" could deny the District Attorney, through the public officials it controlled, the funds necessary for successful opposition.

But here again extraordinary circumstances worked for the "System's" confusion. Not only had the "System" been mistaken in the caliber of the man whom it had permitted to be nominated for District Attorney, but patriotic citizens guaranteed the expenses of effective attack through the District Attorney's office.

Nevertheless, the "System" would ordinarily have been able to laugh at the attack, and render it abortive, by compelling the citizens who were backing the District Attorney to withdraw their support.

Even at San Francisco, the supporters of the District Attorney felt the force of such attack. Those who supported the Prosecution found themselves harassed in their business ventures, and snubbed in the social circles in which they had moved. When Heney, stricken down in the discharge of his duty, lay at the point of death, a minister of the gospel prayed for the wounded Prosecutor's recovery. Immediately from the pews came silent expression of disapproval. That pastor refused to be intimidated, refused to join with his fashionable congregation against the Prosecution. He was eventually compelled to resign his pastorate. Rudolph Spreckels, while accounting for every dollar that the Graft Prosecution had expended, asked to be excused from naming those who had subscribed to the fund, lest they be attacked. Ordinarily, those citizens whose instincts had led them to guarantee the District Attorney their support, would have been forced to abandon him.

But at San Francisco, a few citizens, in spite of ridicule, abuse, social ostracism and business opposition, stood firm for civic righteousness. This made San Francisco's attack upon the "System" possible and stirred the "System" to extraordinary resistance.

The "System," seeing itself threatened, went to the relief of the "boss," its agent, whom even its chief beneficiaries despised. The "boss," through his puppet in the Mayor's chair, declared the office of the District Attorney vacant, and appointed himself to fill the vacancy. The boldness of the move startled the whole community. But the act merely demonstrated the extremes to which the "System" was prepared to go. It was not extraordinary in comparison with what was to follow. Later on, witnesses were to be concealed, intimidated, gotten out of the State; their kidnaping even being attempted. The managing editor of a newspaper opposing the "System" was to be taken on the street in daylight, hurried across the country to a suburban town, forced into a stateroom of an outgoing train, and sent on his way to a distant city. The home of the pivotal witness against the "System"-protected defendants was to be dynamited, the witness and other inmates of the building miraculously escaping with their lives. A public prosecutor was, while conducting one of the "System"-attacking trials, to be shot down in open court. A prisoner at the bar was to arise to denounce the judge on the bench as a partisan and a scoundrel. Thugs were to invade court-rooms while trials were going on, to intimidate "System"-threatening prosecutors and witnesses; men were to be trapped as they offered bribes to trial jurors; agents of the Prosecution were to be bribed to turn over to the defending element the Prosecution's papers and reports. An agent of the Prosecution in the employ of the Defense, working in the interest of the Defense, was to sit at the Prosecutor's side during the selection of a trial jury, to advise the Prosecutor of the character of the men under examination for jurors, and with such advice mislead and confuse.

No; bribe-giving at San Francisco was not so extraordinary as the events which grew out of attempt to punish for bribe-giving.

And now, as we look upon San Francisco beaten, and retarded in her development because of that beating, the hopelessness of her opposition to the "System" is the most startling thing of all. We see now, that with a District Attorney intent upon doing his duty, with funds ample for vigorous prosecution guaranteed, with trial judges of integrity and ability on the bench, none of the accused, so long as he remained loyal to the "System"—so long as he did not "snitch"—was in real danger of suffering the law-provided punishment for the crimes uncovered against him.

Ruef carefully weighed the ability of the Prosecution to save him, against the power of the "System" to punish or to save, and knowing the power of the "System" as few other men knew it, Ruef betrayed the Prosecution and cast his lot with the "System." The outcome would have justified his judgment but for a series of unusual events which none could have foreseen. The most extraordinary incident of the whole Graft Prosecution, we can now, with the "System" uncovered before us, see, was that Abe Ruef went to the penitentiary. With full knowledge of the power, resources and methods of the "System," it is not at all extraordinary that guilty men under its protection should escape punishment. But it is extraordinary—due only to a chain of extraordinary happenings—that one of its agents, who continued faithful, who didn't "snitch," finds himself in prison and unable to get out.

The San Francisco Graft Prosecution uncovered the "System" as it has been uncovered in no other American city, for San Francisco made the hardest, most persistent, and longest continued attack that a municipality has ever made upon it. California has profited greatly because of the uncovering, for while uncovered, the "System" may be proceeded against intelligently, not in the courts, but at the ballot-box. California has been quick to profit by the opportunity which the uncovering of the "System" has offered.

In preparing this volume for the press it is my purpose—so far as lies in my power to do so—*to keep the cover off*.

FRANKLIN HICHBORN.

Santa Clara, Calif., Dec. 25, 1912.

CHAPTER I.

The Union Labor Party Movement.

Eugene E. Schmitz [1] was elected Mayor of San Francisco in November, 1901. He had been nominated by the Union-Labor party. This party was organized after labor disturbances which had divided San Francisco into militant factions, with organized labor on the one side and organized capital on the other. [2]

The convention which had nominated Schmitz was made up in the main of delegates who had affiliations with labor unions and were in close sympathy with the labor-union movement.

But this did not mean that the new party had the unanimous approval of the labor unions, or of the rank and file of organized labor. A considerable faction, with P. H. McCarthy, president of the State Building Trades Council, even then a dominating figure in San Francisco labor circles, at its head, advised against the movement, and opposed the new party candidates not only in 1901,

---

[1] Schmitz, previous to his election, was employed as a musician in a San Francisco theater. His connection with organized labor came through membership in the Musicians' Union. He had no intention of aspiring to the Mayor's chair until Ruef suggested it to him.

[2] The San Francisco labor strike of 1901 arose out of the refusal of the organized teamsters to deliver goods to a non-union express agency. The Employers' Association refused to treat with the men collectively. Other organizations went out in sympathy.

James D. Phelan, who was then Mayor, was the intermediary between the teamsters and their employees. He advocated recognition. The negotiations failed. During the progress of the strike

but in 1903 when Schmitz was a candidate for re-election.

On the other hand, the new party had in the beginning the support of the Coast Seamen's Journal, published at San Francisco, and one of the most influential labor publications on the Pacific Coast. It had, too, the advocacy of several earnest Labor leaders.

Very frankly, such leaders questioned the ultimate consequences of the movement, expressing fears which time was to justify. But to them the situation offered no alternative. Their support and influence went to the new party as an expedient of the times, not as the beginning of a permanent political organization.

But the movement, once started, got beyond their control. During the first five years of Union-Labor party activities in San Francisco many of these original supporters were forced, first into silence and finally into

---

there were constant disturbances. A steamship company, for example, employed prizefighters in the guise of workingmen to seek positions as strikebreakers, and when interfered with to belabor the pickets. Assaults were made upon non-union teamsters carrying supplies to and from railway stations. The Chief of Police, in order to preserve peaceful traffic, placed two policemen upon each truck. Labor leaders asked not only that the police be withdrawn from the trucks, but from the waterfront. This action the Mayor refused to take, on the ground that it was his duty to preserve public order, and that it was in the interest of all to avert rather than suppress trouble. A meeting of representatives of the several factions was held at the Mayor's office, September 23, 1901. The story was circulated that the Mayor had said at the meeting that if the workmen did not want to be clubbed let them go to work. Both sides now admit the statement was not made. Joseph S. Tobin, Henry U. Brandenstein, Lawrence J. Dwyer and Peter J. Curtis, who were present, have set forth in affidavit that "Mayor Phelan did not say at said conference, as has been alleged, referring to the workingmen's strike, that 'if they don't want to be clubbed let them go to work,' nor did he make any statement of like import." At the time, however, feeling was running so high at San Francisco that the most extravagant stories were believed. Opponents of the administration—those representing capital as well as those advocating recognition of the unions—seized upon every opportunity to discredit. Crafty adventurers of the type of Abe Ruef lost no chance to work distrust and confusion. Out of the turmoil came the Union Labor party.

open repudiation of the methods of the Union-Labor party administration.

In the meantime, members of the McCarthy faction, which had resisted the organization of the party, and had opposed it at the 1901 and 1903 elections, became its strong partisans. This element supported the party ticket at the 1905 election; and in 1907, and again in 1909, when McCarthy was himself the Union-Labor party candidate for Mayor.

But the Union-Labor party ticket which McCarthy headed did not have the united support of labor leaders who had organized the movement. Indeed, labor leaders whom the McCarthy faction in 1901 called "scabs" for organizing the Union-Labor party, were, by the same men who had condemned them in 1901, denounced as "scabs" during the 1909 campaign for not supporting the Union-Labor party candidates.

From the beginning, the Union-Labor party had the support of elements outside the labor-union movement. Much of this support came from citizens who, regardless of their attitude on trade-unionism, were dissatisfied with the old parties. The situation offered exceptional opportunity for the political manipulator. But the one man with the political vision to see the possibilities of the third-party movement, was not a member of a labor union. He was a lawyer who had already attained some prominence in San Francisco politics—Abraham Ruef.[3]

---

3 Ruef graduated from the University of California and from the University of California law school with exceptional honors. He was at twenty-one a practicing attorney. With Franklin K.

14   The Union Labor Party Movement

Ruef was quick to see the potentialities of the political Frankenstein which groping labor leaders had brought into being. He knew that *they* could not control their creation; he knew that *he* could. He did not overestimate his powers. He managed the new party's 1901 campaign.[4] Under his direction, success was won for a cause that had been deemed hopeless. The genius of Abraham Ruef made Eugene E. Schmitz Mayor of San Francisco.[5]

Lane, the present Secretary of the Interior, Dean John H. Wigmore of the Northwestern University, and others, he organized a club for civic reform. His first political convention, he tells us in his Confessions, showed him that representative government was a farce. He resolved to devote himself to his law practice. But almost immediately we find him an "errand boy" for Martin Kelly and Phil Crimmins, powerful "bosses" in their day, but now practically forgotten. Ruef continued with Kelly and Crimmins for ten years. He drifted with the machine, securing excellent training for his future career. His opportunity came in 1901, when, in its effort to throw off the yoke of the bosses, the State secured the enactment of a new primary law. Under this law Ruef took his first step to secure control of the State political machine. He seized upon the new law as a vehicle to organize a "reform" movement. His organization took the name Republican Primary League. He secured a large following. He was becoming powerful. He tells us in his Confessions that during this period he was invited to dine at the homes of men of political and social importance, among them William F. Herrin, chief counsel of the Southern Pacific Company, and Patrick Calhoun, president of the United Railroads. But as yet, Ruef had little real influence in the "organization." Then came the labor unrest, and the Union Labor party movement. Ruef managed to combine the Republican Primary League with the Union Labor party movement. This combination was the basis of his campaign for the election of Schmitz.

4 Ruef also provided much of the funds employed in the first Schmitz campaign. In a statement published May 16, 1907, Ruef said: "When Schmitz first ran for Mayor I made his campaign for him, and put up $16,000. My friends told me I was a fool. I guess I was."

5 Out of the 52,168 votes cast for Mayor, at the 1901 election, Schmitz received 21,776. His opponents—Wells (Republican) and Tobin (Democrat)—divided 30,392 between them, Wells receiving 17,718 and Tobin 12,674. Up to the present time (1914) the Union-Labor party has four times been successful in San Francisco mayoralty elections. But only once, in 1905, has its candidate been elected by majority vote. Changes in the San Francisco Charter, ratified at the 1911 session of the State Legislature, place the election of municipal officials on a non-partisan basis, and prevent election by plurality vote. Henceforth all officials must be elected by majority vote.

In practical acknowledgment of Ruef's services, Schmitz issued an open letter, in which he stated himself privileged to consider Ruef his friendly counsellor.[6] The issuance of that letter made Ruef the recognized political representative of the Union-Labor party administration, a position which he held until the estrangement of himself and Schmitz under the strain of the graft prosecution.[7]

---

[6] Schmitz's letter announcing his obligation to Ruef was as follows:

"My Dear Ruef: Now that the election is over and I am to be the Mayor of our native city, I wish to express to you and through you to all your loyal friends and the faithful Republicans who supported my cause, my profound appreciation of the generous, whole-souled, substantial and effective support accorded me in the exciting campaign which has just closed. Viewed from your prominent position in the Republican party, I know the seriousness of the step which you took when you voluntarily and unconditionally offered me your valuable aid, and I cannot in words properly give utterance to my deep feeling in this regard. I can only say that your action is worthy of yourself, and that no higher praise can be accorded you.

"I have now for some fifteen years enjoyed your acquaintance and friendship and your services as my attorney in many capacities, and I say without hesitation or flattery that I have yet to find a more honorable, a more loyal, a more able attorney, or a truer friend.

"I feel that I owe a great deal of my success in this campaign to you and your friends, and I shall not permit myself at any time to forget it.

"Though you have never asked or even suggested it, I shall, with the utmost confidence and with a sentiment of absolute security, feel myself privileged at all times to consider you as my friendly counsellor and to call upon you whenever I may require assistance in the solution of any of the perplexing and complicated questions which must necessarily arise in the conduct of so vast and important an office.

"I trust that you will not hesitate to say that I may do so. Again and again thanking you and your friends, I am,

"Very sincerely yours,
"E. E. SCHMITZ."

[7] Ruef at once availed himself of the opportunities which his position offered. He accepted regular "retainers" from public-service corporations. He testified before the Grand Jury that he was employed by the United Railroads through Tirey L. Ford, just after the first election of Schmitz, at $500 per month, and that he gave receipts to Ford for this money, during Schmitz's first term of office, but received the money always in Ford's office in currency; but that after the second election of Schmitz, he (Ruef) refused to give any more receipts for this money, although he continued to receive it from Ford the same as before with receipts, and that

But the government of San Francisco did not pass entirely under control of the Union-Labor party until four years after Schmitz's elevation to the Mayoralty.

During the era of Union-Labor party power in San Francisco, the Mayor and the eighteen members of the Board of Supervisors were elected every two years.[8] Schmitz, under Ruef's management, was re-elected in 1903. But the Union-Labor party failed at that elec-

---

after the third election his salary was increased to $1,000 per month, which was paid in the same way by Ford without any receipts.

Ruef further testified that he was employed by the Pacific States Telephone and Telegraph Company, immediately after Schmitz's first election, through T. V. Halsey, and that Halsey paid him $1,200 per month in currency without any receipt.

E. S. Pillsbury, general counsel of the Pacific States Telephone and Telegraph Company, testified that he never heard of Ruef's employment until after the indictments were returned against Halsey, and that he, Pillsbury, attended to all of the legal business of the company during the entire time Ruef was under employment. Pillsbury received only $1,000 per month for his own services, and testified that he would have objected to the payment to Ruef of a larger salary than he was getting.

Pillsbury was a stockholder to the amount of $500,000 in his own right, and was a member of the executive committee of the board of directors of the company.

At the trial of The People vs. Tirey L. Ford, No. 817, I. W. Hellman, one of the most prominent of California bankers and at one time a director of the United Railroads, testified: "Some five years ago (the Ford trial was in 1907, which would make the date about 1902) Mr. Holland, who was then the president of the United Railways, came to me to ask my advice whether Mr. Ruef should be employed as an attorney for the United Railways, stating that by employing him peace could be secured with the labor unions, that he had great influence with them, and there would be general peace, and it was to the benefit of the railways company to have such peace. Mr. Ruef then was an attorney of high repute, recognized as a good lawyer, and I said if that could be accomplished it would be for the benefit of the railway company as well as for the public, and I advised yes. Whether he has been employed or not I do not know, because I afterward sold my interest in the company and I never have inquired whether he had been employed or not."

In this connection, it is interesting to note that Ruef in his latest confession, the publication of which was begun in the San Francisco Bulletin in May, 1912, states that his employment by corporations as attorney did not begin until after the second Schmitz election—that is to say, in 1903. Hellman's testimony would indicate that his employment by the United Railroads dates from 1902. Compare with footnote 77, page 74.

8 Under amendments to the San Francisco Charter, ratified by the Legislature of 1911, the Mayor and Supervisors are now elected to four-year terms.

tion, as it had in 1901, to elect a majority of the Board of Supervisors. Many of the commissions, on the other hand, through appointments by the mayor, had, by 1903, passed completely under Union-Labor party control.

Gradually, the opinion grew in San Francisco that the management of the departments was unsatisfactory, if not corrupt. This opinion, in 1905, when Schmitz was for a third time the Union-Labor party candidate for Mayor, found expression in fusion of the Republican and Democratic parties to bring about the defeat of the Union-Labor party nominees.

This fusion was in the name of municipal reform. The organizers of the movement were in the main opposed to machine political methods. When, however, the movement gave evidence of vitality and strength, the political agents of public service corporations became identified with its leadership.[9] The new leaders were soon in practical control. Public-service corporations were largely instrumental in financing the movement. Testimony was brought out before the Grand Jury which conducted the graft investigations, that nearly every public-service corporation in San Francisco

---

9 George F. Hatton, Southern Pacific lobbyist and politician, and political manager for United States Senator George C. Perkins, was one of the principal leaders of the 1905 "reform" movement. He was at one time retained as an attorney by the Empire Construction Company, affiliated with the Home Telephone Company, which was seeking a franchise to establish a telephone system in San Francisco in competition with the Pacific States Telephone and Telegraph Company. The Home Telephone Company contributed to the "reform" campaign fund. Through the "reform" Board of Supervisors, who were to be elected, and whose campaign was thus financed, the Home Company was to get its franchise. But the "reform" candidates were defeated, the Schmitz-Ruef Union-Labor party candidates were elected. The Home Telephone Company thereupon proceeded to secure its franchise by employing Ruef.

contributed to the fusion fund, the average of the contributions being $2,500 for each corporation.[10]

On the other hand, the public-service corporations contributed liberally toward the election of the Ruef-backed, Union-Labor party candidates.[11] Ruef was already on the pay-roll of the law departments of many of them. Thus, generally speaking, it made little difference to the corporations whether the "reform" fusion candidates or the Ruef Union-Labor party candidates were elected. The corporations had captained each side, and in a large measure had financed each side.

The inevitable difficulties of a campaign, financed and officered by public-service corporations, to correct municipal ills for which the corporations were in large measure responsible, were encountered from the beginning. For the head of the reform or fusion ticket, men who had been prominent in the organization of the anti-Ruef crusade were suggested, only to be rejected by the corporation allies who had after the reform

---

[10] William Thomas, of the law firm of Thomas, Gerstle & Frick, attorneys for the Home Telephone Company, testified before the Grand Jury that his company had contributed $8,000 to the "reform" campaign fund. The testimony indicated that this money was used at the primaries. Louis Sloss, one of the leaders of the "reform" movement, testified that after the primaries, Detweiler, who was at the head of the Home Telephone Company enterprise, sent his personal check for $800 additional. Fairfax H. Wheelan, one of the leaders of the "reform" movement, testified before the Grand Jury that the Pacific States Telephone and Telegraph Company, in the name of T. V. Halsey, subscribed $2,000 to the fund; and the United Railroads, concealing its identity under the name "Cash," $2,000 more.

[11] Dr. Charles Boxton was one of the Union-Labor party Supervisors elected in 1905. At the second trial of Louis Glass, vice-president of the Pacific States Telephone and Telegraph Company, for bribery, Boxton testified that during the campaign, T. V. Halsey, political agent for the company, met him on the street and gave him a sealed envelope, saying: "If that will be of any use to you use it."

Boxton found the envelope to contain $1,000 in United States currency.

group's preliminary successes become identified with the movement.

Finally, after several names had been canvassed, John S. Partridge, an attorney of good ability and repute, but scarcely known outside the immediate circle in which he moved, was agreed upon as Mr. Schmitz's opponent. Both the Democrat and the Republican party nominated Mr. Partridge, and with him a complete fusion ticket, including supervisors.

Partridge had a clear field against Schmitz, but his candidacy failed to carry the confidence, or to awake the enthusiasm which brings success at the polls.

The Union-Labor administration was openly denounced as corrupt. Francis J. Heney,[12] fresh from his success in prosecuting the Oregon land fraud cases, went so far as to declare in a speech before one of the largest political gatherings ever assembled in San Francisco that he knew Ruef to be corrupt,[13] and, given opportunity, could prove it.

---

[12] Francis J. Heney when five years old went to San Francisco with his parents. He was educated at the public schools of that city, the University of California, and Hastings Law School. After being admitted to practice he lived for a time in Arizona, where he served as Attorney-General. On his return to San Francisco in 1895, he confined himself to civil practice until, at the solicitation of United States Attorney-General Knox, he undertook the prosecution of the Oregon Land Fraud cases. He was at the close of successful prosecution of these cases, when invited by Rudolph Spreckels, Phelan and others, to participate in the prosecution of the San Francisco graft cases.

[13] Heney's statement was prophetic. The published account of his speech (see Chronicle, November 6, 1905) was as follows:
"If I had control of the District Attorney's office, I would indict Abe Ruef for felony and send him to the penitentiary, where he belongs, for I have personal knowledge that he is corrupt.
"If you elect these people, the graft of this city will become so great that the citizens of San Francisco will ask me to come back and prosecute him. When the time comes I will do as the people request as a matter of civic duty."
Heney's charge brought caustic reply from Ruef. In an open letter to Heney, published November 7, 1905, Ruef said:
"Francis J. Heney:—In the published reports of your speech at

The public generally believed Heney's charges to be justified. But of approximately 98,000 registered voters only 68,878 voted for Mayor, and of these, 40,191 voted for Schmitz. Partridge received only 28,687 [14] votes, being defeated by a majority of 11,504.

Mechanics Pavilion last Saturday night you are represented as saying: 'I say to you, moreover, that I personally know that Abraham Ruef is corrupt, and I say to you that whenever he wants me to prove it in court I will do so.'

"I am not a candidate for office, but as a man I do not propose to leave your false statement undenied.

"In the past I have paid little attention to anything said by hostile papers concerning myself, feeling that the public fully understood the despicable motives underlying the utterances of their proprietors. In your case a different situation presents itself. You have recently acquired considerable repute as a prosecuting attorney for the United States Government. Your statements, if unchallenged, may be given some credence by those not familiar with the true condition of affairs.

"In making the statement that you personally know that I am corrupt you lied. You cannot personally know that which does not exist.

"In making the statement at a time and place which allowed no opportunity for a legal showing before the date of the election which you seek to influence, you showed the same courage which put a bullet into the body of Dr. J. C. Handy of Tucson, Ariz., in 1891, for whose killing you were indicted for murder, and upon trial were acquitted because you were the only witness to the deed.

"You say whenever I want you to prove it in court you will do so.

"I want you to try to prove it, and at once. I demand that you begin at once. I know you cannot prove what does not exist. Why you should wait upon my desire, why you should depend upon my wish to proceed with the performance of what must be to every good citizen a public duty, I do not know.

"But as you declare that you will proceed only with my consent, I give you here and now full consent and authority to proceed, and I go further and ask that you do so.

"I regret that your recent identification with the Citizens' Alliance and with the corporations anxious to encompass the defeat of a candidate in a political campaign should have made you so far forget the regard for truth, justice and decency which should characterize men in our profession, as to have induced you to take the chance of ruining for life the reputation and standing of one who is not rightfully amenable to your charge, and who has not otherwise heretofore given you the slightest private or personal provocation for your savage and mendacious attack.   "A. RUEF.

"San Francisco, November 6th."

14 To hold that only 28,687 electors of San Francisco wished a change in the administration of San Francisco would be unjust. Many who were opposed to Ruef's domination remained away from the polls, through dissatisfaction with the management of the fusion movement. Of the more than 40,000 who voted for the Union Labor ticket, were thousands of union men who were opposed to the

Not only was Schmitz re-elected by overwhelming majority, but the entire Ruef-selected Union-Labor party ticket was elected with him.

Ruef, as Mayor Schmitz's recognized political adviser, and political agent for the Union-Labor party, found himself in control of every branch and department of the San Francisco municipal government.

Schmitz-Ruef element. But Ruef cleverly injected the Citizens' Alliance issue, and the organized labor element was, because of this, made to vote practically solidly for the Ruef-selected candidates. The fact that voting machines were used in every precinct in San Francisco for the first time contributed to this. Members of labor unions did not understand the working of the machines, and were afraid to attempt to vote anything but the straight ticket. This dissatisfied organized labor element, two years later, contributed in no small degree to the election of Mayor E. R. Taylor and the re-election of District Attorney William H. Langdon, thereby making possible continuation until 1910 of the graft prosecution.

CHAPTER II.

THE RUEF BOARD OF SUPERVISORS.

No observer of San Francisco politics, not even Ruef himself, had expected the entire Union-Labor party ticket to be elected. The election of the Supervisors was the greatest surprise of all. Ruef, with his political intimates, had selected the Supervisorial candidates, but more with a view to hold the organized labor vote for Schmitz than with idea of the fitness of the candidates for the duties involved in managing the affairs of a municipality of 500,000 population.[15] Not one of the eighteen elected was a man of strong character.[16] Several were of fair, but by no means excep-

---

[15] At Ruef's trial for offering a bribe to Supervisor Furey, Supervisor James L. Gallagher testified that conferences for selecting the Union Labor party ticket, from Sheriff down, were held at Ruef's office. Gallagher testified of one of these conferences:

"The matter of the nominees for Supervisors was mentioned, and all that I recollect about it is that it was stated that there should be a good representation of prominent Union-Labor men on the ticket, and Mr. Ruef stated that he had that in mind, and that that would be done, and it was also stated that the members on the Board of Supervisors that were Union-Labor adherents should be nominated." See The People vs. Abraham Ruef, No. 1437—Transcript on Appeal, Part 3, Vol. 3, page 1278.

[16] The eighteen members of the Ruef-Schmitz Board of Supervisors were James L. Gallagher, attorney at law; Cornelius J. Harrigan, grocer; James T. Kelly, piano polisher; Thomas F. Lonergan, driver of a bakery delivery wagon; Max Mamlock, electrician; P. M. McGushin, saloonkeeper; F. P. Nicholas, carpenter; Jennings J. Phillips, employed in newspaper circulation department; L. A. Rea, painter; W. W. Sanderson, employed in grocery store; E. I. Walsh, shoemaker; Andrew M. Wilson, employing drayman; George Duffey, contracting plumber; Charles Boxton, dentist; M. W. Coffey, hackman; Daniel G. Coleman, clerk; Sam Davis, orchestra musician; John J. Furey, blacksmith and saloonkeeper.

At the time the graft prosecution opened, Wilson had resigned his position as Supervisor to take up his work as State Railroad Commissioner, an office to which he was elected in 1906; and Duffey to be president of the Municipal Commission of Public Works, to which office he was appointed by Mayor Schmitz.

tional ability. Of this type were Gallagher, an attorney of some prominence who acted as go-between between Ruef and the Supervisors; Wilson, who was a sort of second man to Gallagher, and Boxton, a dentist.

But for the most part they were men who had led uneventful lives as drivers of delivery wagons, bartenders and clerks. Without an exception, they saw in their unexpected elevation to the Board of Supervisors opportunity to better their condition. Some of them would not, perhaps, have sought bribes; few of them knew just how they could employ their office to their best advantage; but from the hour of their election the idea of personal advancement was uppermost in the minds of the majority of the members of the Schmitz-Ruef Board of Supervisors.[17] Their ignorance of the requirements of their office, their failure to appreciate their large responsibilities, and above all their ill-defined ambitions made them promise of easy prey for the agents of the public-service corporations, who were playing for special privileges worth millions.

---

[17] Supervisor E. I. Walsh in a sworn statement made to Heney, March 8, 1907, testified:

"Q. And what was agreed upon there (in caucus) as to programme? A. I couldn't say what was agreed upon with them.

"Q. Wasn't it arranged that every man should be treated alike as to money? A. It wasn't openly suggested that way; it might have been said among the members that way.

"Q. That was the understanding you had. A. Yes, sir.

"Q. That you would be all treated equally and fairly? A. I presume that was the way it was understood."

Supervisor Lonergan had been promised by Supervisor Wilson $8000 for voting to give the United Railroads a permit to operate its lines under the trolley system. At a second meeting Wilson stated the amount would be $4000. Of the scene on this occasion, Lonergan testified at the trial in the case of the People vs. Ford, No. 817:

"Q. What did he (Wilson) say on that occasion? A. There was only $4000 in it for me.

"Q. What did you say. A. I asked him what the hell kind of work that was and what did he mean by it. And he shook his head and said that if I didn't like it, all right; something to that effect."

None realized this better than Ruef. From the beginning, he recognized that the likelihood of individual members of the board yielding to temptation to petty gain [18] threatened his own larger purposes. He let it be known that he would himself personally prosecute any one of them whom he discovered to be "grafting." Ruef was emphatic in his position that the Supervisors should have no financial dealings with those seeking special-privilege advantages. He even defined regular procedure for dealing with persons and corporations that might elect to catch the easiest way to accomplish their purposes by the use of bribe money. To this end he arranged:

(1) That Supervisor James L. Gallagher [19] should represent him on the board. The Supervisors at once

---

[18] Evidence of Ruef's distrust of his Supervisors was brought out at many points in the graft trials. When he discovered that individual Supervisors were, without his knowledge, taking bribes from the Pacific States Telephone and Telegraph Company, he stated to Dr. Joseph S. Poheim:

"I see they have been trying to take my Supervisors away from me, but I have fixed them; I would like to see one of them throw me down." (See Transcript, People vs. Ruef, 1437, Part 3, Vol. 9, p. 4018.) In the midst of the troubles brought upon him by the graft prosecution, Ruef complained that "These fellows (the Supervisors) would eat the paint off a house, and in order to hold them together I had to descend to their level and take them in with me."

Ruef was also jealous of Schmitz's activity. When he learned that Schmitz had promised franchises independent of him, he directed Supervisor Wilson to oppose them. "Butt in on this Parkside business," he said to Wilson. "Mr. Schmitz has promised the Ocean Shore and the Parkside; he is destroying my political influence; these people ought to be made to come and see me."

[19] Gallagher was by far the ablest member of the Ruef-Schmitz Board of Supervisors. He was by profession an attorney at law. In that capacity he had served first as Assistant City Attorney, and finally as City Attorney. For a time he was law partner with Hon. James G. Maguire, whose opposition, as member of Congress from California, to the Pacific railroads refunding measures, won him a national reputation. Maguire was candidate for Governor on the Democratic ticket in 1898, but was defeated. Gallagher had served as Supervisor previous to his election in 1905, and was one of the most experienced members of the Schmitz-Ruef board.

At Ruef's trial on the charge of offering a bribe to Supervisor Furey, Gallagher testified that soon after his election in 1905, Ruef

accepted Gallagher, and dealt with him as Ruef's recognized agent.

(2) Finally Ruef arranged for a regular weekly caucus [20] to be held each Sunday night, on the eve of the regular meeting day of the board, Monday.

The public was not admitted to these caucuses. Those who were admitted were Ruef, Mayor Schmitz, George B. Keane,[21] clerk of the Board of Supervisors, who also acted as secretary of the caucus, and the eighteen Supervisors.

At these meetings, which were held every Sunday evening, Ruef was the dominating figure. Supervisor

---

told him there would be a number of matters coming before the Board of Supervisors in which the corporations and other large concerns would be interested; that there would be a number of large deals coming before the board in which he wanted him (Gallagher) to represent him on the board. Gallagher accepted the agency.

20 Gallagher testified before the Oliver Grand Jury of the nature of these caucuses. From his testimony the following is taken:

"Q. They (the Supervisors) voted in the caucus and you knew how the vote would be. A. Yes, sir.

"Q. And they would be bound by the caucus vote. A. That was understood that a man would vote at the caucus in the way he would vote at the meeting.

"Q. You were understood to represent Mr. Ruef and Mr. Ruef's views. A. That was generally understood by members of the board.

"Q. And whatever way you went meant programme. A. I believe Mr. Ruef told a number of them so, and that circulated among the others; it was generally understood by them."

21 Keane's lasting loyalty to Ruef makes him one of the most interesting characters of the graft cases. He entered Ruef's employ in 1898 as a law clerk. He remained in Ruef's office until January, 1902, when Mayor Schmitz took office. Keane was then made secretary to the Mayor. He served in that capacity until January, 1906, when Ruef gained control of the Board of Supervisors. Ruef then made him clerk of the board. At Ruef's trial for offering a bribe to Supervisor Furey, Gallagher testified that Ruef told him that Keane should be clerk. Gallagher notified the other members of Ruef's decision, and that closed the incident. Keane was, however, much more than a mere clerk. Supervisor Wilson testified at the Ruef trial for offering a bribe to Furey, that he (Wilson) owed his nomination to Keane. Keane was elected to the State Senate where his loyalty to Ruef in foul as well as fair weather made him a conspicuous and somewhat notorious character. At present writing, Keane is foremost in the movement to bring about Ruef's release from State prison.

Wilson, testifying at the graft trials, stated that Ruef took the position of "chief counsel and adviser for the board in matters that were to come before the board."

Keane, as secretary of the caucus, took full notes [22] of the proceedings and sent written notices [23] of the meetings to each of those who were admitted.

The first of these caucuses was held shortly before the Schmitz-Ruef board took office. The organization of the board was provided by the Supervisors authorizing Ruef and Schmitz to make up the committees. Ruef undertook the task. He prepared the committee lists, and submitted his selections to Schmitz and Gallagher. Schmitz and Gallagher suggested unimportant changes. The committees were then announced to the Supervisors at the next caucus. There were objections raised, but these objections, with one exception, were denied in all important particulars. The organization of the Schmitz-Ruef Board of Supervisors was thus perfected.

Ruef's way seemed clear. The committee organization of the Board of Supervisors was his own. The Supervisors were to hold no open meeting until they had met with him in secret caucus to ascertain his

---

[22] At Ruef's trial on the charge of offering a bribe to Supervisor Furey, Keane testified that these notes had been destroyed in the great fire of April 18-19-20, 1906. Keane testified further that Ruef was a constant attendant at the caucuses; that Schmitz was an occasional visitor; that Supervisor Gallagher presided.

[23] Notices of the caucus meetings were sent to Ruef precisely as though he had been a member of the Board of Supervisors. At Ruef's trial for offering a bribe to Supervisor Furey, the following letter of notification was introduced as evidence:

"San Francisco, June 21st, 1906.
"Hon. A. Ruef, San Francisco—Dear Sir: I respectfully beg leave to notify you that the Board of Supervisors will meet in caucus on Sunday evening, June 24th, at 8 o'clock p. m., at Hamilton Hall, Steiner street, near Geary. Your attendance is respectfully requested.
"Yours truly,   GEORGE B. KEANE, Clerk."

wishes. The official clerk of the board, who was also secretary of the caucus, was his tried henchman. Gallagher, the ablest of the Supervisors, flattered at being made his representative, and further bound by mercenary ties, was ready to do his slightest bidding. And never had entrenched boss more fruitful field for exploitation.

But scarcely had the new administration been installed, than a weak point developed in Ruef's position. District Attorney William H. Langdon, who had been elected on the Ruef ticket, gave evidence that he proposed to enforce the law, regardless of the effect upon the administration of which he was a part, or upon Ruef's plans and interests.

The first intimation the public had of Langdon's independent attitude came when gambling games in which Ruef was popularly supposed to be interested were raided under the personal direction of the District Attorney. Langdon had first attempted to close the places through the police department. Failing, he had attended to the matter himself.[24] The gamblers ap-

---

[24] The San Francisco Chronicle in its issue of March 8, 1906, said of the District Attorney's raids on the gamblers:

"The political push and the underworld generally are astonished at District Attorney Langdon's unexpected outbreak. He has descended upon them like a thunderbolt out of a clear sky. For the moment even wrath is less in evidence than surprise. It was not expected. It is not what was paid for. It is like being murdered by one's dearest friend. There is a complete reversal of the usual experience of mankind. In most cities the lid is on and weighed down before election but lifted and thrown away as soon as the votes are counted. To be allowed to run wide open before election and to be closed down and nailed up as soon as the new official is fairly seated is outside of all precedent. And all that after the most liberal contributions. There is a feeling in criminal circles that somebody is guilty of obtaining money under false pretenses. The District Attorney is the one official for whose friendship the law-breakers have the most earnest longings, and behind their closed doors the idle gamblers are trying to figure out what 'lay' this

pealed to Ruef, but Ruef was helpless. Langdon would not be turned from his purpose. The gamblers and capitalists interested in gambling establishments charged Langdon with political ingratitude.

But those who were laboring for the development, and were opposing the exploitation of San Francisco, saw in Langdon's course the first sign that Abraham Ruef was not to have undisputed sway in San Francisco.[25] With Langdon in the District Attorney's office it was still possible that the laws could be enforced— even against Abraham Ruef. The raiding of the gambling dens marked the beginning of the division in San

---

dreadful Langdon is really on, and by what trade he has been induced to ignore all the promises expressed or implied, which those assumed to be able to speak for him dispersed so freely when votes were in demand.

"As for the public, it was for none of these things. Among the decent portion of society the 'motives' of the District Attorney do not arouse even passing curiosity. What does interest them is the present vigor of his work, and the probability of his keeping it up."

[25] Ruef had consented to Langdon's nomination for District Attorney, because he considered that Langdon's intimate acquaintance with the teachers and pupils of the San Francisco public schools would help the ticket. For the three years preceding the campaign Langdon had been Superintendent of Schools at San Francisco. Ruef told Langdon after the election that he had no idea that any one other than Schmitz could be elected on the Union-Labor party ticket that year. When during the campaign Langdon began to develop strength in the contest for District Attorney, Ruef sent him a check for $200 for "campaign expenses," saying that the money had been contributed by Tirey L. Ford of the United Railroads. Langdon returned the check to Ruef with the statement that he preferred to pay his own campaign expenses. During the campaign at every meeting he addressed, Langdon made the statement: "The laws are on the statute books; all may know them. I pledge myself to the enforcement of these laws." To be sure, few if any paid much attention to what Langdon meant, but that was no fault of Langdon's. Everybody was to learn from the hour that he assumed the duties of his office that he meant just what he said. Rudolph Spreckels testified at the Calhoun trial that when Langdon's raids on the gambling dens were made public he felt that "we had a District Attorney who was desirous of doing his duty." The raids were made in February, 1906. Spreckels, Heney, Phelan, Older and others were already considering plans for the exposure and check of the reign of Ruef.

Francisco, with those who approached the Ruef administration with bribe money on the one side, and those
who resisted with the check of law enforcement on
the other.

CHAPTER III.

The San Francisco Ruef Ruled.

The decade ending 1910 was for California an era of extraordinary enterprise and development. A third transcontinental railroad, the Western Pacific, was completed; vast land-holdings as large as 40,000 acres in a body were cut up into small tracts and sold to settlers; waters brought to the land by vast irrigation enterprises increased the land's productiveness three and even ten fold; petroleum fields, enormously rich, were opened up and developed; the utilization of the falling waters of mountain streams to generate electric power, brought cheap light and power and heat to farm as well as to city factory. The Spanish war had brought thousands of troops to the coast. Practically all of them passed through San Francisco. This particular activity had its influence on local conditions. The State's population increased from 1,485,053 in 1900 to 2,377,549 in 1910.

Up to the time of the San Francisco fire, April 18, 1906, San Francisco, of the cities of the State, profited most by this development. San Francisco bank clearances, for example, increased from $1,029,582,594.78 for the year ending December 31, 1900, to $1,834,549,788.51 for the year ending December 31, 1905, a gain of 80 per cent.

San Francisco's increase in population during those five years, can, of course, only be estimated. On the basis of the registration for the 1905 municipal election, approximately 98,000, San Francisco had, at the time of the 1906 disaster, a population of about 500,000, an increase from the population of 342,782 shown by the 1900 census of practically 50 per cent. in five years.[26]

The rapid increase in population, the sustained prosperity of the community, and its prospective development made San Francisco one of the most promising fields for investment in the country.

The public service corporations were quick to take advantage of the San Francisco opportunity. Those corporations already established sought to strengthen their position; new corporations strove for foothold in the promising field. Thus, we find the Home Telephone Company, financed by Ohio and Southern California capitalists, seeking a franchise to operate a telephone system in opposition to the Pacific States Telephone and Telegraph Company, which was already established. And we find the Pacific States Company taking active part in municipal politics to prevent the Home franchise or any other opposition telephone franchise being granted. The corporation holding the light and power monopoly, the Pacific Gas and Electric Company, had by the time of the third Schmitz inaugural, practical control of the San Francisco field. But it was face to face with a clamor for reduction of gas rates. The company was charging one dollar a thousand for gas. The Union-Labor party platform of 1905 pledged the

---

[26] Patrick Calhoun, in a letter to the press, dated March 21, 1906—less than a month before the great fire—stated that the time was near when the San Francisco street-car system would have to serve a million people. The 1910 census, taken four years after the fire, gave San Francisco a population of 416,912.

Board of Supervisors to a seventy-five-cents-per-thousand rate.

Another matter of tremendous importance to the growing municipality was that of the supply of water. The Spring Valley Water Company had a monopoly of this necessity, but demand for municipal water to be brought from the Sierras was strong. A committee of experts had been appointed to pass upon the various sources of supply. Ruef appeared before them as spokesman for the Supervisors. The experts resigned when it was made clear to them that instead of being permitted to make an adequate study of all available sources of supply they were to report upon the Bay Cities project alone.[27] After the ousting of the Schmitz-Ruef administration the Bay Cities project was ignored and bonds authorized to bring water from Hetch-Hetchy valley. The Spring Valley Water Company, however, has been successful in blocking this project, and in 1914, San Francisco seems almost as far away from realizing her ambition for a supply of pure water as in 1905-6 when Ruef and his followers were at the height of their power.

The public-service problem which was attracting the most attention at the time of the great fire, was that of street-car transportation. The principal lines had passed into the hands of the United Railroads.[28] The corporation

27 Ruef testified before the Grand Jury that the water deal would have been the most important pulled off by the Board of Supervisors. He testified that he had told Gallagher to tell the members of the Board there would be more money in it than had been received in any other deal. Ruef gave Gallagher to understand that the amount to be divided would be as much as $1,000,000.

28 The United Railroads was controlled by Eastern capital. Before the entrance of the United Railroads into the San Francisco field, California capital had dominated in purely local public utilities.

had, at the time of Schmitz's election in 1905, practically a monopoly of the San Francisco street-car service.

The company's principal lines were operated by the cable system. But fully five years before the fire, all traction officials as well as the general public, recognized that San Francisco had outgrown the cable road. It was admitted that electric lines must be substituted for the cable, but there was sharp division as to the character of the electric lines which should be installed. The officials of the United Railroads proposed the overhead trolley method of propulsion; the public, so far as it could find expression, declared for the underground conduit system.[29] In taking this position, the public was in reality backing up the municipal engineers, who had been sent to Eastern States to investigate electric transportation systems, and who had found in favor of the conduit and against the trolley.[30]

---

[29] The public's opposition to the overhead trolley system was that the poles and wires would be a disfigurement of what were regarded as the best streets; that the wires were dangerous, and would interfere with the work of firemen in fighting fires; that San Francisco was as much entitled as Washington and New York to the best system. Rudolph Spreckels at the trial of Patrick Calhoun for offering a bribe, testified as to his own opposition:

"I believed that the overhead trolley was unsightly; that it increased the risk of fire; that it was dangerous; that it was noisy and unsightly. I believed from my own observation of the operation of the underground conduit system in other cities that it was preferable, that it was more sightly, just as rapid, and in every way more in keeping with a city of the size and importance of San Francisco. Having been born here, and having large property interests I felt it my duty, as I always have, and hope I always shall, to protect the interests of this community and to protect the interests of its citizens and its property owners. That was my purpose in opposing that franchise and that grant."

[30] As early as 1901, C. E. Grunsky, at that time City Engineer, was directed by the Board of Supervisors to gather data on the operation of electric roads under the conduit system. Grunsky's findings were to the effect that conduit-electric roads were rapidly replacing other types of street railroads.

The city also employed J. C. H. Stutt as consulting engineer,

The San Francisco Merchants' Association, however, apparently dissatisfied with the reports of the engineers employed by the municipality, employed Mr. William Barclay Parsons to report on the relative merits of the trolley and the conduit systems.

Mr. Parsons took issue with the city's engineers, and recommended the trolley as against the conduit.[31]   The directors of the Merchants' Association thereupon declared for the trolley system.

Criticism of this action of the directors was followed by submission of the question to a referendum vote of the Association membership.   The members voted in opposition to the directors, declaring against the trolley and for the conduit.[32]

and sent him to New York and Washington to inspect and report upon the conduit systems in operation in those cities.

He reported that the system was giving satisfaction in both cities, and in many cases was being substituted for the trolley. Engineer Stutt in comparing the two systems said:

"As between the overhead system and the conduit-electric system, it is natural for private corporations to prefer the overhead trolley system on acount of the first cost of roadbed construction, which is more than twice as great for the conduit system.   The conduit system leaves the street open with the view unobstructed by poles, conductors, feed, guard and supporting wires and without the menace to the public and especially to the firemen, always inherent in the bare overhead electric conductor."

This report was widely quoted during the overhead-trolley-conduit agitation that was a feature of a greater part of Mayor Schmitz's administrations.

31 Mr. Parsons found for the overhead trolley on the following general grounds:

(1) That a uniform system was necessary.

(2) That the lines must be extended to the suburbs.

(3) That operation by overhead trolley is more satisfactory than by the conduit system.

(4) That the greater part of the roads could be operated under trolley only.

32 Several questions were presented.   The following is the vote as given in the Merchants' Association Review, the organization's official publication, for February, 1906:

"TOTAL VOTE OF MEMBERS, 364.

"1—Do you favor Mr. Parsons's view of a uniform system of overhead trolley lines throughout the entire city, including a central line of ornamental trolley poles, with lights furnished by the Railroad company between the tracks on Market Street, and a

But the most determined opposition to the installation of the trolley system came from improvement clubs, whose purpose was to promote the best development of San Francisco.

Prominent among these organizations were the Improvement and Adornment Association,[33] the Sutter Street Improvement Club[34] and the Pacific Avenue Im-

---

trolley line with ornamental poles and lights furnished by the Railroad upon Sutter Street?
"Votes received—Yes, 121; No, 204.
"2—Do you favor an overhead trolley system throughout the city except on Market Street?
"Votes received—Yes, 67; No, 212.
"3—Do you favor an underground conduit system for Market Street and for the streets with cable lines leading into Market Street in the central downtown district and in the adjacent residence district, the remainder of the system to be overhead trolley?
"Votes received—Yes, 198; No, 84.
"4—Irrespective of what shall be done on any other streets, which system do you favor for Sutter Street: (a) an underground conduit, or (b) an overhead trolley line if equipped with ornamental poles and lights furnished free by the Railroad company, or (c) an improved cable system?

	"Underground Conduit	Trolley	Cable
"First Choice.............	217	93	5
"Second Choice............	42	83	62
"Third Choice.............	7	14	94

"5—Do you favor changing the cable lines on Nob Hill to electric lines by tunneling the hill and constructing a winding driveway with parks on California Street, as proposed in Mr. Parsons's report?
"Votes received—Yes, 158; No, 140."
This vote was taken after an extended debate at a banquet given by the Association in which Patrick Calhoun, president of the United Railroads, argued for the trolley system, and Frank J. Sullivan, president of the Sutter Street Improvement Club, spoke for the conduit.

33 The Improvement and Adornment Association employed D. H. Burnham to draw plans for the development of San Francisco. These plans, while drawn to attain a maximum of utility, were intended to secure a maximum of beauty as well. Streets were to be widened, boulevards built, parks established. The carrying out of these plans would have made San Francisco one of the most beautiful cities of the world. Their preparation cost the association $17,500. Mr. Burnham volunteered his own services.

34 The objection of the Sutter-Street Improvement Club to the overhead trolley was set forth in the following statement, issued less than a month before the great fire of 1906:
"The Sutter Street Improvement Club is unalterably opposed to the construction of an overhead trolley line on the Sutter Street system. We desire that the public should have no misconception of our position. We propose to contest to the end any attempt to get

provement Club. The membership of these organizations consisted of some of the largest owners of San
Francisco properties. The leaders were comparatively
young men, natives of San Francisco, whose interests

an overhead trolley on the entire Sutter Street system, and for
that purpose we pledge ourselves, and promise to provide the
necessary counsel to maintain our position in the courts. We want
the public with us in this fight, as the fight is being made in the
interests of the whole people.

"Our own investigations make us absolutely certain that if the
public understands the true situation, it will not be misled by the
specious arguments of the United Railroads. The conduit electric
system, despite what the United Railroads and its representatives
may say, is practicable, safe, efficient and superior to an overhead
trolley. We are further satisfied that the company is seeking, by
an offer of $200,000 which they offer to the people, to save itself an
expense of several million dollars, which the conduit electric system
would cost, if it should be required to reconstruct all its lines using
the conduits; but we believe—and we are certain that the citizens
of San Francisco will agree with us in this—that since the United
Railroads, through the watering of its stock, has already made
many millions of dollars out of its properties, and is now taking,
and will take many millions of profits from our people, that it can
afford to contribute to San Francisco the cost of the most attractive
and efficient system of electric railroads. The United Railroads
has put forward many arguments which have been and are easily
met:

"First: It contended, as the public will remember, that the conduit electric system was impracticable on account of the accumulation of rain water in its conduits. This claim it has been forced
to abandon.

"Second: It proclaimed loudly that the added cost of construction of an electric conduit was such that the life of its franchise
would not justify the outlay. Now, they have abandoned this claim,
and assert that it is not the cost of construction, but that there are
other reasons.

"Third: They have declared that a uniform system was desirable. They now admit that a completely uniform system is
impracticable, owing to grades, making it necessary to operate some
lines by cable. Their only contention now is that the overhead
trolley system is more efficient than either the cable or conduit
electric system.

"Mr. C. E. Grunsky is our authority for the statement that in
making the change from the conduit electric to the trolley, in
passing from city to suburbs, there are no objectionable features,
nor danger. Sir Alex. B. W. Kennedy, consulting engineer to the
London County Council, in recommending the adoption of the conduit
electric system for London's municipal street railways, said:
'There is no difficulty in arranging the cars so that they can be
run from the underground (conduit) to the overhead and vice versa,
either with no stoppage at all at the point of change, or with a
stopping of only a few seconds. There is no engineering difficulty
whatever in using a mixed tramway system, i. e., partly underground (conduit) and partly overhead.'

"We would suggest that the public compare the present overhead trolley system, operated by the United Railroads these many
years in this city and county, with the service rendered by the Cali-

were inseparably wrapped up in the community, and
who aimed to promote the best possible development of
the city of their birth and fortunes.

Prominent in this group were Rudolph Spreckels [35]

---

fornia Cable Railway. There is no overhead trolley system in San
Francisco to-day which surpasses the service given by the California Street Company.

"It is claimed that the public will be given a speedier and more
efficient service if the overhead trolley is permitted. We ask the
thousands of citizens who have been compelled to wait for overhead
trolley cars, and to stand up in those overhead vehicles, whether
or not the overhead trolley has thus afforded them satisfactory
service? If we may judge the future by the experience with the
overhead trolley of the past, it means fewer cars (hence less expense
to the United Railroads), overcrowding and discomfort of passengers. The only advantage which thus far has come from the system seems to be to the company itself. It employs fewer men as
a result of that system, but the comfort and convenience of the
public have not been substantially bettered by it as against the
cable.

"Before asking our people to give them an overhead trolley system throughout the whole city, the United Railroads would do well
to show on some one of their overhead trolley lines now in operation a frequent, efficient and satisfactory service to the public. We
do not want for San Francisco an extension and perpetuation of
the unsightly, noisy, dangerous, uncomfortable and inefficient system of overhead trolleys as operated by the United Railroads
to-day.

"Citizens of San Francisco: Be not deceived by the selfish and
specious arguments put forward by the United Railroads. If the
public will stand together, we will win out in this fight; and, if it
should be necessary to that end, the supporters of our organization will put before our citizens a plan for building a complete conduit electric system of railroads for San Francisco, to be built, in
the first instance, by our people, but with a provision giving to the
city an option to purchase the same at any time in the future at
actual cost and interest, so that municipal ownership of the said
system may result just as soon as the city is ready for it.

"All that we ask is that the people stand fast, and save their
city from what we believe would be a calamity from which it would
not recover in the next twenty-five years.

"Respectfully,

"Frank J. Sullivan, Rudolph Spreckels, Julius Rosenstirn, Geo. W.
Merritt, W. D. McCann, Houghton Sawyer.   Edward P. E. Troy,
Secretary."

35 Rudolph Spreckels is a native of San Francisco. At seventeen he was employed in his father's (Claus Spreckels) sugar refinery at Philadelphia. The Spreckels refinery was at the time in
a life-and-death struggle with the "Sugar Trust." Young Spreckels
was given his first lessons in the methods employed by the "trust"
elements to crush competition. His Philadelphia training in large
degree prepared him for the work which later he was to do at
San Francisco. At twenty-two he became president of the Hawaiian Commercial and Sugar Company, owners of one of the
largest sugar plantations of the Hawaiian Islands. The venture
had been a losing one. Spreckels put it on a paying basis within

and James D. Phelan,[36] rated among the heaviest property-owners of San Francisco. These men were ready to join with the United Railroads in any plan which proposed the highest development of the street-car service.[37] On the other hand, they were prepared to oppose

---

a year, and sold it at large profit. Before he was twenty-five he had become a millionaire in his own right. He has been engaged in business at San Francisco for many years, but only when moved by corrupt conditions to take up the fight for honest government did he become active in politics. He financed the graft prosecution. He has since taken active part in California politics, but has steadfastly refused to accept public office, preferring to do his work as a private citizen.

36 James D. Phelan is a native of San Francisco. He is one of the largest owners of real estate in San Francisco and in California. From his youth he has taken keen interest in public affairs. He was chairman of the Charter convention of 1900 which framed San Francisco's present municipal Charter. He was Mayor of San Francisco from 1896 to 1902. After the San Francisco fire he headed the Relief Committee and was largely instrumental in directing the work of rehabilitation. President Roosevelt designated him by proclamation to receive funds for the relief work, and to use the United States Mint as depository. In 1900 the Democratic minority in the State Legislature gave him complimentary vote for United States Senator. In 1914 he was elected to the United States Senate, being the first Federal Senator from California to be elected by direct vote of The People. Senator Phelan has for many years been close friend and business associate of Rudolph Spreckels. He was one of the heaviest backers of the graft prosecution.

37 Rudolph Spreckels testified at the trial of Patrick Calhoun: "I suggested to Mr. Calhoun one thing, that if it was a question of the length of the franchise, of the length of life of the present franchise, standing between the people getting the system which I believed it was entitled to, I would personally be glad to do whatever was in my power to have the Charter amended so that they might enjoy a longer term of franchise, to work out the difference in cost; but that I believed it was all important that San Francisco should have the very best of street-car service obtainable."

United Railroads officials objected to the conduit system on the ground that the conduits would fill with water. Spreckels suggested that property owners agree to drain the conduits without expense to the United Railroads, thus demonstrating their practicability, on the understanding that if the conduit system were found to be practical it should be installed. But in this the United Railroad officials would not acquiesce. (See testimony taken at the Calhoun trial.)   The following is taken from Charles S. Wheeler's testimony given at the Calhoun trial:

"Mr. Heney: Q.   Did not the property owners on Sutter street and the property owners on Pacific avenue, Mr. Rudolph Spreckels and Mr. Phelan in particular, state that they would not oppose the United Railroads obtaining a franchise or permit for the underground conduit on Sutter street?

"Mr. Stanley Moore: That is objected to, if your Honor please,

any attempt to exploit the service to the detriment of San Francisco.[38]

---

as calling for the conclusion of the witness and the mental mind and statement and hearsay of other persons.

"Mr. Heney. I am not asking for their mental mind. I am asking about direct statements at these meetings of committees of the Board of Supervisors.

"The Court: I will overrule the objection.

"Mr. Stanley Moore. We take an exception.

"A. I have [heard] both of them make such statements; Mr. Phelan in substance before the Board of Supervisors, and I have heard Mr. Spreckels make it in the Supervisors' chambers." (See Transcript of Testimony, page 3197.)

[38] Patrick Calhoun, president of the United Railroads, had several conferences with Rudolph Spreckels on the questions involved in the street-car situation. Of these conferences Spreckels testified at the Calhoun trial:

"Mr. Calhoun stated that he was very anxious to obtain the overhead trolley privilege, that he understood that I was actively opposing it, and he wanted to know whether I was open to conviction on the subject. I told him that my mind was entirely free, that if he could prove to my satisfaction that the underground conduit was not feasible that I would have no objection. I told him that the arguments that he had presented, namely, that the Sutter street system could not be converted into an underground conduit system because of the accumulation of water at some number of points—I think 16 were mentioned—was hardly worth while urging since Mr. Holland, a former president of the United Railroads, had, together with Mr. Chapman, urged that reason, and I related to Mr. Calhoun that I had questioned Mr. Chapman and Mr. Holland at length in regard to it and had satisfied myself that their reasons then urged were not legitimate or reasonable; that during the conversation with Mr. Holland I had asked him to state all of the reasons that he had for desiring the overhead and urging against the installation of the underground conduit; that Mr. Holland and Mr. Chapman had both assured me that the only reason was the fact that it was an engineering impossibility; that the accumulation of water in the conduits during the rainy season would prevent the successful operation of the cars, that there would be repeated interruptions and general dissatisfaction as the result. I then proposed to Mr. Holland, I said: 'If that is the only reason and you can convince me that that is true I have no objection to withdrawing my opposition, but I want to propose this: Suppose I, or the property owners on the system involved, agree to pay the expense of the proper drainage of those conduits, and succeed for a period of twelve months in treating the conduit drained at those points you indicate, and succeed during that entire term to keep them free from water, so that you and your engineers will be obliged to admit that there was not one hour during the twelve months during which you could not successfully operate an underground system, will you then agree to install that system?' Mr. Holland and Mr. Chapman looked at one another and finally said 'Well, no, we cannot do that.' Then I said: 'Gentlemen, you are wasting my time and your own because your argument is not the truth and is not the only reason you are urging, or that is prompting you to object to putting in that system.'

"Mr. Holland then proceeded and asked me how I proposed to insure that result and I told him I was not an engineer, but that

A conference of the directors of the Improvement
and Adornment Association with officials of the United

common sense told me and indicated to me that it might be possible to carry off the water at those points through an ordinary stone sewer-pipe and distribute the accumulated waters to the various streets running parallel to Sutter street, and in that way carrying it off and keeping the conduits free from water. Mr. Calhoun said: 'Well, there are other reasons—the question of a uniform system.' He urged very strongly that it would be a very desirable thing to avoid transferring, or it would be an exceedingly nice thing if a man could go to his home without transferring, and have a uniform system of cars operating over all of the system. I told Mr. Calhoun it was hardly a possible thing, that no man would want to stand at any street corner and wait for fifteen or twenty cars to go by until some one car of a particular brand would come along which would take him to the particular part of the city he cared to go to. Then Mr. Calhoun wanted to know if the matter couldn't be compromised, whether I would be satisfied, if the United Railroads would agree to construct an underground conduit system on Sutter street from Market to Powell. He wanted to know also about constructing an underground conduit on Market street, and I told him no, that this did not enter into my calculations, that I was looking to the welfare of the city of San Francisco, that it did not involve merely getting what I wanted in front of the particular properties in which I was personally interested, and I told him that the reasons that had been urged against the granting of an overhead trolley—that it was unsightly, dangerous and noisy and not the most modern system, was my objection, and that it held good for the entire city and not alone on the streets in which I was interested as a property owner. Mr. Calhoun urged further the desirability of the overhead trolley, that it had given satisfaction elsewhere, and I suggested that he might first make the street cars then operated by the overhead trolley in San Francisco a success and satisfactory to the people; that I felt that it was far from a success, and personally, as one of the largest propery-owners on Ellis street, I would emphatically prefer the ordinary cable system to the electric lines that they were then operating. Mr. Calhoun asked for another appointment and it was had I think on the following morning, a meeting at the same place, at the Canadian Bank of Commerce; I think our meeting on that occasion was held in the office of the manager, Mr. Kains.

"Q. What was said there? A. I will not be absolutely certain as to whether all that I have related occurred at the first interview, or whether some that I will relate as having occurred now, did not occur on the first interview. The two meetings were close together, and the subjects that I will relate may have occurred, some of them in the previous meeting and some in the latter. Mr. Calhoun proceeded to ask me about Pacific avenue. He said: 'Would you be satisfied if we agreed to operate the underground conduit system on Sutter to Powell, on Market to Valencia, running it, if we changed the system on the Pacific avenue line—to agree to put in the conduit there, otherwise maintaining the cable?' And he also proposed that it might be a nice thing to withdraw the entire street railway system from Pacific avenue, making of that street a boulevard, and placing overhead trolley on Broadway where there was no car line. He said, 'Of course, Mr. Spreckels, you are an owner of carriages and automobiles, and I suppose you don't use the street-cars, and it would be more desirable from the standpoint of a property owner to have your residence under those circum-

Railroads was finally arranged.[39]   The meetings were
held in March, 1906, less than a month before the great
fire.   There were, before the attempted adjustment was
abandoned, several sessions.

The citizens urged Patrick Calhoun, president of the
United Railroads, to give up his trolley design for
Market and Sutter streets.   As a compromise, he substantially agreed to build the underground conduit as
far as Powell on Sutter, and as far as Valencia on
Market, picking up the trolley on Valencia, McAllister,
Hayes and Haight streets.   The Adornment Committee
directors wanted the conduit system on Sutter street
extended as far as possible, and held out for Van Ness

stances on a boulevard than on a street having a street-car service
with the attending objections.'   I told Mr. Calhoun that my fight
was not a selfish one, that I did have carriages and automobiles,
that I did not use the street-cars and had no need for them, but that
I had in mind the rights of other people living on the street—that
there were many people living on the street who were not so fortunate as I, who did not own carriages and did not own automobiles and had undoubtedly been brought to buy their property
on Pacific avenue because of the fact that it had a street-car
service there.   Mr. Calhoun also in one of these interviews said
that he would tunnel Powell street hill commencing at Sutter and
make that the most important transferring point in San Francisco.
I asked Mr. Calhoun at the time whether it was because I was
interested in property at the corner of Sutter and Powell.   Mr.
Calhoun expressed surprise and said he didn't know that I was an
owner of property there.   I think that in substance was the conversation as I remember it."

39 Patrick Calhoun, Tirey L. Ford and Thornwell Mullally were
among the officials representing the United Railroads at the conference.   At the meeting, first mention of $200,000 in connection
with the proposed change in the street-car system was made.
Citizens had contended that the objection of the United Railroads
in opposing the conduit system was the difference in the initial
cost of installation.   This point came up, and President Calhoun
stated that he would, if the trolley system were allowed, give the
difference between the cost of installing the two systems, for any
public purpose.   This difference, Calhoun stated, would be about
$200,000.   Turning to James D. Phelan, of the Adornment Com-
mittee, Calhoun stated that the money could be used in extending
the so-called Park Panhandle, part of the Burnham plans, and a
matter in which Phelan was greatly interested.   Phelan replied
that San Francisco would not accept money for any such purpose,
and was able to construct the Park Panhandle if the people
wanted it.   (See testimony of James D. Phelan at the trial of The
People vs. Patrick Calhoun for offering a bribe, page 2750.)

avenue. Calhoun would not consent to install the conduit beyond Powell.

In the midst of this deadlock, the San Francisco Chronicle published what purported to be reports of the several conferences. Up to that time there had been no publication of the meetings.

Following the Chronicle publication, Calhoun, in a letter to members of the Adornment Association, declared the information contained in the Chronicle article to be inaccurate,[40] and offered to let the people decide whether they wanted a conduit system on Market street to Valencia, and on Sutter street to Powell, or a uniform all-trolley system throughout the city.

Mr. Calhoun's suggestion seemed reasonable until he stated in an interview that by the people he meant the Board of Supervisors.

He was asked how he proposed to ascertain the wishes of the people.

"I should suggest," he is reported as replying, "that the matter be referred to the decision of the Board of

---

[40] The Chronicle in its issue of March 23, in referring to Mr. Calhoun's letter practically charged him with lack of good faith. The Chronicle said:

"The alleged 'inaccuracy' of the Chronicle's interesting report of the compromise reached by the United Railroads and the Society for the Adornment of the City proves to be that the electric conduit in Sutter street is to stop at Powell street instead of extending to Polk street, as proposed, and which is the least which should have been accepted if any compromise whatever was to be made. We shall be greatly surprised if when the changes are finally made there is not a great deal less conduit than Mr. Calhoun now seems to agree to. We gravely doubt whether Mr. Calhoun expects to construct a foot of conduit in this city. However, he does agree to do so under certain conditions and we shall see what we shall see. . . . It does look as though some settlement of the matter would be reached, as the United Railroads have receded from their iron-clad determination not to consider the electric conduit at all. When that is accomplished we shall speedily see the last of the cables south of California street, a consummation as devoutly wished by the people as was the introduction of the cable in place of the horse-car a quarter of a century ago."

Supervisors. The Board of Supervisors is a public body selected by the people, and represents the ideas and wishes of the people of the city."

The reply was not well received. The Supervisors were even then under suspicion of corruption. Less than a fortnight before, March 10, the Examiner had called the board's action on an ordinance which was supported by the Home Telephone Company "suspicious," and had stated that the board had "made the mistake of acting as a bribed Board of Supervisors would have acted." [41]

---

[41] It was openly charged that money had been used to put this franchise through the preliminary steps necessary for its granting. The Examiner in its issue of March 10, some five weeks before the fire, said:

"The Supervisors owe it to themselves to bring back the telephone franchise order for further consideration. Since the hasty vote on the ordinance last Monday ugly rumors have been the measure. The regard of the Supervisors for the good name of the Board demands that they should clear the record of the SUSPICIOUS CIRCUMSTANCES that surround the vote on the order.

"The present Board of Supervisors was elected on a platform that pledged its members to a municipal ownership programme. Among the purposes specifically announced was the ACQUISITION OF A TELEPHONE PLANT to be owned and operated by the city.

"Yet the FIRST ACT OF THE BOARD in dealing with a public utility question is to favor an ordinance granting a franchise for fifty years to a private corporation without proper compensation to the city and WITHOUT ANY CONTRACT that would enable the city to buy out the plant at a just appraisement when the time comes to acquire a municipal telephone system.

"The bill was introduced after a brief hearing and passed to print on the 26th of February. On the 5th of March it was passed to a vote in the Board of Supervisors without discussion. One of the members of the Board who rose to explain his vote was shut off with such indignity that he left the Supervisors' chamber. Nor, indeed, did all the members know what they were voting on; for one of the Supervisors later in the session asked if the telephone franchise was not to be called up, and was surprised to be told that it had already been passed upon.

"This sort of 'gum-shoe' legislation will not do for San Francisco. It inevitably rouses the suspicions of crookedness that have been hawked about the streets since Monday last.

"A telephone franchise is not a matter to be treated lightly. It is an affair of more moment than passing a street or even of fixing a water rate. It deserves the deepest consideration, for the division of service between two companies creates a confusion in business that should be taken carefully into account. It is only the wretched service given by the old company that has brought the backing of a certain popular support to the advent of a new

Later on, the Supervisors themselves confessed to having been bribed to grant the telephone franchise. The public, not at all blind to what was going on, believed, even at the time Mr. Calhoun made his suggestion, although there was no proof, that the Supervisors had been bribed.

San Francisco was opposed to any plan that would put trolley cars on the city's best streets. Submission of the issue to the people would have been popular. Mr. Calhoun's proposal that it be left to the Supervisors was met with suspicion, and open distrust of Mr. Calhoun's motives.

In answer to the criticism which Mr. Calhoun's suggestion had aroused, Mr. Calhoun, in a second letter to the Adornment Association, withdrew his offer to submit the question to the people, and announced the intention of his company to proceed with preparation of a plan for a uniform trolley system to be installed wherever the grades would permit.[42]

---

company. The manner in which the obvious evils of a division of service can be lessened requires much more thought than has yet been given, and many changes in the ordinance should be made unless the last state of the San Francisco telephone service is to be worse than the first.

"It is the duty of the Supervisors to recall the ordinance, answer the rumors of crooked work by seeing that everything is carried on above board and in the open, and treat the franchise in accordance with their anti-election pledges to the people. They cannot afford to rest under appearance of evil that now surrounds the late vote on the order.

"We do not wish to believe that any undue influence was used, but the Supervisors must have heard the rumors that are frequent in the streets, and they must realize that they have made the mistake of acting as a bribed Board of Supervisors would have acted. They have broken their pledge, but happily it is not too late for them to correct the gross error."

42 Mr. Calhoun's second letter, as introduced as evidence at his trial for offering a bribe (page 2775, Transcript, The People vs. Calhoun), was as follows:

"San Francisco, March 23.—Messrs. James D. Phelan, R. B. Hale, Herbert E. Law, Rufus P. Jennings and others—My dear Sirs: You will recall that the only condition on which I consented

This second letter was made public in March, 1906, less than a month before the fire. The position taken by the United Railroads was generally condemned.[48]

to even consider the introduction of an underground conduit on Market street from the ferries to Valencia, and on Sutter from Market to Powell, was to secure harmony and unanimity of action in the development of San Francisco. You will further recall that I distinctly stated that 'if all sides to this controversy are not willing to faithfully and loyally abide by what the people of San Francisco may determine on this subject, the United Railroads prefers to urge, in the interest of the development of San Francisco, a uniform system of overhead trolley operation.'

"The development of the last few days, the threatened litigation against my company, and the action of the Sutter-Street Improvement Club, demonstrate that harmony and unanimity of action, so much to be desired, cannot be obtained, and that the United Railroads cannot expect all parties to the controversy 'to faithfully and loyally abide by what the people of San Francisco may determine on this subject.' On the contrary, if the people should elect to put an overhead on Sutter street, the address of the Sutter-Street Improvement Club distinctly states 'we pledge ourselves and promise to provide the necessary counsel to maintain our position in the courts.'

"In view of these facts, I desire to inform you that the United Railroads will proceed to prepare a plan for the improvement of the transportation of San Francisco. The essential feature of which plan will be a modern, up-to-date, efficient and uniform system of electric propulsion, through the introduction of the overhead trolley system wherever the grades of the streets of the city will permit. When this plan is perfected it will be presented to the proper authorities of the city for their consideration. We will be very glad to go over it with you. Under the circumstances, it will be useless for me now to furnish the preliminary plan of which we spoke.

"In conclusion, permit me to express my appreciation of the motives which led you to seek a conference with me, and the earnest desire of every gentleman who participated in that conference to reach a basis of harmonious action in order that the development of San Francisco might not be obstructed and delayed. "Very truly yours,   PATRICK CALHOUN, President."

48 The Chronicle commented upon Mr. Calhoun's new position as follows:

"The letter written by Patrick Calhoun of the United Railroads to the committee of citizens who have sought to induce him to change his attitude on the subject of overhead trolleys was not in good taste. It exhibited corporative arrogance in its most exasperating form. Mr. Calhoun is too well bred, or perhaps too cautious a man to tell the public to be damned, but every line of his communication breathes the spirit of the insolent utterance of William K. Vanderbilt, and the community will take it that way. . . .

"There is an ill-concealed menace in Mr. Calhoun's declaration that the United Railroads has a plan in preparation which, when perfected, 'will be presented to the proper authorities of the city for their consideration.' As he plainly tells us that this plan provides for an 'efficient and uniform system of electric propulsion through the introduction of the overhead trolley system wherever the grades

But the opposition took more practical form than mere denunciation. A group of capitalists, headed by Claus Spreckels, father of Rudolph Spreckels, Rudolph Spreckels and James D. Phelan, announced their intention to organize a street-railroad company, to demonstrate the practicability of operating electric cars in San Francisco under the conduit system.

The plan was given immediate endorsement both by press and general public. The project was explained in detail to Mayor Schmitz, who in a published statement gave the enterprise his unqualified approval.[44]   But

of the city will permit,' the announcement is equivalent to a notification that 'the proper authorities of the city' will be appealed to for permission to carry out such a scheme, whether the people like it or not. His defiant attitude suggests that he feels pretty sure that the authorities will be on the side of the United Railroads against the people, but he may be mistaken on that score. There is a point beyond which even complaisant authorities would not wish to press the matter to oblige a corporation which shows so little regard for the desires and needs of a community from which it extracts over eight million dollars annually." (See San Francisco Chronicle, March 25, 1906.)

[44] Mayor Schmitz in his statement, said:
"If Claus Spreckels can see his way clear to carry out his great purpose, the fact stands that he must be known more than ever as he has been known in the past, as the greatest public benefactor of the West. I will say, if he can see his way clear, reservedly, for I doubt that any citizen of this city or State can point to any understanding that he has announced he would accomplish, that he has failed to accomplish. Not only is his determination, but within his control is the money to carry out his determination, and I have yet failed to find the man that can say that any object can fail of accomplishment when determination and money walk hand in hand.

"If Mr. Spreckels can carry out his announced desire to network San Francisco with railroads operated by the underground conduit system, I can only say that through his wonderful ambitions of purpose San Francisco will take a stride forward that is wonderful to contemplate. Such action upon the part of Mr. Spreckels would place San Francisco not only in advance of any city in America, but would place it in advance of any city in the world in the battle for public control of utilities operated for the public benefit. The offer of Mr. Spreckels is not only one that must awaken the amazement, but the approbation of every public-spirited citizen. While the rest of the great cities of the world (as well as San Francisco before Mr. Spreckels made his offer) are puzzling to find means through which they can accomplish the great purpose of municipal ownership, Mr. Spreckels has come forward and has offered, for the good of the people, to demonstrate the efficiency of a system that will mean that not only shall the

when the incorporators sought further interview with
Mayor Schmitz, they found themselves unable to secure
a hearing.

The company, under the name of the Municipal
Street Railways of San Francisco, was formed with
Claus Spreckels, James D. Phelan, George Whittell,
Rudolph Spreckels and Charles S. Wheeler as incorporators. The capital stock of the company was fixed at
$14,000,000. Of this, $4,500,000 was subscribed, ten
per cent. of which, $450,000, was paid over to the
treasurer.[45]

---

beauty of San Francisco be not sacrificed, but that the public
desire for rapid transit shall be fulfilled. Backed with the millions he controls, his offer is significant, and is one that we cannot
contemplate lightly.

"As Chief Executive of the city I can only express the hope
that something will happen that will permit Mr. Spreckels to carry
out his object. At one stride this would place San Francisco at
the head of the world in the titanic struggle now waging between
the people and the corporations for the control of those utilities
in which the people are interested for comfort and the corporations
for profit. Great as is his offer, it adds not only enthusiasm, but
rekindles hope in my always expressed desire that my administration would mark the first victory of the municipality in its fight
to control those things that are theirs.

"The people are on the eve of winning for themselves those
things that are theirs. If the offer of Mr. Spreckels can be carried
out, and I see no reason why it cannot, the battle is ended. Not
only will San Francisco be the victor, but from the battle she
will emerge, her beauty unmarred and her railways standing as
exemplifications of the fact that what in science is possible is
capable of actual and practical accomplishment." (See San Francisco Call, March 24, 1906.)

But in spite of this approval, after the organization of the new
company was assured, Rudolph Spreckels found the Mayor's door
closed to him when he attempted to secure an interview. (See
Rudolph Spreckels' testimony at the Calhoun trial.)

45 The purposes of the incorporators were brought out at the
graft trials. At the Calhoun trial, when James D. Phelan, former
Mayor of San Francisco, and one of the incorporators, was under
cross-examination, Calhoun's attorney referred to other public
utility ventures in which Claus Spreckels had been interested, and
asked:

"Q. You knew of the matter of the rival gas or competing gas
lines, and the rival and competing electric lines, and the rival and
competing steam railroads down the valley at the time you went
into the corporation to put in the People's Street Railroad? A. I
knew, and I know the effect they had; they reduced rates in both
cases; and if our system accomplished the purpose of bringing Mr.
Calhoun's railroad to a realization of the public desire to have a
conduit system, our purpose would have been accomplished. It

With this $450,000 an experimental line, under the conduit system, was to be built on Bush street.[46]

The articles of incorporation provided that the franchises acquired under them should contain provisions for the acquisition by the City and County of San Francisco of the roads thus built.[47]

The new company filed its articles of incorporation with the Secretary of State at Sacramento on April 17, 1906.

In the early morning of the day following, April 18, came the San Francisco earthquake and fire. For the moment the public forgot all differences in the common disaster. But the lines of division between exploiter and builder could not be wiped out, not even by the destruction of the city. The contest, which had, without any one realizing its full significance, been fast coming to a head before the fire, was to take definite shape after the disaster.

was the last resort. I looked upon it, as an incorporator, as the last resort. We had negotiated in a friendly way for months, and I saw the fruit of all the conferences fade away and believed that arrangements had been made by Mr. Calhoun with the city administration, and the only resort left to us to do was to build a road of our own to demonstrate that it was practicable and possibly profitable—a conduit system."

[46] As early as April 3, 1906, a petition was circulated for signatures among residents and property owners on Bush street, asking the Board of Supervisors to grant a franchise to operate street-cars on Bush street under the electric-conduit system.

[47] The San Francisco Examiner of March 31, 1906, set forth that "an important feature (of the plans for competing street railways) was that the city should have the right at the end of ten years or any shorter period that might be preferred, to take over the system and operate the same itself, the terms of the transfer to be such as would be just both to the builders and to the municipality."

Among the purposes for which the Municipal Street Railways of San Francisco was formed, was set forth in the articles of incorporation the following: "To accept and acquire franchises for street railroads, elevated railroads and subways, containing provisions for the acquisition thereof by the City and County of San Francisco, or such other conditions as may be lawfully inserted therein."

CHAPTER IV.

San Francisco After the Fire.

The great San Francisco fire was brought under control Friday, April 20, 1906. The Sunday following, the first step was taken toward getting the scattered Board of Supervisors together. George B. Keane, clerk of the board, is authority for the statement that the meeting place was in a room back of Supervisor McGushin's saloon.[48] The ashes of the burned city were still hot; the average citizen was thinking only of the next meal and shelter for the night for himself and dependents. But the public-service corporations were even then active in furthering plans which had been temporarily dropped while San Francisco was burning.

At the McGushin-saloon meeting, Keane found with the Supervisors Mr. Frick of the law firm of Thomas, Gerstle & Frick. Mr. Frick was on hand to represent the petitioners for the Home Telephone franchise, which, at the time of the disaster was pending before the board.

For months previous to the fire, no subject affecting a San Francisco public-service corporation had, with the single exception of the United Railroads' scheme for substituting electric for cable service, created more discussion than the Home Telephone application for

---

48 See Keane's testimony in The People vs. Ruef, No. 1437, Part 3, vol. 1, page 455.

franchise. There had been allegations that the progress which, previous to the fire, the Home Company had made toward securing its franchise, had been paid for,[49] but for weeks after the fire few citizens had time to think about it. The people forgot for the time the issues which had before the disaster divided the city. But the agents for the public-service corporations did not forget. We find a representative of the Home Telephone Company picking his way over the hot ashes of the burned city to McGushin's saloon to meet the Supervisors that the interests of his company might be preserved. The developments of the graft prosecution indicate that even as the Home Company was seeking out the Supervisors, the United Railroads was getting into touch with Ruef.[50]

But if the corporations were quick to avail themselves of the situation to secure privileges denied them

---

[49] See footnote 41, page 43.

[50] Supervisor Gallagher testified in the case of The People vs. Ruef, No. 1437, that about a week before the fire "Mr. Ruef stated that the United Railroads wanted to secure a permit to use electricity upon their lines and asked me to speak to the members of the Board of Supervisors about it and let him know whether it could go through the Board, and about what amount of money it would take. I told him that I would do so." (See Transcript on Appeal, page 850.) Similar testimony, to show that the United Railroads was dealing with Ruef during the month preceding the fire, was brought out at trials of other defendants in the "graft" cases. This would make the date of Ruef's activity on behalf of the United Railroads about the time of Mr. Calhoun's announcement that he would proceed to present plans for the trolley system, to the "proper representatives" of the People (the Supervisors), who were even then, through Ruef, receiving bribe money from public-service corporations.

Gallagher testified further (see same transcript, page 853) that within a week after the fire Ruef stated to him that the United Railroads still wanted its electric permit, and directed that Gallagher find out whether such a permit could be put through the Board. Gallagher testified that he saw members, put the question to them, and reported back to Ruef that in his judgment the permit could be put through by paying each member of the Board the amount which Ruef had specified, $4,000.

before the fire, they were also active in the work of rehabilitation—so far as such activity served their plans and purposes.

This was well illustrated by the course of the United Railroads. Within a fortnight after the fire, that corporation had established efficient service over a number of its electric lines. For a time, passengers were carried without charge. On April 29 and 30, however, fares were collected from men, but not from women and children. With the beginning of May, fares were collected from all persons. For a time, in a glare of much publicity, the United Railroads contributed these collections to the fund for the relief of the stricken city.

The Home Telephone Company had no plant to restore nor authority to establish one; but on Ruef's suggestion it, too, contributed to the fund for the relief of the stricken city—$75,000.[51]

The United Railroads' activity in restoring its electric roads, was in curious contrast to its failure to take advantage of the possibilities offered by its cable systems. As some excuse for this inactivity, the corporation's representatives alleged that the cable slots had been closed by the earthquake, making restoration of the cable roads impractical.

The alleged closing of the slots was even used as argument against the conduit electric system.[52]   But

---

[51] Supervisor Gallagher testified at graft trials that Ruef had told him the payment of this $75,000 to the Relief Fund was a good thing, as it would tend to shut off adverse criticism. But the Home Company people had asked that the money be not turned over to the Relief Fund until such time as the ordinance granting the franchise had been approved or the matter definitely determined.

[52] As early as May 5, C. E. Loss, a railroad contractor, came out with the proposition that the city should abandon all idea of

as a matter of fact, there were many to testify that the damage done the cable slots was not from the earthquake, although the slots in the burned district had been warped more or less by the heat of the fire. But this damage was easily remedied. On the Geary-street road, for example, cars were run for an hour or more after the earthquake. The fire warped the Geary-street cable slot, but this was easily and cheaply remedied by a force of men with cold chisels and hammers.[53]

conduit systems, because the cable slots had been closed by the earthquake. In this, Loss was disputed by City Engineer Thomas P. Woodward. Woodward, in an interview printed in the Examiner on May 5, 1906, said:

"I think Mr. Loss was mistaken when he said the earthquake closed the cable slots. I have not made a careful examination of the various roadbeds in San Francisco, but from what I have seen as I have gone about the city, I am inclined to think that no injury was done the cable slots by the earthquake.

"The lines on Sacramento, California, Geary, Sutter and Haight streets appear to be all right outside the burned district. Where the metal was subjected to the intense heat, the slots are warped out of shape, and in some places closed."

Loss's allegations called forth the following editorial comment in the Examiner of May 5th:

"Even an earthquake shock and a conflagration do not long obscure the vision of certain wealthy gentlemen where there is a chance to turn a calamity to their individual account.

"Before the catastrophe, San Francisco had indicated with great emphasis to the United Railroads that it would not permit the reconstruction of the cable system into an overhead trolley, but would insist upon a modern up-to-date conduit electric railroad, the safety, utility and efficiency of which had been demonstrated in New York and other Eastern cities.

"The emergency created by the destruction of the traffic systems in the city has compelled permission for a temporary trolley line because it could be constructed more quickly than any other.

"It is not intended, and the United Railroads must be made to realize that it will not be permitted, that the unsightly poles and dangerous wires will be allowed to cumber the new and more beautiful San Francisco, any more than it will be permitted that the rough shacks and sheds which temporarily shelter the people in parks and streets and otherwise vacant lots shall remain after the emergency which called them into being has ceased."

53 A. D. Shepard, vice-president and secretary of the Geary-street Railroad Company, gave the following statement to the Examiner as to the condition of the Geary-street roadbed:

"We can run cars as far as the road goes, but the power-house is not ready for business. The smokestack at Geary and Buchanan streets must be built up to comply with the ordinance of the city before we can get a permit to build fires under the boilers. The smokestack should be repaired by the end of this week, and cars will probably be run over the road then. I cannot say just

Statements from officials of the United Railroads, now of record, indicate that the company's cable lines suffered no greater damage than did other cable systems. An affidavit of Frank E. Sharon, for example, who before the fire was superintendent of cables and stables belonging to the United Railroads, made in the adjustment of fire losses sustained by that corporation, sets forth that the company's principal cable power house and repair shops situate on Valencia street were damaged but little by the earthquake.[54] Although the

---

what day we will begin to run cars. All depends upon the smoke-stack and the Board of Public Works.

"Our line was not injured by the earthquake, and we ran cars for some time after the shake. It was the fire that drove us out of business. The heat warped the slot, making it narrow in places and wide in other spots, but this is easily remedied." (See Examiner, May 30, 1906.)

[54] Sharon's affidavit was introduced at the graft trials. It was as follows:

"State of California, City and County of San Francisco—ss.

"Frank E. Sharon, being first duly sworn according to law, deposes and says: That he was for many years prior to April 18, 1906, the superintendent of cables and stables belonging to the United Railroads of San Francisco, and situate at the corner of Market and Valencia streets; that on the property situate at said Market and Valencia streets were located what is known as the Market and Valencia Power House and Shops, consisting of power-house, stables, machine shops, special machine shops, mill, offices, store-rooms, sheds, etc.; that he was such superintendent on April 18, 1906; that on the morning of April 18, 1906, immediately following the earthquake he proceeded to the above described premises, arriving there at about 8 a. m.; that none of the buildings above described were materially damaged by the earthquake; that the walls of all the buildings were standing and intact; that the roofs of all the buildings were on and uninjured by the earthquake, with the exception of the roof of a portion of what is known as the power-house, which was damaged by reason of a small portion of the chimney adjoining the power-house on the west falling thereon; that the greater portion of said brick from the top of said chimney fell toward the south or east into the driveway; that extending from the base of said chimney to the crown thereof and on the east and west side thereof are cracks which were in said chimney for many years prior to the earthquake of April 18, 1906, which cracks were opened somewhat by said earthquake; and the boilers in said power-house were not injured to any extent and steam was kept under said boilers for some time after the earthquake; that in his judgment the building as a whole was intact and the machinery not injured in any material part of the earthquake; that the building caught fire from the adjoining buildings on the east

buildings were damaged by the fire, the damage to the contents, including the machinery by which the cable cars were operated, was, according to statements made by the United Railroads in fire-loss adjustment, comparatively small. The company placed the sound value upon this machinery and contents, after the earthquake, but preceding the fire, at $70,308.80. The salvage was placed at $60,933.80, leaving a total fire loss of $9,375.[55]

The cable cars, with few exceptions, were saved. The most serious loss of cars was on the Powell-street system, where sixty-four were destroyed. Only one Valencia-street car was burned. After both earthquake and fire, the United Railroads had available at least 150 cable cars for its Market and Powell-street systems. This does not include the cable cars available on the Hayes and McAllister roads. The power-houses of these two last-named systems were not destroyed by fire. The allegation has been made that the McAllister-street cable was kept running for several hours after the earthquake.

But whatever the possibilities for the restoration of

---

and southeast late in the afternoon of April 18, 1906; said buildings were not dynamited nor backfired for any purpose.
"F. E. SHARON.
"Subscribed and sworn to before me this 10th day of August, A. D. 1906.
"CHARLES R. HOLTON,
"Notary Public in and for the City and County of San Francisco, State of California."

[55] The loss included $25 damage to two engines which cost new $24,000; $2,000 damage to six boilers, new cost $30,000; $210 water-tank, cost new $350; $500 damage to pipes, valves and fittings, which cost new $10,500; material in store-room worth $2,000, a total loss; $4,800 loss of two tension carriages used for taking up slack of the cable. These tension carriages could very easily have been restored. This loss, $4,800, and the $2,000 stock loss, deducted from the total of $9,375, leaves a total loss of $2,575 to the machinery of a plant estimated to have cost $115,848.

the United Railroads' cable properties, no steps were taken toward that end. Instead, trolley wires were strung over the tracks of cable systems. Street-car service was one of the greatest needs of the first few weeks following the fire. Statements that cable properties could not be restored were generally believed; the trolley service was accepted as a matter of expediency; few thought, however, that it was to be permanent.[56]

---

[56] As late as November 13, 1906, seven months after the fire, the San Francisco Call published an editorial article on the trolley permits which showed that even then their nature was not fully understood. The Call said:

"The insolent disregard of public rights in the streets by the United Railroads is inspired, of course, by ulterior purpose to entrench the corporation in the possession of privileges, permits or franchises granted at a time of stress and confusion whose legality may and probably will be questioned later.

"The Call does not desire to assume an attitude of hindering or hampering progress. We recognize fully that every new street-car line adds materially to the value of property within its tributary territory. In a word, the growth of a city or a neighborhood is, to a considerable degree, dependent on facilities for urban transit.

"But it does not follow from these considerations that franchises should be granted for nothing to any and every applicant who is able to construct a street railway. The right to use the streets is the most valuable privilege possessed by a municipality. It should be made to yield a corresponding revenue.

"All this might seem so obvious as scarcely to require statement, but in practice the principles here laid down have been virtually disregarded in San Francisco. In no instance was there more flagrant disregard of public rights than in the wholesale grants of permits or franchises to construct overhead trolley lines made after the fire.

"The United Railroads at the time professed to regard these permits as merely temporary, but that profession was not very long maintained. The company now declares that many, if not all, of these permits amount to absolute franchises in view of the capital invested in making the necessary changes. That is the explanation of the outrageous disregard of public rights shown in tearing up some five or six miles of streets at once and in different parts of town. This process is obviously wasteful as a financial proposition, and is calculated besides to arouse general indignation. We find these weighty considerations disregarded on the advice of the corporation's lawyers, to bolster up an invalid claim to the possession of franchises obtained by trick and device in an hour of public confusion.

"What the extent of the corporation's claim under these permits may be we are not advised, and there is no immediate means of finding out as long as the administration which granted these hole-and-corner permits remains in power. The same influences that made the Mayor and Supervisors so complaisant to the will

Within two weeks after the fire, the United Railroads had trolley wires strung over the cable tracks on Market street. The little objection made to this course went unheeded. The Market-street trolley cars, two weeks after the fire, were as welcome to The People of San Francisco as were the temporary shacks which were being erected upon the sites of the old city's finest buildings. Market-street trolley cars gave as sorely-needed transportation as the shacks gave needed shelter.

The opening of the Market-street trolley line was made subject for rejoicing throughout the city. In the midst of this good feeling toward his company, President Calhoun gave out that if allowed to place overhead wires on Sutter and Larkin streets, he would place 2,000 men at work and have both these lines in operation within thirty days.[57]

But the era of good feeling was not of long dura-

---

of the United Railroads are still operative. It was only the other day that another permit for a street-car line was granted, and granted illegally. This administration stays bought.

"Therefore, the streets are torn up in a dozen different parts of town and left in that condition untouched for months with the full consent of the administration. But this political condition is not permanent. Some of these people will go to jail. They will all be ousted at the next election. San Francisco has had enough of them.

"The United Railroads is endeavoring to fortify one wrong by committing another. These things will not be forgotten in a, hurry. We are convinced that the corporation is pursuing a shortsighted policy. Costly litigation must ensue to test the validity and extent of the overhead trolley permits. The people will not consent to see their most valuable property traded away by a lot of conscienceless boodlers, and if it should prove that the United Railroads has been able to make two wrongs constitute one right, it is very certain that a movement of irresistible force will follow for a reduction of street-car fares.

"We are convinced that it will pay the United Railroads to be fair and decent with the people of San Francisco. The present policy is neither fair nor decent. The service is bad, public rights in the streets are outraged, and, worst of all, the corporation is the most malign, corrupting influence in the politics of our municipal government. There will come a reckoning."

[57] See statement printed in San Francisco Examiner, May 4, 1906.

tion. On May 14, less than a month after the fire, the Supervisors received a communication signed by President Calhoun as President of the United Railroads, setting forth that if the board would permit the use on the cable lines of the standard electric system in use on the company's other lines, the United Railroads would be glad to put all of their lines in commission as rapidly as could be accomplished by the most liberal expenditure of money and the largest possible employment of men.[58]

That very day, the Supervisors took the initial step toward granting to the United Railroads a blanket per-

---

[58] Calhoun's letter to the Supervisors read:
"United Railroads of San Francisco.
"President's Office.
"San Francisco, May 14, 1906.
"To the Honorable Board of Supervisors of the City of San Francisco—Gentlemen: The United Railroads of San Francisco respectfully represents that, notwithstanding its urgent and earnest efforts to provide adequate street railway transportation on the lines being operated, constant pressure is being applied and innumerable requests are being presented to it to increase its transportation facilities.

"The company is anxious to please the people, and is willing to do its part in the immediate upbuilding of the Greater San Francisco, but owing to the unavailability of material and machinery for operating its cable systems, as well as the great length of time necessary to rebuild destroyed power-houses and reconstruct its cable conduits, a long time would necessarily elapse before the cable systems could be operated so as to give the required relief to traffic congestion.

"If your Honorable Board will permit the use on the cable lines of a standard electric system such as is now used on the company's other lines, we will be glad to put all of our lines in commission, and will agree to have them in complete operation wherever grades will permit as rapidly as the most liberal expenditure of money and the largest possible employment of men will accomplish. The necessary expenditure for labor and materials to do this work will run into the millions, and will afford much-needed employment to several thousand deserving men.

"We believe the prompt reconstruction of your lines of transportation will inspire confidence in all investing capital and greatly aid in the prompt rebuilding of your city.

"We submit these suggestions for your consideration at the request of many of our citizens from every walk of life.
"Respectfully,
"PAT. CALHOUN, President."

mit, authorizing that corporation to substitute the trolley system for all its cable lines.

Immediately, San Francisco's opposition to the trolley system was revived. All classes joined in condemning the action of the board. The Sutter Street Improvement Club, representing large down-town interests and property holders, adopted resolutions demanding that the Supervisors refuse to grant the permit. The San Francisco Labor Council, representing over 100 affiliated unions, with a membership of more than 30,000 wage earners, declared as strongly against such action. The press charged the United Railroads with taking advantage of the city's distress to force the trolley upon her.[59]

---

59 The trolley permit was passed to print on May 14. The Examiner, in its issue of May 15, said:

"The United Railroads, with the rapacity for which it has ever been noted, is seeking to capitalize the city's woe to its own advantage.

"Before the disaster of April 18 it had been balked in its purpose to make San Francisco a trolley town. The protests of citizens who knew that the underground system is better than the cheap, unsightly trolley system and had been proved safer, had blocked the United Railroads project. And it seemed certain that the scheme to cumber Market street and Sutter street with poles and wires was definitely stopped.

"The emergency which demanded the swiftest possible establishment of a transportation system, gave the United Railroads its opportunity to revive the discreditable scheme. As an emergency service nobody could object to the overhead trolleys. But it was understood that the service was absolutely temporary in its character and should only obtain during the pendency of present conditions.

"Yesterday, however, there appeared out of the void of forbidden things an ordinance that was hastily passed to print, granting a franchise to the United Railroads to trolleyize its whole system.

"It was expected evidently that this iniquitous measure could be sneaked through under cover of the present stress and excitement without people realizing until it was too late what had been done.

"When the scheme was flushed it was still attempted to make it appear that this was a temporary measure, a representation absolutely varying with the language of the ordinance.

"But the scheme has not succeeded yet.

"It was to be expected that, like the looters who have to be kept from other people's property by soldiers and police, San Francisco's misfortune would bring out a horde of corporate ghouls

Then came explanations and defense. Mayor Schmitz in public interviews set forth that the proposed permit was not a permanent measure, nor under its provisions could the United Railroads indefinitely operate trolley cars in Market street.[60] The Labor Council which had at first adopted resolutions condemning the policy of granting the permit, adopted resolutions of confidence in the "present city administration." President Calhoun himself solicited citizens to attend the meeting of the board at which a vote was to be taken on the proposed permit, to urge action favorable to the United Railroads.[61]

---

eager to snatch privileges during the time of disorder. But it was likewise to be expected that the city administration, which has been so alert to protect private property, would be equally alert to protect the precious possessions of the city.

"The railroads can only do what the city permits, and a strong official scrutiny of the ordinance which was yesterday passed to print should result in its final defeat.

"No matter what other claims an administration may have to the gratitude and respect of the citizens of San Francisco, it cannot afford to be known as the administration that put trolley poles on Market street."

[60] The day that the ordinance granting the trolley permit was ordered printed, Mayor Schmitz stated in an interview as published in the Examiner:

"The proposed franchise is merely a temporary measure. It does not mean that the United Railroads can indefinitely operate their cars by the overhead trolley in Market street, or in the streets formerly occupied by cable roads. It is necessary now to have transportation. The cable roads cannot be repaired, I am told, for some time. Meanwhile, the franchise to string overhead wires has been granted. It can be revoked."

[61] At the Calhoun trial, William H. Sanderson testified to having been introduced to Calhoun by Ruef at a public meeting, a few days before the trolley permit was granted. He was then asked:

"Q. What, if any, conversation then ensued between yourself, Mr. Ruef and Mr. Calhoun? A. Well, I stated—Mr. Calhoun was at that time sitting at a large table in the room, where the committee had held its session, and he rose out of his seat, and the three of us held a conversation following that introduction. I stated to Mr. Calhoun—I asked him when the people of North Beach were or might expect railroad facilities, that the population was coming back to that portion of the city, and that other portions of the city were provided with facilities, and that we were compelled to walk through miles of burned district in order to get anywhere; and Mr. Calhoun said in reply, that if the people of

Long before the board met to take final action it was recognized that in spite of opposition the permit

---

San Francisco desired railroad facilities, they should co-operate with the railroad company that was here to provide them with the same; and I said to Mr. Calhoun that I thought that we were ready to do anything that the company desired us to do, and asked him what in particular he wished us to do, and he said: 'There is that trolley privilege matter before the Supervisors; that comes up next Monday, and you people of San Francisco ought to come down before that Board, that the people of San Francisco, or you, are vitally interested in the matter of this trolley permit.' Mr. Ruef then said: 'Come down before the Board next Monday, Sanderson, and make a talk on behalf of your organization in favor of the trolley permit. We will see that you get the privilege of the floor. A number of citizens of San Francisco will be there, and we propose to show the press that the people of San Francisco are behind this permit.' I said to Mr. Calhoun: 'The papers tell me that this is a very valuable franchise and you ought to pay the city something for it.' And Mr. Calhoun said in substance that he thought that the company would be paying all that the privileges was worth if it built the road. Then I suggested to him that perhaps that sentiment which objected to the disfigurement of Market street and Sutter street by the erection of poles and wires, ought to be placated to some extent, and I asked him why he would not at least put the feed-wires under ground; and he said that that would entail an expense which the company at that time was not or did not think it advisable to meet. And then I asked him why he would not put the poles 200 feet apart instead of 100 as—or 200 feet apart, as was done in European cities, and he said that the 100-foot system was the more advisable in his opinion. And then Mr. Ruef said to me: 'The passage of this permit will mean immediate work for 5,000 men. We will be able to take them out of the camps and put them at work.' And I said to Mr. Ruef: 'That is all very well, Mr. Ruef, but it seems to me that there is another side to this question—a political side. The people of San Francisco are at last all behind your administration. What they need in this crisis is leadership, and we will have to take such leadership as you give us; and now that everybody is with you, and even the Bulletin has quit, it is not good policy on your part to stir up another newspaper war. The Examiner has been your friend ever since Schmitz was first elected, and it will not swallow the trolley proposition in its present form, and it is charging your administration with corruption. If it persists in its fight it will eventually break your back. It seems to me that it would be a comparatively easy matter to placate this opposition by exacting some compensation for this permit, either in the way of cash or by way of a percentage of the proceeds of the road, or you might limit it as to time; give them a permit for five or ten years. You have them at your mercy and they are bound to accept whatever terms you prescribe.' Mr. Ruef then said: 'To hell with the Examiner, no public man can afford to swallow that paper. This thing will go through on Monday. It is all settled.' And then I said: 'You don't need me then,' and Mr. Calhoun said: 'I don't think we do, Mr. Sanderson.' That is all the conversation, or that is substantially all the conversation that took place in regard to that matter."

would be granted.[62] And it was granted. On May 21,
the Supervisors passed the ordinance which gave the
United Railroads authority to convert its cable systems,
wherever grades would permit, into trolley lines. For
this privilege, no money compensation, nor promise of
compensation, was made the city.[63]

Demand that Mayor Schmitz veto the ordinance
granting these extraordinary privileges followed. Nevertheless, the Mayor affixed his signature to the trolley
permit-granting ordinance.

Fair expression of the feeling this action engendered
will be found in the San Francisco papers of the latter
part of May, 1906. "Mayor Eugene E. Schmitz," said
the Examiner, for example, "has betrayed the trust
reposed in him by the people, violated his solemn pledge
in favor of an underground conduit system, and joined
Abe Ruef and the United Railroads in the shameless
work of looting the city at the time of her greatest
need."

The Ruef-Schmitz administration protested at the

---

[62] Said the Examiner in its issue of May 16, 1906: "It looks
very much as if Patrick Calhoun, Thornwell Mullally and their pals
of the United Railroads had sneaked up behind San Francisco just
as she lay wounded from earthquake and conflagration. In the
guise of helping her, they were caught picking her pocket. If the
Supervisors aid and abet them, the people will be warranted in
setting up their effigies in lasting bronze, a group of everlasting
infamy, with the inscription: 'THESE MEN LOOTED SAN FRAN-
CISCO AT THE TIME OF THE GREAT FIRE OF 1906.'"

[63] Of the failure to exact pay for the franchise, the Examiner
of May 17, 1906, said:
"Mayor Schmitz and the Board of Supervisors must know, and
if they do not know they are now informed, that the franchises
they propose to give away to the United Railroads are worth a
great deal of money to the city of San Francisco, and they certainly do know that the city never was so greatly in need of money
as now. To give away so much of value at such a time is so
hideous a crime that it will leave a scar upon the reputation of
everybody concerned in it, no matter what that reputation has been
up to the time of the infamy."

criticism. The eighteen Supervisors, seventeen of whom were within a year to confess that they had accepted bribes and all of whom were to be involved in the scandal, joined in a letter [64] to the Examiner, announcing that such criticism was unwarranted, and injured the city. The letter contained veiled threat that questioning of the Supervisors' motives would not be tolerated. The threat, however, intimidated nobody. Criticism of Ruef and the administration continued.

But in spite of the hostility toward him, Ruef controlled the San Francisco delegates who were named that year to attend the Republican State convention. The convention met at Santa Cruz. Ruef held the balance of power. He was the most sought man there.

---

[64] The Supervisors' letter to the Examiner was as follows:
"San Francisco, Cal., May 26, 1906.

"To 'The San Francisco Examiner,' City—Gentlemen: The Board of Supervisors of the City and County of San Francisco, regretting the hostile stand which your journal has in these distressing times assumed toward the rebuilding of our destroyed city, by indiscriminately attacking every vested interest and all intending investments of capital in this city, respectfully submits for your consideration the propriety of joining with instead of assailing those who are in good faith and with their energy and ability striving to restore and rebuild our beloved city.

"Irrespective of any personal feeling caused by your wanton attacks on his Honor the Mayor, and on this Board, we ask of you, as citizens of San Francisco and as the legislative branch of our government, to cease your thoughtless and dangerous efforts to drive away from our city every interest which has expressed its intention to assist in our rebuilding and which has manifested a practical confidence in our future. Otherwise, the day will certainly not be far distant when the people, realizing the result of your course, will seek to protect the city against its further continuance.

"In all good faith for the city's interests and without any personal rancor, these suggestions are submitted to your careful attention.

"Respectfully, James L. Gallagher, Max Mamlock, Chas. Boxton, L. A. Rea, F. P. Nicholas, Andrew M. Wilson, Geo. F. Duffey, J. J. Furey, M. W. Coffey, Daniel G. Coleman, C. J. Harrigan, J. J. Phillips, P. M. McGushin, E. I. Walsh, Sam Davis, Jas. T. Kelly, Thomas F. Lonergan, W. W. Sanderson."

He had the nomination for Governor in his hands. He gave it to James N. Gillett.[65]

While the convention was in session, a dinner was given the State leaders of the Republican party at the home of Major Frank McLaughlin, then Chairman of the Republican State Central Committee. Ruef was one of the select few present. A flash-light picture of that banquet board shows him seated in the place of honor at the center of the table, the remaining guests with the exception of the host, McLaughlin, who is seated at Ruef's side, standing.

At Ruef's back stands James N. Gillett, who had just received, with Ruef's assistance, the party nomination for Governor, his hand resting upon Ruef's shoulder. Others in this flash-light group are George Hatton, political manipulator, whose connection with the 1905 mayoralty campaign in San Francisco has already been noted; J. W. McKinley, head of the Southern Pacific Law Department at Los Angeles, who was chairman of the convention; Rudolph Herold, a politician prominent in the counsels of the old "Southern Pacific machine"; Justice F. W. Henshaw of the California Supreme Bench, who was nominated at the convention for re-election;[66] Walter F. Parker, political agent for the

65 Ruef, in his story of his political career, "The Road I Traveled," states that in an interview with William F. Herrin, chief of the Southern Pacific law department, previous to the primary campaign, the necessary expenses of the primary campaign and of the primary election were discussed. Herrin, according to Ruef's account, agreed not to oppose the Ruef tickets. "As agreed prior to the primary," Ruef goes on to say in his narrative: "Herrin paid me $14,000 for the purpose of securing for his organization the certainty of the votes of the San Francisco delegation." See San Francisco Bulletin, August 31, 1912.

66 Henshaw was re-elected. After Ruef had been convicted and the Appellate Court had refused to grant him a new trial, Henshaw, before the briefs had been filed in the matter of the appeal

Southern Pacific Company; Warren R. Porter, who had just received the nomination for Lieutenant-Governor; Congressman J. R. Knowland, prominent in the counsels of the "machine" that at the time dominated the State, and Judge F. H. Kerrigan of the Appellate Bench, whose decision in favor of the Southern Pacific Company while on the Superior Bench, in the so-called San Joaquin Valley railroad rate case, made him a conspicuous figure in California public life.[67]

The group represented the most effective forces at the time in California politics. Ruef, at the Santa Cruz convention, reached the height of his power. He left Santa Cruz planning a State organization that would make him as great a factor in State politics as he was at the metropolis.

But on his return to San Francisco, Ruef found himself harassed by criticism and beset by opposition. At every point in the municipal administration, with the exception of the District Attorney's office, was suggestion of graft and incompetency. The police department could not, or would not, control the criminal element. Merchants, in the middle of the day, were struck down at their places of business and robbed. Several were fatally injured in such attacks, being found dying and even dead behind their counters. Street robberies were of daily occurrence.

In the acres of ash-strewn ruins, was junk worth hundreds of thousands of dollars. The police seemed

from the Appellate to the Supreme Court, signed an order granting Ruef a new hearing. See Chapter XXIX.

67 See decisions in Edson vs. The Southern Pacific Co., 133 Cal. Reports and 144 Cal. Reports.

utterly powerless to protect this property.   It became
the loot of unchecked bands of thieves.

A reign of terror prevailed.   Citizens feared to appear on the streets at night.   Merchants charged that their
business was seriously injured by these conditions.   On
all sides, blame was placed upon the Schmitz administration which Ruef was known to control.[68]

Then again, Ruef's toll from the tolerated gambling,
saloon and social evil interests was getting too heavy
for his own safety.[69]   The public was given hint of this
when the newspapers quoted George Renner, a prominent businessman, as asserting that a liquor license could
be secured if the applicant "put the matter into Ruef's
hands and paid a fat little fee."   Ruef, in his reply,
stated that the liquor people were nuisances anyhow.
Ruef had long acted as attorney for the California
Liquor Dealers' Association.   The Association, after

---

[68] Nor was this criticism confined to San Francisco; it was general throughout the State. The Sacramento Bee, in describing the
conditions prevailing at San Francisco, said:
"In the hold-ups which are now terrorizing the people of San
Francisco the citizens are seeing the effects of a loose or dishonest
municipal administration. The form of lawlessness now prevailing
in San Francisco follows upon bad local government as inevitably
as night follows day."

[69] Definite figures, alleged to be the graft schedule enforced
in the San Francisco tenderloin after the fire, were published. The
Chronicle of April 24, 1907, said on this score:
"After the great disaster of last April, or so soon as the new
tenderloin began to build up and the Barbary Coast district began
to establish itself, a schedule of prices for protected vice was formulated. This schedule has been rigidly adhered to. In the case
of houses of ill-fame, the proprietors were required to pay the policemen on the beat the sum of $5, the sergeants $15, the captains
$25, and the chief of police $75 to $100 every week for the privilege
of conducting their nefarious business. The gambling houses were
assessed according to their ability to pay, but the average price
for police protection, according to Heney, was about the same as
the houses of prostitution. The dives along Pacific street and in
the Barbary Coast district were required to pay $50 every week to
the police captain and the chief, those two functionaries presumably
dividing the money. The sporting saloons where women of the
night life congregate were taxed a similar amount."

Ruef's flippant characterization of the liquor people, boldly dispensed with his services and employed another attorney, Herbert Choynski, in his stead. Choynski made no effort to placate Ruef. On the contrary, he gave out interviews to the press charging that Ruef had received $500,000 for the trolley permit, and that each Supervisor had been given $4000 or $5000 for his vote.

This story was given some credit, although few realized the amount of truth it contained.

The Supervisors were spending money freely. Men, who in private life had earned less than $100 a month, and as Supervisors were receiving only that amount, gave evidence of being generously supplied with funds. Supervisor Coffey, a hack driver, took a trip to Chicago. Lonergan, driver of a delivery wagon, announced plans for a tour of Ireland with his wife and children. Wilson planned a trip through the Eastern States. The official head of the administration, Mayor Schmitz, left on a trip to Europe, leaving Supervisor Gallagher as acting Mayor.[70] Reports printed in San Francisco papers of Schmitz, the orchestra player, as guest of the most expensive European hotels, did not tend to lessen the opposition to the administration.

---

[70] Ruef advised strongly against Schmitz leaving San Francisco. In an interview printed in the San Francisco Call, May 16, 1907, the day after he had plead guilty to a charge of extorting money from French restaurant dives, Ruef said:

"The great mistake of this whole thing began with the Mayor's trip to Europe. The Mayor had been proclaimed as the man of the hour after the disaster of last April. He was suddenly seized with the desire of making a trip to Europe, where he expected to be received as one of the crowned heads. He thought his fame would spread throughout the world and he hoped to be lionized abroad and, incidentally, gain social prestige. The whole thing was a mistake. I begged him not to go. I pointed out to him that the city was in ruins and the place for the Mayor was at home. He persisted, and all my pleadings were in vain."

The general dissatisfaction with the administration finally found expression in a mass meeting intended to inaugurate a movement to rid the community of Ruef's influence.[71] The meeting was called in the name of various promotion associations and improvement clubs. It was to have been held in the rooms of the California Promotion Association, a temporary shack that had been erected in Union Square, a public park in the business district. But the crowd which gathered was so great that the meeting had to be held in the park itself.

When the committee in charge met to complete final preparations, preliminary to calling the meeting to order, Ruef and Acting Mayor Gallagher, with astonishing assurance, appeared before the committee and offered their co-operation in the work in hand. Their presence does not appear to have been welcome. Nevertheless, before the resolutions which the committee had under consideration were read before the crowd, all harsh references to Ruef and the municipal administration had been expurgated. In effect, the expurgated resolutions called upon commercial organizations, clubs, labor unions and similar bodies to form a committee of 100 for public safety.

In the meeting which followed the expurgation of the resolutions, the organizers of the movement lost control. Their counsel was for moderation in a situation where all elements were at work.

---

[71] At a preliminary meeting of the organizers of this movement, held in the office of the California Canners, October 10, 1906, responsibility for the state of affairs in San Francisco was charged to Ruef. It was stated at this meeting, and given out to the press, that convincing evidence had been secured against Ruef which warranted his prosecution.

The crowd was made up of Ruef claquers who shouted everybody down; members of **Labor Unions** who had been led to believe that the purpose of the gathering was to break down the unions; and of radicals who were for proceeding immediately to clean up the town. Those responsible for the gathering appeared appalled at its magnitude, and showed themselves unable to cope with the situation.

William A. Doble presided. Samuel M. Shortridge, an attorney who was to play a prominent part in the graft trials, stood at Doble's side and acted as a sort of director of the proceedings. The expurgated resolutions were read by the President of the Merchants' Association, E. R. Lillienthal. The ayes were called for and the resolutions declared to have been adopted. The next moment announcement was made that the meeting stood adjourned.

An angry demonstration followed. The people had met to discuss lawlessness. They refused to be put off. The adjourned meeting refused to adjourn. There were cries of **Drive Ruef out of Town**. One speaker, A. B. Truman, denounced Ruef as a grafter. For the moment an outbreak seemed imminent. At this crisis, Acting Mayor Gallagher appeared.

"I would suggest," he announced,[72] "that you disperse to your respective homes."

---

[72] Acting Mayor Gallagher was emphatic in declaring that no vigilance committee should disgrace San Francisco. The interior press, which was following the San Francisco situation closely and from an independent standpoint, advised Mayor Gallagher that the best way to prevent organization of such a committee would be to enforce the laws. Said the Stockton Record:

"If Acting Mayor Gallagher and his associates wish to abate the agitation in favor of a committee of safety for San Francisco, they should do less talking and take more energetic action against

Citizens who did not care to participate in what threatened to become a riot began leaving the park. But Ruef's henchmen did not leave.

Ruef, who had cowered in fright when the crowd was denouncing him, was concealed in a room in the so-called Little St. Francis Hotel, which after the fire had been erected in Union Square Park. From his hiding place he could see the crowd without being seen. At the right time, he appeared on the steps of the building which were used for the speaker's stand. His followers, now in a majority, cheered him wildly. The next moment, Ruef was in control of the meeting which had been called to protest against the conditions in San Francisco, for which the administration, of which he was the recognized head, was held to be accountable.[73]

---

the thug element. The police department of the afflicted city is now virtually on trial. It is even under suspicion of offenses graver than that of inefficiency. One or two more crimes of violence with well-known people as victims will fire the public indignation of San Francisco to a point where incapable officers will be forced aside and an authority created to meet the grave emergency confronting respectable citizenry."

The Stockton Independent went even further. Said that paper of the San Francisco situation:

"Acting Mayor Gallagher of San Francisco declares there shall be no vigilance committee and no lynching in San Francisco. If he and the police are unable to prevent daily murders, or attempted murders, by single criminals, how can he prevent good citizens in hundreds of thousands from lynching those criminals if they catch them? Perhaps some of the purblind members of the police force may be among the first to be lynched."

[73] After Ruef's capture of the Union Square meeting, Rev. P. C. Macfarlane, pastor of the First Christian Church at Alameda, said in a sermon (October 21, 1906) of the San Francisco situation:

"Let a few resolute, clean-handed business men of San Francisco who are not cowards, who are not quitters or grafters, get together and make a purse of twenty, fifty or a hundred thousand dollars, then employ the ablest attorney to be had and set quietly to work to find the graft and punish the grafters. They could make chapel exercises on Sunday afternoon in San Quentin look like a political rally in San Francisco inside of two years.

"Thus Eugene E. Schmitz stands before the world as a man who tried to reform and could not. He is a moral inebriate. He is a welcher. He is a wanderer on the face of the globe, a man without country, expatriated by his own cowardice. This is Dr. Jekyll.

"But there are some who see in Schmitz Mr. Hyde. These do

The first serious attempt to oust Ruef from his dictatorship had failed.

But while the protestants against prevailing conditions were hot with the disappointments of this failure, District Attorney Langdon issued a statement that he had determined to seize the opportunity presented by the impanelment of a new Grand Jury to inaugurate a systematic and thorough investigation into charges of official graft and malfeasance in office. To assist in this work, he announced, Francis J. Heney had been requested to become a regular deputy in the District Attorney's office, and had accepted. That the investigation might not be handicapped by lack of funds, Mr. Langdon stated Rudolph Spreckels had guaranteed that he would personally undertake the collection from public-spirited citizens of a fund to provide for the expenses necessary to make the investigation thorough.[74]   It be-

---

not give the Mayor credit for even a spasm of virtue and say that the great work of the morning of April 18 was done by General Funston and prominent citizens of their own volition.   These people say that he has now gone from San Francisco, taking with him vast sums of money gained through the granting of the trolley franchise, plotted even while the embers smoldered, and that he will never return.

"The United Railroads is universally believed to have acquired its trolley franchises by corrupt means. It is said that prominent merchants will crane and crook and bow and scrape to get a nod of recognition from Abe Ruef. Ruef has used the advantages given him by the state of affairs to corrupt the greatest city in California. Ruef owns the Board of Supervisors. The Police Commissioners belong to him. The saloon-keeper who wants a license, a corporation that wants a favor from the Board of Supervisors, has only to retain Ruef as an attorney at a fee sufficiently large."

Dr. Macfarlane gave expression to what many thoughtful men were thinking, but of which few with interests at San Francisco dared to admit openly.

74 Mr. Langdon's statement was published October 21, 1906.   It was in full as follows:

"In view of the present extraordinary conditions prevalent in the City and County of San Francisco, the unusual increase in crime, which threatens to grow worse as the winter sets in, and in view of the numerous charges of official graft and malfeasance in office, I have determined to seize the opportunity presented, by the impanelment of a new grand jury, which has been set down for next

came known that William J. Burns, who had been
associated with Heney in the Oregon land-fraud cases,
had been retained to direct the investigation, and that
for several months his agents had been quietly at work.
The effect of these announcements was immediate.

Wednesday by Hon. Thomas F. Graham, the Presiding Judge of the
Superior Court in the City and County of San Francisco, to inaugurate a systematic and thorough investigation into these conditions. It is my official duty to do so, and in pursuance of that duty
and in view of the magnitude of the task, I have decided to seek
the best assistance obtainable. It is my purpose to set at rest
these charges of official graft by either proving them false or convicting those who are guilty. If the charges be untrue, their falsity
should be demonstrated to the world, so as to remove the impres-
sions which have been circulated to the injury of the credit and
fair name of the city. If they be true we should show to the country that there is enough strength, virtue and civic pride in our
people to enable the regularly constituted machinery of justice to
re-establish conditions on a clean, righteous and just basis, without
resort to any extraordinary expedients outside the law. This is to
be an honest, fair, thorough and searching investigation. We shall
protect no man. We shall persecute no man, but we shall prosecute every man who is guilty, regardless of position or standing in
the city. In order that we may have the benefit of expert services
in this work I have requested Mr. Francis J. Heney, who has won
national fame for his work in the prosecution of the Oregon land
fraud cases, to become a regular deputy in my office. Mr. Heney
has accepted. It is unfortunate that this work should be commenced during a political campaign, but the conditions in San
Francisco to-day require that radical action be taken at once, and
though I may be charged with instituting this investigation at this
particular juncture for political advantage, I must ask the public
to judge me by the results attained, which will be the best answer.
"I am not unmindful of the great difficulties involved in this
investigation. It will be both laborious and costly. The money
available under the appropriations made to the District Attorney's
office and the grand jury is, of course, utterly inadequate. Often
previous investigations by other grand juries have been made abortive because of this lack of necessary funds to meet expenses. In
the present instance we shall not suffer this severe handicap. I am
authorized to announce that Mr. Rudolph Spreckels has guaranteed
that he will personally undertake the collection from public-spirited
citizens of a fund to provide for the expenses necessary to make
the investigation thorough and so that good results may ensue.
The city is in deep affliction consequent upon the dreadful calami-
ties of last spring; it is in danger from certainly increasing inva-
sion of desperate criminals from all over the world; some of the
public departments are undoubtedly in bad hands, and I appeal to
my fellow-citizens to give this investigation their moral support,
so that the innocent may be protected, so that the guilty may be
punished, and so that San Francisco may be helped to her feet and
started again on the high road of prosperity in her material conditions, and have restored decency, efficiency, honesty and honor in
her public affairs.

"WILLIAM H. LANGDON, District Attorney."

All talk of "vigilante committee" and "lynching" ceased. The case of The People of San Francisco vs. the Schmitz-Ruef Administration was to be presented in an orderly way in the courts.

And the united press of San Francisco, legitimate business interests, and a great majority of the people welcomed the alternative.

CHAPTER V.

GRAFT PROSECUTION OPENS.

Three days after the announcement of his plans, District Attorney Langdon appointed Heney to a regular deputyship. But even before Langdon had taken office, as early as December, 1905, Fremont Older, editor of the San Francisco Bulletin, had suggested to Heney that he undertake the prosecution of those responsible for conditions in San Francisco.

The Bulletin had been the most fearless and consistent of the opponents of the Schmitz-Ruef regime.[75] After Ruef's complete triumph at the November election in 1905, he boasted that he would break the Bulletin with libel suits. With every department of government in his control, Ruef appeared to be in a position where, even though he might not be able to make good his threat, he could cause the Bulletin much annoyance if not great financial loss.

Older went on to Washington to engage Heney to

---

[75] The persecution of the Bulletin during this period was characteristic of Ruef's methods and reflected the state of lawlessness which prevailed in San Francisco. R. A. Crothers, proprietor of the paper, was assaulted and badly beaten. The newsboys organized into a union. The boys were sincere enough, but the movement was in reality engineered from the tenderloin. Soon a strike of newsboys against the Bulletin was inaugurated. Copies of the paper were snatched from the hands of citizens who purchased it. Bulletin carriers and agents were assaulted. Tugs of its delivery wagons were cut. When the paper was delivered to stores, sticks and stones were thrown in after it. The police did not interfere. The manifestations of lawlessness went unchecked. Libel suits were brought against the Bulletin. Business boycotts were attempted against it.

defend the paper, should Ruef attempt to make his boast good. Heney gave Ruef's threats little credence. "I would be very glad to defend you," he told Older, "but I am afraid I'll never get a chance to earn that fee." [76]

Incidentally Older stated that he believed a fund could be raised to prosecute the corrupters of the San Francisco municipal government, and asked Heney if he would undertake the prosecution, if such a fund could be secured.

Heney replied that he would be glad to undertake it, but stated that at least $100,000 would be required. And even with this amount, Heney pointed out to Older, all efforts would be futile, unless the District Attorney were genuinely in sympathy with the movement to better conditions.

On Heney's return to California early in 1906, Older brought him and Rudolph Spreckels [77] and James

---

[76] See address made by Heney before Citizens' League of Justice in October, 1908.

[77] Rudolph Spreckels, although connected with large enterprises, had steadfastly refused to employ Ruef as an attorney, or to join with him in any way. Given control of the San Francisco Gas Company, for example, although he was importuned to do so, Spreckels refused to employ Ruef as attorney for that company. Spreckels testified at the trial of The People vs. Patrick Calhoun. that he had first realized the necessity of proceeding against Ruef and the Ruef-Schmitz administration when Ruef proposed to him to organize a syndicate to purchase San Francisco municipal bonds. Spreckels testified that Ruef set forth his plan as follows:

"He (Ruef) asked me if I would get together a syndicate for the purpose of bidding on these bonds; that he would guarantee that if I did get up such a syndicate, our bid would be a successful bid; that we would not be obliged to bid above par, and that he would guarantee that we would be the successful bidders. My reply to Mr. Ruef was that I could not understand how anybody could make such an agreement or promise, and how did he propose to make such a statement—to carry out what he had stated. He said: 'Why, that is a simple matter. You know my connection with the Labor Unions and the Labor Union party. Just at the time that the bids are about to come in, I will arrange to tie up this town; we will have the biggest strike that the community has ever known.

D. Phelan together. Heney and Spreckels met for the
first time. Phelan vouched for Langdon's [78] integrity
and honesty of purpose. Indeed, Langdon was already
giving evidence of his independence of the Ruef organization. Up to that time no attempt had been made to
raise the funds necessary to conduct a practical investigation. Phelan stated that he would subscribe $10,000
and Spreckels agreed to give a like amount. Spreckels
undertook to look the field over and expressed confidence that he could get twenty men who would subscribe $5000 each, making the $100,000 which Heney
had declared to be necessary for the undertaking. The
question of Heney's fee was then raised.[79]

---

and I would like to see any of your bankers or your capitalistic
friends bid on the bonds under those circumstances, excepting
yourself, those that are in the know'—words to that effect, was
his expression. I said to Mr. Ruef: 'Do you mean to say, Mr.
Ruef, that for the purpose of making money you would bring about
a strike which might entail even bloodshed, for the mere sake of
making money?' And Mr. Ruef flushed up and said: 'Oh, no; I
was only joking.' And he soon withdrew from my office."
It is interesting to compare Spreckels' attitude toward Ruef
with that of I. W. Hellman, as shown by Hellman's testimony at
the trial of Tirey L. Ford. See footnote 7, page 15.

[78] Heney, in his address on the work of the Graft Prosecution,
October, 1908, paid Langdon the following high tribute:
"Mr. Langdon, as soon as we laid the matter before him and
convinced him it was in good faith and not to serve private interests, said: 'Yes, I will appoint Mr. Heney assistant in my office
and give him full sway to make a thorough investigation, on one
condition, and that is that I am kept personally in touch with
everything going on at all times. I am District Attorney and I
propose to be District Attorney and to act upon my own judgment.'
And there never has been a time that Mr. Langdon didn't have absolute sway over all matters, and did not wholly consent to what
was done, and he has had the final say in everything, and I wish
to say that there is more credit due to him than to any of us. He
had a greater personal sacrifice to make.
"The first thing he had to take into consideration was that he
had gone into office as the candidate of the Labor party, and he
knew he would be called a traitor and denounced if it appeared
that any man who had been on the same ticket as he had been
elected upon had been grafting. He had to possess more moral
than physical courage, and a higher kind of moral courage, and
that courage was exercised to the credit of San Francisco as well
as to the credit of Mr. Langdon."

[79] The Graft Defense labored without success to make it appear

"If there be anything left out of the $100,000 we will talk about fee," Heney replied. "But I don't think there will be anything left and I will put up my time against your money."

It was practically settled at this meeting that Heney should devote himself to the prosecution of corruptionists against whom evidence might be secured. He returned to Washington early in March to wind up his affairs there. Before he could return to San Francisco, came the earthquake and fire.

Heney got back to San Francisco April 25, one week after the disaster. He had another conference with Spreckels.[80] Spreckels told him that he wanted the investigation begun at the earliest possible moment, and that he (Spreckels) would himself guarantee the expenses which might be incurred.[81] Heney notified

that Heney was compensated for his service. Out of the Prosecution fund, the expenses—rental, clerical hire, etc.—of offices, so far as they were maintained especially for the work of the Graft Prosecution, were paid. These were known as "Heney's offices." When Rudolph Spreckels was on the stand at the Calhoun trial, he testified under Heney's announcement that the Defense could ask him any question it chose and no objection would be made. Earl Rogers, for Calhoun, endeavored to make it appear that Heney was getting pay.

"Mr. Spreckels," Rogers asked, "in addition to paying Mr. Heney's office expenses, amounting to five or six hundred dollars a month, have you paid other expenses for Mr. Heney?"

"No, sir," Spreckels replied.

Heney, the testimony all through shows, received not a dollar to compensate him for his services to the city; moreover, it shows that he had given up business which would have brought him large fees, that he might be free to conduct the Graft Prosecution. See transcript Calhoun trial, pages 3837 and on, 3746, 3743, etc.

The efforts of well-compensated attorneys for the Defense to make it appear that Heney was paid for his work, furnish one of the amusing features of the graft trials.

80 The conference was held on May 10 or 11. This was four days before the Supervisors took the preliminary steps toward granting the United Railroads its overhead trolley permit, and several months before the bribe money was paid.

81 See testimony of Rudolph Spreckels at trial of The People vs. Patrick Calhoun, No. 1436.

Burns, and as early as June [82] Burns had begun the investigation that was to result in the downfall of Ruef, and the scattering of his forces.

By the middle of the following October, Heney had so arranged his affairs as to be free to devote himself to the San Francisco investigation. His appointment as Deputy District Attorney followed.

In view of one of the principal defenses advanced by Ruef and his allies, namely, that the graft prosecution was undertaken to injure the United Railroads, these dates are important. The services for which the bribe money which got the United Railroads into difficulties was paid, were not rendered until May 21, 1906, long after final arrangements had been made for Burns to conduct the investigation and Heney to assist in the prosecution. The actual passing of the United Railroads bribe money was not completed until late in August [83] of that year. Burns was at work, and had

---

[82] Al McKinley was the first detective put to work for the Graft Prosecution. On May 25, 1906, Chief Burns detailed him to watch Ruef. Later, June 19, 1906, Burns directed Robert Perry to shadow Ruef. Perry did so until nearly a year later, when Ruef was placed in the custody of an elisor.

[83] That prosecution of officials of the United Railroads was not thought of when the graft prosecution was begun, was brought out at the trial of The People vs. Patrick Calhoun, No. 1436. The following, for example, is taken from Rudolph Spreckels' testimony:
"Mr. Heney—Q. At the time that Mr. Phelan agreed to contribute the $10,000, Mr. Spreckels, what did you say, if anything, about contributing yourself? A. That was in the first meeting, I think, Mr. Heney, and I told him that I was ready and willing to contribute a similar amount; that I believed it would be possible to get others to join and contribute.
"Q. At that time was anything said by any person about prosecuting Mr. Calhoun? A. Absolutely no.
"Q. Or any person connected with the United Railroads Company? A. The discussion was entirely confined to the administration, the corrupt administration as we termed it.
"Q. At that time did you have any purpose or intention of prosecuting Mr. Calhoun? A. I had not.
"Q. Did you have any reason to believe that Mr. Calhoun at

received pay for his services before the bribe-giving for which United Railroad officials were prosecuted had taken place.[84]

Langdon's announcement that he would appoint Heney as a Deputy District Attorney, to assist in investigating into charges of official corruption, brought upon him the condemnation of the municipal administration and of the leaders of the Union-Labor party. P. H. McCarthy and O. A. Tveitmoe, who, from opposing the Union-Labor party movement in 1901-3 had, by the time the Graft Prosecution opened, become prominent in its councils, were particularly bitter in their denunciations. At a Ruef-planned mass meeting held at the largest auditorium in the city October 31, 1906, for the purpose of organizing a league for the protection of the administration, Langdon was dubbed "traitor to his party," a man "who has gone back on his friends," "the Benedict Arnold of San Francisco."

---

that time had committed any crime? A. I had no indication of such a crime.
"Mr. Moore—Was that time fixed, Mr. Heney?
"Mr. Heney—Yes, it was fixed; the first conversation, and he has fixed it as nearly as he could.
"The Court—Have you in mind the testimony on that point, Mr. Moore? There was some reference to it in an earlier part of the examination.
"Mr. Heney—Q. When you had the talk with Mr. Heney in April, 1906, did you say anything about prosecuting Mr. Calhoun, or anybody connected with the United Railroads? A. I did not.
"Q. Did you at any time tell Mr. Heney that you desired to have him prosecute Mr. Patrick Calhoun? A. I did not, at any time.
"Q. Did you tell him at any time that you desired to have him prosecute any person connected with the United Railroads Company? A. I did not." See transcript The People vs. Patrick Calhoun, No. 1436, page 3730.

84 Rudolph Spreckels testified at the trial of The People vs. Patrick Calhoun, No. 1436:
"Mr. Perry was employed to get information in regard to Mr. Abraham Ruef and the city administration as early as June, 1906, and his efforts and of one other man employed at that time were directed toward that and that only."

Heney was denounced as "the man from Arizona." On the other hand Mayor Schmitz was called "the peerless champion of the people's rights," and Ruef, "the Mayor's loyal, able and intrepid friend."

Thomas Egan, one of the organizers of the Union-Labor party, stated of the graft prosecution: "This movement, led by Rudolph Spreckels and engineered by James D. Phelan, conceived in iniquity and born in shame, is for the purpose of destroying the labor organizations and again to gain control of the government of our fair city."

Ruef, in an earnest address, insisted upon his innocence of wrongdoing. "As sure as there is a God in heaven," he announced solemnly, "they have no proof as they claim." [85]

Acting Mayor Gallagher issued a statement in which he took the same ground as had Egan at the Dreamland Rink mass meeting, that the prosecution was a movement on the part of the Citizens' Alliance to disrupt the labor unions.[86]

---

[85] See San Francisco newspapers, November 1, 1906.

[86] Gallagher's statement was in full as follows:
"It seems to me that these assaults that are being made upon Mayor Schmitz are exceedingly reprehensible. It is strange that the gentlemen who are making the attacks did not see fit to make them while Mayor Schmitz was here. Especially does this apply to Langdon, who, by reason of past association with Mayor Schmitz, and favors received by him from the Mayor, should have been the last man to attempt to besmirch the Mayor in his absence. I am satisfied that all these attacks upon the administration officials have their origin in the long-continued attempt on behalf of the Citizens' Alliance to disrupt the labor organizations of the city. An administration that is friendly to organized labor is an impassable obstacle in the way of such a purpose. The enormous amount of labor of all kinds that will have to be performed in this city during the next few years has undoubtedly prompted the organizers of the old Citizens' Alliance to renew their assaults upon the officials elected by the Union Labor party in the hope that they may thereby themselves secure control of the municipal administration

From another angle, officials of public service corporations charged those identified with the investigation
with being in league with the labor unions. In one of
his statements to the public, Patrick Calhoun, president
of the United Railroads, set forth that, "I confidently
expect to defeat alike the machinations of Rudolph
Spreckels, his private prosecutor, with his corps of hired
detectives, and Mr. Cornelius, president of the Carmen's
Union, the leader of anarchy and lawlessness, and to see
fairly established in this community the principles of
American liberty, and the triumphs of truth and justice." [87]

Then, too, there were points at which the two supposed extremes, corporation magnates and Labor-Union
politicians, touched in their opposition to the prosecution. At a meeting held on November 2, 1906, less
than two weeks after Heney's appointment, John E.
Bennett, representing the Bay Cities Water Company,
read a paper in which Heney and Langdon were denounced as the agents of the Spring Valley Water
Company. The Chronicle, in its issue of November 3,
charged that the paper read by Mr. Bennett was type

---

and thus work out their own will in the matter of the conditions
under which labor shall perform the task of rebuilding this city.

"So far as I am concerned personally, I consider that the dis-
ruption of the labor organization would be a great sacrifice of the
interests of all of the people. The city must be built up; but the
Citizens' Alliance and all organizations and individuals in sympathy
with it may as well understand, first as last, that the work will
only be done through organized labor, and not by the employment
of pauper labor in competition with the mechanics and artisans of
the labor unions.

"That this view of the situation is well recognized by the labor
organizations of the city is shown by the action of the Building
Trades Council last night in approving and indorsing my action in
removing Mr. Langdon."

[87] Contained in a statement published May 18, 1907. See San
Francisco papers of that date.

proof of a pamphlet that was to be widely distributed, and that the proof sheets had been taken to the meeting by George B. Keane, secretary of the Board of Supervisors.[88]

On the other hand, practically the entire press of the city,[89] the general public and many of the labor

---

[88] The nature of the attacks upon the supporters of the Prosecution is shown by the proceedings in the libel suit brought by the San Francisco First National Bank against the Oakland Tribune. Rudolph Spreckels was president of the bank; the Tribune was one of the stanchest of the opponents of the prosecution. The Tribune charged that the Graft Prosecution had for one of its objects the unloading of the Spring Valley Water Company's plant upon San Francisco, and that the First National Bank was burdened with Spring Valley securities. Among other things the article set forth:

"The recent disclosures of the methods by which it was sought to unload Spring Valley's old junk, called a distributing system, together with its inadequate supply of inferior water, on the city at an outrageous figure by the swinging of the 'big stick' has not enhanced the value of the securities of the corporation in the view of the national examiners. Even the efforts to cloud the real purposes of the promoters of the Spring Valley job by calling it a civic uprising to stamp out municipal graft is said to have failed to mislead the Federal experts. The suggestion that the 'big stick' would force the city to purchase the plant of the decrepit corporation for $28,000,000 after its real estimate was appraised by an expert at $5,000,000 and held by the bondholders to be worth, as realty speculation, $15,000,000, has not enthused the Federal bank examiners in relation to the value of Spring Valley bonds as security for a national bank."

The First National Bank did not hold Spring Valley Company securities. As the Tribune's charges were calculated to injure the bank, action for libel followed. At the hearings, it developed that the articles had been furnished the Tribune by the political editor of the San Francisco Chronicle, who testified that he was paid fifty dollars a week for his Tribune articles. This was more than his salary as political editor of the Chronicle. He admitted on the stand that he had heard what he stated in his article, "only as a matter of gossip."

[89] The San Francisco Call, in an editorial article, printed October 22, expressed the general sentiment in San Francisco. The Call said:

"San Francisco will welcome the undertaking by Mr. Francis J. Heney of the duty to search out and bring to justice the official boodlers and their brokers that afflict the body politic. Public opinion is unanimous in the belief that Supervisors have been bribed and that administrative functions such as those of the Board of Works and the Health Board have been peddled in secret market. Even the Board of Education is not exempted from suspicion.

"These convictions, prevailing in the public mind, call for verification or refutation. The sudden affluence of certain members of the Board of Supervisors, the current and generally credited reports that the United Railroads paid upward of $500,000 in bribes to grease the way of its overhead trolley franchise, the appearance of

unions gave the prosecution unqualified endorsement,
welcoming it as opportunity, in an orderly way, either
to establish beyond question, or to disprove, the charges
against the administration of incompetency and corruption.[90]   Rudolph Spreckels's statement, that "this is

public officials in the guise of capitalists making large investments
in skating rinks and other considerable enterprises—these and other
lines of investigation demand the probe. If there has been no dishonesty in office the officials should be the first to insist on a
thorough inquiry.
    "If it is true, as we believe, that official boodling has been the
practice, a systematic inquiry will surely uncover the crimes. It is
impossible to commit such offenses where so many are concerned
without leaving some trace that can be followed and run to earth.
The crimes of the gaspipe thugs seemed for the moment hidden in
impenetrable mystery, but patient search discovers the trail that
leads to conviction. Criminals are rarely men of high intelligence.
They betray themselves at one or other turn of their windings.
We are convinced that some of our Supervisors and not a few of the
executive officials appointed by Schmitz are in no degree superior
in point of intelligence and moral sense to the gaspipe robbers.
    "Mr. Heney's record as a remorseless and indefatigable prose-
cutor of official rascals is known. He will have the assistance in
his new work of Mr. William J. Burns, who did so much to bring
to light the Oregon land frauds. Those crimes were surrounded and
protected by fortifications of political influence that were deemed
impregnable. When the inquiry was first undertaken nobody believed it would ever come to anything. It was a slow business,
even as the mills of the gods grind slowly, but if fine the grist
of the criminal courts of Oregon is large and satisfying.
    "The people of San Francisco have been sorely tried. Fire and
earthquake we cannot help, but the unhappy city has been made
the prey of a set of conscienceless thieves who have done nothing
since our great calamity beyond promoting schemes to fill their
own pockets. Our streets, our sewers, our schools and our public
buildings have been neglected, but the sale of permits and franchises, the working of real estate jobs and the market for privileges
of every variety have been brisk and incessant. Officials have
grown rich: Some of them are spending money like a drunken
sailor. It is time for housecleaning and a day of reckoning. Heney
and Burns will put the question: 'Where did they get it?' "

    90 Bishop Montgomery, of the Roman Catholic Church, in an
interview in the San Francisco Call, October 20, 1906, said in reference to the San Francisco graft prosecution:
    "Mere accusations have been so long and so persistently made
that the public has a right to know the truth; and, above all, those
who are innocently so charged have a right to a public and complete
vindication. Nothing now but a thorough and honest investigation
can clear the atmosphere and set us right before the world and
with ourselves.
    "I have such confidence in the courts of California that I believe
no innocent man needs to fear that he will suffer from them, and
no guilty man has any just right to complain.
    "I believe the investigation has been undertaken in good faith
for the best interests of the city, and that it will be conducted
thoroughly and honestly."

no question of capital and labor, but of dishonesty and justice," [91] was generally accepted as true expression of the situation.

Those directly connected with allegations or suggestion of irregular practices, issued statements disclaiming any knowledge of irregularity or corruption. General Tirey L. Ford, chief counsel of the United Railroads, in a published interview,[92] stated that no political boss nor any person connected with the municipal ad-

---

[91] Mr. Spreckels' statement was contained in an interview printed in the San Francisco Call, October 28, 1906. It was as follows:

"This is no question of capital and labor," he said, "but of dishonesty and justice. There is no association of men, capitalists or others, behind what we have undertaken, and it cannot be made a class question. No one knows that better than Ruef. And it will be impossible for him to fool the workingman by these insinuations.

"I want the workingmen of this city to recall that meeting which was recently held in Union Square. I was asked to attend that meeting and be its chairman. I refused to preside, to speak or go there unless I could be assured that it was not to be a movement of the capitalistic class on the one hand against the workingmen on the other. And because I did not receive that assurance I did not attend. Mr. Heney stayed away for the same reason.

"Now, who was it that originated that meeting? Sam Shortridge. Who was it who drew the resolutions; who was it who prompted the speakers and the chairman? It was Sam Shortridge.

"Mr. Ruef says that meeting was dominated and arranged by the Citizens' Alliance. Very well. Then let Mr. Ruef explain to the workingmen why it was that a few days afterward he hired Sam Shortridge as his attorney.

"I believe that it is impossible to fool the laboring men of this city now. Absolutely and definitely I want to say to them that there is nothing behind this movement but the desire for a clean city. It is absolutely regardless of class. Every man who owns a home, who has a family, is as much interested in what we have undertaken as is the wealthiest citizen."

[92] See San Francisco Examiner, October 28, 1906, from which the following is taken: "Of course there was no bribery (said General Ford), nor offer to bribe, nor was there anything done except upon clean and legitimate lines."

"Q. General, if any bribe, or offer to bribe, had been made by your company to any person connected with the San Francisco municipal administration, or to any political boss having control of the same, or if any member of the Board of Supervisors, or of the municipal government had benefited to the extent of one dollar financially by the agreement to grant to the United Railroads the privilege desired, you, in your official capacity, would undoubtedly be aware of it, would you not? A. I am certain that I would; I am, therefore, equally certain that no such thing was ever done or contemplated."

ministration had benefited financially to the extent of
one dollar in the trolley permit transaction, and that
had any one profited thereby, he (Ford) in his official
capacity would have known of it. Those connected
with the administration were as vigorous in their denials.[93] Many of them expressed satisfaction at the
prospect of an investigation. Supervisor Kelly went
so far as to suggest that the municipality give $5000 to

[93] The following are excerpts from interviews published in the
San Francisco Examiner, October 23, 1906:

Abraham Ruef: "I am satisfied that if Mayor Schmitz had known
that this investigation was afoot he would have postponed his trip
abroad and would have remained here to disprove all allegations
of graft."

Supervisor Andrew Wilson: "I shall be glad to welcome any investigation as to my official acts or as to my official conduct. I
never took a dishonest dollar in my life."

Supervisor Patrick McGushin: "The more they investigate, the
better I shall like it. I do not believe Mr. Heney has any evidence
of graft. Speaking for myself, he can investigate me or my bank
account if he likes."

Acting Mayor James L. Gallagher: "So far as the administration is concerned from the statements I have received, everything
is straight. So far as the Police Department is concerned no one
can tell. I can not tell."

Supervisor Jennings Phillips: "This investigation will be a good
thing. There has been so much talk of graft and so many accusations that it all will be settled once and for all. If Mr. Heney has
any evidence I know nothing of its nature nor against what part of
the administration it is directed."

Supervisor Edward Walsh: "As a Supervisor I have tried to do
my best. I court an investigation. I do not pay much attention to
Mr. Heney's statements. I have been here thirty-seven years and
I can hold up my head, as can every other member of this Board."

Supervisor Michael Coffey: "Nothing would afford me more
pleasure than to have them investigate my integrity and my official
acts. I hope they'll make a full and thorough investigation and clear
us all of the slurs that have been cast upon us."

Supervisor S. Davis: "I think there is nothing to this whole
thing. If Mr. Heney can find out anything let him do it. It is hard
to have insinuations cast at you. My personal connection with the
administration has been straight."

Supervisor F. P. Nicholas: "There has been so much noise about
graft that it will be a good thing to go thoroughly into the matter.
Personally I court an investigation of my official acts. If Mr. Heney
has any evidence of corruption I know nothing of it."

Supervisor Daniel Coleman: "These loud cries of graft that have
been current of late will be silenced through this investigation. It
should be thoroughly gone into so that the purity of the administration cannot hereafter be questioned."

Supervisor Max Mamlock: "I do not think it is worth my while
to think about this investigation. I do not see where Mr. Burns or
Mr. Heney could get any evidence of graft."

assist in the inquiry. "Let us," said Supervisor Lonergan, "get to the bottom of this thing. These cracks
about graft have been made right along, and we should
have them proved or disproved at once."

But in spite of this brave front, the developments
of the years of resistance of the graft prosecution
show the few days following Heney's appointment as
Assistant District Attorney to have been a period of
intense anxiety to Ruef and his immediate advisers.
Ruef held daily consultations with Acting Mayor Gallagher, Clerk Keane, and his attorney, Henry Ach.
The public knew little of these consultations, but a
rumor became current that Mayor Gallagher would suspend District Attorney Langdon from office. Little
credence was given this, however. Nevertheless, on the
night of October 25 Acting Mayor Gallagher suspended
Langdon from office, and appointed Abraham Ruef to
be District Attorney to conduct the graft investigation.[94]

---

[94] Acting-Mayor Gallagher's order removing Langdon is printed
in full in the appendix. One of the charges alleged against
Langdon was that he had appointed Francis J. Heney to be his
deputy for ulterior purposes. Of Heney it was alleged that he had
"in a public speech in said city and county (San Francisco),
aspersed the character and good name of a prominent citizen of this
community (Abe Ruef), and stated that he knew him to be corrupt, etc."

Acting-Mayor Gallagher's order of removal was made in per-
suance of Sections 18 and 19 of Article XVI of the San Francisco
Charter, which read as follows:

"Sec. 18. Any elected officer, except Supervisor, may be suspended by the Mayor and removed by the Supervisors for cause;
and any appointed officer may be removed by the Mayor for cause.
The Mayor shall appoint some person to discharge the duties of the
office during the period of such suspension.

"Sec. 19. When the Mayor shall suspend any elected officer he
shall immediately notify the Supervisors of such suspension and the
cause therefor. If the Board is not in session, he shall immediately
call a session of the same in such manner as shall be provided by
ordinance. The Mayor shall present written charges against such
suspended officer to the Board and furnish a copy of the same to
said officer, who shall have the right to appear with counsel before
the Board in his defense. If by an affirmative vote of not less than

The following morning the San Francisco Call, under a large picture of Ruef, printed the words: "THIS MAN'S HAND GRIPS THE THROAT OF SAN FRANCISCO."

---

fourteen members of the Board of Supervisors, taken by ayes and noes and entered on its record, the action of the Mayor is approved, then the suspended officer shall thereby be removed from office; but if the action of the Mayor is not so approved such suspended officer shall be immediately reinstated."

CHAPTER VI.

RUEF'S FIGHT TO TAKE THE DISTRICT ATTORNEY'S OFFICE.

The impaneling of the Grand Jury was to have been completed on October 26. Heney was appointed Assistant District Attorney on October 24. Ruef, to secure control of the District Attorney's office before the Grand Jury could be sworn, had little time to act. But he was equal to the emergency. Gallagher removed Langdon and named Ruef as District Attorney the day after Heney's appointment and the day before the impaneling of the Grand Jury was to have been completed.

Ruef had, however, considered Langdon's suspension from the day of the District Attorney's announcement of his plans for investigating graft charges. Gallagher testified at the graft trials that Ruef had, several days before Langdon's suspension, notified him it might be necessary to remove Langdon from office.[95] The Acting Mayor expressed himself as ready to carry out whatever Ruef might want done.

Gallagher testified that the names of several attor-

---

[95] Gallagher testified at the trial of The People vs. Ruef, No. 1437, to the conversation at Ruef's law offices when Ruef first broached the matter of Langdon's removal, as follows: "The substance of the conversation was that Mr. Ruef stated that it might become necessary to remove Mr. Langdon from the office of District Attorney, and to appoint somebody else. I replied that that was a matter for him to make up his mind on; if he determined it had to be done, I would do it; words to that effect, I cannot give the exact language."

neys, including that of Henry Ach, Ruef's attorney and close associate, were canvassed as eligible for appointment as Langdon's successor. Nothing definite was decided upon, however, until the day that Langdon's position was declared vacant. On that day, Gallagher received word from Ruef to call at his office. There, according to Gallagher's statement, he found Thomas V. Cator, a member of the municipal Board of Election Commissioners. Henry Ach came in later.

Ruef told Gallagher that he had decided it was necessary to remove Langdon, and that he had decided to take the place himself. Gallagher assured Ruef that whatever Ruef decided in the matter he, the Acting Mayor, would stand by. The papers removing Langdon had already been prepared. Gallagher read them over, for typographical errors, he states in his testimony, and signed them.

The Board of Supervisors was to have met that day at 2:30 P. M. in regular weekly session. Gallagher, as Acting Mayor, was to preside. But it was well after 6 P. M. when Gallagher arrived, from Ruef's office, at the council chamber.

He appeared worried and disturbed. The Supervisors, who had been waiting for him for nearly four hours, were called to order. The communication removing Langdon was read and adopted without debate or opposition.[96] Gallagher then announced that he had appointed Ruef to be Langdon's successor.

---

96 The San Francisco Chronicle, in its issue of October 26, thus describes the proceedings attending Langdon's removal:

"Gallagher took the chair at 6:30 p. m. and there was ten minutes' perfunctory business.

"His honor seemed uneasy, but at the careful prompting of

How completely Ruef dominated the municipal departments was shown by the fact that he filed his bond, his oath of office, and his certificate of appointment at the various municipal offices without hint of what was going on reaching the public. Ruef had commanded secrecy, and secrecy was observed. After Gallagher had announced Ruef's appointment in open meeting of the Supervisors, the filing of the papers was made public.

Although the Supervisors, in open board meeting, endorsed Gallagher's action without apparent hesitation, nevertheless the abler among them did so with misgivings. Supervisor Wilson went straight from the meeting of the board to Ruef's office. He told Ruef that in his judgment a mistake had been made; that the papers would call the removal of Langdon confession of guilt.[97]

Secretary Keane, he called for 'communications from executive officers.'

"Keane then announced, 'From his honor, the Mayor,' and read Gallagher's letter suspending District Attorney Langdon 'for neglect of duty' and sundry other charges.

"During the reading of the long document there was no sound in the hall save the hoarse voice of Secretary Keane, and on its completion Supervisor Sanderson arose.

"Gallagher explained that Langdon would 'be given an opportunity next Thursday afternoon at 2:30 o'clock to appear before the board and defend himself against the charges.'

"He then recognized Sanderson, who offered a motion accepting the communication from the Mayor and directing that Langdon be directed to appear to answer.

"Supervisor Wilson seconded the motion.

"Upon the call for the 'ayes,' although the Supervisors usually let silence indicate their consent, there was a chorus of approval, and upon the call for the 'noes' there was dead silence.

"Supervisors L. A. Rea and J. J. Furey were not present."

97 At the trial of The People vs. Ruef, No. 1437, page of Transcript 2654, Wilson testified: "I told him (Ruef) that I thought it was a bad move at this time and that the papers in the morning would state it was simply a confession of guilt; and I said that I had stood there and taken my program on the matter, but I felt it would ruin my chances in the face of an election, running for Railroad Commissioner, and he said I would feel better after I had something to eat, and we went over to Tait's and had supper. On the way over he (Ruef) sent Charlie Hagerty in to notify Mr. Heney of his removal."

But Ruef laughed at his fears, and to cheer him up, took him to a popular restaurant for dinner.

But before leaving his office, Ruef performed his first act as District Attorney. He wrote a curt note to Heney, dismissing him from the position of assistant.[98] Later in the evening he appointed as Heney's successor Marshall B. Woodworth.

The order of dismissal was delivered to Heney within ten minutes. Heney's answer reached Ruef as he sat at dinner with Supervisor Wilson and Henry Ach, who had joined the group. Heney's reply was quite as pointed as Ruef's letter of dismissal. Heney stated he did not recognize Ruef as District Attorney.

The battle between the two forces was fairly on. Ruef and his associates, as they sat at dinner, discussed the advisability of taking possession of the District Attorney's office that night, but concluded to wait until morning. In this Ruef suffered the fate of many a general who has consented to delay. When morning came, District Attorney Langdon had his office under guard, and San Francisco was aroused as it had not been in a generation.

Supervisor Wilson had not misjudged the interpretation that would be placed upon Langdon's suspension. The Call the following morning denounced Ruef as "District Attorney by usurpation; a prosecuting officer to save himself from prosecution." The Chronicle set forth,

---

[98] Ruef's order dismissing Heney was as follows:
"Mr. Francis J. Heney: You are hereby removed from the position of Assistant District Attorney of the City and County of San Francisco.
"Dated, October 25, 1906.   (Signed) A. RUEF,
                                        "Acting District Attorney."

in a biting editorial article, that "as long as they (the Ruef-Schmitz combine) felt safe from prosecution, they jauntily declared that they would like to see the accusations fully justified, but the instant they began to realize the possibility of being sent to San Quentin, they turned tail and resorted to a trick which every man in the community with gumption enough to form a judgment in such matters will recognize as a confession of guilt."

The Examiner called the removal of Langdon and the appointment of Ruef, "the last stand of criminals hunted and driven to bay."

"They have," said the Examiner, "come to a point where they will stop at nothing. . . . William H. Langdon, the fearless District Attorney, and Francis J. Heney, the great prosecutor, have driven the bribe-seekers and the bribe-takers to a condition of political madness. In hysterical fear they last night attempted their anarchistic method of defense."

The Bulletin devoted its entire editorial page to Ruef's new move, heading the article, "Ruef's Illegal Action is Confession of Guilt."

"Nothing," said the Bulletin, "in the history of anarchy parallels in cool, deliberate usurpation of authority this latest exhibition of lawlessness in San Francisco. . . . Government is seized to overthrow government. Authority is exercised in defiance of authority. The office of the District Attorney is seized deliberately, with malice aforethought, with strategy and cunning and used as a fort for thieves to battle down the forces of citizenship. The criminals, accused of felony, after inviting investigation and pretending to assist, have shown their hypocrisy by committing an act of anarchy which, while it might be tolerated for the time being in San Francisco, would result in the execution of these men in any government of Europe."

Gallagher's action, while upheld by the Union-Labor party leaders, and by the unions which these leaders dominated, was condemned by independent labor organizations.

The Building Trades Council, with which all the building trades unions were affiliated, dominated by P. H. McCarthy, promptly endorsed Gallagher's action in removing Langdon. But many of the affiliated unions not only withheld endorsement, but some of them repudiated the action of the central body.

The Bricklayers and Masons' Union, for example, with 800 members present, and without a dissenting vote, adopted resolutions declaring that "the President and Secretary [99] of the Building Trades Council are not fit persons to be at the head of the Union movement in San Francisco," and denouncing the course of the municipal administration, which the Building Trades Council had approved, as "high-handed defiance of the law."[100]

In spite of this repudiation by the unions, Ruef issued

---

[99] P. H. McCarthy and O. A. Tveitmoe, respectively president and secretary of the Building Trades Council.

[100] The resolutions adopted by Bricklayers' and Masons' International Union No. 7, were as follows:

"Whereas, The office of District Attorney of San Francisco County has been declared vacant by the Acting Mayor and Supervisors at a time when the said District Attorney was preparing an investigation into the official acts of the said Supervisors and others; and

"Whereas, One of the persons accused by the said District Attorney of being guilty of criminal acts, has been appointed by the Acting Mayor and Supervisors to fill the office thus vacated; and

"Whereas, The Building Trades Council of San Francisco has indorsed the action of the administration, and the president and

a statement in which he denounced the prosecution as a movement "to destroy the Union Labor organization and to control the situation in San Francisco in the interest of those who are opposed to the success of the wage-earning classes." He announced further, "I have accepted this office, the first political position I ever held in my life, because I believe it to be my duty to the public to bring to an end this constant defamation and to stop the publication of matter detrimental to the city's growth and material interest."

"I do not intend," he said, "to make any changes in the personnel of the District Attorney's office until it is determined what fate Mr. Langdon shall meet, with the exception that Mr. Heney will not be retained. I will not have Mr. Heney in my office because I do not believe that his moral standing is equal to the position." [101]

---

secretary of said Council has aided and abetted said usurpation of power to the utmost of their ability; therefore, be it

"Resolved, That this Union condemn the action of the Council in this matter, and that we condemn the president and secretary of the Council for lending or selling their aid to help to prevent the investigation of the public acts of officials who have thrown themselves open to suspicion, and thereby placing the honest union men of San Francisco in the false light of indorsing such high-handed defiance of the law; and be it

"Resolved, That we deny that the proposed prosecution of the present administration is an attack on organized labor; and further, be it

"Resolved, That it is the sense of this Union that the president and secretary of the Building Trades Council are not fit persons to be at the head of the Union movement in San Francisco, and that the delegates representing this Union in the Council are hereby instructed to use every honorable means to carry out the spirit of this resolution; and further, be it

"Resolved, That a copy of these resolutions be furnished by the corresponding secretary to each and every Union affiliated with the Council, so that they will consider this an invitation from this Union to assist in ridding the central body of officers whom we believe have done all in their power to bring unionism into disrepute."

Similar resolutions were adopted by Journeymen Plumbers, Gas and Steam Fitters' Local, No. 442.

101 See Ruef's statement as published in the San Francisco Chronicle, October 26, 1906.

District Attorney Langdon was out of the city when Acting Mayor Gallagher announced his suspension from office. Langdon hurried back prepared to resist the executive's action.[102] Even while Ruef and his associates were debating the advisability of taking possession of the District Attorney's office that night, attorneys for the prosecution were at work on papers in injunction proceedings to restrain Acting Mayor Gallagher, the Supervisors and Ruef from interfering with the District Attorney in the discharge of his duties. The papers were not ready before 5 o'clock of the morning of the 26th. At that hour, Superior Judge Seawell signed an order temporarily restraining Ruef from installing himself as District Attorney, and from interfering with Langdon in the discharge of his duties as District Attorney. By eight o'clock that morning, Presiding Judge Graham of the Superior Court had assigned the case to Judge Seawell's department; a police officer and two deputy sheriffs had been installed in the District Attorney's office with instructions to enforce the restraining order. For the time, at least, District Attorney Langdon was secure in his office.

Ruef appeared two hours later. He was that morn-

---

102 Mr. Langdon, on arriving in San Francisco, issued the following statement:

"No person in California believes that my alleged suspension is due to neglect or inefficiency. No dissent is necessary before the people. It is plain that my removal is deemed necessary by Ruef and Gallagher to prevent an honest, searching investigation of conditions that prevail in municipal affairs in San Francisco. Their plan will come to naught, however.

"As District Attorney I shall pursue this investigation to the end. I deny the legal right of the Mayor or the Board of Supervisors to suspend or dismiss me. The provision of the Charter purporting to give that authority is clearly unconstitutional. The citizens must determine whether or not they will countenance this high-handed proceeding in a community which is supposed to be governed by the law, and not by the will of a boss and his puppet."

ing to have represented the defendant in a murder trial, The People vs. Denike, but began the day by formally withdrawing from the case on the ground that as District Attorney he could not appear for the defense. He appeared in the police courts ready to prosecute a libel suit which he had brought against the proprietor of the San Francisco Bulletin, but the justice had been served with Judge Seawell's restraining order and the libel-case hearing was postponed. In Judge Dunne's department of the Superior Court, Ruef received something of a set-back. The Court made a special order permitting one of Langdon's deputies to prosecute in a criminal action then pending, regardless of who might be District Attorney. The restraining order kept Ruef and Woodworth out of the District Attorney's office. By noon it was evident that at the big event of that eventful day, the impaneling of the Grand Jury, Langdon, and not Ruef, would, as District Attorney, represent The People.

CHAPTER VII.

Oliver Grand Jury Impaneled.

The hard fight of the morning of October 26th to prevent Ruef taking possession of the District Attorney's office had been carried on practically without the general public being aware of the proceedings. Langdon had been suspended early in the evening of the previous day. The temporary order restraining Ruef from interfering with the District Attorney had been signed at 5 o'clock in the morning. The general public found by the morning papers that Ruef had attempted to seize the office, but of the steps taken to stay his hand the papers had nothing. The question on every man's lip was: Will Judge Graham recognize Ruef or Langdon as District Attorney at the impaneling of the Grand Jury?

The court was to meet at 2 o'clock. Long before that hour arrived, the halls of Temple Israel, a Jewish synagogue in which several departments of the Superior Court met during the months following the great fire, were packed with citizens. The street in front of the building soon became jammed with a struggling mass of men demanding entrance. The crowd became so great that none could enter or leave the building.

Plain-clothes men were on all sides, and succeeded in clearing a space about the entrance. The work of clearing the building of all who could not show that they had business there, then began. In this work, deference was shown Ruef's adherents. Notorious saloon-keepers, ex-prize fighters and strong-arm men friendly to Ruef were permitted to remain. Opponents of the administration who protested against removal were unceremoniously thrown out.

Although little groups of partisans of the administration appeared in the crowd, the citizens assembled were in the main clearly in sympathy with the prosecution.[103] The arrival of Langdon, Heney and Spreckels was signal for outbursts of applause. Ruef apparently appreciated the feeling against him. He appeared guarded by two detectives of the regular police department,[104] and a body-guard of partisans. The crowd began to press about him. Several of his followers made motions as though to draw revolvers. Ruef hurried into the building. To add to the confusion, there was, planned or without planning, misunderstanding as to the room in which the hearing was to be held. The representatives of District Attorney Langdon's office finding themselves misinformed as to the meeting place, forced their way from hall to hall seeking reliable information. When

---

[103] The San Francisco Chronicle in its issue of October 27 thus described the crowd: "Every man the police put out of the building was cheered by the crowd and every time policemen laid hands on anyone they were hissed. However, it was evident that the citizens who gathered outside the Temple Israel yesterday afternoon did not come prepared to fight with the police force. In the crowd standing outside almost every man prominent in the business and professional life of the city could be seen. Manufacturers, merchants, lawyers, doctors, men engaged in all the various lines of wholesale and retail business, and all the professions, included among the latter being many Protestant ministers, Catholic priests and Jewish rabbis. Here and there in the great concourse of people were scattered little groups of men of the type that may be seen hanging around the tenderloin."

[104] Detectives Steve Bunner and Tim Riordan. These men accompanied Ruef for nearly a month. Late in November, after Ruef had been indicted, they were sent back to active duty.

4

the room was finally located, it was found to be packed
with Ruef followers. The sheriff ordered the doors
closed. The Court's attention was called to this. District Attorney Langdon insisted that the doors be opened
and the crowd permitted to enter to the capacity of the
room. He pointed out that some had been admitted and
others kept out, and insisted there should be no discrimination. This course was taken. The crowd poured
in until every available foot of standing room was occupied.[105]

Eighteen of the nineteen citizens required under the
California law for Grand Jury service had already been
drawn at former sessions of the court. As soon as
order had been secured, the name of the nineteenth was
taken from the jury box.

This detail over, Heney called the Court's attention
to the provision of the California law, that no person
whose name does not appear on the assessment roll of
the county in which he serves is eligible for Grand Jury
service, and that the courts have held further, that bias
or prejudice of a Grand Juror against a person indicted
is sufficient grounds for setting aside the indictment.
Heney then stated that he wished to examine the nineteen men as to their qualifications as Grand Jurors.

Ruef, announcing himself as an officer of the court,

---

105 While the crowd was pressing into the room, a deputy sheriff
undertook to search Heney for concealed weapons. Heney complained of the officer's conduct, protested vigorously. "That is the
man standing there," cried Heney, "he did so at the request of Abe
Ruef."

"Who was informed that Mr. Heney was armed," responded
Ruef.

It developed that Heney was not armed, and the incident went
no further. But it indicated the sharpness of the division between
the two factions.

arose to speak. Heney objected to Ruef appearing, if by officer of the court he meant District Attorney or Acting District Attorney. Ruef answered that he appeared only in his capacity as member of the bar. On this showing he was allowed to proceed.

Ruef contended that the procedure proposed by Heney was irregular; that if followed the validity of the Grand Jury would be imperiled. He stated that he did not want to see the Grand Jury made an illegal body.

Heney replied that he intended, as Assistant District Attorney, to present felony charges against Ruef, and desired to examine the prospective Grand Jurors as to their bias for or against Ruef. Furthermore, Heney insisted, the Court had authority to excuse a juror if he were not on the assessment roll. To accept as Grand Jurors men whose names were not on the assessment roll, or men biased or prejudiced against Ruef would, Heney insisted, make the proceedings a farce.[106]

---

[106] The Chronicle of October 27, 1906, contains the following account of Heney's reply to Ruef: " 'I now announce to the court,' said Heney fervently, 'that I intend as Assistant District Attorney, to present charges of felony and misdemeanor against Abraham Ruef, and I desire to examine the members of this panel to determine if any member entertains bias or prejudice for or against Abraham Ruef in the matter of the charges which are to be presented by the District Attorney's office. I understand that there is no question as to Abraham Ruef's right to have the indictment set aside if any member of the Grand Jury is biased or prejudiced against him. It would be a farce,' Heney went on, his voice swelling, 'it would be adding to the comedy of errors enacted last night (the attempted removal of Langdon from office), if we have a Grand Jury which is biased or prejudiced. It has become public through the newspapers—to some extent, at least—that Abraham Ruef is to be investigated. The People have the same right as the defendant to examine the members of the panel as to their qualifications. I know that a number of the members do not possess the qualifications provided by the statute, as they are not on the assessment roll, and I desire to question them on that point. The Court has the right to excuse a juror if he is not on the assessment roll. The Supreme Court has decided that a man has the right to be investigated by a Grand Jury of nineteen men who are qualified according to the statute and none others. It is not necessary to take for grand jurors the nineteen whose names are first

In reply to Heney, Ruef defied him to produce any evidence "in open court before an untutored Grand Jury for an indictment." Ruef charged Heney further with employing abuse "to make the Grand Jury illegal so that nothing might come of any indictment."

At this point, the Attorney General of the State, U. S. Webb,[107] addressed the Court. At his suggestion

---

drawn from the box. We should examine them, so that a member who has a bias or prejudice as to a particular person may be instructed that he shall not participate in the investigation of that person.' "

[107] Under the California law, the Attorney-General may at his discretion, take the prosecution of a criminal case out of the hands of a District Attorney. It was within General Webb's province to have taken charge of the San Francisco graft trials. In a statement given wide publicity at the time, General Webb stated that he had no intention of taking charge of the graft trials unless Ruef succeeded in seizing the District Attorney's office. Long after, however, Heney, in an affidavit filed in the case of The People vs. Patrick Calhoun, Thornwell Mullally, Tirey L. Ford, William M. Abbott, Abraham Ruef and Eugene E. Schmitz, No. 823, set forth a statement made to him by Ruef when Ruef was pleading for immunity, in which Webb's presence at the impaneling of the Grand Jury was touched upon as follows:

"Ruef said in reply in substance, 'You are prejudiced against me, Heney, ever since we had that quarrel during last election. You know that the public-service corporations are responsible for the conditions which exist in San Francisco and that I can help you send some of the officials of those corporations to the penitentiary, and I can also help you to clean up this city and make it impossible for corruption to get a foothold here again for a long time. You are afraid to trust me, but you are making a mistake. The moment it becomes known that I have gone over to the prosecution the most powerful influences in this State will all be arrayed against us, and particularly against me. The moment you attack Pat Calhoun you in fact attack Herrin. You don't know the relation between these parties and the corporation as well as I do. I am very fond of Tirey Ford, but I don't care a rap about Pat Calhoun, and would just as soon testify against him as not. But the moment it becomes known that I am ready to do so my life will no longer be safe. I will have to stick to the prosecution from the moment I start in with it. You don't know what desperate means these people are capable of resorting to. My life will not be safe. If they keep me in the county jail with O'Neil as Sheriff they will kill me to a certainty. You don't know how many influential people are involved in this thing. You and Burns think you know, but there are a lot of people whom you don't know anything about who are mixed up in it. I tell you that the combined influence of all these people will make it next to impossible to secure convictions, and will make it very dangerous for all of us. It will not do to lessen the weight of my testimony any by having me plead guilty in that extortion case. Besides that, the Court would not allow me bail after I had pleaded guilty, and the Supreme Court may

the Grand Jurors were excused for the day. General Webb then stated that he knew of no law for the procedure which Mr. Heney suggested. He admitted, however, that such procedure would be desirable, and advised that no hasty action be taken in coming to a decision.

Heney in reply read from California decisions to. show that The People have the authority to make examination of Grand Jurors, and continued:

"The only question remaining is as to when this examination shall be made. Suppose the foreman of the Grand Jury is biased or prejudiced. Does it require any argument that now is the time to make this examination instead of waiting until we have presented our evidence to the Grand Jury? Shall we first have to give those whom we accuse time to bribe witnesses and get them out of the country? Shall we let the defendant come in and quash the indictment, if there is any bias or prejudice, and then be enabled to protect himself against prosecution?

"After the miserable fiasco (the attempted removal of

---

knock out the elisor, and then I would be absolutely in the hands of the other people, and they would surely kill me. Sheriff O'Neil is loyal to me now, but the moment he knew I was going to testify against Schmitz he would be very bitter against me, and would do whatever those people wanted him to do. Moreover, Herrin will get Attorney-General Webb to come down and take these cases out of the hands of Langdon and yourself, and he will declare the immunity contract off upon the ground that the District Attorney has no power to make one and will prosecute me on some of the bribery cases now pending against me, and if they convict me Herrin will see to it that I am not pardoned by the Governor. He now controls the Governor and the chances are he will continue to name the Governor and control him for the next twenty years. Webb was a deputy in Ford's office when Ford was Attorney-General, and it was Ford who got him to come down here and 'butt in' at the time you were impaneling the Grand Jury. I know you fellows thought it was I who got him to come down here, but as a matter of fact I did not know any more about it than you did until he appeared there, and I am sure it was Ford who did it."

Langdon) which occurred last night," Heney went on, "what more important duty for this Court to perform than to say immediately that the law is more powerful than any man or any set of men in San Francisco?"

As Heney concluded, the packed courtroom burst into applause. The crowd outside heard, took it up and cheered wildly. As soon as order was restored, Henry Ach, one of the attorneys appearing for Ruef, suggested that Heney, the Attorney General and himself, get together to present the question of whether Langdon or Ruef were District Attorney to the Supreme Court. Ach stated that he feared if Langdon or Heney attended a session of the Grand Jury and Ruef were to be found to be District Attorney, then the acts of the Grand Jury might be invalidated.

Heney replied that in acting as prosecutor it had been his rule "to have no conferences, treaties or alliances with persons charged with crime, or with their attorneys." On this ground, Heney declined Mr. Ach's proposition.

Judge Graham made no rulings that day on any of the points raised, but ordered a continuance until the following Monday.

After adjournment of court, the appearance of Langdon and Heney at the entrance of the building brought forth cheers from the crowd that all through the proceedings had waited outside. A speech was demanded of Langdon.

"My friends," he replied, "we have no speeches to make. We have a duty to perform and we will perform that duty."

Immediately behind Langdon came Ruef, closely guarded by police and detectives. He was pale and worn and clearly frightened. The crowd pressed about him. Threats came from his followers to shoot into the crowd if it pressed too closely. Ruef finally reached his automobile and was driven away.[108]

The topic of discussion of the two days that elapsed before Judge Graham decided the questions that had been raised by Heney's proposal to proceed with the examination of the Grand Jurors, was whether Graham would allow such examination. It was alleged that no less than four of the citizens drawn for Grand Jury service were not on the assessment roll. There were,

---

[108] While Ruef was struggling through the crowd to reach his automobile Dr. Shadwick O. Beasley, Instructor in Anatomy at the Cooper Medical College, was assaulted by some unidentified person. Dr. Beasley turned, shook his first at Ruef and hissed him. The doctor was immediately placed under arrest. Dr. Beasley, on his part, swore out a warrant charging an unknown deputy sheriff with battery. Beasley was then made subject of petty persecution. He was, for example, held up on the street by a deputy sheriff and charged with carrying a concealed weapon. He was searched by two men, but nothing more deadly than a case of surgical instruments was found upon him. Dr. Beasley complained bitterly of the rough treatment from the officers.

The San Francisco Chronicle, in its issue of October 27, 1906, thus describes the scene which followed Ruef's appearance before the crowd:

"With fists and clubs Chief of Police Dinan and his squad from the Central Police Station fought off the crowd of angry citizens assembled about the Temple Israel who sought to lay violent hands on Abe Ruef when the curly-headed usurper of the functions of the municipal government was leaving the scene of the Grand Jury meeting yesterday afternoon. And in the wake of the police were the Ruef heelers from the tenderloin with their hands on their pistols, threatening to shoot down the citizens of the city of San Francisco who should dare to approach too near the sacred person of their tenderloin idol.

"It was one of the most remarkable scenes ever witnessed in any city of this country. Stung with the outrageous assumption of the powers of the public prosecutor when he was about to be placed on trial himself for crime, the citizens of the city, among whom are names that stand highest in business and professional circles, sought to make him realize the impudence of his conduct. That he escaped a swift punishment for his arrogant seizure of the office of the District Attorney is solely due to the presence and strenuous efforts of the police."

too, charges that Ruef controlled several of them. Some of the papers printed the names of those whom it was alleged were either under obligations to Ruef or connected with his political organization.

A second crowd filled courtroom, building and street when Judge Graham's court was called to order the following Monday. Mounted policemen, plain-clothes men and detectives, directed by two captains of police, were, however, on hand to preserve order.[109] There were no demonstrations. Judge Graham announced from the bench that after due deliberation, he had concluded that the District Attorney had the right to interrogate the Grand Jurors as to their qualifications. He stated further that inasmuch as Langdon was the de facto District Attorney, Langdon would conduct the examination.

The prosecution had won the first skirmish in the years-long fight upon which San Francisco was entering for the enforcement of the law.

The next move came from Attorney Samuel M. Shortridge. Shortridge appeared with Ruef's attorney, Henry Ach, and Marshall B. Woodworth. Ruef had named Woodworth, it will be remembered, as Heney's successor in the District Attorney's office.

Mr. Shortridge read Acting Mayor Gallagher's order suspending Langdon and appointing Ruef, and also called the Court's attention to the fact that Ruef had filed his official bond as District Attorney. Shortridge

---

109 In sending his officers to handle this crowd, Chief of Police Dinan gave the following instructions:

"The captains, sergeants and officers so detailed are instructed that they are sent to the place designated for the purpose of doing strict police duty. They will see that the streets and sidewalks are not obstructed, and that no violations of the law are permitted."

stated that the matter was pending before Judge Seawell, and asked the Court, "in deference to Judge Seawell," to postpone proceedings until the District-Attorney controversy should be decided. Shortridge expressed himself as fearful that, if the examination of the Grand Jurors went on, Judge Seawell's decision might invalidate the Grand Jury proceedings.

W. T. Baggett, Assistant City Attorney,[110] followed Shortridge. Mr. Baggett read a letter from the Acting Mayor, setting forth the fact of Langdon's removal, and joined with Shortridge in pleading for delay. But the pleas of both gentlemen were denied. Judge Graham repeated his opinion given earlier in the day that Langdon should be recognized as the de facto District Attorney, and ordered the impaneling of the Grand Jury to continue.

Shortridge thereupon announced his desire to participate in the examination of the Grand Jurors. Heney objected to Shortridge appearing as a representative of the District Attorney's office. Shortridge replied that he respected Judge Seawell's order, and had no intention of violating it. He asked if he would be permitted to act in the capacity of amicus curiæ [111] in examining jurors. This privilege was accorded him.

The examination of the Grand Jurors occupied more

---

[110] Under the San Francisco municipal charter, the District Attorney has charge of criminal cases, and the City Attorney of civil cases in which the city is concerned. The City Attorney also acts as adviser to the Mayor and Board of Supervisors. The two are independent offices.

[111] Shortridge stated that as amicus curiae, it was his duty to see that the proceedings were without flaw. Heney refused to take him seriously, however, referred to him facetiously as the "curious friend of the Court," and suggested that the Court unassisted might be able to determine what was competent evidence.

than a week. Several of the nineteen were excused, it being found that their names were not on the assessment roll.

The examination was concluded [112] on November 7th and the Grand Jurors sworn. B. P. Oliver was appointed foreman. From him the body received its name of Oliver Grand Jury. The Grand Jury organized by electing C. G. Burnett secretary. But one important question remained to be decided, namely—Was Ruef or Langdon to represent The People at the investigation into graft charges which the Grand Jury was ready to begin?

---

[112] The following nineteen citizens composed the Grand Jury that conducted the investigation of San Francisco "graft" charges: E. J. Gallagher, photographic supply dealer; Frank A. Dwyer, real estate; Herman H. Young, baker and restaurant proprietor; Mendle Rothenburg, liquor dealer; James E. Gordon, merchant; Alfred Greenebaum, merchant; Wallace Wise, haberdasher; Jeremiah Deasy, insurance agent; Rudolph Mohr, brewer; C. G. Burnett, capitalist; Charles Sonntag, merchant; Morris A. Levingston, liquor dealer; B. P. Oliver, real estate; W. P. Redington, druggist; Christian P. Rode, drayman; Ansel C. Robinson, merchant; Dewey Coffin, real estate; F. G. Sanborn, law book publisher; Maurice Block, merchant.

CHAPTER VIII.

Ruef Loses the District Attorney's Office.

While the impaneling of the Grand Jury was going on before Judge Graham, Ruef was disputing Langdon's title to the office of District Attorney before Judge Seawell. In these proceedings Samuel M. Shortridge appeared with Ruef's attorney, Ach, and Deputy City Attorney Baggett, not as amicus curiæ, but as Ach's associate in the legal contest to force Langdon out of office.

The principal feature of Ruef's case was the introduction of affidavits, signed by sixteen members [113] of

---

[113] The Supervisors who signed the affidavits exonerating Ruef and themselves were: Charles Boxton, Jennings J. Phillips, W. W. Sanderson, F. P. Nicholas, L. A. Rea, Edward I. Walsh, Andrew M. Wilson, J. J. Furey, Sam Davis, C. J. Harrigan, James T. Kelly, P. M. McGushin, Thomas F. Lonergan, Daniel G. Coleman, Max Mamlock and M. W. Coffey. Each of them made declaration as follows:

"This affiant has never committed a felony of any kind or character, and has never been a party thereto, and there is not and can be no evidence presented of or concerning any felony committed by the undersigned or threatened by the undersigned. It is not true that this affiant has ever been party to the commission of any crime or any misdemeanor.

"This affiant further says that any and all charges, assertions and innuendoes contained in the complaint and contained in the public press of and concerning any alleged felonies, misdemeanors or wrongful acts committed or alleged to have been committed by this defendant are absolutely untrue and false, and this affiant has never been guilty of any violation of the law, and, so far as the knowledge of this affiant is concerned, each and all of the other defendants named herein are absolutely innocent of the commission of any crime or felony or offense against the laws of the State of California; and this affiant further says that he has no knowledge, direct or indirect, of the commission of any felony or or any misdemeanors or of any violations of the laws of the State of California, or any thereof, or of the City and County of San Francisco, by either or any of the defendants named herein."

At the graft trials it developed that the Supervisors had signed this affidavit without reading it. At the trial of The People vs. Glass, No. 675, Supervisor Michael Coffey testified that "On the afternoon that affidavit was signed, I came down late to a meeting

the Board of Supervisors, in which the Supervisors denied committing felony of any character. Later, after the Supervisors had confessed, these affidavits were to be used by the defense at practically all the graft trials in efforts to break down their testimony against the bribe-givers.

During the examination, Ach endeavored to force from Langdon and his deputies a statement of what evidence they had against Ruef. In this Ach failed. On the other hand, the prosecution sought to bring out testimony that Ruef had directed Gallagher to suspend Langdon.[114] To this end Heney placed Ruef on the stand. But Judge Seawell stated [115] that he did not at that time wish to go into question of motive and the point was not pressed.

---

of the board and the members of the board were in the Notary Public's office. I went over there and met Mr. Keane, and Mr. Keane produced that paper and asked me to sign it, and I signed it and gave him a dollar to pay the Notary fees. I did not read the affidavit at that time. It was not read aloud to me while I was there. I did not talk with any person about what was in this affidavit before it was prepared. I did not know who prepared it." See page 237 of transcript on appeal.

Supervisor Wilson testified: "Mr. Ruef got up that affidavit, I believe. I signed it because there was a rumor going about that some of the Supervisors had gone over to the prosecution. It was so stated in the public press and there was a little excitement among the members of the board and we understood this was sent down by Mr. Ruef to stiffen them up and to find out if that was so. It was not read at the notary's office while I was there. I did not read it before signing it." See Transcript on Appeal The People vs. Glass, page 278.

Supervisor Boxton testified: "I signed the affidavit just shown me at the request of the clerk of the Board of Supervisors, Mr. George Keane. I do not know who prepared the affidavit. No one had talked with me as to the facts that were to be put in it. I knew nothing about its contents at all. It was supposed generally amongst the members there was some talk about it, that there was some of the members there that were a bit weak-kneed, and would probably tell all they knew, so this affidavit was framed up, as I understand it, to tie them down a little tighter." See Transcript on Appeal, The People vs. Glass, page 251.

Practically the same testimony was given by other Supervisors at the various graft trials.

114 See footnote 95, page 87.

115 The passage between Heney and Ruef's lawyers which fol-

The outcome of the proceedings was a second victory for the prosecution. The injunction against Ruef was granted;[116] Langdon was left in peaceful possession of the District Attorney's office.[117] Later, Judge Seawell issued a permanent writ of prohibition against the Board of Supervisors restraining that body from removing Langdon from office.

Langdon and his deputies, after a three-weeks fight, were free to proceed with the graft investigation.

---

lowed Judge Seawell's ruling is thus set forth in the San Francisco Chronicle of November 3rd:

" 'You can ask Mr. Ruef if he is guilty of any crimes or felonies,' Ach suggested to Heney.

" 'I suppose he'll plead guilty here?' responded Heney skeptically.

"Samuel M. Shortridge, of Ruef's legal staff, took this remark to heart and hotly said to Heney, 'You'll plead guilty before he does.' The Judge informed Shortridge that Heney obviously spoke in jest, but Shortridge thought it a poor joke. Ruef considered Heney's whole proceeding a joke."

116 Judge Seawell in his decision said:

"I am clearly of the opinion that the Charter, in so far as it relates to removal and suspension, does not apply to the District Attorney. I am firmly convinced that neither the Mayor nor the Board of Supervisors has any power to remove or suspend him. The District Attorney should not be left to the investigation of the municipal authorities. I can conceive how he might be compelled to proceed against the very persons who might be conducting an inquiry. I will grant the injunction as prayed for against Mr. Ruef."

117 A movement to secure Heney's dismissal from the District Attorney's office, on the ground that he had accepted a fee in addition to his salary as Assistant District Attorney, to act as prosecutor was started. But the allegation was not sustained and another failure was scored by the defense.

CHAPTER IX.

Ruef and Schmitz Indicted.

Within twenty-four hours after organizing, the Grand Jury had begun investigation into graft charges. Tenderloin extortion, especially in connection with the so-called "French Restaurants," was the first matter taken up. The inquiry involved both Schmitz and Ruef.

The term "French Restaurant" in San Francisco is used in connection with a particular type of assignation house. These establishments contain a restaurant on the ground floor, and sometimes banquet hall and private rooms without assignation accompaniments. The stories overhead are devoted to private supper bedrooms. Some of these assignation places are several stories in height. Before the fire, among the establishments alleged to be "French Restaurants" were Marchand's, Delmonico's, the New Poodle Dog, the Bay State and the Pup. The extent of the business conducted by these places is indicated by the testimony of A. B. Blanco, who stated under oath at the graft trials that he had $200,000 invested in the New Poodle Dog, while Joe Malfanti testified that he had about $400,000 invested in Delmonico's.[118]

French Restaurants had long been a scandal in San Francisco. Toward the close of 1904, the Police Com-

---

[118] See Transcript on Appeal The People of the State of California vs. Eugene E. Schmitz, pp. 500 and 557.

mission, then absolutely under domination of Schmitz and Ruef, gave evidence of proceeding against such places. The commission, as a beginning, revoked the liquor license of a "French Restaurant" known as Tortoni's. Without a license to sell liquor a "French Restaurant" could not continue in business. These licenses had to be renewed once every three months. The Police Commission had arbitrary power to grant, or to refuse, application for renewal. One by one renewal applications of other French Restaurants were held up. It became a matter of common report that all the "French Restaurants" were to be treated as Tortoni's had been, namely, driven out of business by having their licenses to sell liquors revoked.

And then Abe Ruef appeared before the Police Commissioners as attorney for the "French Restaurant" keepers.[119] Ruef asked that consideration of the French Restaurant cases be postponed for two weeks. This was accorded him. But his request that during those two weeks the places be permitted to conduct their business as before, namely, that they be allowed to sell liquors

---

119 Ruef stated that he appeared as attorney for the French Restaurant Keepers' Association. But those who paid him the money for his efforts in this instance testified at the trial of The People vs. Eugene E. Schmitz that they held membership in no such organization, nor had they heard of it. In May, 1907, Ruef stated to Heney that he had closed the bargain with the French-restaurant keepers to represent them on JANUARY 6, 1905. He insisted that he had at first flatly refused to represent them; that he had had no intention whatever of so doing until the San Francisco Bulletin denounced him for having had the licenses held up and challenged him to take the cases and to attempt to defend himself upon the theory that the money so obtained by him was received as an attorney's fee.

Heney examined the Bulletin files and found that the first time the Bulletin had mentioned the French-restaurant hold-up as an attempt on the part of Ruef to extort money from the restaurant proprietors was in the last edition of The Bulletin for JANUARY 7, 1905. (See Heney's affidavit in the case of The People vs. Patrick Calhoun, et als., No. 823, pp. 141 to 143, inclusive.)

in the private supper bedrooms, was denied by a tie vote, two commissioners of the four voting for Ruef and two against him.

Before the two weeks' extension of time which Ruef had secured had expired, Mayor Schmitz had removed from office one of the commissioners who had opposed [120] Ruef's request that the sale of liquors in "French Restaurant" bedrooms be continued.

The opposing commissioner out of the way, the board by a vote of two to one, adopted certain rules submitted by Ruef for the management of French Restaurants.[121] By the same vote, the commission then granted the French-Restaurant licenses, action upon which had so long been delayed.

All this was done before the public. There were, of course, charges of graft and extortion, which most people, although without definite proof, believed. Heney, nearly a year later, in his speech in the Partridge campaign, referred to in a previous chapter, charged graft. A Grand Jury had made [122] an honest attempt to get to the bottom of the scandal. The efforts of this early Grand Jury came to nothing.

---

120 Commissioner Harry W. Hutton.

121 These Ruef-provided rules directed that no liquors be served in supper bedrooms on the first and second floors of the establishments, and required the French restaurants to take out hotel licenses and to keep registers the same as hotels. What the keepers of the places thought of the regulations came out at the Schmitz trial. Joe Malfanti of Delmonico's, for example, testified: "They (the Ruef rules) made no change in the running of my business—not a single change. I had a hotel license for years before and I always had a register, so there was no change in my place whatever."

122 The Andrews Grand Jury, named from its foreman, T. P. Andrews. The work of the Andrews Grand Jury was not lost, however. It served as basis for much of the investigation conducted by the Oliver Grand Jury.

The Oliver Grand Jury had not been in session a fortnight, however, before the whole miserable story of Ruef's connection with the French Restaurant cases had been spread before it.

Thomas Regan, who had served as Police Commissioner during the Schmitz administration, testified that as early as the summer of 1904 Schmitz had told him that the "French Restaurants" were bad places and should not be permitted to exist. When Tortoni's was closed, Schmitz stated to Regan, according to Regan's testimony, that the French Restaurants were all run alike, and should all be closed. Acting upon the Mayor's suggestion, the Police Commission ordered the investigation into the methods of the French Restaurants which created such a sensation in San Francisco during the closing months of 1904. Licenses were denied in some cases. In others, hearings of applications for renewals were postponed from time to time. Some proprietors were called upon to show cause why their licenses should not be revoked. Of all of which, Commissioner Regan testified, he kept Mayor Schmitz informed.

The course of the commission threw the keepers of the French Restaurants into a panic. Their attorneys found themselves helpless and could give their clients no encouragement. Marcus Rosenthal, for example, who appeared before the commission on January 3, 1905, on behalf of the Bay State Restaurant, testified at the Schmitz trial, that he was not permitted to say anything; that the commissioners would not listen to him, nor hear testimony. After that meeting he had advised his client, and a little group of "French Restaurant" keepers who had gathered about him, that it would be useless for them to appeal to any court, because under the law there could be no review of the action of the Police Commissioners; that the commission could arbitrarily dispose of any saloon-keeper, and he could not seek remedy in the courts.

And then, having explained the situation fully, Rosenthal told them, what every observer in San Francisco knew, "There is only one man who could help you, and that is Mr. Ruef." [123] The French Restaurant keepers received this advice from all sides. Joe Malfanti testified at the Schmitz trial that "numerous friends advised me to see Ruef."

And to Mr. Ruef the "French Restaurant" keepers finally found themselves compelled to go—at the urgent suggestion of a fellow French Restaurant keeper, Jean Loupy.

Loupy was proprietor of the French Restaurant known as the "Pup." At Loupy's place Ruef maintained a sort of headquarters. There he took his dinner practically every night, entertained friends and received his henchmen.

Ruef had from time to time acted as Loupy's attorney. He had also loaned Loupy money. At the time

---

[123] Rosenthal testified at the Schmitz trial: "I told them from my observations and how things were going in the city and had been going for some years, that there was only one man who could help them—it was a question of life and death with them—and I said there is only one man who could help you, and that is Mr. Ruef."

Rosenthal, when examined on this point before the Grand Jury, refused to testify on the ground that conversation between attorney and client was privileged. Adler got into trouble with the Grand Jury over his testimony on this point. Both Rosenthal and Adler, however, testified at Schmitz's trial.

of the French Restaurant troubles, Loupy, according to his testimony, owed Ruef $1000.

When the closing of the French Restaurants seemed inevitable, this Loupy brought word to the French Restaurant proprietors that Ruef would represent them all before the Police Commission for $7000 a year,[124] on a contract for two years. The sum was finally cut to $5000,[125] $10,000 for the two years. For the first year "Marchand's," "Delmonico's," "The New Poodle Dog" and the "Bay State" paid $1175 each. Loupy for the "Pup," on the grounds that he had been put to considerable expense and was a poorer man than the others, paid only $300.[126]

---

[124] N. M. Adler, proprietor of the Bay State Restaurant, testified at the Schmitz trial as to Loupy's negotiations. Loupy called upon him twice. "The first time he came," Adler testified, "he told me that things were very serious, and we would have to put up some money and hire Mr. Ruef; that he was the only man that could help us. I told him that I could not understand the proposition; that I had run my business for twenty years, and didn't think that they could do me any harm. At that time Ruef was making his headquarters at the Pup restaurant. I could see that from my place across the street. He went there regularly."

Then Adler testified to the meeting before the Police Commissioners, at which his attorney, Rosenthal, had not been permitted to speak, and continued: "Afterwards, Loupy came to me again, and told me that Tortoni had closed up, and that we should put up the money or we would be all closed. This was after we had been to the meeting of the Police Commissioners."

[125] The testimony brought out at the graft trials showed that Ruef received $8500 from the French restaurants, $5000 the first year from the five in the combine; $3000 the second, and $500 additional from Camille Mailhebeau. Ruef stated to Heney later and so testified at the Schmitz trial, that half of the $8000 received from the combine he turned over to Schmitz.

[126] The five restaurant keepers were asked at the Schmitz trial whether they had employed Ruef because he was a lawyer or because of his recognized power as political boss. They testified as follows:

A. B. Blanco of the "New Poodle Dog"—"Well, being a political boss we thought he had influence enough to get our licenses."

N. M. Adler, of the "Bay State"—"Well, the way I took it, Mr. Ruef is a boss. He had an influence over the commission. He was the only man who could help us." On cross-examination: "I understood that if I did not employ Ruef I would not get my

The money being paid over to Ruef,[127] Ruef appeared before the Police Commissioners, as has already been told, with his plan for regulating the French Restaurant business in San Francisco.

Ruef's arrangements with the French Restaurant

---

license. I understood that Mr. Ruef was the only man who could get my license."

Michel Debret of "Marchand's"—"Well, I agreed to (pay the money to Ruef) because having consulted we saw we had no way to get out of it unless we paid Ruef, as he was a political boss, to protect ourselves." "Because we thought—we thought if we didn't pay the money we would be treated like Tortoni's, we would be closed; we had no way to get out of it." "I believed that Ruef and the Mayor controlled the Police Commissioners."

Joe Malfanti of "Delmonico's"—"I did not pay this $1175 for fun; I had to save my license. I had about $400,000 invested there. I never figured on what effect it would have upon my business if I did not get a license. If it was for myself alone I would close the place, but I figured on my partners, what they had paid. They had a lease for five years and could not go through with it and I did it as a favor. If I was alone I would close. I would not make any fight. Numerous friends advised me to see Ruef." "I went to Ruef—Ruef was the man that controlled the administration—Ruef was the one that could do the thing. His relation with the Mayor was so he could do what he pleased."

Jean Loupy was asked by Heney: "Did you go to him (Ruef) because he was a lawyer or because he was a political boss?" "Because he was a political boss," replied Loupy.

[127] Ruef would not take a check, neither would he accept gold —he insisted upon having currency—neither would he give a receipt. The money was taken to him by Pierre Priet, a French-restaurant keeper. Regarding the transfer of the money, Joe Malfanti, at the Schmitz trial, gave the following testimony:

"Mr. Heney—Q. What did he say you were to get for the five thousand dollars, Priet? A. Yes.

"Q. Yes, what did Priet say you were to get for your money? A. We were going to get the license.

"Q. For two years? A. No, we were going to have no trouble for two years about a license.

"Q. Five thousand dollars a year? A. Yes, sir.

"Q. Now, then, what was said about how the money was to be paid? What did Priet say about how the money was to be paid? A. In currency.

"Mr. Campbell—That is under the same objection and exception.

"The Witness—And that two people, not three, only two people, not three.

"Mr. Heney—Q. What do you mean, that no one was to go with him to Ruef? A. Yes.

"The Witness—Priet said the money should be brought there in currency and paid with two people.

"Q. Did Priet get you a receipt? A. I don't think he ever looked for any. I asked him about that when he came back. He said: 'Well, you should be glad to get his word of honor.' That is what I got from Priet."

keepers were concluded during the first week in January. Police Commissioner Regan testified that sometime after January 3, Mayor Schmitz asked him to vote to restore the French Restaurant licenses.[128]   Regan objected on the ground that it was not right to ask him to vote first one way and then another.   With Commissioners Regan and Hutton voting against issuing the licenses, the licenses could not be granted.   Either Hutton or Regan had to change their attitude, or one of them had to be removed from office.   Police Commissioner F. F. Poheim testified at the Schmitz trial that at a conference on the French Restaurant problem held early in January, 1905, which he and Schmitz attended, Schmitz announced: "We will have to give these people (the French Restaurant proprietors) their licenses if we can.   If we cannot do anything else we will have to remove Hutton."

And during the week following Ruef's first appearance before the commissioners as representative of the French Restaurants, Mayor Schmitz removed Hutton.[129]

---

128 Regan testified at the Schmitz trial:
"The Mayor asked me to vote for the French liquor licenses. The first time he did so he put it on political grounds. He requested me to vote for them, saying it would hurt him politically if the license was not granted; and that they had so many friends and so many rich people frequented those places that it would be a very unpopular thing to take the licenses away, and he requested me to vote for them. That it would be unpopular to take them, the licenses, away, as they, the restaurants, had so many friends and so many rich people frequented the places. I said I didn't think it was right, that he knew he got me to close those places up. That I could not vote for them, as they were immoral and should be closed. The second conversation was all of the same tenor."

129 Commissioner Poheim took papers from Ruef's office to the Mayor on the day of Hutton's removal. Poheim testified at the Schmitz trial:
"I took papers from Mr. Ruef's office that I believe were the papers of removal. He told me that they were. That was the day of Hutton's removal."

The licenses were then issued to the "French Restaurant" keepers.[130]

Much of the story of these transactions was presented to the Grand Jury. But the evidence was not secured without effort. Many of the witnesses were unfriendly; others afraid of the consequences of frank statement of facts. Witnesses disappeared and could not be found. Several known to have testified were threatened and even assaulted. One French Restaurant keeper, before the investigation had been concluded, had been indicted for perjury. Three attorneys who were more or less in touch with the tenderloin situation had been cited for contempt for refusing to answer questions put to them in the Grand Jury room. But point by point the evidence was presented.

---

[130] The Chronicle in its issue of February 1, 1907, thus summarized the evidence against Schmitz and Ruef, and the nature of their defense:

"Those operations are these: There are in this as in all other cities certain dens of vice, ranging from the very fashionable down to those patronized by the dregs of society, which can exist only when licensed to sell liquor. To give or withhold the license is within the discretion of the Police Commissioners, and from their action there is no effectual appeal. Since Ruef got control of the majority of these commissioners they have been mere puppets, giving or withholding the licenses of these places as directed by Schmitz. That being the case, when renewals of licenses were necessary, the applicants were refused. That meant the ruin of their business. In the end, either from their general knowledge, or because as advised, they applied to Ruef. When the fee was settled and paid—in the case of the French restaurants $5,000 a year—Ruef notified Schmitz, who, as the prosecution is evidently prepared to prove, then directed the licenses to issue, and they were issued. In the aggregate, enormous sums were annually collected from these places by Ruef or his agents, and without that payment they could not have continued business. The revenues thus obtained were evidently the sources of Schmitz's suddenly acquired wealth. Presumably some small share was paid to the subordinates.

"Certainly that is extortion, and extortion of the most villainous kind. To the ordinary reader it is completely covered by the language of the statute. The contention of Ruef and Schmitz is not that they did not get the money, or that it was not a villainous thing, but merely that it was not a villainy expressly forbidden by statute, and that therefore to indict them for it is 'persecution.' If there are any people in the city who uphold or condone such things they are no better than Ruef or Schmitz themselves."

The Grand Jury, on the evidence, indicted Schmitz and Ruef on five counts for extortion.[131] Bonds were fixed at $10,000 on each charge, $50,000 for each defendant.

Ruef [132] was released on $50,000 bail.

---

131 The press throughout the State was a unit in approving the Grand Jury's action. The San Francisco Chronicle fairly expressed the general sentiment. It said:

"Every decent man in San Francisco breathes freer to-day. The fact cannot be concealed that there was an uneasy feeling in the community that the machinations of the boss would again secure immunity for himself and those who were with him in the grafting business. The facility with which he turned the Grand Jury preceding the present one into an instrument to accomplish his own purposes inspired the fear that by hook or crook he may have obtained control of the one now sitting; but the promptitude with which the first indictment was brought allays all apprehension and converts it into confidence that the body now in session is in deadly earnest and that it will earn the gratitude of its fellow citizens and cover itself with glory by striking an effective blow which will put an end to flagrant venality in office and restore the good name of San Francisco."

The San Francisco Examiner said of the indictment of Schmitz and Ruef: "The light breaks, the reign of political terror seems at an end. Mayor Eugene E. Schmitz and Abe Ruef, his mentor and master, have been indicted for extortion. The move of political regeneration and civic reform that has been sweeping the country has hit San Francisco with the force of all the other successes behind it. In other cities and other States the powerful rascals as well as their satellites have been sent to prison. Evidently San Francisco and California are to rid themselves of the arch political criminals. . . . Thursday, November 15, 1906 (the day on which Ruef and Schmitz were indicted), is a day to be remembered. It marks the beginning of San Francisco's regeneration. It is a day of heroic events to be told to children and grandchildren. It is the day of the declaration of independence of California's great metropolis."

132 Ruef denounced his indictment as absurd, insisting that he had merely taken fees for services rendered. In an interview published in the San Francisco Chronicle of November 16, 1906, he said:

"The whole thing is absurd. I was simply acting in the relation of attorney to a client. I took my fee for rendering legal services. I was retained by a contract as attorney by the restaurant keepers. If it is extortion for an attorney to accept a fee from his client, we all might as well go out of business. This is exactly the same charge that was made against me once before and was found baseless. I have nothing to fear."

On November 17 the Chronicle, touching upon Ruef's defense, said: "Every branch of the city government which is controlled by Ruef men is known to be utterly rotten. The only question has been whether under the advice and direction of low legal cunning, the grafters have kept themselves immune from the law. And the question is about to be settled."

Schmitz, the day after the indictments were brought, was reported to have started for home from Europe.

Schmitz's probable reception on his arrival at New York apparently gave keen anxiety at San Francisco.

Heney states that Justice F. W. Henshaw called at his (Heney's) office and asked Heney, as a favor, to tell him whether Schmitz would be arrested upon his arrival in New York, as William J. Dingee of the Contra Costa Water Company, wanted to arrange for Schmitz's bail in New York City. William F. Herrin of the Southern Pacific Company is credited with interesting himself in Schmitz's behalf in arranging for the bond that was furnished when Schmitz reached San Francisco. Schmitz's bond was furnished by Dingee and Thomas Williams, president of the New California Jockey Club. The New California Jockey Club operated the notorious Emeryville racing and gambling establishment. Mr. Dingee was at the time one of California's most prominent capitalists.

CHAPTER X.

Fight to Evade Trial.

The indictments against Schmitz and Ruef were returned November 15. Schmitz reached San Francisco on his return from Europe on November 29.[133] He at once joined with Ruef in the fight to prevent the issue raised by his indictment being presented to a trial jury.

---

133 On his arrival in New York after being indicted for extortion in the French Restaurant cases, Mayor Schmitz in an interview widely published at the time gave his attitude toward the French Restaurants. The Mayor explained that these restaurants had existed so long in the city that they had become a recognized adjunct of a gay life of a gay town. He had not favored their suppression, and whenever the Police Commissioners agitated the revoking of their liquor licenses, he had opposed them.

"The French restaurants did no great harm," he is quoted as saying, "and to destroy them would be to ruin the men who had invested money in them." The character of some of the heavy investors in these establishments was brought out in the report of the commission appointed by Mayor E. R. Taylor to ascertain causes of municipal corruption in San Francisco, as disclosed by the investigations of the Oliver Grand Jury. The report set forth:

"The business (of the French restaurants) is very prosperous, and, as is usual, the landlord shares in its prosperity. People of social prominence were known to accept a portion of the profits of such establishments, through the extremely liberal rentals paid, and the system is received with easy toleration. One of the largest of these assignation places was located on a prominent corner of the downtown shopping district where hundreds of women daily passed its doors. The building, five stories in height, had four stories devoted to the private supper bedrooms. The land was owned in trust by one of the largest, if not the largest, trust company in the West. A lease was sought and obtained by a man notorious in the line of business above described; the building was constructed by the trust company according to plans satisfactory to him for this purpose, and the enterprise was conducted there for seven years until the building was destroyed by fire. The significant thing about such a transaction is, not that there are people who are willing to accept money from such a source, or financiers willing to put trust moneys to such uses, but that the facts, though well known, did not seem to detract in the slightest from the social recognition accorded to the persons so taking a share of the profits, while the officer of the trust company which made the lease of that particular house situated in the shopping district, was appointed a regent of the State University."

The two defendants were to have been arraigned on
December 3, but at their earnest solicitation arraignment [134] was continued until December 6.

On that day the plans of the defendants became apparent. It was seen that they would divide the defense,
demanding separate trials; and it was quite as evident
that their first move would be an attack upon the validity
of the Grand Jury.

Attorneys Frank C. Drew and John J. Barrett appeared for Schmitz, while Ruef was represented by
Samuel M. Shortridge and Henry Ach. At the close of
the proceedings, Ach asked that subpoenas be issued for
the members of the Grand Jury to appear in court the
following Monday to testify for the defendants. This
meant the examination of the Grand Jurors for bias.

---

[134] During the reading of the first of the five indictments,
Schmitz stood, but Ruef remained seated. When the second indictment was read, both the defendants kept their seats. Heney demanded to know what was going on. Judge Dunne announced that
the arraignment must proceed as in ordinary cases. During the
reading of the remaining indictments both defendants remained
standing, but Ruef kept his back turned toward the court. Commenting upon this incident, the Chronicle, in its issue of December
8, 1906, said in an editorial article:

"In Judge Dunne's court a rogue on trial insolently refused to
stand and be arraigned like any other criminal, apparently on the
assumption that a political boss was above the courts. He was
finally compelled to stand and let his shame be seen. He sat, however, through one arraignment, and the people have reason to complain that the trial Judge did not earlier enforce the respect due to
the majesty of the law. In another instance there is a more grave
offense. A lawyer presumed to bandy words with the Judge on
the bench, and is reported to have said to the Court in a loud and
insolent tone, evincing evident disrespect, 'And I have heard considerable oratory from you.' Nothing was done about it, and Judge
Dunne owes it to the people to explain why he did not promptly
commit the insolent fellow to jail. The Judge on the bench represents the majesty of the law. He sits for the people in solemn
judgment on offenders. He is expected to enforce due respect for
the tribunal, and for that purpose is invested with the power of
summary punishment for contempt. Our alleged administration of
criminal justice is disgraceful, and the evil permeates the entire
machinery, from the policeman on his beat to the highest tribunal."

The long technical fight to disqualify the Grand Jury had opened.[135]

In the attack upon the Grand Jury, Joseph C. Campbell joined with Schmitz's attorneys, Drew and Barrett, while Frank J. Murphy and Charles H. Fairall appeared with Shortridge and Ach for Ruef. Ach, in moving to set aside or quash the indictments, stated that the motion was made for Schmitz and Ruef jointly, but that the defendants reserved the right to plead and to be tried separately.

---

135 The attack upon the Grand Jury had, however, been begun the day before, and was progressing in another department of the court even as Ruef and Schmitz were arraigned. Investigation into graft conditions had by this time got beyond the tenderloin. Several minor indictments had been brought. Supervisor Fred P. Nicholas had been indicted for accepting a bribe of $26.10. As chairman of the Public Building and Grounds Committee, the Grand Jury found he had accepted a 10 per cent. commission on $261 worth of furniture purchased for the city. Several witnesses had been indicted for perjury in connection with the graft investigation. That the investigation was going far was now conceded. The defense concentrated to disqualify the Grand Jury. On behalf of Nicholas and Duffy, the Grand Jurors were haled into Judge William P. Lawlor's court December 5, the day before Schmitz and Ruef were arraigned. The defendants were represented by Frank J. Murphy, who was to play a prominent part in the graft defense. The following taken from the examination of Foreman B. P. Oliver, as printed in the San Francisco Chronicle of December 7, is a fair sample of the nature of the inquiry:

"Did you say to anyone that this is just the beginning of the investigation of municipal corruption?"

"I have said that from the statements I have heard in the Grand Jury room that the corruption of the municipal administration was so great that the present Grand Jury could hardly expect to make any impression upon it. As to when and where I made that statement I cannot tell," replied Oliver, who proceeded: "As to myself, the mere testimony I have heard in the Grand Jury room has filled me with horror and disgust."

"Does it fill you with such horror that you believe everyone connected with the administration is corrupt?" asked Lawyer Fairall of counsel for the defense. "I do not believe anyone to be corrupt until he is proved to be so."

"Could you act fairly and impartially, as a Grand Juror, while having your present feeling of horror and disgust?" "Yes, absolutely so, for I have a conscience."

"You feel that your conscience would enable you to act fairly?" "I do. If I erred at all it would be on the other side, so as to be sure that I did the accused no injustice."

This examination went on for several days. The same examination of the Grand Jurors followed in the case of Ruef and Schmitz, and was repeated for the third time on behalf of public-service corporation agents who were indicted later.

Ach's motion was based on nineteen counts. The point most insisted upon was that Grand Juror Wallace Wise was disqualified because of his having been on a petty trial jury panel during the current year. Wise, being thus disqualified, Ach argued, the whole indictment failed as much as though the whole nineteen Grand Jurors were disqualified.[136]

Judge Dunne, after a three days' hearing, swept aside the multitude of technical objections which the various attorneys for the defense had advanced. In particular did he refuse to declare the whole nineteen Grand Jurors disqualified, because of the alleged disqualification of Juror Wise.

The prosecution had gained another point in its fight to bring the defendants to trial on the merits of their cases.

But the attack upon the Grand Jury had scarcely begun. After Judge Dunne's ruling, the nineteen Grand Jurors were to be put on the stand and examined one by one for bias.[137] The defense went further, and had

---

[136] The question of the eligibility of Grand Juror Wise was finally decided by the State Supreme Court in the matter of the application of A. Ruef for a writ of habeas corpus (150 California, p. 665.) The Court held that the presence on the Grand Jury of a member who had served and been discharged as a juror by a court of record within a year of the time that he had been summoned and impaneled to act as a grand juror does not affect the validity of an indictment found by the Grand Jury.

[137] The Chronicle, in its issue of December 18, 1906, said of the attack upon the Grand Jury:

"The fact that the felons whom we are trying to convict are officials has nothing to do with their demonstration of the fact that it is impossible, under the laws, to put thieves in the penitentiary, when there is a large band rounded up at one time and they all fight. Under our laws the half-dozen rascals who have already been indicted for their share in the orgy of official plunder in this city can block our criminal courts. The disgraceful farce of putting the Grand Jurors and the District Attorney on trial instead of the scoundrels who have been indicted can apparently be protracted for weeks. Happily the Legislature meets early next month, and if

Rudolph Spreckels up to question him as to his motives in guaranteeing a fund for the investigation of graft conditions.[138]   District Attorney Langdon was also placed on the stand to be examined as to his motive in appointing Heney his assistant.   He denied most emphatically that he had appointed Heney for the sole purpose of instituting criminal proceedings against Ruef and Schmitz.

The examination of Grand Jurors, prosecutors and citizens lasted from December 17 until January 22.   On the last named date, Judge Dunne denied the motion to set aside the indictments for bias.   The prosecution had gained another step toward bringing the defendants to trial.

Judge Dunne stated that he was ready to set the cases for trial the next day.   But the defendants had

---

it does not put a speedy end to it we are mistaken.   We are getting an object lesson which, perhaps, was needed.   The whole miserable machinery of obstruction must be swept away.   Whoever is indicted by a Grand Jury must go to trial, unless, in the opinion of the trial Judge, extraordinary conditions indicate that some inquiry should be made to be conducted solely by himself.   The public will be satisfied with nothing short of that, nor will it be satisfied with that.   The abuses of appeal must be ended."

138 Mr. Spreckels testified in part as follows: "I am not interested in the downfall of any man, either Eugene E. Schmitz or Abraham Ruef.   I did guarantee the sum of $100,000 to detect any wrongdoing whatsoever in the city of San Francisco.   I indicated that to Mr. Heney.   I cannot recollect as to dates, but I think it was a short while before the commencement of these proceedings. It was since the calamity of April 18.   I had been interested for a long while before that in starting an investigation. . . .   I did not guarantee to Mr. Heney $100,000, but I did guarantee that for the purpose of investigation for the collection of evidence, I would personally guarantee $100,000 for the expenses. . . .   My object was merely to ascertain the truth or falsity of things that had been generally stated.   Some of the things I had known of myself. I knew there was an effort made in the city here of doing things in the past.   Mr. Ruef, himself, had had a conversation with me which indicated that he was in a position to do certain things, and knowing these things I was willing that an investigation should proceed to the bottom, and to furnish the money necessary to collect the evidence.   I have stated publicly relative to this fund of $100,000."

another delaying play. They demurred to the indictments. The demurrers were not disposed of until February 18.

In the meantime, the defense had made several complicating moves. The first of these was an application to Judge Graham to have the case against Schmitz transferred from Judge Dunne's court. At the same time Schmitz surrendered himself to the Sheriff, and applied to the Supreme Court for a writ of habeas corpus, and a writ of prohibition, setting up the points already raised in Judge Dunne's court against the indictments. The Supreme Court finally decided against Schmitz.

But there remained another way of having the case transferred from Judge Dunne's court. The law governing changes of venue could be changed by the Legislature. The 1907 Legislature had convened early in January. A measure was introduced in both Senate and Assembly under the terms of which a defendant in a criminal action was permitted to secure a transfer of his case from one court to another by merely filing affidavit of his belief that he could not get fair trial in the court in which his case was pending.[139] The measure was

---

139 The San Francisco Chronicle, in its issue of January 17, 1907, said of the Change of Venue bill:

"Assemblyman Grove L. Johnson of Sacramento, and Senator L. A. Wright of San Diego, have introduced identical bills which provide in brief, that in any criminal trial the accused may displace the Judge upon his mere affidavit that he 'believes he cannot have a fair and impartial trial.' Upon the filing of such an affidavit the services of some other Judge must be secured, provided that in counties having more than one department of the Superior Court the case shall be transferred to some other department of the same county. The bill provides that the act shall take effect immediately upon its passage. The obvious intent of the law is to enable the indicted boodlers of this city to select the Judge who shall try them, to set aside all that has thus far been done to get them before a jury and have their cases retried from the beginning."

known as the "Change of Venue Bill." Its chief supporter in the Legislature was George B. Keane.

Keane was not only clerk of the Board of Supervisors, but he was a member of the State Senate representing a San Francisco district. Keane championed the "Change of Venue Bill." [140] The measure passed the Assembly, but failed of passage in the Senate. Ruef in his efforts to escape trial before Judge Dunne had lost again.

Early in February, when the efforts of Schmitz and Ruef to evade trial were being pressed the hardest, agitation against the Japanese gave Schmitz opportunity not

---

[140] Ruef had, as early as 1904, secured a hold on the State Legislature, by putting up and electing a Union Labor party legislative ticket. "I told the legislators," said Ruef in a statement published after he had entered San Quentin prison, "to vote on all labor questions and legislation directly involving labor interests always for the labor side. I told them on all other questions to follow the Herrin program. Herrin was appreciative. He expressed his sense of obligation."—Abraham Ruef's "The Road I Traveled," published in San Francisco Bulletin, July 6, 1912.

Keane, at the trial of The People vs. Ruef, No. 1437, admitted that he had supported "The Assembly bill providing for changes of place of trial in certain cases," at the special request of Ruef. See transcript on appeal, part 3, book 1, pages 442-3. Keane was also active in the advocacy of other measures changing the law governing criminal cases. One of these practically forbade public comment on a criminal trial from the impaneling of the Grand Jury until the rendering of the verdict. Commenting upon this anti-publicity bill, E. H. Hamilton, in a dispatch from Sacramento to the San Francisco Examiner, published in that paper March 5, 1907, said: "This bill had been sneaked through the Senate the other night when no one was paying any attention, but Senator Boynton moved to reconsider the vote by which the bill was passed, and brought up the matter to-day, asking that the bill be given a free discussion before it was acted upon. He showed that it was directly in opposition to the Constitution of the United States and the Constitution of the State, because it was aimed directly at the freedom of the press and intended to prevent newspapers from publishing accounts of criminal trials.

"Senator Sanford of Mendocino said that it was an attempt to muzzle the press and to prevent people from ascertaining what was going on in criminal lawsuits, but the Senate refused to reconsider the vote by which it had passed the unconstitutional bill."

Keane also pressed an amendment to the codes to prevent stenographers and bookkeepers testifying against their employers. During the discussion in the Senate Committee on the Change of Venue bill, Keane offered an amendment to make this measure take effect immediately.

only to absent himself from the State, thus bringing the proceedings so far as they applied to him, to a standstill, but to restore his prestige. Schmitz was quick to avail himself of the situation.

The question of admitting Japanese to California schools was then under consideration at Washington. A request was extended the San Francisco Board of Education, through California Congressmen, that the members of the board go to Washington for conference with the government authorities. Members of the board held consultation with Schmitz, after which word was circulated about the State that in defense of the public schools against the Japanese, Schmitz must, on behalf of San Francisco and California, go to Washington.

A telegram was received from Congressman Julius Kahn, a close supporter of Ruef and Schmitz, who represented a San Francisco district in Congress, stating that "at the request of the President and Secretary of State we ask you to come here immediately for a conference with them and the California delegation."

Schmitz started for Washington on February 3.[141] He was absent from San Francisco until March 6. He did not, however, as had been predicted, return amid popular acclaim. The outcome of the Washington negotiations was not satisfactory to California. There was

---

141 On the way across San Francisco Bay to take the train at Oakland, in the words of newspaper reports of the incident, members of Mayor Schmitz's personal following who accompanied him, "were frankly delighted with the prospect of the indicted Mayor returning from the national capital covered with glory, and acclaimed the savior of the country from a war with Japan."

Ruef regarded the incident cynically. "As soon as Schmitz got aboard that train," said Ruef on the day of the Mayor's departure, "the nation was saved."

popular belief that the Mayor's mission had failed. At the State line Schmitz received the startling word that Ruef was a fugitive from justice; that Sheriff O'Neil had failed to discover the fugitive's whereabouts and had been disqualified. During the month of his absence from San Francisco, the Mayor was soon to learn, events of tremendous importance to himself and to his administration had occurred.

CHAPTER XI.

Ruef a Fugitive.

Three months [142] after his indictment in the "French Restaurant" extortion cases—three months of continuous fighting to evade the issue—Ruef found his last technical obstruction, as far as the State courts were concerned, swept away, and was forced to enter his plea to the charge contained in the indictment. He pleaded "not guilty." His trial was set for March 5.

Up to the day before the date fixed for the trial to begin, nothing had come up to indicate further delay. On March 4, however, Ruef's bondsmen surrendered him into the custody of the Sheriff. Ruef then applied to Superior Judge J. C. B. Hebbard for a writ of habeas corpus. The application was based on the allegation dealt with in a previous chapter, that Grand Juror Wise was ineligible, because he had been drawn as a trial juror within a year before the impanelment of the Grand Jury of which he was a member. On the ground that Wise was ineligible for Grand Jury service, Ruef's attorneys contended, their client's restraint was in violation of the Fifth and Fourteenth amendments to the Federal Constitution, thereby raising a Federal issue and paving the way for appeal to the Federal courts.

---

142 Ruef and Schmitz were indicted November 15, 1906. The date of Ruef's plea of "Not guilty" was February 18, 1907.

In opposing Ruef's new move, Hiram W. Johnson,[143] who had been employed to assist the District Attorney in the "graft" prosecution, pointed out that the cases named in the petition were pending in a co-ordinate branch of the Superior Court; that they were set for trial the following day; that the points, including the Federal points, had been made subject of extensive arguments before Hebbard's colleague, Judge Dunne, and in the course of those arguments every question presented in the proceedings had been passed upon.

Ach, representing Ruef, denied that the Federal question had been presented. Johnson insisted that it had. An unfortunate scene followed.[144]   Hebbard showed symptoms of intoxication.   Johnson, Langdon and Heney finally refused to participate further in the proceedings and walked out of the courtroom.[145]

---

[143] Hiram W. Johnson is a native of California, having been born at Sacramento. He was educated at the Sacramento public schools and the University of California. At twenty-one he had been admitted to practice at the California bar. He was active for years against the corrupt political conditions in California before he came into prominence as one of the prosecutors at the graft trials. In 1910 he was selected to lead the movement against the political machine which dominated the State. As primary candidate for Republican nomination for Governor, he visited practically every community in California, making one pledge to be carried out in the event of his election, "to kick the Southern Pacific out of political control of the State." He was nominated and elected. His election resulted in political revolution in California. (See "Story of the California Legislature of 1911" and "Story of the California Legislature of 1913.") He was one of the founders of the Progressive party at Chicago in 1912, and was that year candidate for Vice-President with Roosevelt on the National Progressive ticket. In 1914 he was re-elected Governor of California with overwhelming vote. Johnson is the first Governor since 1853 to secure re-election in California.

[144] See Heney's affidavit in The People vs. Ruef, No. 823.

[145] "Again we protest," said Johnson when the final break came, "in behalf of the District Attorney of this city and county, and in the name of the people of California. We do not believe in this; we will not participate in it; and we take our leave of this court. We will not participate in any proceeding which does not, according to our ideas, comport with the dignity of justice, the dignity of this court, or our own dignity."

The withdrawal of the District Attorney and his assistants did not delay Judge Hebbard's decision. He denied the writ Ruef prayed for, but he allowed an appeal from his order to the Supreme Court of the United States, and admitted Ruef to bail pending that appeal.

One of Ruef's attorneys filed the writ of error issued by Judge Hebbard with the clerk of the Federal Circuit Court. May 2 was set as the date for the appearance on the writ of error before the United States Supreme Court at Washington.[146]

The Aetna Indemnity Company had furnished Ruef's bond. This company surrendered Ruef to the Sheriff in the forenoon. In the afternoon it furnished the bail that had been imposed by Judge Hebbard.

Ruef, in Hebbard's order granting him opportunity to take his case to the Federal Courts, had basis for further struggle in the courts to evade trial. But he undertook a new move. After leaving Hebbard's courtroom on the afternoon of March 4, Ruef dropped out of sight as completely as though the earth had opened and swallowed him.

For three days the regular peace officers of San Francisco searched San Francisco for him but they did not find him.

---

146 On March 25, 1907, Ruef's appeal in the habeas corpus matter was dismissed by the Supreme Court of the United States. Of this move, Frank J. Murphy, one of Ruef's attorneys, is quoted in a published interview: "We have instructed our representative in Washington to withdraw the writ of error filed by us. This decision was reached on account of the decision of the State Supreme Court to the effect that the participation of an incompetent juror does not affect the validity of an indictment."

This action left the Prosecution free to proceed with Ruef's trial without any possibility of the proceedings being questioned later.

When Ruef's case was called for trial in Judge Dunne's department on the morning following the proceedings in Judge Hebbard's court, Ruef's attorney, Samuel M. Shortridge, was present, but not the defendant.

Shortridge was in the position of an attorney in court without a client.[147] After a wait of four hours, to give Ruef every opportunity to make his appearance, Heney moved that the bonds of the absent defendant be declared forfeited, specifying the bonds originally given

---

[147] Judge Dunne ruled that Ruef, being a fugitive from justice, and his trial one for felony, at which the defendant must be present at every stage of the proceedings, there was no trial before the court. Shortridge was in the position of counsel without a client. During the examination of Coroner Walsh, after his failure to find Ruef, Shortridge insisted upon interrupting the examination. Judge Dunne after repeated warnings, found Shortridge guilty of contempt of court, and sentenced him to serve twenty-four hours in jail. The Chronicle of March 9, 1907, contains the following account of the incident:

"Have you not said," Walsh was asked by Heney, "that you hoped he (Ruef) would be acquitted and that you would do all you could for him? Are you not in sympathy with him?"

Again the Coroner quibbled and Judge Dunne ordered: "Answer the question. Do you sympathize with him or not?"

Still the witness hesitated, and again the Judge asked with vigor: "Are you in sympathy with him?"

"If he is innocent I am in sympathy with him, if he is guilty I am not."

"I suppose you wish it to appear that you are not in sympathy with him so that you may take charge of the jury," suggested Heney.

Samuel M. Shortridge, one of Ruef's lawyers, here said that he objected on behalf of his client to the line of examination.

Heney proceeded without paying any attention to Shortridge's interruption. Shortridge again entered an objection, and Judge Dunne ordered him to take his seat.

"But I wish to be heard on behalf of my client," persisted Shortridge.

"Take your seat, Mr. Shortridge, or I will order the Sheriff to cause you to do so or remove you from the court room," declared Judge Dunne.

"Am I to understand that I am not to be heard in this court?" demanded Shortridge with play of great indignation.

"Mr. Shortridge, your conduct is boisterous and offensive and tends to interfere with the orderly conduct of the court. I declare you guilty of contempt and sentence you to be confined in the County Jail for twenty-four hours. Mr. Sheriff, take him into custody."

as well as those furnished in the proceedings before Hebbard.

Judge Dunne, in ruling upon Heney's motion, stated that he was proceeding as though the proceedings before Judge Hebbard had not occurred. Those proceedings, he announced, he felt were under a species of fraud. He ordered Ruef's original bonds forfeited and took the question of the forfeiture of the bonds in the proceedings before Judge Hebbard under advisement. He considered it his duty, he said, to proceed with the trial of the case until ordered to desist by the Supreme Court or by the Court of Appeals.

Attorney Shortridge announced to Judge Dunne that in proceeding with the hearing he might find himself in contempt of the Supreme Court of the United States. Judge Dunne stated that that would not embarrass him, and in any event, he would not proceed with the matter until the defendant was in court.

The day passed without the defendant's whereabouts being discovered. Sheriff O'Neil reported that he had been unable to find the fugitive, but expressed his belief that he would be able to do so eventually. With that understanding court adjourned for the day.

The day following, Ruef's attorneys appealed to the State Appellate Court [148] for a writ of prohibition to prevent Judge Dunne and others from further proceeding against Ruef in the extortion cases, and to show cause

---

[148] The two principal points on which the defense based their applications for writs of habeas corpus and of prohibition were:

(1) That Juror Wise, having sat on a petty jury within a year, was disqualified to act as a Grand Juror, and hence the indictments were fatally defective.

(2) That the matter was before the Supreme Court of the United States on a writ of error.

why the writ should not be made permanent. Ruef being
in hiding, the application was not signed by the peti-
tioner. The Appellate Court, after twenty-four hours,
denied the petition. Ruef's representatives then went
before the State Supreme Court with the same representations. And here, again, eventually, Ruef lost.

In the meantime, Ruef had not been found. The day
following his disappearance, Judge Dunne disqualified
the Sheriff and named the next officer in authoritative
sequence in such matters, the Coroner, W. J. Walsh, as
elisor, to arrest Ruef and bring him into court.

Coroner Walsh had no better success than had Sheriff
O'Neil. Ruef had disappeared on the night of Monday,
March 4. On Friday, March 8, after three days of
unavailing search by O'Neil and Walsh,[149] Judge Dunne
disqualified Walsh and appointed William J. Biggy [150]
as elisor to arrest the fugitive.

Within two hours Biggy, accompanied by Detective
William J. Burns, had located Ruef at a road-house in
the San Francisco suburbs and had placed him under
arrest.[151]

---

149 Heney, in his affidavit in contention that an Elisor should
be appointed to bring Ruef into court, indicated the conditions
which were handicapping the prosecution.

150 Biggy afterwards became Chief of Police of San Francisco.

151 Ruef was with one of his henchmen, Myrtile Cerf, when arrested. Long after, when he had plead guilty to one of the extortion charges, Ruef stated in an interview published in the San
Francisco Call, May 16, 1907, that it had been his purpose "to wait
until the Legislature had acted on the Change of Venue Bill," which
was considered in a previous chapter, and which at the time of
Ruef's flight was being engineered through the Senate by George
Keane in his capacity as Senator. Ruef, in his interview, stated
further: "We had expected that this bill would go through. Naturally we were surprised when we learned that Campbell, the May-
or's (Schmitz's) attorney, was at Sacramento lobbying against the
bill. What his object was I do not know. He even went to George

Having taken his man,[152] the elisor was at a loss to know what to do with him. To put him in the city prison was to turn him over to the police; to put him in the county jail was to turn him over to the Sheriff. The Chief of Police was even then under indictment with Ruef, a co-defendant; the Sheriff had been disqualified. The only alternative was for Biggy himself to hold Ruef until the court could act. Biggy accordingly secured suitable quarters at the Hotel St. Francis, and there held Ruef a prisoner until the following Monday, when he was taken before Judge Dunne.

Judge Dunne refused to admit Ruef to bail, remanded him to Elisor Biggy's custody, and continued his trial until the following morning, Tuesday, March 12.

Ruef immediately made application to the Supreme Court for a writ of habeas corpus, asking to be released from the custody of Elisor Biggy and placed in charge of the Sheriff. But here again Ruef was defeated. Elisor Biggy continued his keeper for many months following.

Ruef, after his appeal to the Federal Supreme Court, had exhausted every legal device known to himself and his attorneys to escape trial in the extortion case pending

---

Keane, who had charge of the bill, and tried to switch him to the other side."

During the period of Ruef's disappearance, his attorneys had insisted that they were unaware of his whereabouts. Myrtile Cerf, his companion in flight, refused to say before the Grand Jury with whom he had telephonic communication while at the roadhouse, on the ground that such testimony might incriminate him.

152 Ruef's arrest threw the administration into the greatest confusion. Supervisor Wilson testified at the trial of The People vs. Ruef, No. 1437, Part 3, Vol. 7, p. 3175, that at 2 o'clock of the morning following Ruef's capture, he went down to Henry Ach's apartment to ascertain if the rumor that Ruef had been found were true.

before Judge Dunne.[153] His last recourse gone, Ruef found himself brought face to face with trial before a jury. On March 13 the selecting of jurors to try Ruef began in Judge Dunne's court.

But events of far greater moment than petty extortion had the attention of San Francisco. Even as Ruef was in hiding, Detective Burns and his assistants had trapped three members of the Board of Supervisors in bribery. This opened up the most fruitful field of the graft

---

153 Of the procedure which made possible Ruef's long technical fight to escape trial, the San Francisco Chronicle on November 10, 1906, said:

"The disgraceful condition of our criminal laws permits guilty men to put off their doom almost without limit. Where money makes unscrupulous talent available that course is invariably taken by those caught in the toils of justice. There are many objects to be gained by these delays. Witnesses may die or be spirited away. Most important of all the public becomes wearied and finally forgets or loses its zest for the enforcement of the law. When that stage is reached the 'pull' comes into play. By the connivance of the District Attorney, and especially of the Judge, continuance after continuance can be granted until proof becomes impossible and the case is dismissed. The adoption of such a course by any accused person of bad reputation is moral evidence of guilt which is conclusive with the public. We have had in this city many disgraceful criminal trials. We have had many obvious miscarriages of justice. There have been wealthy men whom everybody feels should be in the penitentiary who have hardly ceased for a day to flaunt their faces in decent society. We have never had a case in which the obstruction to the cause of justice began so early as Ruef began it, or was conducted with such brazen effrontery. It is not within our recollection that any accused person of whose guilt there was reasonable doubt had adopted such a course. Its adoption is the recognized sign of guilt.

"But while our laws affecting court practice are very bad, they do afford the means of ultimately bringing criminals to trial and convicting them if the evidence is sufficient and the jury unbiased and uncorrupted. It only requires that the public maintains its interest and thereby sustains its officials in their efforts to secure justice. In this case the advantage is with the public. There is no possibility of a 'pull' with the District Attorney. His assistant, Mr. Heney, is himself a master of the criminal law and in notable cases elsewhere has triumphed over similar efforts for delay made in behalf of criminals of far higher social and political standing than Ruef. In fact Ruef has no standing of any kind in the community in any way different from that possessed by other political bosses supposed to be corrupt. The indignation of this community is a righteous indignation and it will never abate until under the due processes of law the truth in respect to Ruef and his roustabouts is dragged out in open court."

prosecution, and immediately the extortion cases became of comparative unimportance. The trapping of the three Supervisors led to confessions from fourteen others, which involved not only Ruef in enormous bribery transactions, but also prominent members of the bar, and leaders in the social, financial and industrial life of California.

CHAPTER XII.

Trapping of the Supervisors.

Months before the Oliver Grand Jury was convened, it was common gossip in San Francisco that the members of the Board of Supervisors were taking money from the public service corporations.[154] Belief of this had got beyond the stage of mere newspaper accusation. It had become the firmly-settled conviction of the law-abiding element of the community. For this reason, as the

---

[154] At the trial of The People vs. Ruef, No. 1437, Supervisor Andrew M. Wilson testified to a conversation which he had had with Ruef at Ruef's office early in September, 1906. He was asked to state what he had said to Ruef on that occasion. Wilson replied:

"A. I told him Mr. Choynski was across the street; I pulled the blind aside at his office, and showed him Mr. Choynski talking to Jesse Marks; that he had stated to Marks the exact amount on the trolley proposition.

"Mr. Sullivan: Q. Who had stated to Marks the exact amount on the trolley proposition? A. Mr. Choynski, and that I had advised him a few weeks before that not to continue that fight for the attorneyship of the Liquor Dealers.

"Q. Advised who? A. Mr. Ruef; and that Mr. Choynski was telling him what he had said to McGushin at one of the meetings regarding the $4,000 on the trolley.

"Q. That who had said what he had told Mr. McGushin? A. Yes, sir.

"Q. That who had said it? A. That Mr. Choynski had said that McGushin looked paralyzed when he mentioned the exact amount, but denied it; and I says to Mr. Ruef, 'He has the correct amount on the trolley,' and he stated that there must be a leak somewhere in the Board; and I told him I thought——

"Q. (Interrupting). Who stated that there must be a leak somewhere in the Board? A. Mr. Ruef; and I stated that I thought it came through Morris Levy, and that possibly he got his information through Supervisor Kelly, as they were very friendly.

"Mr. Ach: Q. Who said that, you or Ruef?

"Mr. Sullivan: Q. Who said that? A. I stated that to Mr. Ruef, that I thought the source of the leak was through Supervisor Kelly telling Morris Levy, and Morris Levy telling Choynski."
—See Transcript, page 2643.

months wore away in technical wrangling in the "French Restaurant" extortion cases, the public became impatient that time and energy should be expended in comparatively unimportant matters, while big graft went unprobed.

Partisans of the administration took advantage of this sentiment to belittle the prosecution.

Under this sort of hammering, the prosecution, during the months of February and March, 1907, unquestionably lost ground in public opinion.

But with Ruef holding the Supervisors to rigid accounting, and agents of public-service corporations lynx-eyed [155] to detect any weakness in their position, and quick to report with warning and advice to Ruef at any suggestion of danger, Burns and his associates were able to make little headway in securing evidence of big graft that would justify indictmenf or warrant trial.

The Supervisors looked to Ruef absolutely. Some of them took bribe money from others than himself in spite of his warning, but when they scented a trap they hurried to Ruef for advice.

When he directed them to return the bribe money

---

[155] Supervisor James L. Gallagher testified at the trial of The People vs. Ruef, No. 1437, of a note which had been delivered to him by Mr. Abbott, attorney for the United Railroads, from Tirey L. Ford, head of the United Railroads law department, to be delivered to Ruef. The substance of the note, Gallagher testified, was that "The Grand Jury is taking up the investigation of the charges concerning the United Railroads permit; not much headway has been made; it is intended to endeavor to trap some of the Supervisors."

Gallagher, unable to find Ruef, went back to Ford, according to Gallagher's testimony, and asked if the note were so important that Ruef should be hunted up. Ford had directed him to open the envelope and read the note. Gallagher did this, made a shorthand memorandum of it. and read the message to Ruef later. See transcript, The People vs. Ruef, Part 3, Vol. 2, pp. 976 to 983.

they promised to do so, and in some cases actually returned it.

Ruef was a competent captain over men who had all confidence in his ability to keep them out of trouble. So long as he was in touch with the Supervisors his position so far as the Supervisors was concerned was almost impregnable. When, however, Ruef was caught in a position where he could no longer consult freely with his men, advise them and reassure them, his organization went to pieces in a wild scramble of every member thereof to save himself.

This occurred when Ruef was placed in the custody of Elisor Biggy.

Ruef fully appreciated this weak point in his position. He realized from the beginning of the Graft Prosecution the danger of members of the Board of Supervisors being trapped in independent bribery, and himself becoming involved through their confessions. Even before his flight from trial in the extortion case, he knew that his fears bade fair to be realized.

Some fortnight before Ruef's flight, Supervisor Lonergan had been to Ruef with confession of having taken $500 from Golden M. Roy. Roy was proprietor of a well-known cafe and was counted by men in Lonergan's position as one of the supporters of the administration. But the more astute Ruef at once suspected betrayal. Ruef bluntly informed Lonergan that he had been trapped, directed him to return the money Roy had given him and warned him of the risk he ran in accepting bribes.

Ruef's fears were well founded. Roy, in his dealings

with Lonergan, was acting for Detective William J. Burns.

The trap which Burns had prepared for the eager Lonergan was plausibly baited.

Roy was a restaurant keeper with several side enterprises, among them interests in a skating-rink. An ordinance regulating skating-rinks was pending before the Supervisors. Roy, acting under direction of the District Attorney, approached Lonergan with a statement that he wished the ordinance defeated. Lonergan accordingly met Roy at the skating-rink office. In an adjoining room, placed so they could see and hear, were Detective William J. Burns and two others. From their places of concealment the three men heard the bargain, and saw Roy pay Lonergan $500 to defeat the skating-rink ordinance.

Roy, acting for the District Attorney, then attempted to trap Gallagher. He offered Gallagher $1000 for his work on the skating-rink ordinance. Gallagher refused to take any money and said that Roy was a friend of the administration and it should not cost him anything. Roy urged Gallagher to accept the money, alleging that it came from a pool; that Gallagher was entitled to it; that he, Roy, had given money to several Supervisors already. Gallagher asked him to tell which ones. Roy refused, saying, "You would not expect me to tell on you."

Gallagher immediately suspected Lonergan and told his suspicions to Wilson, and the two hunted up Lonergan and charged him with getting the money.

Gallagher hurried Lonergan to Ruef much the same

as they would have rushed a man showing the symptoms of a deadly malady to a physician. Ruef warned him and advised him. The thoroughly frightened Supervisor assured Ruef that he would be careful in the future, and that he would return the money he had received from Roy.[156]

But even as Ruef was dealing with Lonergan, Supervisor Edward I. Walsh was walking into a trap set in duplication of that into which Lonergan had fallen.

Walsh, at the skating-rink, with the eyes of Burns and others upon him, accepted $500 from Roy—who was working as before under direction of the District Attorney—as the price of his vote on the skating-rink ordinance.

The third Supervisor to fall into the District Attorney's trap was Dr. Charles Boxton.

Dr. Boxton [157] was a different type from Lonergan and Walsh. He had had the advantage of superior education and training. A specially prepared trap was set for him at Roy's house. Boxton was introduced into the front room separated from the dining-room by folding doors. The dining-room had been darkened, and the folding doors left slightly ajar. Burns, with his assistants, was concealed in the dining-room, where they

---

156 An interesting incident of this transaction grew out of word being carried to Roy, that Ruef had told Lonergan that Roy was a stool pigeon for Burns. Roy went to Ruef's office with a show of great indignation, demanding to know what Ruef meant by such a charge. Ruef apologized and denied.

157 Boxton is thus described by Ruef, in his account of the graft cases: "Dr. Boxton was a dentist; he held the position of dean and professor of dentistry in an established medical and dental college. He was a popular man about town; had been one of the grand officers of the Native Sons' organization; an officer of the First California Regiment in the Philippines, and had been several times elected Supervisor by large and popular votes."

could see all that took place in the front room, as well as hear what was said. They saw Roy offer Boxton the money; heard him tell Boxton that the ordinance was to be defeated; saw Boxton take the money.

The trap was to be sprung once more, with Lonergan, for the second time,[158] the victim.

Lonergan, instead of returning the $500 he had accepted in the skating-rink transaction, as he had promised Ruef he would do, accepted an additional $500 from Roy. As before, Burns and his men witnessed the transaction.

Roy had told Lonergan of an ordinance authorizing the establishing of an oil refinery in which Roy claimed to be interested. He promised Lonergan $500 to support the measure. The ordinance had been cleverly prepared, with an acrostic in the title, spelling the word "Fake." [159] Roy had interested Boxton in the measure as well as Lonergan. Boxton had introduced it at a regular meeting of the Board of Supervisors. On March 7, while Ruef was a fugitive, Lonergan went to Roy's house to get the money to be paid him for the support of the "Fake" ordinance.

---

[158] The reason for springing the trap on Lonergan the second time was that the plan of Burns's had miscarried on the first trap. Burns had put a man in partnership with Lonergan, who was to induce Lonergan to cash a draft for $200, shortly after Lonergan had received the $500 in marked currency.

When Lonergan was asked to cash the draft, he said all right, but that he would have to go home and get the money. He went home and brought back gold. About this time the Chronicle published a story to the effect that several Supervisors had been trapped.

[159] The acrostic was made by skipping two lines to the third, the first word of which began with "F," then skipping two lines to the sixth, skipping two lines to the ninth, and finally skipping two lines to the twelfth; the first letter of the first word of each of these lines spelt the word "Fake."

The same arrangements had been made for Lonergan as for Boxton. Burns and his men were concealed in the darkened dining-room; the folding doors were ajar. Lonergan took the money.

"What," he demanded of Roy, "have you in the next room?" and advanced toward the partially-open folding doors. At that Burns threw the doors open.

"You see," said Burns, "what he has in there."

"I want you to arrest this man," cried Lonergan, indicating Roy. "He bribed a Supervisor."

"Yes, I saw him do it," replied Burns. "But you did not tell me to arrest him when he bribed you down at the skating-rink."

Lonergan at first denied the skating-rink incident, but finally admitted it. Langdon and Heney were sent for, and joined the party at Roy's house. Lonergan was urged to tell what he knew of graft of the Schmitz-Ruef administration. He finally consented. It was not a long story. Supervisor James L. Gallagher had acted as go-between, Lonergan stated, from Ruef to the Supervisors. From Gallagher, Lonergan testified, he had received $475 to influence his vote in the ordinance granting permits to the organized prize fight promoters to hold fights once a month; $750 to influence his vote in fixing gas rates at 85 cents per thousand instead of 75 cents, as had been pledged in the Union Labor party platform on which he had been elected; $3500 in the matter of granting the Home Telephone Company's franchise; $4000 for his vote in granting the United Railroads its permit to establish the overhead trolley system. Lonergan stated further that Gallagher had promised him $750, and later $1000, to influence his vote in the matter of passing an ordinance for the sale of a franchise applied for by the Parkside Realty Company, with the "biggest thing yet" to come, when the deal was consummated, by which the city would accept the plans of the Bay Cities Water Company.

In addition to the sums received from Gallagher, Lonergan confessed to receiving $5000 from T. V. Halsey, representing the Pacific States Telephone and Telegraph Company. Halsey had paid Lonergan the money, the Supervisor said, to oppose the granting of a franchise to the Home Telephone Company.

Walsh and Boxton were sent for. On their arrival at Roy's house they were closely questioned, and urged to confess, but neither would make a statement that night. Boxton insisted that he would admit nothing unless the other Supervisors made statements. But on the following day, March 8, Walsh made a statement under oath to the District Attorney and Heney, in which he confessed to receiving bribes from Gallagher, except in the Home Telephone bribery, in the same amount and under like conditions that Lonergan had stated bribes had been paid him.

Startling as these confessions were, they as a matter of fact involved none but Lonergan, Walsh, Gallagher and Halsey. At no point did they touch Ruef, or Schmitz, or those who had furnished the bribe money. Boxton with Walsh and Lonergan had been trapped in bribery. Two had confessed to receiving money from Gallagher, but even though the third, Boxton, added his confession to theirs, it would not have provided sufficient to convict. The confessions of the three were uncorroborated as to each bribe. The remaining fifteen Supervisors would to a certainty have sworn they voted for the several measures without inducement. With such testimony from the fifteen, no motive could have been shown for Gallagher to bribe Lonergan, Walsh and Boxton; the measures could, with the votes of the fifteen, have been passed without the votes of the three Supervisors trapped. To make out even a fairly good case against Ruef, it was absolutely essential to have Gallagher's testimony, and in addition thereto, the testimony of a majority of the members of the Board of Supervisors.[160]

The prosecution had made progress in trapping the three Supervisors, and in getting confession out of two of them. But at best it was only an opening wedge. The least slip would have lost all the ground gained. The three trapped Supervisors might be sent to State Prison. Had they been, Schmitz with the fifteen Supervisors remaining would have filled their places by appointment. The situation would then be more difficult for the prosecution than ever.

While the agents of the District Attorney were dealing with the complicated problems which the first break in the line of the graft defense brought upon them, Ruef

---

[160] With the testimony of all the Supervisors, including Gallagher, the prosecution subsequently found great difficulty in convicting Ruef. In the Parkside case, all the Supervisors testified in regard to two promises made to them, and all the officials of the Parkside Company testified to negotiations with Ruef and to the payment of money to him. In addition thereto, William J. Dingee, who was an entirely disinterested party, testified to a conversation with Ruef, which was highly incriminating in its character, and which amounted to an admission on the part of Ruef that he was receiving money in the Parkside matter.

With all this evidence before it, the jury stood six for acquittal and six for conviction.

continued a fugitive. Gallagher, Ruef's immediate representative, realized the seriousness of the situation. He had no real loyalty for Ruef. His one thought was for Gallagher. He could for the moment see no hope for himself, except in the defeat of the prosecution. He accordingly exerted himself to block Burns, and to prevent the conditions of graft in the Board of Supervisors from becoming public.[161]   Supervisor Wilson was assisting him. As encouragement, the anxious Ruef had sent Gallagher word by his sister to remain firm. But the leader was gone; Ruef's grip was loosened. From Gallagher down to the wretched Lonergan, the Supervisors were thinking of saving themselves alone.

Ruef's word, sent by his sister to Gallagher, was for Gallagher "to sit on the lid." Gallagher soon after observed to Wilson that "the lid was getting a little warm"; that he thought he would get in touch with the prosecution to see what could be done with the other

---

161 Wilson testified at the trial of The People vs. Ruef, No. 1437, of the anxiety of the Supervisors during this period. Although Wilson had resigned from the board to accept the office of State Railroad Commissioner to which he had been elected, he went to a conference of the Supervisors to decide what should be done. The following is from Wilson's testimony:

"Q. You were not then a Supervisor, were you? A. No, sir.

"Q. Who told you to go there? A. I was helping Mr. Gallagher.

"Q. Helping Gallagher do what? Don't you know? A. Sit on the lid, that is what we called it.

"Q. Helping Gallagher sit on the lid? A. Yes, sir.

"Q. What does 'sitting on the lid' mean? That is a bit of the vernacular that I am not acquainted with.

"Mr. Dwyer: That is vernacular authorized by the President-elect of the United States, I suppose it is good English?

"Mr. Ach: Well, he is a big man; I suppose he might sit on something that might be a lid. The Court: Finish your answer.

"Mr. Ach: Q. What do you mean? A. Trying to keep the facts of the condition of the Board of Supervisors from becoming public.

"Q. What do you mean by that? A. The condition of the Board, the graft matters."

side. Wilson assured Gallagher that he considered such a move would be a wise one.

Gallagher's first definite word that as many as three Supervisors had been trapped reached him through Dr. Boxton's attorney, H. M. Owens. Owens told Gallagher that Boxton had made full statement of the situation to him and that he was convinced, and so was Boxton, that if Boxton went to trial he would be convicted.

The effect of this information upon Gallagher can be appreciated when it is realized that Gallagher, acting as Ruef's go-between, had himself paid Boxton money. Owens stated further that the question of giving the Supervisors immunity, provided they made complete confession, had been broached, and the suggestion had been made that Gallagher meet some member of the prosecution to discuss this point. The names of Langdon and Burns were suggested, but Gallagher did not care to meet them. He finally agreed, however, to an appointment with Rudolph Spreckels.

Before the meeting between Gallagher and Spreckels took place, Langdon, Heney, Spreckels and Burns had a conference. It was suggested that Spreckels might indicate to Gallagher that the prosecution would like to have his confession and statement, and that the District Attorney would unquestionably be able to extend to him immunity [162] on the strength of his giving full and free,

---

162 At the trial of The People vs. Patrick Calhoun, No. 1436, Spreckels testified to his own attitude on the question of immunity. He said: "I would be willing to grant immunity to any man who would bring to bar a man of great wealth who would debauch a city government, and who would use his wealth to corrupt individuals and tempt men of no means to commit a crime in order that he might make more money."—See transcript of testimony, page 3326.

truthful testimony concerning crimes in which he was involved while acting as a Supervisor in connection with the public service corporations and others.

Three meetings were held between Spreckels and Gallagher before the matter was concluded. The meeting-place was in the grounds of the Presidio, the military reservation at San Francisco.

The first of the three meetings was preliminary only. Spreckels explained to Gallagher the aims and purposes of the prosecution.[163]   Gallagher would make no admissions, and indicated that under no circumstances would he consider the District Attorney's immunity proposition unless all the Supervisors were included within its provisions.

After this preliminary meeting, Spreckels conferred with Langdon and Heney. It was agreed that Gallagher's testimony was essential. He was, indeed, the

---

[163] At the trial of The People vs. Ruef, No. 1437, Gallagher testified that Spreckels told him in substance as follows:

"Mr. Spreckels then stated that he was not actuated by vindictiveness in the matter, that he did not wish to make any more trouble or cause any more distress than was necessary in carrying out what he had undertaken, and that his purpose was to endeavor to stop the unlawful transactions,—dealings of corporations and large interests in this city with public officials; that his reason, that his view of the matter was that in order to accomplish that, that it would be necessary, or that he did not desire unnecessarily to injure anyone, and that the members of the Board of Supervisors and those who were engaged with them in the matter, outside of those who represented the corporations and big interests, were not as important from his standpoint as those who had, as those in control of those interests, because the members of the—the public officials and political bosses would come and go, but that the corporations and big interests remained; that they were, as he thought, the source of the trouble, and therefore, he did not consider it important, or so important, to punish the officials as to reach those that were in his judgment primarily responsible for the conditions, that he felt that the District Attorney would grant immunity to the members of the Board of Supervisors if they would tell the whole truth of their transactions with the corporations and other persons, large interests, that had had any dealings with them of an unlawful character. I think I then said to him I would consider the matter and would talk with the members of the Board of Supervisors about it."

pivotal witness. The confessions of Lonergan, Boxton and Walsh showed that he had carried the bribe money from Ruef to the Supervisors. Furthermore, the testimony of a majority of the Supervisors would be necessary. Under the circumstances it was decided that immunity could very properly be extended to all the Supervisors.

This decision Spreckels took back to Gallagher. Gallagher called his leaderless associates together.

By this time it was generally known among the Supervisors that Lonergan, Walsh and Boxton had been trapped, that at least two of them had made statements to the prosecution. Furthermore, there were rumors that other members had been to the prosecution and made confessions.

Gallagher explained the seriousness of the situation.[164] He explained to them the immunity proposition which the prosecution had made, and stated that the matter rested in their hands. He said that he was will-

---

164 Gallagher at the trial of The People vs. Ruef, No. 1437, made the following statement of what he said to the Supervisors:

"My best recollection of the statement is that I said to them that some of the members of the Board of Supervisors had been trapped in accepting money on some matters before the Board, and that they had made statements to the prosecution, as I understood, or were about to do so, and that I had seen Mr. Spreckels and talked with him concerning the other members of the Board of Supervisors, and that Mr. Spreckels had stated to me that the purpose was not to prosecute the members of the Board of Supervisors provided they would make statements, full and true statements, of their relations in the transactions with the quasi-public corporations and large interests in the city that they may have had unlawful dealings with; that Mr. Spreckels had stated that the public officials were coming and going, and that the political bosses were coming and going; his object was to reach the source of the condition that he was trying to eradicate; that the corporations and these other interests remained all the time, and that he felt that they were the ones that should be the object of his efforts at eradicating that condition in the city. Mr. Spreckels stated that he was not actuated by vindictiveness in the matter; in other words, Mr. Ach, as nearly as I could, I repeated the statements of Mr. Spreckels to me."
See Transcript on Appeal, page 1471.

ing to sacrifice himself, if necessary, but that the whole matter was with them to decide.

Wilson and Boxton urged that the terms offered by the prosecution be accepted.[165]

The Supervisors present were at first divided. Some of them announced that they would take the attitude of denying all graft.

"Very well," replied Gallagher, "any one who wants to take that attitude will be excused from further discussion."

But none of the troubled officials left the room.

Boxton stated that he would involve Gallagher in a statement, and that Gallagher would have to testify to all the money transactions he had had with the board. The Supervisors knew, even then, that Gallagher had already been involved by the confessions of Walsh and Lonergan. Under the urging of Gallagher, Wilson and Boxton, they finally decided to make confession.

Ruef was not present at that last secret caucus of the Schmitz-Ruef Board of Supervisors.

Gallagher took back word to Spreckels that he had communicated to the Supervisors the message which Spreckels had delivered to him from the District Attorney, to the effect that immunity would be granted to the Supervisors, provided they would make sworn dec-

---

[165] "I told them," said Wilson in his testimony in the case of The People vs. Ruef, No. 1437, "that I had always taken orders from Mr. Ruef, that I looked upon him as the political captain of the ship, that I had followed out his orders; that I did not feel that I should sacrifice myself, or ask Mr. Gallagher to sacrifice himself through the condition that had been brought about; that I thought it would be unreasonable for any Supervisor to ask Mr. Gallagher to sacrifice himself, that some of the others might walk the streets and feel that they were honest men; that I did not feel he should be sacrificed alone in the matter."

laration of the crimes in which they were involved, giving a truthful account of all matters. The Supervisors, Gallagher told Spreckels, had decided to accept the proposition, and would meet the District Attorney for the purpose of making their statements.

Gallagher rather tardily asked immunity for Ruef, but Spreckels stated that he had not discussed this feature with the District Attorney, and that Gallagher would himself have to take the matter up with the authorities directly.

In considering this immunity arrangement with the bribed Supervisors, the fact should not be overlooked that during the five months which had passed since the opening of the graft prosecution, Spreckels and Heney had been meeting officials of the public service corporations involved practically every day at luncheon. But the corporation officials would give no assistance in exposing the corruption which was undermining the community.[166]

---

[166] The public service corporation officials were encouraged by Spreckels and Heney to give information which would lead to the indictment and conviction of Ruef and Schmitz, and thus clean up the city. Instead of giving such information, they pretended that the rumors in regard to bribery were all baseless.

At the Pacific Union Club, where they generally lunched, Spreckels and Heney were the recipients of many kind words of encouragement and of congratulation, up to the time that Ruef plead guilty in the French-restaurant case. Immediately thereafter the atmosphere commenced to change. The indictment of some of the prominent members of the club was not pleasing. During the first trial of Glass, he and his attorneys constantly lunched at the Pacific Union Club, and many men, prominent in finance, would stop and chat ostentatiously with Glass and his lawyers, and would then ignore Spreckels and Heney, who would be sitting at a near-by table.

An attempt to keep Rudolph Spreckels out of membership in the Bohemian Club was almost successful about this time, while Drum was elected a director of the Pacific Union Club while still under indictment, and Thomas Williams, of the New California Jockey Club, one of the bondsmen for Schmitz, was elected President.

CHAPTER XIII.

Confessions of the Supervisors.

The resignation of Supervisor Duffey to take charge of the municipal department of public works, and of Supervisor Wilson [167] to take the office of State Railroad Commissioner, left sixteen members of the elected Schmitz-Ruef Board of Supervisors at the time of the exposures of the graft prosecution. The sixteen, after the surrender at their last secret caucus, made full confession of their participation in the gains of the organized betrayal of the city.

Supervisor Wilson added his confession to the sixteen. Thus, of the eighteen Union Labor party Supervisors elected in 1905, four years after the organization of that party, seventeen [168] confessed to taking money from large combinations of capital, the very interests which the party had been brought into being to oppose. The public service corporations, confronting a party organized primarily to control municipal government to

---

[167] To the places thus vacated, Mayor Schmitz appointed O. A. Tveitmoe and J. J. O'Neil. Tveitmoe and O'Neil assumed their duties as Supervisors after the bribery transactions were completed. They did not become involved in the graft exposures, but served to the end of the terms for which they had been appointed.

[168] The eighteenth Supervisor, who made no confession, was Duffey. Duffey, according to Gallagher's confession, participated with the others in the graft distributions. In the hurry of the final arrangements for the confessions, however, Gallagher gained the impression that confession was not to be required of Duffey. Rather than give appearance of lack of good faith, the prosecution decided to abide by the impression which Gallagher claimed he had formed.

the end that equitable conditions in San Francisco might be guaranteed those who labor, by the simple process of support before election and bribery after election, secured as strong a hold upon the community as their most complete success at the polls could have given.

These large interests, approaching the new order with bribe-money, found politicians operating in the name of organized labor, ostensibly to promote the best interests of labor, to be not at all formidable. And when the exposure came, and the bribe-giving corporation magnates were placed on their defense, their most potent allies in the campaign which they carried on to keep out of the penitentiary, were found in the entrenched leaders of the Union-Labor party.

The Supervisors' confessions corroborated the statements previously made by Lonergan, Walsh and Boxton.

The bribery transactions to which the seventeen Supervisors confessed, came naturally under two heads:

The first class included the briberies carried on through Ruef, who dealt directly with those who furnished the bribe money. Ruef employed Gallagher as agent to deal with the Supervisors. Thus Gallagher did not come in contact with those who furnished the money, while the Supervisors were removed still further from connection with them. Ruef, on his part, in passing the money, did not come into immediate contact with the Supervisors except in Gallagher's case. It was bribery reduced to a fine art. In this group of transactions were included the bribery of the Supervisors to grant to the United Railroads its trolley permit; to the Home Telephone Company, its franchise; to the Pacific Gas and Electric Company, an 85-cent gas rate; to the prize fight combine, monopoly of the pugilistic contests in San Francisco. In this class, too, is properly included the Parkside Transit Company, which had, at the time the exposure came, paid Ruef $15,000 to secure a street railroad franchise, with a promise of $15,000 more when the franchise had been actually granted. The Supervisors received nothing in this transaction, but they had been told by Ruef's agent, Gallagher, there would be, first $750 each for them in the Parkside matter. Later on they were told the sum would be $1000 each.

The second class of bribes included those which were paid directly to the Supervisors. They included the bribes paid by T. V. Halsey, agent of the Pacific States Telephone and Telegraph Company to a majority of the Supervisors to prevent their awarding the Home Telephone Company its franchise. Gallagher did not participate in these bribery transactions, and could only indirectly throw light upon them. But in the other cases Gallagher was the pivotal witness. He received the bribe money from Ruef, and, after taking out his share, he paid the balance to the other Supervisors.

With a wealth of detail, Gallagher told how he had received the money, when and where, and went into the particulars of its distribution among his associates. He had received from Ruef in all, $169,350.[169] Of this, he

---

[169] This was the amount that Ruef turned over to the Supervisors. It represented a comparatively small part of what he received from the Public Service corporations. From the United Railroads alone, because of the granting of the trolley permit, he received $200,000. In addition he was drawing a regular fee of $1,000 a month from the United Railroads.

The Supervisors were not always satisfied with the amount Gal-

had retained $27,275 for himself; the balance, $142,075, he had divided among his associates on the board.

This enormous corruption fund which Gallagher divided with the Supervisors had come from four sources. The so-called prize-fight trust had furnished $9,000 of it; the Pacific Gas and Electric Company, $13,350; the Home Telephone Company, $62,000, and the United Railroads, $85,000.

The first money that passed from Ruef to Gallagher and from Gallagher on to the Supervisors, the confessions showed, was for the prize-fight monopoly. This particular bribery seems to have been intended as a trying-out of the several members to ascertain which of them would take money in connection with the discharge of their duties as Supervisors.

Every member of the board accepted the package of bills which Gallagher tendered him. Indeed, several of them displayed surprising alertness to secure all that was their due. Ruef, it became known among them, had given Gallagher $9000, which evenly divided, meant $500 for each of the eighteen Supervisors. But Gallagher gave them only $475 each. An explanation was de-

lagher gave them. There were times when they entertained the idea that Ruef had sent more than Gallagher gave. They accordingly delegated Supervisor Wilson to ascertain from Ruef whether all the money intended for them was reaching them. Ruef refused to discuss the matter with Wilson. Wilson, at the trial of The People vs. Ruef, No. 1437, testified:

"I told him (Ruef) that the Supervisors had asked me to call and see him; that they wanted other information to confirm Mr. Gallagher's reports to the Board on these money matters. He said that he did not care to discuss that with anyone other than Mr. Gallagher; that it took up time and that whatever Mr. Gallagher did on the Board was with his full knowledge and consent; that the matters were being handled satisfactorily by Mr. Gallagher, and when anything arose, any other condition confronted him, he would look elsewhere for a leader, but he did not want to go in at that time and discuss those matters with anyone."

manded of him. He stated that he had taken out 5 per cent. as his commission.

So strong was the dissatisfaction created by the holding out of this 5 per cent. that Ruef arranged to pay Gallagher a larger amount than the others received to compensate him, no doubt, for his extra services as bribe-carrier.

The new arrangement for the compensation of Gallagher was followed when the Supervisors were paid after fixing gas rates at 85 cents per thousand cubic feet, instead of 75 cents,[170] the sum pledged in their party platform.

One of the Supervisors, McGushin, refused to break his platform pledge, and held out for the 75-cent rate. In distributing the gas money, Gallagher paid nothing to McGushin.[171]

But to each of the remaining sixteen Supervisors, Gallagher confessed to giving $750. Following the new rule that he was to have extra compensation, Gallagher kept for himself $1350.

At the time of the gas-rate bribery, Supervisor Rea was making it unpleasant for his associates. Mr. Rea

---

[170] About the time the 85-cent gas rate was fixed, one of the Pacific Gas and Electric Company's stations was burned. Ruef stated to Gallagher that the fire would be used as one of the reasons for fixing the .85-cent rate; that it would probably appeal to the public as an excuse for fixing the rate at 85 cents when the platform of the party had mentioned 75 cents. See Transcript, The People vs. Ruef, No. 1437, page 784.

[171] When McGushin refused to follow directions and give the Pacific Gas and Electric Company an 85-cent gas rate, Gallagher went to Ruef about it. At the trial of The People vs. Ruef, No. 1437, Gallagher testified: "I told him (Ruef) that McGushin was rather demurring at receiving the money, at taking the money, and that I had told Mr. McGushin that he had better go down and talk with Mr. Ruef. He (Ruef) said, "All right, if he comes around I will talk with him.""

had accepted $475 prize-fight money from Gallagher, without, he testified before the Grand Jury, knowing what it was for. A few days later he told Schmitz of the matter. Schmitz contended that no such work was going on. Rea, when he received his $750 in the gas-rate case, went to Schmitz with a statement that money was used to have the gas rate fixed at 85 cents. Rea asked Schmitz what he was to do with the money. He testified before the Grand Jury that Schmitz replied: "You keep quiet. I will let you know."

That was the last Rea heard from Schmitz on the subject. Rea testified before the Grand Jury that he still had the money Gallagher had paid him in the prize-fight and gas-rate cases.

Rea's trip to Schmitz seems to have kept him out of the division of the Telephone and the United Railroads money.

The Telephone bribery was somewhat complicated by the fact that rival companies were in the field bidding for Supervisorial favor. It developed that eleven of the Supervisors [172] had accepted from T. V. Halsey, representing the Pacific States Telephone and Telegraph Company, bribes to block the granting of a franchise to the

---

172 The Supervisors who accepted money from Halsey, acting for the Pacific States Telephone and Telegraph Company, to prevent a franchise being awarded an opposition company were: Boxton, Walsh, Wilson, Coleman, Nicholas, Furey, Mamlock, Phillips, Lonergan, Sanderson and Coffey. The amount paid in each instance was $5,000. Halsey promised several of the bribed members from $2,500 to $5,000 in addition to be paid them, if they remained faithful, after their terms had expired. The money, the several members testified, had been paid to them by Halsey in an unfurnished room in the Mills Building which had been temporarily engaged for Mr. Halsey's use by Frank G. Drum, a director of the Pacific States Telephone and Telegraph Company. Examples of the methods employed to corrupt the laboringmen Supervisors who suddenly found themselves placed in a position of trust and responsibility will be found in the appendix.

Home Telephone Company. On the other hand, the Home Telephone Company had paid Ruef $125,000 [173] to be used in getting favorable action on its application for a franchise. Ruef gave Gallagher $62,000 for the Supervisors. Ruef states that he divided the remainder with Schmitz. In this way, the administration was bribed to grant the Home Telephone franchise, while eleven [174] of the Supervisors, a majority of the board, were bribed not to grant it.

The complications which this created almost disrupted the Ruef-Schmitz combine. The difficulty was threshed out in a Sunday night caucus. Those who had received money from the Pacific States people, with Supervisor Boxton at their head, insisted that the Home franchise

---

[173] This is the amount given by Ruef in his "confession." He states that he received $25,000 when he agreed that the Home Telephone Company should have the franchise; and $100,000 when the franchise was granted. According to his statement he gave $65,000 to Gallagher for the Supervisors; $30,000 he gave Schmitz; $30,000 he kept himself. Gallagher testified on several occasions that he received but $62,000 from Ruef. The details of Ruef's confessions are not dependable. On Ruef's own statement of the basis of division of this particular bribe money among the Supervisors, Gallagher received only $62,000 of Home Telephone money from him.

[174] Ruef was himself to blame for the complication, for he had given certain of the Supervisors to understand that the purpose of the Pacific Telephone and Telegraph Company was to prevail, and that the Home Telephone Company would not be granted its franchise. The Supervisors in taking the Pacific Telephone and Telegraph Company's money, not unreasonably supposed they were taking from the favored of the administration. Supervisor Wilson in his confession said: "The first conversation I had with Mr. Ruef, affecting money matters, was on the Pacific States Telephone matters. I told him that I had been out to dinner with Mr. Halsey, and I understood that everything was going to be satisfactory with their company. He (Ruef) said that it would terminate that way."

Acting upon this hint, Wilson accepted $5,000 from Halsey. Later he told Ruef of having got the money. Ruef told him that he should not have taken it. Wilson has testified that he offered to return it. "No," he claims Ruef replied, "don't do that just now. Wait and see. I will let you know later. You might get into a trap by giving it back; you had better wait."

Ruef claims, however, that he advised Wilson to return the money.

should not be granted. On the other hand, Ruef and Schmitz, with the thousands of the Home Company in view, insisted that it should be. Both Ruef and Schmitz warned the Supervisors that they were perhaps at the dividing of the ways.

"Well," replied Boxton significantly, "if men cannot get a thing through one way they might try and get it through in another."

Mayor Schmitz demanded of Boxton what he meant by that. "Well," Boxton replied vaguely but defiantly, "you know there are other ways of reaching the matter." [175]

But Boxton was unable to prevail against the support which Ruef and Schmitz were giving the Home Telephone Company. Although eleven of the Supervisors had taken money from the Pacific States Company to oppose the granting of a franchise to the rival Home Telephone Company, all but four of those present at the caucus decided to stand by Ruef and Schmitz, and voted in caucus to grant the Home Company its franchise. [176]

The next day, in open board meeting, with Boxton still leading the opposition, the franchise was awarded to the Home Telephone Company.

---

[175] For description of this "dividing of the ways" scene, see testimony of Supervisor Wilson, Transcript on Appeal, The People vs. Ruef, page 2843.

[176] Gallagher in his confession said of the decision of the Supervisors to stand by Ruef and Schmitz: "Mr. Wilson talked to a number of those boys (Supervisors who had taken money from the Pacific States's agent), he being one of those who had taken this money, and he told me that notwithstanding the fact that they had taken this money that he didn't feel that he wanted to stand out from the leadership of Mr. Ruef and wanted to act with him and myself in the matter and said that he would talk to the other boys about it, and see how they felt about the proposition of voting for the Home Telephone franchise anyhow."

The division of the money received from the Home Telephone Company people was one of the hardest problems in bribe distribution which Ruef and Gallagher were called upon to face.

The first plan was to pay the Supervisors who had at the last supported the Home Telephone franchise, $3500. At once those Supervisors who had, from the beginning remained faithful to the administration's support of the Home Company and had refused to accept money from Halsey, pointed out that they would receive $3500 only, while the Supervisors whom Halsey had bribed would get in all $8500; that is to say, $3500 from Gallagher for voting to grant the franchise and $5000 from Halsey not to grant it. It was, those who had remained true contended, inequitable that Supervisors who had been faithful to Ruef and Schmitz from the beginning should receive only $3500; while those who had been temporarily bought away from the administration received $8500.

The "justness" of this contention appealed to all. A compromise was finally arranged, under which those who had stood out to the end against granting the Home franchise, should receive no part of the Home Telephone bribe money; those who had received $5000 from Halsey but finally voted for the Home franchise, were to return $2500 of the $5000 to Halsey, and receive $3500 from Gallagher, making the total of the telephone bribe money for each $6000; those who had received nothing from Halsey were each to be allowed $6000 of the Home Telephone money. In this way each Supervisor who had voted for the Home franchise would get $6000 for his vote. In the case of four of the Supervisors the entire $6000 came from the Home Company. Gallagher, too, was one of this class, all his compensation being Home Telephone money. But Gallagher received $10,000. Eight of the Supervisors had received money from Halsey, and yet voted to give the Home Company its franchise. These received $3500 Home Company money from Gallagher and were allowed to keep $2500 of the Pacific States Telephone and Telegraph Company money that Halsey had given them. Thus the Pacific States was forced to pay the Supervisors part of the bribe money they received for granting its rival a franchise. Incidentally, some of the Supervisors did not return half the $5000 to Halsey. But this is a phase of the ethics of bribery upon which it is unnecessary to touch.

Ruef regarded this unique discipline of the Pacific States as just punishment for its offense of trying to buy his Supervisors away from him.[177]

Following the telephone bribery, came that of the United Railroads to secure the much-opposed over-head trolley permit. On account of this permit, Gallagher testified, Ruef had given him $85,000 to be distributed among the Supervisors.

Of this $85,000, Gallagher kept $15,000 for himself,

---

[177] In his confession, Gallagher stated that under this arrangement he paid $3,500 each to Coffey, Coleman, Furey, Lonergan, Mamlock, Nicholas, Phillips and Wilson; $6,000 each to Davis, Duffey, Harrigan and Kelley, reserving $10,000 for himself. Those who received no part of the Home Telephone Company money were Boxton, Sanderson, Walsh, McGushin and Rea. Of the five, Boxton and Sanderson received $5,000 each from Halsey of the Pacific Company, and Walsh, according to his recollection, $3,500. McGushin and Rea received none of the bribe money paid by the two telephone companies.

gave Wilson $10,000,[178] and to each of the other Supervisors with the exception of Rea,[179] $4000.

Gallagher's testimony relative to the offer of a bribe in the matter of the Parkside Realty Company franchise was quite as explicit. He swore that Ruef had stated to him there ought to be $750 for each Supervisor in this. Later on, with a change in the proposed route,[180] Ruef had told Gallagher that the amount would be $1000 to each Supervisor. Gallagher had conveyed this information to the Supervisors. At the time of Ruef's flight, arrest and the attending breaking up of his organization, the Supervisors were impatiently waiting for this money to be paid.[181]

---

[178] Gallagher testified before the Grand Jury, that the additional compensation had been given Wilson because he was more useful than any other member, besides himself, in keeping the Supervisors in line and in passing information regarding prospective bribe money.

[179] Gallagher testified before the Grand Jury that he had paid Rea nothing, because he had no confidence in Rea's judgment and self-control. "I told Mr. Ruef," Gallagher testified, "I did not care to, that I wouldn't take the responsibility of dealing with Mr. Rea. I believe he was talking and had talked about matters dealing with me and did not care to have any dealings with him. He (Ruef) said, 'Very well, I'll attend to him,' or 'I will see to that myself,' or some such expression as that."

[180] The original plan was to have this road on Twentieth Avenue. But to grade Twentieth Avenue would take time, and cost upwards of $100,000. On the other hand, Nineteenth Avenue had been graded, macadamized, and accepted as a boulevard. The Parkside people asked a change in the purchased franchise, to give them the boulevard. But the Charter prohibited grants of franchises over declared boulevards. Ruef concluded this provision could be overcome by ordinance. He feared criticism, but finally yielded to the Parkside people's request. Then went word to the Supervisors of increase in compensation in this particular transaction.

[181] Gallagher's testimony before the Grand Jury regarding the promised bribes in the Parkside franchise undertaking was as follows:
"Q. Now, then, the Parkside trolley, was there an understanding in regard to money being paid on that? A. The Parkside realty company's franchise for street railway on Twentieth Avenue, that is what you refer to—on Nineteenth Avenue, that is correct; it was originally intended for Twentieth, afterward changed to Nineteenth; that is right there was nothing paid to any member of the Board upon that that I know of. There were some rumors about

One by one, sixteen of Gallagher's associates went before the District Attorney and made full confession. In every detail they bore out Gallagher's statements. When they had done, the District Attorney had statements from seventeen [182] of the eighteen Supervisors,, that they had received large sums of bribe money to influence their votes in matters in which public service corporations were concerned; he knew the purposes for which the bribe money had been paid; he had a statement from Gallagher, corroborated at many points by the testimony of the other Supervisors, that the money had been furnished by Ruef. Ruef's testimony would bring the bribery transactions directly to the doors of

---

it and Mr. Ruef spoke to me about it and said there ought to be a payment of $750 to each member on it and afterward said that if the thing was changed from Twentieth Avenue to the Nineteenth Avenue, that there ought to be $1,000 each paid.

"Q. About when did he say it ought or he would be able to pay them? A. He said that he expected to, yes, sir. He did not say he was ready to do so, on the contrary, has always denied that he had the money to pay it with.

"Q. He never said he had the money before on the other matters? A. No.

"Q. He would just say there will be this much coming? A. Yes, sir.

"Q. And the same way in regard to this also? A. Yes, sir.

"Q. $1,000? A. Yes, sir.

"Q. And you passed it out in the same way? A. Yes, sir.

"Q. And it was put through with that understanding? A. Yes, sir.

"Q. The only definite, was it, it hasn't come? A. Not yet.

"Q. Do you know why the money hasn't been given to you yet by Ruef? A. No, sir.

"Q. Has he given you any reason? A. Mr. Ruef said that the amount has not been paid to him.

"Q. You heard complaints from the members that they had been so long about coming through? A. Yes, indeed.

"Q. Did you make complaint to Ruef about it? A. Yes, sir.

"Q. What did he say? A. He made that excuse consequently that he didn't have it.

"Q. Never said that he did not expect it? A. Did not."

[182] The anxiety on the part of the confessing Supervisors to tell the truth was pathetic. When McGushin began his story he was asked: "Of course this statement you make is free and voluntary." "Yes," replied McGushin, simply, "Mr. Gallagher himself told me to tell the truth."

those who had bribed.   This testimony could have been had, had the prosecution agreed to give Ruef complete immunity.

Ruef was a prisoner in charge of an elisor.   He knew that the Supervisors had confessed.   In an agony of indecision he sent for Gallagher and Wilson to learn from them all that had occurred.[183]   They told him that full statements had been made to the District Attorney.   Ruef complained that Gallagher should have tried to get into touch with him before making statements.   To which Gallagher replied that such a course would have been impossible.[184]   Both Gallagher and Wilson advised Ruef to make terms with the District Attorney.   Ruef replied that he would think it over.   Little came of the conference.   The statements of the two Supervisors, however, must have shown Ruef how thorough the undoing of his organization had been, and how hopeless was his own case.   But Ruef, sparring for time, and pleading for complete immunity, did not make immediate confession and, as a matter of fact has not, up to the

---

[183] "I want to learn from your own lips," he told Wilson, "if what I have already heard is true regarding your making a statement to the prosecution."

"I have been thoroughly informed," said Ruef in an interview given out later, "of everything that the members of the Board of Supervisors are reported to have told the Grand Jury, and I have no comment to make upon their alleged confessions at this time. Later, however, I will issue a statement which will furnish more sensations in connection with municipal graft than anything that has been made public."

[184] Gallagher left the conference first.   Wilson testified at the graft trials that after Gallagher had gone Ruef stated that "had he been in Gallagher's place he wouldn't have made those statements to the prosecution."

"You can never tell what one will do until he is placed in Mr. Gallagher's position," replied Wilson, "we discussed the matter fully for two or three days before he took that step."

present writing, told the full story of his connection with the public service corporations.[185]

After the confessions of the Supervisors, the District Attorney left Ruef to himself and hastened the Supervisors before the Grand Jury, where they repeated their miserable stories.[186]

And then the Grand Jury took up the task of tracing the bribe money from those who had received it, to those who had paid it.

---

[185] The nearest Ruef has come to a statement of his connection with the public service corporations is contained in his story, "The Road I Traveled," which appeared in the San Francisco Bulletin. The account is inaccurate and incomplete. Nothing, for example, is told by Mr. Ruef, of the proposed Bay Cities Water Company deal, which at one time he claimed to be the most important of all he had in view.

[186] The Supervisors were all examined before the Grand Jury on the same day. Heney in an affidavit, filed in the case of The People vs. Calhoun et al., No. 823, states that "one of the reasons which actuated me to examine all of said Supervisors on the same day was that the newspapers had discovered that they had made confessions on the preceding Saturday, and I wanted to make sure that no one of them was tampered with by anyone who might be interested in changing his testimony before I succeeded in getting his testimony recorded by a stenographer in the Grand Jury room."

CHAPTER XIV.

The Source of the Bribe Money.

After the confessions of the Supervisors, the Grand Jurors had definite, detailed knowledge of the corruption of the Union-Labor party administration. The Grand Jurors knew:

(1) That bribes aggregating over $200,000 had been paid the Supervisors.

(2) That of this large amount, $169,350 passed from Ruef to Gallagher and by Gallagher had been divided among members of the board. The balance, the evidence showed, had been paid to the Supervisors direct by T. V. Halsey of the Pacific States Telephone Company.

(3) The amount of each bribe; the circumstances under which it was paid; even the character of the currency used in the transaction.

(4) The names of the corporations benefited by the bribery transactions, as well as the character of the special privileges which their money had bought.

With the exception of the Home Telephone Company, the names of the directors of these benefiting corporations were readily obtainable.[187]

---

187 The following persons sat on the Boards of Directors of the several corporations involved in the graft disclosures, either during 1906 when the briberies were committed, or during 1907 when the exposures came:

Pacific Gas and Electric Company—N. W. Halsey, E. J. de Sabla, John Martin, Frank G. Drum, Wm. H. Crocker, N. D. Rideout, Frank B. Anderson, John A. Britton, Henry E. Bothin, Louis F.

With this data before them, the Grand Jurors proceeded to trace the source of the bribe money.

Naturally, men who had long held places of respectability in the community were slow to admit having given Ruef vast sums, even under the transparent subterfuge of paying him attorney's fees.[188] Some of them, when haled before the Grand Jury, testified reluctantly, and only under the closest questioning. Others frankly stood upon their constitutional rights, and with pitiful attempt to smooth out with studied phrases the harshness of the only acceptable reason for their refusal, declined to testify on the ground that their testimony would tend to incriminate them.

Monteagle, Jos. S. Tobin, G. H. McEnerney, Cyrus Pierce, Carl Taylor, F. W. M. McCutcheon.

Pacific States Telephone and Telegraph Company—Henry T. Scott, Louis Glass, F. W. Eaton, Timothy Hopkins, Homer S. King, F. G. Drum, E. S. Pillsbury, Percy T. Morgan, all of San Francisco; J. C. Ainsworth, P. Bacon, J. H. Thatcher, C. H. Chambreau, E. H. McCracken, C. B. McLeod, C. E. Hickman, J. P. McNichols, R. W. Schmeer, all of Portland.

Parkside Company—W. H. Crocker, Wellington Gregg, Jr., C. E. Green, J. J. Mahony, W. H. Cope, A. F. Morrison, Hugh Keenan, Wm. Matson, J. M. O'Brien, Douglas S. Watson, J. E. Green.

United Railroads—Patrick Calhoun, G. F. Chapman, Geo. H. Davis, Tirey L. Ford, Benj. S. Guiness, I. W. Hellman, Chas. Holbrook, A. C. Kains, J. Henry Meyer, Thornwell Mullally, Jos. S. Tobin.

The names of the board of directors of the Home Telephone Company, during the period of the bribery transactions, has not, so far as the writer knows, been made public. A. C. Kains resigned from the directorate of the United Railroads, and Jos. S. Tobin from the directorates of the United Railroads and the Pacific Gas and Electric Company, about the time of the disclosures.

188 The inconsistency of the "attorney fee plea" is well illustrated in the United Railroads transaction. Ruef received $200,000 from the United Railroads because of the trolley permit. General Tirey L. Ford, head of the United Railroads law department, to which he devoted all his time, was credited with receiving a salary of $10,000 a year. Thus Ruef's single "fee" was as much as the United Railroads would have paid its head lawyer in twenty years, almost a lifetime of professional service. And Ruef, it must be remembered, in addition was getting $1,000 a month from the United Railroads—more than the chief of that corporation's legal department was receiving.

Nevertheless, the Grand Jury succeeded in wringing from the officials of the several corporations involved, damaging admissions; admissions, in fact, quite as startling as had been the confessions of the Supervisors. The refusal of some of those not unreasonably under suspicion, to testify was, too, quite as significant.

In the matter of the bribery of the Supervisors by T. V. Halsey, agent of the Pacific States Telephone and Telegraph Company, the Grand Jury had information that eleven Supervisors had been paid over $50,000 to oppose the granting of a franchise to the Home Telephone Company. A majority of the payments were made in an unfurnished suite of three rooms in the Mills Building. Frank Drum, a director of the company, admitted having engaged the rooms at Halsey's request. E. J. Zimmer, auditor for the company, testified that Halsey held the position of General Agent of the company. Halsey's duties, the testimony showed, were assigned him by Louis Glass, vice-president and general manager, and for a time acting president of the company. Halsey, under the company's organization, reported to Glass. Zimmer testified that Halsey could not spend the company's money except on the proper approval of the executive officer of the company. From October, 1905, when President Sabin of the company died, until February, 1906, when Henry T. Scott, Sabin's successor, was elected, Glass acted as president and as executive officer. He had, according to Auditor Zimmer, authority to approve expenditures made by Halsey. After Scott's elevation to the presidency, either Glass or Scott could have approved such expenditures. Zimmer testified further to giving Halsey, at Glass's order,[189] as high as $10,000 at a time. Halsey [190] gave no vouchers for these large sums; they did not appear on the books; [191] they were carried on tags.

Zimmer stated that he did not know for what the funds were used; had merely followed out Glass's instruction, and given Halsey the money.

The testimony of Thomas Sherwin threw some light

---

[189] Zimmer insisted at first that the total of the amounts which he turned over to Halsey would not exceed $20,000. Later he admitted that he had not kept track of the amounts, and the total might have been $30,000. This he increased to $35,000, and finally stated that it was "not over $40,000, if it was that." He admitted that it would have been possible for Executive Officer Glass to have paid out $70,000 without his knowledge. "Checks," he said, "could have been signed without going through me; could have been carried just the same as this tag account was."

William J. Kennedy, cashier and assistant treasurer of the company, who had charge of the "tags," stated that during February, 1906, considerable amounts were drawn out in this way, which might have totalled as high as $70,000.

[190] Regarding the manner in which money was furnished to Halsey, Zimmer testified before the Grand Jury as follows:

"Q. This $10,000 that you gave him (Halsey) under direction of Mr. Glass, in what shape did you hand it to him? A. Currency.

"Q. Did you have the currency on hand or send out and get it? A. Sent out and got it. I went out and got it.

"Q. Where did you get it? A. I don't remember, I had to go to several banks.

"Q. Did Mr. Glass tell you he wanted you to give it to him in currency? A. Yes, sir."

[191] These admissions led to close questioning of Mr. Zimmer. The following is taken from his testimony given before the Grand Jury:

"Q. Now, in what way did that money appear in the books? A. Didn't appear in the books.

"Q. How was it taken care of? A. No voucher was ever made for it.

"Q. How would your cash account for it? A. It wasn't taken out of the cash account, so far as I know.

"Q. What was it taken from? A. By check issued on the regular bank account.

"Q. Who was the check made payable to? A. Eaton, treasurer, the same as other coin checks are issued, coin or currency.

"Q. It would have appeared somewhere in the books, that check, that amount would be deducted from the bank account? A. Yes, sir; but carried in the expense account of the cash suspense.

"Q. Leave a tag with you? Leave a tag, would you? A. Yes."

upon the bookkeeping methods followed. Sherwin had been traveling auditor for the American Bell Telephone Company, which concern owned 51 per cent. of the stock of the Pacific States Telephone and Telegraph Company. Later he took Zimmer's place as auditor of the Pacific States Company.

Mr. Sherwin admitted that some of Mr. Halsey's "special expenses," at least, were finally charged to the company's legal department.[192]

Passing from the investigation of the bribery transactions of the Pacific States Telephone and Telegraph Company to the activities of the Home Telephone Company, the Grand Jury examined prominent business men of Los Angeles as well as of San Francisco.

The plan of operation followed by the capitalists behind this enterprise was to organize a construction company, whose part was to establish the plants, put them

---

192 Before the Grand Jury, Sherwin was closely questioned as to one of Mr. Halsey's "Special expense" claims. The following is from his testimony:

"Q. Now, then, that shows that it was charged against what fund? A. That got in the legal expense finally, we charged it to Reserve for Contingent Liabilities, and each month we credit that account, I have forgotten maybe $2,000, and charge it to legal to make it run even in the expense each month.

"Q. Why does it go to legal? A. Because—instead—to what else would it go?

"Q. What makes it legal? A. Oh, that's just a subdivision of our expense.

"Q. Was this $600 legal expenses? A. I don't know what it was.

"Q. Who told you to put it under legal expenses? A. You mean who told us to put it in that account?

"Q. There is nothing on that paper that indicates that it goes into legal expense? A. No.

"Q. Now, then, you say it was finally charged to the legal department. Why? A. Simply because everything that is charged to that reserve finally gets into legal expense.

"Q. Everything that is charged to that reserve fund? A. Yes, that reserve fund is charged off for legal expense.

"Q. And what is the reason for that? A. For charging it to legal?

"Q. Yes. A. For charging it to legal—because—I don't know the reason—it is always done that way."

into operation and turn them over to the operating companies, taking their pay in the securities of the local operating company. Thus, at San Francisco, the Empire Construction Company played an important part in the Home Telephone Company enterprise.

As Heney put it, the Empire Construction Company received the most benefit from the granting of the Home Telephone franchise. The Empire Construction Company furnished at least part of the money that went into the fusion campaign fund in 1905. Investigation showed that 25 per cent. of the stock of the Empire Construction Company belonged to men who were in the construction solely, while 75 per cent. was in the hands of men who were financing the enterprise. This last block of stock at the time of the investigation was divided among James H. Adams and Thomas W. Phillips of the Adams-Phillips Company, A. B. Cass, Gerald S. Torrance and A. K. Detweiler. Detweiler could not be found. Adams, Cass and Torrance, after answering some of the questions put to them, availed themselves of their constitutional privilege, and refused to make further answers. The books of the Adams-Phillips Company disappeared and employees of that company undertook to evade answering questions regarding the disappearance, on the ground that they might incriminate themselves. But a sharp order from the Superior Court brought out their testimony. However, none of them gave testimony that led to the discovery of the missing volumes.

But the general trend of the testimony went to show that the responsible agent for the Empire Construction Company and the Home Telephone Company in San

Francisco was A. K. Detweiler. The testimony showed Detweiler to have been at Ruef's office in consultation with Ruef and Supervisor Gallagher; he was active in every move that was made on behalf of the Empire Construction Company and of the Home Telephone Company in San Francisco, and had the disbursing of the funds.

Incidentally, through the testimony of Dr. Fred Butterfield, a representative of Adolphus Busch, the brewer, the Grand Jury learned that a third telephone company. the United States Independent, seeking a franchise to do business in San Francisco, would have bid for the franchise which the Home Company received, had not the franchise been so worded that only the telephone system controlled by the Home people could be operated under it. Butterfield stated that his company, made up of responsible capitalists, considered the franchise worth something over a million dollars, and was prepared to bid up to a million dollars, if necessary, to get it. The Home Company paid San Francisco $25,000 for the franchise. Butterfield testified that his company had intended to invest $4,500,000 in the San Francisco enterprise, and that Ruef knew of the extent of the company's plans. With such testimony, the assertions of Ruef's partisans that opposition to the Ruef-Schmitz administration retarded development of the community compare curiously.[193]

The Grand Jury could not secure the attendance of Mr. Detweiler, for about the time of the investigation Mr. Detweiler mysteriously disappeared. The investiga-

193 See Supervisors' letter to the Examiner, footnote 64, page 62.

tion into the affairs of the Home Company had, therefore, to be concluded without Mr. Detweiler's testimony.

Following the policy of the stockholders of the Empire Construction Company, the officials of the United Railroads refused to testify. President Patrick Calhoun [194] and Thornwell Mullally, assistant to the president, when given opportunity to state their side of the case under oath, stood upon their constitutional rights, and declined to give evidence that might incriminate them.[195] They were accordingly excused from the Grand Jury room.

---

[194] Calhoun returned to San Francisco April 10. In interviews published in the San Francisco papers of April 12, Calhoun emphatically denied all knowledge of the bribery transactions. In his interview in the Chronicle he said:

"I wish to go on record before the people of San Francisco as stating that not one of the officers or legal counsel of the United Railroads of San Francisco or the United Railroads Investment Company of New Jersey ever paid, authorized to be paid, approved of paying or knew that one dollar was paid to secure the passage of the trolley franchise ordinance by the Board of Supervisors, and if I had known that one dollar was paid for the purpose of securing this franchise I would not have accepted it."

[195] The refusal of Calhoun and Mullally to testify created a sensation, even in those sensational times. The Chronicle in its issue of May 4, 1907, printed the following account of the incident:

"For the first time in the history of the examination of witnesses before this Grand Jury, Heney was careful not to instruct the prospective witnesses as to their legal rights. Instead he merely asked them if they were already familiar with their rights under the law.

" 'I am aware,' said Calhoun, who was the first to be called, 'that anything I might tell this body might be used against me.'

" 'With that understanding are you willing to become a witness before this Grand Jury?' asked Heney.

" 'I am not,' was Calhoun's response.

"The jurymen who had leaned forward as the reply of the president hung on his lips sank back in their seats.

" 'That is all, Mr. Calhoun,' said Heney to the president, and then going to the door he said to the bailiff, 'Call Mr. Mullally.'

"Mullally's examination was identical with that of his superior's and he was permitted to go. Neither President Calhoun nor Assistant Mullally will be called again to the jury room."

Calhoun issued the following statement of his refusal to testify:

"When called before the Grand Jury this afternoon and informed that it had under investigation the alleged bribery of public officials by the United Railroads, we declined to be sworn and in

But the employees of the company did not escape so easily. When, for example, George Francis, William M. Abbott, George B. Willcutt and Celia McDermott refused to answer questions put to them in the Grand Jury room, they were haled before the Superior Court, where they were informed that they must testify.

In spite of the hostility of these witnesses, the prosecution succeeded in securing a wealth of data regarding $200,000 which passed into the hands of Tirey L. Ford and, according to the theory of the prosecution, from Ford to Ruef.

The prosecution established the fact that two days before Mayor Schmitz signed the trolley permit, that is to say, on May 22, 1906, Patrick Calhoun, as president of the United Railroads, received by telegraphic transfer from the East to the United States Mint at San Francisco, $200,000.[196] Two days later, the day the trolley permit was signed, President Calhoun took Ford

order that our action may not be misconstrued, I call your attention to these facts:

"For months past the public prints have been full of charges traceable to certain persons connected with the prosecution that they had positive evidence that the United Railroads had spent not less than $450,000 in bribing the officials of this city. I have repeatedly stated that neither I nor the United Railroads, nor any official of the United Railroads, had bribed anyone, authorized any bribery, knew of any bribery or approved of any bribery. This statement I now fully reaffirm. It is not for us nor any officer of our company to disprove these grave charges. It is for those making them to prove them. We do not now care to discuss their motives. We know that they cannot produce any truthful evidence connecting us or any officer of the United Railroads with this alleged crime.

"We relied, in declining to be sworn, upon the broad Constitutional right of every American citizen that a defendant cannot be called as a witness, and upon the justice, fairness and common sense of the Grand Jury, to whom we look for complete vindication without offering one word in our own behalf."

196 For several weeks after the great fire of April 18-19-20, 1906, the banks were closed at San Francisco. Money could, however, during this period, be transferred to San Francisco, through the United States mint.

to the Mint and instructed Superintendent of the Mint Leach to give Ford $50,000 of the $200,000. Ford told Leach that he wanted currency. The currency was finally secured by exchanging gold for bills at the Mint headquarters of the relief work then being carried on in San Francisco. These bills, it was shown, were all in small denominations, having been sent to San Francisco from all parts of the country by individual subscribers to the relief fund.

This money was taken away from the Mint, the testimony showed, by Ford and William M. Abbott.

Soon after, Ruef loaned Supervisor Rea [197] $3500. By a curious trick of fate Rea had leased a piece of property from Rudolph Spreckels. In payment on this lease he used the money that Ruef had loaned him. This money was all in bills of small denominations. Late in July Ruef gave Gallagher $45,000, all in bills of small denominations, as partial settlement with the Supervisors for granting the trolley permit. Gallagher gave Wilson of this money $5000, and the other Supervisors with the exception of Rea $2000 each. They all understood that it was because of the trolley franchise deal. The balance Gallagher retained for himself.

The confessing Supervisors, with the exception of Wilson and Rea, testified that their first payment on account of the trolley permit was $2000 each, in bills of small denominations. Wilson testified to having received $5000.

Later, Ford, making two trips to the Mint, drew out

---

[197] Gallagher had notified Ruef that he would not deal with Rea in the trolley transaction. Ruef, Gallagher alleged, had agreed to attend to Rea's case himself. See Chapter XIII.

the $150,000 balance of the $200,000 that had been telegraphed to Calhoun's credit. As before, the Mint paid
him in gold, and as before, Ford exchanged the gold
for currency. But instead of getting bills of small de-
nomination, on the two trips which Ford made for that
$150,000, he secured fifty and one hundred-dollar bills.

On the day that Ford drew the last of that $200,000
from the Mint, an agent in the employ of the prosecution followed Ruef from his office to the car barns in
which Ford's office was then located. A few days later
Ruef gave Gallagher $40,000 in fifty and one hundred-
dollar bills, the greater part of which Gallagher distributed among the Supervisors as second and final payment on account of the granting of the trolley permit.

In the Parkside deal, the Grand Jury had little difficulty in tracing the money involved. William H.
Crocker,[198] a capitalist of large affairs, who owned the
largest interest in the company, showed astonishing ignorance of the management. The Grand Jury learned
little from him.

But those interested in the enterprise with Crocker
not only told how half the money was paid Ruef, but
how the books had been manipulated to conceal the
payment.

---

[198] Crocker testified before the Grand Jury, however, that he
had known Ruef for many years. "He (Ruef) and my brother-in-
law, Prince Poniatowski," said Crocker, "both being French, and
both being pretty clever men, struck up quite a friendship together and through that means I used to see more or less of Ruef
and that was one of those peculiar friendships that spring up with
people who are not identified and not connected in any way whatever in any business enterprise, sprang up between Ruef and myself, and when he told me that in my office it didn't surprise me
a bit."

Crocker had testified that Ruef had promised to do all he could
to get him his franchise, and wouldn't want a dollar from Crocker,
or from the institution with which Crocker was connected.

Ruef, according to the testimony of officials of the company, had first demanded $50,000 as price for his employment to put the franchise through, but had finally agreed to take $30,000. This amount, officials of the company testified, was provided by drawing two checks, one in favor of H. P. Umbsen and the second in the name of Douglass S. Watson, secretary of the Parkside Company. Umbsen and Watson thereupon deeded to the Parkside Company two parcels of land. The transaction was then charged to the purchase of property.[199]

---

199 Of this manipulation of the books, President J. E. Green, of the Parkside Company, testified before the Grand Jury as follows:

"Q. How was the transaction to appear in the books? How was the property account to be charged with it? It would have to show some property. A. It was charged for a block that was purchased from Watson and Umbsen, a block of land.

"Q. Did you tell Watson to do that? A. I believe I did.

"Q. How did they get paid for the land? A. They deeded this block which they had to the company and the company in turn executed a deed to them, returning the land to them, simply a matter of bookkeeping.

"Q. Was the company's deed put on record? From them to the company? A. I rather think so.

"Q. What was the purpose of that? A. To get a charge to the property account for the expenditure of that amount of money.

"Q. What was the reason for charging it to property account? A. Every expenditure that was made was charged to property account with the idea the property had to pay it back.

"Q. Did you always go through the form with every expense that wasn't actually a piece of property, did you go through a form of deeding a piece of property and then deeding it back? A. No, sir.

"Q. What was the reason of doing it in this instance? A. Because—other things—there was a case—grading, sewering or fencing the blocks when they spoke for itself.

"Q. I don't see how it helped you; it went to the property account and the property went right out; don't see how it helped you any. A. It had to be charged to something, Mr. Heney.

"Q. Why couldn't it be charged to what it was, attorneys' fees? A. Because attorneys' fees were charged against property account.

"Q. Were Morrison & Cope's fees charged up as a piece of property and did they go through a rigmarole of deeding a piece of property too? A. No; their fees or any other expense against the property interests.

"Q. Didn't they go into the books as a fee for Morrison & Cope and charged as expenses against property? A. Charged direct to property.

"Q. As expense? A. Don't know as expense; it was charged to property, showing that we had that much money in property;

The property was deeded back to Umbsen and Watson at the same time, but these last deeds were not immediately recorded.

Watson cashed the checks at the Crocker-Woolworth Bank, of which William H. Crocker was president. He testified that he received currency for them.

The $30,000 he took to G. H. Umbsen. Half the $30,000 Umbsen paid Ruef.

At the time of the exposure, Umbsen [200] testified he

---

when we got through selling anything over, that was profit in our favor.

"Q. It appeared on the books as having been paid to Morrison & Cope for attorneys' fees? A. Can't say without seeing the books.

"Q. Ordinary way of keeping books? A. Yes.

"Q. You didn't cover up anything you paid to Morrison & Cope by putting through the hands of the secretary? A. No, sir.

"Q. Why did you cover up this in connection with Ruef? A. I don't know; suppose the property account is probably the proper one to charge it to.

"Q. Only explanation of it? A. Yes, sir."

[200] Early in the graft investigation Detective William J. Burns, with studied carelessness, dropped a remark in the presence of a salesman of the Parkside Company, that he had heard money was being used in the Parkside case. Soon after, Thomas L. Henderson, secretary of the company, received word from William I. Brobeck, of the law firm of Morrison, Cope & Brobeck, attorney for the Parkside Company, to call at that firm's law office. Of the incident, Henderson testified before the Grand Jury as follows:

"Q. His first question to you was what? A. We went in there. He said, Mr. Henderson, I am going to talk to you about Parkside and he said, have you an attorney? I said, no. I have no attorney. He says, it might be well for you to get an attorney. I said, all right, Mr. Brobeck, I will take you for an attorney. He said, all right, I will take you for a client.

"Q. Then what was said? A. Then he spoke, he said, you know about that remark made by Mr. Burns at Nineteenth and H. I replied how I got the remark from Hooper who was the salesman out there and I had passed it off, saying I did not want to talk about it. Then he said to me, I can't remember just the words, but his advice to me was not to say anything about it. I told him certainly, I would not. Then he spoke about Umbsen. Could I communicate with Gus? And I told him I could on the 4th of the month, he was then between Havana and Florida, and would arrive in New York about the 4th. Do you think it would be advisable to telegraph or write to him not to say anything? I said: Oh, no, I don't see any necessity for doing that.

"Q. What was the remark as you heard it that Burns made? A. We were coming down on the Sutter street car, Mr. Kernan and myself, when Ed Hooper, salesman, spoke to us and said:

was withholding the second payment until the franchise should be put through.[201]

In the gas-rate case, the Grand Jury found that the corporation that would, in the final analysis, benefit by the increase in gas rates, was the Pacific Gas and Electric Company. The four responsible men in this company were found to be N. W. Halsey, John Martin, Eugene de Sabla and Frank G. Drum. Halsey was out of the State for the greater part of the time and Cyrus Bierce, acting as treasurer of the corporation, looked after his interests. This narrowed the responsibility down to de Sabla, Martin and Drum.

I had a distinguished visitor yesterday. I said, who; he said, **Mr. Burns, the detective.** He said, I knew something about the telephone cases. I say what he said, a little something. He asked me about that and started for the automobile and when he got there, he turned around and said, another thing, I want to ask you about, I heard Ruef got $30,000 from Parkside. Who would be the man to see. I am only out here selling land and don't know anything about that. I had been here with Watson when he was agent and when Umbsen took charge he kept me in the same job. He was the salesman out there, that was at that time they had this automobile race and I turned around and said: I see the Oldsmobile won the race in Los Angeles, because I didn't want to continue the conversation with him.

"Q. Did Brobeck, in his conversation, tell you where he got the information that Burns had been out there? A. No sir, he did not.

"Q. Did he tell you that he knew what Burns had said? A. The impression I got was that he knew. I don't remember his saying in just so many words.

"Q. He referred to the statement made by Burns? A. He may have made the remark that you know about what was said out there.

"Q. At the time you talked about your having an attorney did he tell you to send him some money? A. After we finished he said, 'Mr. Henderson, you had better send me pay for this interview.' I said what? and he said five or ten dollars and when I got to the office, I mailed him a check for $10."

201 Ruef's version of the affair, as Ruef gave it before the Grand Jury, was: "Mr. Umbsen stated to me that with a great deal of difficulty, he had been able to persuade the people interested to allow me this fee. I thereupon told Mr. Gallagher that I had made arrangements to secure for myself an attorney's fee in the matter and I would allow him something over $13,500 as his proportion of the fee. Mr. Gallagher estimated what it would require for his services in the matter and we had discussed would the Supervisors accept that amount."

De Sabla testified before the Grand Jury that Ruef was not, to his knowledge, at any time on the pay roll of the company. Martin swore that he knew of no money that had been expended in connection with the fixing of the gas rates, and expressed himself as being as surprised as anyone at the confessions of the Supervisors to having received money after the gas rates had been fixed. Later, after Ruef had plead guilty to extortion, both de Sabla and Martin refused to testify further before the Grand Jury.[202]

Mr. Frank G. Drum, when called before the Grand Jury, stated that he had had no conversation with Ruef in reference to the fixing of the gas rates.[203] But later Ruef told the Grand Jury that the money which he had turned over to Gallagher in the gas-rate transaction had come from Drum.[204]

---

[202] John Martin's statement, when he refused to testify, furnishes fair example of the attitude of those who became involved in the graft scandal. The Grand Jury record shows:
"John Martin recalled.
"Foreman (to witness). You have already been sworn, so you can consider yourself under oath. Mr. Martin: I desire to stand on my constitutional right and not to testify further.
"Mr. Heney: If you feel that your testimony might have a tendency to subject you to prosecution—. A. (interrupting). No, not that. I am not so advised that that is necessary. My constitutional rights are broader than that, I am advised.
"Q. Then you don't desire to testify? A. No, sir.
"Mr. Heney: All right."

[203] Mr. Frank G. Drum testified as follows:
"Q. Do you know Abraham Ruef? A. Met him.
"Q. Did you have any conversation with him about that time? A. No, sir.
"Q. I mean a conversation with reference to the rates? A. No, not that I know anything about."

[204] Ruef on this point testified before the Grand Jury as follows:
"I received from Mr. Frank G. Drum, $20,000 as an attorney's fee as spoken of between ourselves, about the time that the gas rates were being fixed. Of that money, I gave to Mr. Gallagher for the Board of Supervisors about, as I remember it now, $14,000. It may have been a few hundred dollars more or less. I think about $14,000. Mr. Drum spoke to me about employing me in the service of the company some month or two before, I believe,

The first to be indicted because of these transactions was Ruef. Sixty-five indictments were on March 20 returned against him. Eighteen were based upon the bribing of Supervisors in the so-called fight trust matter; seventeen upon the bribing of Supervisors in fixing the gas rates; thirteen upon the bribing of Supervisors in the matter of the sale of the Home Telephone Company franchise; seventeen in the matter of granting the over-head trolley permit.

On the same day, ten indictments were returned against Theodore V. Halsey, of the Pacific States Telephone and Telegraph Company, for the bribery of Supervisors to prevent the sale of a franchise to a competing telephone company. A number of indictments were found against A. K. Detweiler, for bribing Supervisors in the matter of the sale of the Home Telephone fran-

---

and engaged me as attorney to represent the interests, as I understood it from him, which he represented in the company, at $1000 a month, of which I received, I believe, for two or three months. At the time of the fixing of the gas rates some of the Supervisors, as I was informed by Supervisor Gallagher, insisted upon fixing an extremely low rate, such a rate as would have been ruinous to the business of the company, a rate which neither I nor any one who had looked up the question would have considered under any circumstances to be reasonable, proper or maintainable, and said they were determined absolutely to reduce those rates. The matter was brought up at one of the Sunday evening caucuses and some of the members of the Board of Supervisors insisted that the board had been pledged by its platform to a rate of 75c. per thousand feet; they thought that was even too much and made some strong speeches and others maintained the 75c. rate and they contemplated fixing the 75c. rate that evening, that is to say, agreeing to do it at the proper time which I suppose was a week thereafter. In the meantime, the company sustained a heavy fire loss, not the fire of April 18th, but the previous fire, which caused them a great deal of damage, and I told Mr. Drum that it would be necessary for me, in order to protect the interests of the company and the interests which he represented, to have an additional attorney's fee and I told him that I thought it would require $20,000. He considered the matter and one day, a day or two afterward, he agreed to pay me the additional attorney's fee of $20,000 which I thereafter received.

"Q. Where did the conversation take place in which you told him about the necessity of having the $20,000? A. At his office in the Mills Building."

chise. The Detweiler indictments, thirteen in number, were based upon payments of money by Ruef to Gallagher, and by Gallagher to different members of the board. On March 23, the Grand Jury returned nine indictments against Louis Glass, vice-president of the Pacific States Telephone and Telegraph Company, based upon the bribing, through Halsey, of Supervisors to prevent the granting of a competing telephone franchise.

During the two months that followed, the Grand Jury continued at the steady grind of graft investigation. Finally, on May 24, one additional indictment [205] was brought against Halsey and two against Glass. On that

---

205 Although the Graft Prosecution was to be effectively opposed by Union Labor party leaders, the San Francisco Labor Council, made up of representatives of practically every San Francisco labor union, on the night of March 23, 1907, adopted resolutions declaring for the prosecution of bribe-givers as follows:

"Whereas, The indictments issued during the past few days by the San Francisco Grand Jury against certain individuals involve specific charges of flagrant and widespread corruption on the part of many members of the present city government; and whereas, said government, having adopted the name of 'Union Labor' has professed particular concern for the welfare of the working class, as represented by organized labor, and has sought and secured election upon pledges of loyalty to the principles, economic and political, to which organized labor everywhere is committed; and whereas, the alleged conduct of the city government is not only grossly repugnant to the principles of organized labor, but violates every rule of common honesty; and whereas, the conduct of the 'Union Labor' government and the inevitable association thereof with the character of the labor movement is calculated to lead to public misconception of the latter and thus to injure it and lessen its efficiency in its chosen field, therefore be it

"Resolved, By the San Francisco Labor Council, that we declare that every corruptionist, briber and bribed, should be prosecuted and punished according to law, and hereby pledge our co-operation to that end; further

"Resolved, That we reassert the position of the San Francisco Labor Council as a body organized and conducted for purely economic purposes, having no connection, direct or implied, with the Union Labor party or any other political party or organization, and therefore being in no way responsible for the conduct or misconduct of any such party or organization; further

"Resolved, That we also reaffirm our belief that the private ownership of public utilities constitutes the chief source of public corruption, and is in fact a premium thereon, and therefore ought to be displaced by the system of public ownership of public utilities."

date, fourteen indictments were returned against Patrick Calhoun, Thornwell Mullally, Tirey L. Ford, William M. Abbott,[206] Abraham Ruef and Mayor E. E. Schmitz, indicted jointly, for the bribery in connection with the granting of the over-head trolley permit.

The day following, May 25, G. H. Umbsen, J. E. Green, W. I. Brobeck and Abraham Ruef were jointly indicted fourteen times on charges of offering a bribe to fourteen Supervisors in the Parkside franchise matter. The same day, fourteen indictments were returned against Frank G. Drum, Abraham Ruef, Eugene E. Schmitz, Eugene de Sabla and John Martin on charges of giving and offering bribes to fourteen Supervisors in the matter of fixing the gas rates.

Still another series of graft indictments were to be found. Three prize-fight promoters, W. Britt, "Eddie" Graney and "Jimmie" Coffroth were, on nine counts, indicted jointly with Schmitz and Ruef for bribery in connection with the awarding to them of virtually a monopoly of the promotion of prize fighting in San Francisco.

---

206 At the time Patrick Calhoun held the office of President of the United Railroads; Mullally was assistant to the President; Ford general counsel for the corporation. Abbott was Ford's assistant.

CHAPTER XV.

Ruef Pleads Guilty to Extortion.[207]

While the Supervisors were making full confessions of their participation in the bribery transactions, and the Grand Jury was dragging from unwilling promoters, capitalists and corporation employees information as to the source of the corruption funds, Ruef's days and nights were devoted to consideration of plans for his own safety. Ruef, after his arrest and confinement under Elisor Biggy, became one of the scramblers of his broken organization to save himself.

But Ruef was more clever, more far-seeing than any of the Supervisors. His course from the beginning indicates that, in considering confession, he carefully weighed against the power of the regularly constituted authorities of San Francisco to protect him if he testified for the State, the ability of organized corruptionists to punish for betrayal. Ruef realized that although the all-powerful State "machine," labeled Republican, of which the San Francisco organization labeled Union Labor, which he had built up, was but a part, had for the moment lost control of the San Francisco District Attorney's office, but the "machine" still dominated the other departments of the municipal government, as well

---

207 The statements contained in this chapter are based on affidavits filed in the case of The People vs. Patrick Calhoun et al., No. 823. Many of the statements are qualified, and in many instances denied, in affidavits filed by Ruef, his friends, associates and attorneys, in the same proceedings.

as of the State government.[208]   Ruef realized that Langdon might die; that the State Attorney General might set Langdon aside and himself conduct the graft prosecution.   And he realized that some day a district attorney other than Langdon would be prosecutor in San Francisco.   In any of these events, what would be the lot of the man who had betrayed the scarcely-known captains of the powerful machine?

On the other hand, the hour when the evidence which the District Attorney had accumulated against him would be presented before a trial jury, approached with deadly certainty.

Such considerations led to Ruef devoting his days to resistance of the proceeding against him in the trial court, where a jury to try him on one of the five extortion charges on which he had been indicted, was being impaneled, while his nights were given to scheming to wring from the District Attorney immunity from punishment for the extortions and briberies which had been brought to his door.

The period was one of activity for both District Attorney and Ruef.   On the whole, however, the District Attorney had the liveliest time of it.

To be sure, Ruef had been brought before the trial judge; that is to say, the impaneling of a trial jury had

---

208 In this connection, in discussing the difficulties in the way of bringing criminals to trial, the San Francisco Chronicle, in its issue of March 14, 1907, said:

"The penal laws of California are admirable, and cover almost every transaction deserving moral reprobation.   The only reason why all our people are not either virtuous or in jail is that the same Legislatures which have so carefully defined crimes and prescribed punishments have been still more careful to enact codes of criminal procedure that nobody can be convicted of any crime if he has the cash to pay for getting off.   And what the legislatures have failed to do in this direction the courts have usually made good."

begun, but Ruef's technical fight had not been abandoned for a moment.

The appearance of Ruef under arrest was signal for
a fight to have him admitted to bail. But release under
bonds Judge Dunne denied him on the ground of the
immediate approach of his trial, and because he had attempted to put himself beyond the process of the court.
Ruef's attorneys appealed to the United States District
Court for a writ of habeas corpus, but this was denied
them. His attorneys filed affidavits alleging bias and
prejudice on the part of Judge Dunne against Ruef,
and demanding a change of venue. And with these
various motions, all of which the District Attorney was
called upon to meet, was the appeal from Judge Hebbard's order to the Federal Supreme Court, which was
considered in a previous chapter.

The actual work of drawing a jury to try Ruef began
on March 13,[209] eight days later than the date originally
set for trial. The State was represented by District Attorney Langdon, Francis J. Heney and Hiram W. Johnson. At the defense end of the table with Schmitz and
Ruef were Attorneys Joseph C. Campbell, Samuel M.
Shortridge, Henry Ach, Charles A. Fairall and J. J.
Barrett. But it developed that one of the four citizens
drawn for jury service was not in the courtroom. The
defense objected to proceeding during the absence of the
venireman. The hearing was accordingly postponed.
Because of one technical obstruction and another, the
work of impaneling the trial jury was delayed until

---

209 Four years later to a day, March 13, 1911, Ruef was taken
to the penitentiary at San Quentin to begin service of his fourteen-
year term for bribing a Supervisor.

April 2.. Even after that date there were interruptions, but the work of securing the jury [210] went on until May 13, when the twelfth man to try Ruef was accepted.

But while Ruef was making this brave fight in public to head off trial on the extortion charge, behind the scenes he was imploring representatives of the Prosecution to grant him immunity from punishment in return for such confession as he might see fit to make.

As early as March 20, Ruef sent word to Heney through Burns [211] that he was willing to make confession, provided he were given immunity from punish-

---

[210] As the impaneling of the Ruef jury proceeded, that Ruef's nerve was breaking became apparent to all who saw him. The Chronicle, in its issue of March 18, 1907, thus describes his condition:

"Ruef's nerve is breaking down. He is a prey to doubts and fears which never troubled him in those days when he could see his political henchmen every day and bolster up their confidence in his ability to fight off the prosecution. Reports reach his ears of confessions of guilt on the part of some of his official puppets, of the sinister activities of Burns and his agents and treachery on the part of those whom he considered his most devoted adherents, and fill him with alarm.

"It was different when he could hold his Sunday evening caucus with the members of the Board of Supervisors, and reassure them that all would be well. He knows the men he used in his political schemes and their weaknesses."

[211] Heney, in instructing Burns as to his policy regarding Ruef, took occasion to state to the detective his attitude toward the broken boss. In an affidavit filed in the case of The People vs. Calhoun et al., No. 823, Heney sets forth that he told Burns: "Ruef was not a mere accessory or tool in the commission of these briberies. He is a man of extraordinary brain power, keen intelligence, fine education, with the choice of good environment, great power of persuasion over men, dominating personality, great shrewdness and cunning, coupled with a greedy and avaricious disposition. He has not been led into the commission of these crimes through weakness, but on the contrary has aided in the initiation of them and has joined hands with the most vicious and depraved elements in the city to secure unlawful protection for them in conducting their resorts of vice, and has joined hands with the special privilege seeking classes to place improper burdens upon the people of this city by granting franchises to public service corporations which ought never to have been granted, and by fixing rates which may be charged by them in excess of the amounts which such rates ought to be, and thus indirectly robbing the poor people of this city of a large part of their meagre earnings, and that to let Ruef go free of all punishment under such circumstances would be a crime against society."

ment for all crimes which he had committed or in which he had participated.

Heney refused absolutely to consider any arrangement which involved complete immunity for Ruef. Negotiations on the basis of partial immunity followed.[212]

Heney, on the ground that he did not trust any of Ruef's lawyers, refused to discuss the matter with them, but stated that he would meet any lawyer in whom he had confidence to negotiate terms of partial immunity, provided that Ruef's representative were permitted:

(1) To give the names of Ruef's accomplices who would be involved by his testimony.

(2) To give the general nature of the offenses in which the various accomplices were involved.

(3) To be prepared to assure Heney that Ruef's evidence against his accomplices could be corroborated, and was sufficient to sustain a conviction.

Ruef at first appeared to be well satisfied with the plan. He sent for a list of San Francisco attorneys, and set himself enthusiastically to the work of selecting a list of the names of attorneys to be submitted to Heney. But he failed to make a selection, urging all the time to Burns that Heney accept Henry Ach. Ruef's insistence that he deal with Ach convinced Heney that Ruef was not acting in good faith, and he

---

212 Running through the affidavits which resulted from the differences between the forces of the prosecution and the defense concerning these negotiations, is a thread of suggestion that individual members of the prosecution differed as to the policy that should be followed toward Ruef. Burns, the detective, leaned toward granting him complete immunity. Heney was unalterably opposed to this course. Langdon, on the whole, sided with Heney.

refused to yield to Burns's urging that he give way to Ruef in this particular and accept Ach as Ruef's representative.[213]

Under Ruef's temporizing, negotiations dragged until April 2, the day that, Ruef's technical obstructions in the main set aside, his trial was to be resumed before Judge Dunne.

On that day, a new actor appeared in the person of Dr. Jacob Nieto, a Jewish Rabbi of some prominence in San Francisco.

Nieto, according to Burns's statement to Heney, asked the detective if he had any objection to his (Nieto's) calling upon Ruef. Nieto stated further that he believed that he could get Ruef to confess, and volunteered the theory that the "higher-ups" were endeavoring to make Ruef a scapegoat for all the boodling that had been committed.

Burns reported to Heney that he not only replied to Nieto that he had no objection to Nieto's visiting Ruef, but would be glad to have the Rabbi endeavor to get Ruef to tell the truth.

When Burns told Heney of this conversation, Heney did not show himself so well pleased with the arrangements as Burns might have expected. The prosecutor took occasion to warn Burns against Nieto. Heney had already had unpleasant experience with Rabbi Nieto.[214] Nevertheless, Nieto visited Ruef.

---

213 See Heney's affidavit in the matter of The People vs. Patrick Calhoun et al., No. 823.

214 Nieto, according to Heney, had endeavored to make it appear that race prejudice entered into the prosecution of Ruef. Heney, in an affidavit filed in the case of The People vs. Calhoun et al., No. 823, tells of Nieto's interference even when the Oliver Grand Jury was being impaneled. Heney says: "During the latter part of

Members of Ruef's family were called into consultation.   Conferences were held between Ach, Ruef an
Burns.   Heney states in his affidavit that he did n
attend these meetings.   Finally Burns brought Hene
word that Ach and Ruef wanted citations to sho
that the District Attorney had authority to grant im
munity.   Heney sent back word that he was confide
that the District Attorney had no such power, but wit

October or the first week in November, 1906, while said Grand Ju
was being impaneled, Dr. Jacob Nieto introduced himself to me i
the court room of Department No. 10, where I had noticed th
he was a constant attendant and close observer of the proceeding
connected with the impaneling of the Grand Jury.

"Some days after he had introduced himself to me he steppe
up to me, just as court had adjourned and after I had been exam
ining some of the grand jurors as to their qualifications, and sa
in substance:

" 'Mr. Heney, it seems to me that you discriminate somewh
against the Jews in examining jurors, and I think that in yo
position you ought to be more careful not to exhibit any prejudi
against a man on account of his religion.'

"I asked what in particular I had done to cause him to critici
my conduct in that way, and he referred to some question whic
I had asked a grand juror, but which I cannot now recollect.
then said to him in substance:

" 'Why, Doctor, you are supersensitive.   Some of the best frien
I have in the world are Jews, and some of the best clients I ev
had in my life were Jews, and I have no prejudice against ar
man merely on account of his religious belief.   I am sorry that yc
have so misapprehended the purpose and motives of my questio
to jurors.'

"On a subsequent day, during the time the Grand Jury wa
being impaneled, Dr. Nieto again approached me after an adjour
ment of the court and again reproached me for having again show
prejudice or discrimination against some grand juror of the Jewis
faith by the questions which I asked him * * * and I said to hi
in substance, in a very emphatic tone of voice: 'Dr. Nieto, I ha
heretofore told you that I have no prejudice against any man wha
ever on account of his religion.   All I am trying to do in this ma
ter is to get fair grand jurors, and I am just as willing to tru
honest Jews as honest Christians, but I want to make sure that
man is honest, whether a Jew or Christian, and it looks to me a
if you are trying to find some excuse to line up in opposition to th
prosecution.   I do not see why you need to seek for excuses if th
is what you want to do.   I am conscious of my own singleness
purpose and purity of purpose in examining grand jurors, and it
wholly immaterial to me, therefore, what you or anybody else ma
think of my method of questioning them.' "

As a matter of fact Jews not only sat on the Oliver Grand Jur
but were among the most earnest and effective in sifting the gra
scandal to the bottom.   But that the false cry that Ruef was perse
cuted because he was a Jew influenced many of his fellow Jews
his favor is unquestionably true.

the further statement that if the terms of the immunity agreement were reasonable and in the interest
of justice, that the Court, provided it had confidence
in the District Attorney, would unquestionably follow
such recommendation as that official might make.

Burns brought back word to Heney that Ruef and
Ach continued to insist upon complete immunity.

Heney sent back an ultimatum to the effect that
Ruef must plead guilty to the extortion case then
on trial before Judge Dunne [215] and take his chances
with the sentence that would be given him; that if
Ruef did this, Heney was willing to arrange for complete immunity in all the other cases, provided Ruef
showed to Heney's satisfaction that his testimony could
be sufficiently corroborated and would sustain a conviction of his accomplices other than Supervisors, in
cases where members of the Board of Supervisors had
been bribed.

In the meantime, the work of selecting a jury to
try Ruef on the extortion charge was going on with
the deadly certainty of the slide of the knife of a
guillotine. The second week of the examination of
prospective jurors brought Dr. Nieto to Heney's office.
Burns accompanied the Rabbi.

Nieto [216] described himself as no particular friend

---

[215] This case was numbered from the indictment, 305. Schmitz
was indicted jointly with Ruef in this indictment, and later was
convicted under it and sentenced to five years in the penitentiary.
See Chapter XVI. The testimony at the Schmitz trial showed that
Ruef had taken the extortion money from the French-Restaurant
keepers, after Schmitz had acted with him to imperil the French-
Restaurant keepers' liquor licenses, and had given part of the proceeds of the enterprise to Schmitz.

[216] In his affidavit, Heney quotes Rabbi Nieto as saying in
substance: "I do not care to get publicly mixed up in the Ruef
case, because among other things, I am not a particular friend of
Ruef's, and am not interested in the matter as an individual but

7

of Ruef. He expressed the opinion that Ruef should be punished; that he should restore his ill-gotten gains. Heney stated to Nieto his attitude toward Ruef, as he had expressed it many times before. From that time on Dr. Nieto was a frequent caller at Heney's office, always for the purpose of discussing the question of Ruef's confession. During all these meetings Heney did not depart a jot from his original position that the extortion charge against Ruef should not be dismissed.

Later on, a second Rabbi, Dr. Bernard M. Kaplan, joined Nieto in these visits to Heney's office. Kaplan continued active in the negotiations to secure immunity for the fallen boss.[217] Finally Nieto, Kaplan and Ach sent word to Heney and Langdon by Burns that they desired to meet the District Attorney and his assistant

---

only in the welfare of this community. I think that Ruef has grievously sinned against this community and that he can do a great deal to undo the wrongs which he has committed and to clear up the situation, and I have told him that it is his duty to himself and to his family and to the city of his birth to do so. I want you to understand, Mr. Heney, that I have not come here to ask you to let Ruef go free and without punishment. I think he ought to be punished, and I think he ought to give a large part of the money which he obtained from these corporations to the city to improve its streets. He ought to give $300,000 for that purpose, but Ruef thinks more of money than he does of his family, or even of his liberty, and I think he would rather go to the penitentiary than give up any very large amount of it."

217 Heney, in his affidavit, makes the following statement of his impression of Kaplan: "Dr. Kaplan appeared to be far more interested in finding out just what would be done to Ruef, provided he plead guilty in the French Restaurant case than he was in the moral issue which was involved in the discussion, or in the beneficial effect which the testimony of Ruef might have upon the deplorable situation then existing in San Francisco on account of its municipal corruption.

"This was evidenced more from his manner and form of questioning than by anything which he said. I immediately became convinced that he was influenced by no motive or purpose other than that of getting Ruef off without any punishment if possible; but I also formed the opinion that he was honest and unsophisticated."

at Heney's office to discuss the immunity question. Heney and Langdon consented and the meeting was held in the latter part of April.

Ach insisted upon complete immunity, but admitted that he had advised Ruef to take the best he could get.[218] Neither Langdon [219] nor Heney would consent to complete immunity, nor to material change in the stand which Heney had taken. Ach wanted assurance that the Judges before whom the bribery cases were pending would, on motion of the District Attorney, dismiss them as to Ruef, and suggested to Heney that he go to the judges and get them to consent to the proposed agreement. To this Heney made emphatic refusal, stating that the utmost he would do would be to go with Ach to Judges Dunne and Lawlor and ask each of them whether he had confidence in him (Heney) and what the Judge's general practice was in relation to matters of this kind, generally, when they came before his court.

Other conferences [220] were held, at which Ach continued to urge complete immunity for Ruef, which

---

218 Heney, in his affidavit, states: "During the conversation Ach stated, in substance: 'You can't convict Ruef in this French Restaurant case, but I realize that you are sure to convict him in some of the bribery cases, and I think it is useless for him to stand out and fight any longer, he had better take the best he can get, and I have told him so. He insists, however, that he ought not to be required to plead guilty in the French Restaurant case, or to submit to any punishment.' "

219 In the course of the interview, Langdon stated to Ach and the two Rabbis that he had authorized Heney to conduct the negotiations for him, but that he wanted it to be distinctly understood by everybody that he had the final say in the matter and would exercise it, and that no agreement could be concluded without his personal sanction.

220 Heney, in his affidavit describing these meetings, states that Ach, Kaplan and Nieto habitually came in the back way so they would not be seen by newspaper reporters who at the time frequented the front halls of the private residence in which Heney,

finally brought out emphatic statement from Heney that he did not trust Ruef and would enter into no agreement with him which did not leave it in the power of the District Attorney to send him to the penitentiary if at any time the District Attorney and himself concluded that during the progress of the matters Ruef was acting in bad faith, or that the information which he might give was not of sufficient importance to the people of the city and the State equitably to entitle him to go without punishment.

Heney takes pains all through his affidavit to make it clear that he treated with Nieto and Kaplan at all times upon the theory that they were Ruef's special pleaders and special representatives, who believed that Ruef was sure to be convicted upon as many of the felony bribery charges as the District Attorney tried him on, and that he would go to the penitentiary for a term of years equivalent to life.

On the night of April 21,[221] when the work of se-

---

after the fire, had his offices. Ach, Heney states, was desirous of not being known as party to the negotiations. Heney in his affidavit says: "In this same conversation (at the first conference) Ach said in substance: 'I want everybody here to agree that the fact that I participated in this conference, or had anything to do with advising Ruef to turn state's evidence, shall never be made known; it would absolutely ruin my business if it became known. A lot of the people whom Ruef will involve as accomplices are close friends of clients of mine. Of course I do not know just whom he will involve, but I do have a general idea. For instance, while he has never told me so in so many words, I understand that he will involve William F. Herrin. Now just to illustrate to you how it would affect me in business if it was known that I participated in urging Ruef to do this I will tell you that I am attorney for one company, an oil company, that pays me ten thousand dollars a year as a salary for attending to its business, and Herrin is one of the directors of the company and undoubtedly has sufficient influence with the other directors to take this client away from me. This is only one instance, and there are many others.'"

221 See affidavits of Francis J. Heney and Judge William P. Lawlor on file in the case of The People vs. Patrick Calhoun et al., No. 823.

lecting a jury to try Ruef was nearing completion, Ach, Kaplan and Nieto visited Heney's office with assurance that Ruef had about concluded to accept Heney's terms. But, they explained, a new difficulty had come up. Rabbi Nieto was to leave San Francisco the next morning for a trip to Europe. Neither he nor Dr. Kaplan was familiar with the practices of the courts, and while the judges would no doubt consider favorably any recommendation which was made by Mr. Langdon or by Mr. Heney, nevertheless, the two Rabbis would like to hear from Judge Dunne and Judge Lawlor statement as to what the practice of each of these judges was in that respect before they urged Ruef any further to accept the terms which had been offered him. As Dr. Nieto was to leave for Europe early in the morning, they wanted to see the judges that night.

Heney assured his visitors that owing to the lateness of the hour, he was afraid it would be impossible for them to see the judges before morning. But they insisted. Burns was finally sent out to find the judges if he could. He succeeded in locating Judge Lawlor at the theater. Judge Lawlor at first refused to see Nieto and Heney that night, stating that they could appear at his chambers the next morning. But Burns explained that Nieto had to leave for Europe the next morning, adding that he was sure that both Nieto and Heney would consider it a great favor if the Judge would see them that night, as the matter was very important. Lawlor finally consented to see them, but stated that he would do so only at his chambers, if, as he understood it, Heney and Nieto wanted to see him about his duties as judge. Burns took word back to Heney's office that they could go to Judge Lawlor's chambers, where the Judge would go as soon as the theater was over.

Heney, Kaplan and Nieto met Lawlor at his chambers. Heney went straight at the purpose of the meeting.

"Judge," Heney sets forth in his affidavit he said in substance, "we come up here tonight to ask you what the practice of your court is in criminal cases in relation to recommendations which may be made by the District Attorney?"

Judge Lawlor replied in effect that the District Attorney represents the public in the prosecution of crime, and that under the law it was the practice for that official to submit to the court recommendations concerning persons who turn state's evidence; that the law vests the authority in the Court to determine all such recommendations and that it is proper for the District Attorney to make them; that such recommendations should be carefully considered by the Court; and if they are in the interests of justice they should be followed, otherwise not. Judge Lawlor stated further that he would not consider or discuss any cause or case of any individual except upon a full hearing in open court, and that it would be determined alone upon what was so presented. Final decision, he said, would in every case rest with the Court, and if the application was in the interest of justice, it would be granted, but if not it would be denied.

Immediately after having made this statement

Judge Lawlor excused himself and left the building.

Judge Dunne, when finally found by Burns, objected as strongly as had Judge Lawlor to going to the courtroom that night, but finally yielded to the same representations as had been made to Judge Lawlor.

All parties at the meeting with Judge Dunne at the courtroom were agreed and the incident was quickly over.

Heney asked the Judge, in effect, to state for the benefit of Nieto and Kaplan the practice of his court in criminal matters in relation to any recommendations which may be made by the District Attorney's office in the interest of justice when the defendant becomes a witness on behalf of the State against his accomplices. Heney stated further that the two Rabbis would also like to know whether or not Judge Dunne had confidence in District Attorney Langdon and himself.

Judge Dunne replied in substance: "I have confidence in you, Mr. Heney, and in the District Attorney, and while I have confidence in the District Attorney, whenever a recommendation or suggestion is made by him in a case pending in my department, it is my practice to entertain and be guided by it, provided, of course, it is in the interest or furtherance of justice."

Kaplan wanted to know what the course would be should a man plead guilty and afterwards ask to change his plea.

"You have heard what I have said, gentlemen, as to my practice," replied Judge Dunne. "Of course, in all cases of such recommendations, and which I insist shall always be made in open court, whenever the District Attorney fails to convince me that he is well advised, or that good and sufficient grounds exist for his motions, it must be remembered that the final determination must always rest with me. But, of course, I would give great weight to any recommendation either you, Mr. Heney, or Mr. Langdon might make."

From the courtroom Nieto, Kaplan and Burns went to Ruef, but Ruef still insisted that he should not plead guilty to the extortion charge, "backed and filled," as Burns expressed it.

Ruef sent word to Heney by Burns, asking an interview. But this Heney refused to grant, bluntly stating that should he meet Ruef, Ruef would misrepresent anything that he might say. Heney instructed Burns to tell Ruef that he could accept the proposition that he had made to him or let it alone as he pleased, that no more time would be wasted on him; that trial of the extortion charge would be pressed to conclusion and regardless of whether conviction were had or not, Ruef would be tried immediately on one of the bribery charges.

Nevertheless, the persistent Ruef got an interview with Heney. He secured it in this way:

After Heney had retired on the night of May 1st, Burns called him up on the telephone, to state that if Heney would give Ruef a moment's interview that Burns was confident that Ruef would accept Heney's proposition. Heney granted the hearing.

Ruef plead for complete immunity. He argued that for him to plead guilty to the extortion charge would weaken his testimony in the bribery cases. He urged that public opinion would approve his release. He charged Heney with being prejudiced against him.

Heney listened to him patiently, but refused to consider any suggestion that he alter the original proposition.

By this time ten jurors had been secured to try Ruef. Ruef begged for an interview with Langdon. It was granted, with Heney and others present. The same ground was gone over again; the same denials made. And then Heney bluntly told Ruef in substance: "You must plead guilty in case No. 305 and take your chances on the sentence which will be imposed in that case. This is our ultimatum and you must agree to this before the first witness is sworn in case No. 305, or we will withdraw our proposition and will never again renew it, or any other proposition looking to any sort of leniency or immunity for you."[222]

The day following, Burns brought word to Heney that Ruef had concluded to accept the Prosecution's proposition, and had begun his confession by reciting the particulars of the United Railroad's bribery. Burns recited what Ruef had told him. Burns's enthusiasm suffered a shock from Heney's cool analysis of Ruef's statement.[223]

Heney pointed out that Ruef had made no revelation which the Prosecution had not known before, and

---

222 See Heney's affidavit in the case of The People vs. Patrick Calhoun et als., No. 823.

223 Ruef in this confession to Burns stated that he had received $200,000 from General Tirey L. Ford, head of the United Railroads law department. Of this amount, he said $50,000 he had given to Schmitz and retained $50,000 for himself. Ruef, five years later, in his story "The Road I Traveled," published in the San Francisco Bulletin, again stated that he had received $200,000 from Ford, of which he gave to Schmitz $50,000, to Gallagher his share for the Supervisors, and retained $50,000 for himself. Gallagher received $85,000. This leaves a balance of $15,000 which Mr. Ruef does not account for.

further that Ruef was certainly concealing part at least of what had occurred between him and General Ford. Heney was now convinced of Ruef's treachery.[224] Ruef's future course tended to strengthen this conviction.

Having agreed to make full statement of his connection with the bribing of the Supervisors, Ruef haggled over the form of immunity contract. He endeavored to force upon the Prosecution a contract of his own drawing. Failing in that he tried to persuade Heney and Langdon to enter into a stipulation that he might withdraw his plea of guilty in the extortion case.

In neither move was he successful. Heney refused to depart a jot from his original proposition. Ruef finally accepted the immunity contract which Heney had submitted.[225]

Even after the immunity contract had been signed, Ruef continued to urge Burns that he be not required to plead guilty. The prosecution was not sure what Ruef would do. The examination of jurors to try him went on. The jury was completed on May 13,[226] and

224 It is significant to note in this connection that Heney did not call Ruef as a witness before the Grand Jury in the United Railroads cases until after the Grand Jury had found indictments against the officials of that corporation. In the opinion of the Grand Jurors, the testimony, exclusive of that of Ruef, justified these indictments.

225 The immunity contract signed by Ruef and the District Attorney will be found in full in the appendix.

226 At the completion of the Ruef Jury, the Chronicle, issue of May 15, 1907, said:
"The Ruef jury is complete and we are now in a way to learn all the truth about the particular crime for which Ruef is this time on trial, but which, compared with most other crimes for which he has been indicted, is a mere peccadillo. That Ruef got the money is proved, for he has confessed. His defense, of course, will be that the French-Restaurant proprietors voluntarily presented him with it. The state will have to prove, in order to secure a conviction, that they did not give the money voluntarily, but yielded it

was sworn. But the actual taking of testimony was delayed by Ruef demanding change of venue from Judge Dunne's court. This motion after the filing of numerous affidavits by both sides, was denied.

However, Ruef's last motion delayed the taking of testimony for two days more.

Upon Judge Dunne's ruling the next move would have been the placing of witnesses on the stand. But before this could be done, Ruef whispered to his attorney, Ach. Ach arose and addressed the Court.

"I am requested by our client, your Honor," Ach said in substance, "that it is his desire to have a conference with his counsel. I would like to draw your Honor's attention to the fact that up to this time Mr. Ruef has not had a single opportunity to confer with his counsel alone. If the elisor, or the guards, were not in the same room they were quite close by. I think, in view of this fact, that we might be granted an adjournment until say two o'clock of this afternoon so that Mr. Ruef may have this privilege of conferring with us."

Heney promptly denied Ach's statement. "What Mr. Ach has stated is not a fact," said Heney. "Mr. Ruef has always been granted privacy in his conference with counsel."

On Langdon's suggestion, a half hour's recess was

up under threats which they believed it to be in his power to execute. If the state fails to prove that Ruef will stand before the community merely as a moral leper, loathsome to be sure, and despicable almost beyond human conception, but yet not proved guilty of that for which the law prescribes punishment in state's prison. If proper proof cannot be made he must, of course, be acquitted of this crime and at once put on trial for another. Nothing is gained by society by the conviction even of the most unmitigated scoundrel on insufficient testimony. But when the proof is sufficient the salvation of society demands punishment, and more particularly of punishment of the rich criminal."

granted to allow Ruef to confer with counsel. With his attorneys, Henry Ach, Samuel M. Shortridge, Frank J. Murphy and Judge Fairall, Ruef went into Judge Dunne's chambers for conference.

On their return to the courtroom, Ach and Short-ridge, with Ruef's consent, withdrew from the case on the ground that they could not agree with Ruef as to the manner in which the case should be conducted. Fairall and Murphy remained by their client.

And then Ruef, the tears streaming down his face, addressed the Court. He stated his intent to acknowledge whatever there may have been of wrong or mistake in his record, and pledged himself, so far as it lay in his power to make it right.[227]

---

227 Ruef's statement was in full as follows:

"If your honor please, with the permission of the court, I desire to make a statement. I do so after only a short consultation with my attorneys, to whom I have only within the last half hour disclosed my determination, and against their express protest. I take this occasion to thank them for their services, fidelity and friendship. Notwithstanding the Court's finding yesterday that this trial might safely be carried on without serious injury to my health, physical or mental, I wish to assure you that my personal condition is such that I am at the present time absolutely unable to bear for two or three months daily the strain of an actual trial of this case, the constant, continual, nightly preparations therefor, the necessary consultation and conversation with my attorneys in regard thereto, to say nothing of other cares and responsibilities.

"Moreover, the strain of these proceedings upon those whom I hold nearest and dearest of all on earth has been so grave and severe that as a result of these prosecutions their health has all been undermined, they are on the verge of immediate collapse and their lives are indeed now actually in the balance.

"I have occupied a somewhat prominent position in this city of my birth, in which I have lived all my life, where are all my ties and interests, whence, when the time shall come, I hope to pass into the eternal sleep. I have borne an honored name. In my private and in my professional life there has been no stain. In my public affiliations, until after the municipal campaign of 1905 and the election of the present Board of Supervisors, the abhorrent charges of the press to the contrary notwithstanding, no action of mine ever gave just ground for adverse criticism or deserved censure; but the assaults of the press and its failure to credit honesty of purpose, a desire to hold together a political organization which had been built up with much effort, the means of otherwise holding them, did after the election of this Board of Supervisors in a meas-

"I desire," concluded Ruef, "to withdraw my plea of not guilty heretofore entered, and to enter the contrary plea, and at the proper time submit to the Court further suggestions for its consideration.[228]

ure influence me and the high ideals for which I had heretofore striven.

"During the past few weeks I have thought deeply and often of this situation, its causes and conditions. To offer excuses now would be folly. To make an effort at some reparation for the public good is, however, more than possible; to assist in making more difficult, if not impossible, the system which dominates our public men and corrupts our politics will be a welcome task.

"I have decided that whatever energy or abilities I possess for the future shall be devoted even in the humblest capacity to restoring the ideals which have been lowered; shall, as soon as opportunity be accorded, be re-enlisted on the side of good citizenship and integrity. May it be allotted to me at some time hereafter to have at least some small part in re-establishment on a clear, sane basis, a plane of high civic morality, just reciprocal relations between the constantly struggling constituent element of our governmental and industrial life.

"In the meantime I begin by earnestness of purpose, a purpose to make the greatest sacrifice which can befall a human being of my disposition to make, to acknowledge whatever there may have been of wrong or mistake and so far as may be within my power to make it right.

"I reached this final determination last night after careful reflection and deliberation. Where duty calls I intend to follow, whither hereafter the path of my life may lead and however unpleasant and painful may be the result. I make this statement so that the Court and the whole world may know at least the motives which have guided me in the step I am about to take.

"As an earnest I have determined to make a beginning, I am not guilty of the offense charged in this indictment. I ask now, however, that this jury be dismissed from further consideration of this case. I desire to withdraw my plea of not guilty heretofore entered and to enter the contrary plea, and at the proper time submit to the Court further suggestions for its consideration."

[228] The Chronicle, in its issue of May 16, said of Ruef's confessions:

"Abraham Ruef should have thought of his family before he entered upon his career of crime. They are innocent and the public need not, as indeed it cannot, withhold its sympathy for them. The most terrible punishment which is inflicted on such criminals is the distress which their crimes brings upon the innocent persons who have been accustomed to respect and honor them. But it is the inexorable doom which crime brings upon itself.

"For Ruef himself the only sympathy possible is that which one might feel for a wolf which, having devastated the sheep fold, has been pursued, brought to bay and, after a long fight, finally disposed of. It is not a case in which the safety of society permits leniency to be shown. Ruef has corrupted every branch of the city government which he could get hold of and brought the city almost to the verge of ruin. Seldom has a man occupying an unofficial station in life been able to achieve so much evil. It will be many a year

"If the defendant wishes to change his plea of 'not guilty' to 'guilty,'" said Heney, "the prosecuting attorney will consent to the discharge of the jury, as he requests, but we think the indictment should first be re-read so that he may enter the plea as he wishes."

The indictment was read.

"What is your plea?" asked Judge Dunne of the prisoner.

And Ruef replied, "Guilty."[229]

---

before San Francisco can outlive the shame which the man Ruef has brought upon her.

"He has not been ingenuous even in his confession, for while pleading guilty as charged, he professes to be not guilty of this particular crime—meaning merely by that that he did not extort the money by threats within the meaning of the law. Witnesses, however, would have sworn that he did so. It is unthinkable that such sums should have been paid him voluntarily by the restaurant keepers. All that Ruef can mean by his profession of 'innocence' while pleading guilty, is a claim that he succeeded in terrifying the restaurant men into submitting to blackmail without the use of words which the law would construe as a threat. There is no moral difference between what Ruef would claim that he did and the crime to which he has pleaded guilty.

"Ruef also shows his disingenuousness by attributing his situation to 'the assaults of the press.' Doubtless he has been assaulted by the press. But the press has accused him of nothing but what he has confessed and intimated. What fault has he to find with that? Shall the press remain silent while thieves plunder a distressed city and rob it of its good name? Ruef fought the forces of decency until he could fight no longer. No man is strong enough to stand up against the wrath of an outraged community. His physical collapse was inevitable and the only mantle which charity can throw over him is that his physical weakness broke down his mental faculties and caused the self-contradictions in what is a virtual confession of all that he has been charged with."

229 The position of the Prosecution was most difficult. Every department of the municipal government, with the exception of the District Attorney's office, was controlled by the corrupt administration, of which Schmitz was the official head. The necessity of dealing with Ruef, and the question of immunity arose primarily and almost entirely, from the fact that there was practically no evidence against Schmitz, except in the French restaurant case, and that there was no evidence in that case that Schmitz received any of the money which was collected by Ruef. Consequently without Ruef's testimony no conviction of Schmitz was possible at all, except in the French restaurant case, and in that case his conviction was not at all certain. Union Labor party adherents were naturally unwilling to believe Schmitz guilty until he had been so proven. The big public service corporations and Herrin of the Southern Pacific were all still in sympathy with him and ready to back him

for re-election.   An election was approaching early in November.
The redemption of the city depended upon taking its control away
from Schmitz.   The Police Commission and the Board of Public
Utilities were part of the corrupt and discredited administration.
During the rebuilding of San Francisco it was of vital importance
to have these two boards honest.   Hence the Prosecution felt justified in going to unusual length to secure the additional testimony
against Schmitz, which ought to make his conviction certain in the
French restaurant case, and thus immediately depose him from office
and place the entire city government in the hands of honest men.
The new Mayor could appoint a new Board of Supervisors, new
Police Commission and new Board of Public Works, as well as
many other important officials; and such new Mayor and Supervisors
would be reasonably sure of re-election.   Agents of the Public
Service corporations realized to the full extent the importance of
preventing the conviction of Schmitz, and of forcing the prosecution
to submit to the appointment of a new Board of Supervisors before
any conviction of Schmitz could possibly be secure, so that the new
Board of Supervisors, so selected through Schmitz by themselves,
would have the power of appointing the new Mayor in case Schmitz
were convicted.   This new Mayor could appoint a new Police Commission and it in turn a new Chief of Police, and the new officials
would be controlled by the same interests which controlled the old
ones.

CHAPTER XVI.

SCHMITZ CONVICTED OF EXTORTION.

One week after Ruef had plead guilty to the charge of extortion, his co-defendant, Mayor Eugene E. Schmitz, indicted jointly with Ruef, was brought to trial, under indictment No. 305, to which Ruef had entered his plea of guilty.

Hiram W. Johnson and J. J. Dwyer appeared with Heney and Langdon for the Prosecution. The defense was represented by the firm of Campbell, Metson & Drew, assisted by John J. Barrett and Charles Fairall, all prominent at the San Francisco bar.

The preliminaries were not unlike those of the Ruef trial, which, at the point where testimony would have been taken, was stopped by Ruef's plea of guilty. There were the same allegations of bias, the same attempts to secure change of venue, the same appeals to the higher courts in habeas corpus proceedings. But these moves availed Schmitz as little as they had Ruef. Point by point the upper courts found against the indicted Mayor; step by step he was dragged to proceedings before a trial jury.

The selection of the jury occupied two weeks. But with the swearing of the twelfth juror, Schmitz did not stop proceedings with tearful confession and a plea of guilty. Doggedly the troubled Mayor let the trial go on. The Prosecution called its witnesses to the stand.

One by one Schmitz's former associates as well as the restaurant men from whom, through Ruef, he had received money, took the stand and told the sordid story of the corruption of the Schmitz-Ruef administration.

The specific charge under which Schmitz was tried was that of extortion from Joseph Malfanti, Charles Kelb and William Lafrenz, proprietors of Delmonico's Restaurant, of $1,175. The sum was Delmonico's share of the $5,000 paid to Ruef in 1905, by the French-restaurant keepers to prevent the liquor licenses, without which their establishments could not be successfully conducted, being taken from them.

The testimony showed:

(1) That Schmitz had used his power as Mayor over the Police Commissioners to compel them in the first instance, to withhold French-restaurant liquor licenses, and that later in the latter part of January, 1905, he had exerted himself as actively and effectively to have the licenses granted, even removing from office Police Commissioner Hutton, who was standing out against the French restaurants.

(2) That attorneys, appearing before the Police Commissioners, to present the claims of the French-restaurant keepers for licenses, were unable to secure a hearing. One of these testified to having advised his client, and other French-restaurant keepers that "there is only one man who can help you, and that is Mr. Ruef."

(3) That a French-restaurant keeper who owed Ruef money, and at whose establishment Ruef had his headquarters, approached his fellow French-restaurant

keepers and told them that for $7,000 a year Ruef would represent them and keep them secure in their business for two years. The $7,000 demand was finally reduced to $5,000, $10,000 for the two years.

(4) That the French-restaurant keepers raised $8,000 of the $10,000 demanded, and sent it to Ruef, $5,000 the first year and $3,000 the next.

(5) That Ruef refused to receive anything but currency, would give no receipt for the money, and would deal with one man only.

(6) That Ruef claimed to receive the money as a fee from the "French Restaurant Keepers' Association," but that no such association existed in San Francisco.

(7) That after the French-restaurant keepers had satisfied Ruef, Ruef appeared for them before the Police Commissioners and, after Commissioner Hutton had been removed from office by Mayor Schmitz, secured for them their licenses.[230]

Having established its case thus far, the Prosecution rested.

The move was unlooked for. Ruef was known to have confessed; it had been confidently expected that he would be placed on the stand to answer the question, in whatever form it could be forced into the record: Did you divide the money which you received from the French-restaurant keepers with Mayor Schmitz?

But Ruef was not put on the stand. The public marveled, but those behind the scenes knew that Ruef was not the willing witness for the Prosecution that the public thought.

---

[230] For fuller discussion of this testimony see Chapter "Ruef and Schmitz Indicted."

Ruef had confessed to Heney that he had given half the $8,000 which he had received from the French-restaurant keepers to Mayor Schmitz. But Heney, having trapped Ruef in deception, had very good reason for being distrustful of him.

Ruef, forever seeking to justify himself, had told Heney that he had refused to appear before the Police Commissioners on behalf of the French-restaurant keepers, until the San Francisco Bulletin had challenged him to dare represent them, and claim the money he received from them was a fee. Ruef insisted that the Bulletin's challenge led him to take the case.

In this Heney trapped Ruef in his trickery.

Ruef's purported contract with the mythical "French Restaurant Keepers' Association," under which the French restaurant keepers had paid him $8000, bore date of January 6. Ruef insisted to Heney that January 6 was the true date upon which the contract was signed. The oral agreement had been made January 5. Heney then confronted Ruef with files of the Bulletin which showed that the Bulletin had not mentioned Ruef as appearing on behalf of the French-restaurant keepers until January 7. This was one day after Ruef had signed the purported contract with the mythical French Restaurant Keepers' Association.

A stormy scene between Ruef and Heney followed this exposure.[231] Heney charged Ruef with falsehood

---

[231] "You have not," said Heney to the trapped boss, "told us all the truth in the United Railroads case. You have not told us all the truth in the case of the gas rate matter. You have not told us all the truth in the Bay Cities Water deal. You have not told us all the truth about the deal with Herrin in relation to the delegates from this city to the Santa Cruz convention. You have not told us all the truth in the telephone franchise matter. You lied to

and deception, and declared the immunity agreement canceled. Heney then ordered Ruef from the room, and did not, until long after the Schmitz trial had closed, have conversation with him again.

When Schmitz's trial opened, District Attorney Langdon, Hiram Johnson, all the rest of Heney's associates, urged that Ruef be put on the stand, insisting that the case would be greatly strengthened if it could be proved by Ruef that Schmitz had received half the extortion money.

Heney conceded the strength of this contention, but held, on the other hand, that Ruef would lie so much about other things that he would do more harm than good to the case. Personally, Heney insisted, he wanted nothing to do with him.

Thus, in making his opening statement to the jury in the Schmitz case, Heney refrained from stating that he expected to prove Schmitz received any part of the money which had been paid to Ruef.

But of the break between Heney and Ruef, the pub-

---

us in the Parkside matter, and I caught you at it before the Grand Jury. You tried to protect Will Crocker in that matter and told Burns before you went into the Grand Jury room that you had never spoken to him on the subject. You swore to the same thing in the Grand Jury room until you cunningly guessed from my questions that Will Crocker himself had told the truth to the Grand Jury, and that I was getting you in a bad hole; you then suddenly pretended to just remember that you had held one conversation with Will Crocker on the trolley franchise matter at the Crocker National Bank that lasted a half an hour, and that you had held another conversation on the street with Will Crocker on the same subject at the corner of California and Kearny streets, which lasted an hour. You had not forgotten either of those talks, but you did not think Will Crocker would testify to them and you wanted to curry favor with him by thus making him think you wanted to protect him, and you did it because he is rich and powerful. You wanted his influence hereafter to help keep you out of trouble, because you have no idea of acting in good faith with the prosecution. I don't believe you ever acted in good faith with anybody in your life, but you have over-reached yourself this time."—See Affidavit of Francis J. Heney, in The People vs. Patrick Calhoun et als., No. 823.

lic knew nothing. San Francisco looked to see Ruef
put on the stand. When the Prosecution rested without
calling this supposedly star witness, even the Defense
was taken by surprise and had to ask continuance until
the following day before calling witnesses.

Schmitz took the stand in his own behalf. He denied
the statements which his former Police Commissioners
had made against him. The Mayor's story of denial
was soon told. Heney, on cross-examination asked:

"Did Ruef pay you any part of the $5,000 that has
been testified he received from the French restaurants?"
and Schmitz replied: "I didn't know that Mr. Ruef got
any $5,000, nor did I receive any part of it."[232]

And then, in detail, Schmitz denied that he had
received any money from Ruef, or had had any conversation with him regarding a "fee" which Ruef had received from the French-restaurant keepers.

In rebuttal, Ruef was called to the stand.[233] "Did
you," questioned Heney, "in January or February, 1905,
in this City and County of San Francisco, at the house
of Eugene E. Schmitz, the defendant, at number 2849
Fillmore street, give to Eugene E. Schmitz any money,
and if so how much, and in what kind of money?"

"I did," answered Ruef, "$2500 in currency."

---

[232] This answer came in the face of strong objection from
Schmitz's counsel. Mr. Campbell went so far as to direct Schmitz
not to answer. Mr. Barrett's objection was expressed in a way
that caused Judge Dunne to order him to his seat. The several
objections were overruled and the witness was directed to answer
the question.

[233] Heney, in an affidavit filed in the case of The People vs.
Patrick Calhoun et al., No. 823, says of Ruef's appearance: "I did
not at any time see or speak to Ruef, except when he was on the
witness stand, and then only from a distance and in open court in
the regular course of the trial and in the performance of my duty as
a prosecuting officer."

"Did you, then and there, tell him," pursued Heney, "that it was his share of the money you had received from the five French-restaurant keepers?" "I didn't say to him," replied Ruef, "that it was his share of the money which I had received from the French restaurants. I did say to him that I had received from the French restaurants the sum of $5,000, and that if he would accept half of it I should be glad to give it to him. Thereupon I gave it to him."

Ruef testified further to paying Schmitz $1500 early in 1906, half of the second payment made to him by the French-restaurant keepers.

The jurors before whom Mayor Schmitz was tried took one ballot only. They found the defendant guilty of extortion as charged in the indictment.

Following the verdict, Schmitz, who eighteen months before had, for the third time been elected Mayor of San Francisco, was, as a convicted felon, confined in the county jail.[234]

---

[234] Where Schmitz spent the night of Thursday, June 13, the night of his conviction, is a matter of dispute. Sheriff O'Neil insists that he spent the night in jail. This has been denied. The statement has been made, apparently on good authority, that all of Friday following, Schmitz, accompanied by Dominic Beban, a deputy sheriff and State Senator from San Francisco, was about town in an automobile. But on Saturday, Judge Dunne warned the sheriff that Schmitz was to be treated as any other prisoner. After that day, pending his appeal to the higher courts, Schmitz was confined in the county jail. Attorney J. C. Campbell made a hard fight to keep his client out of jail. Among other things, Mr. Campbell held that the Mayor had so much official business to attend to that it was practically necessary for him to be in his office all the time for the next month.

Schmitz, under this conviction, was sentenced to serve five years in the penitentiary.

CHAPTER XVII.

Schmitz Ousted From Office.

The confession of the Supervisors to bribery had no sooner become known than angling for control of the municipal government under its prospective reorganization began.[235]

The public-service corporation that had during the 1905 municipal campaign contributed to the campaign funds of both the Union Labor party and the opposing "Reform" fusion organization, had no care as to who reorganized, or in what name the reorganization was accomplished, so long as they continued in control. These corporations had larger interest in public affairs than ever; there was prospect of their officials being indicted for felonies. But so long as Schmitz continued to be Mayor, neither those who aimed to reorganize for the best interests of San Francisco, nor those who were

---

235 As early as March 20, 1907, two days after the Supervisors gave their confession to the Grand Jury, The Chronicle touched upon the growing resistance to the prosecution. It said:

"In the leading political clubs there is talk of Governor Gillett removing Mayor Schmitz and appointing a successor. This is in the line of gossip, however, for there is a legal question involved, the framers of the municipal Charter having provided no means for the removal of the head of the municipal government should he be found criminally derelict. There is also some talk of Schmitz resigning if Heney will vaccinate him and render him immune from punishment for his offenses, as he is said to have done with the Supervisors. Another angle of the gossip in this regard is that the Mayor will appoint a Board of Supervisors picked by prominent merchants and professional men who have organized for the purpose of redeeming San Francisco from the toils of the grafters."

plotting to continue the old order with new men, in the interests of the corporations, could act. The old order controlled Schmitz; the opposition, having whipped confessions out of the Supervisors, controlled the board. Neither element could undertake reorganization until in control of both Mayor's office and Supervisors.

This deadlock was brought about by charter provisions empowering the Board of Supervisors to fill vacancies occurring in the mayoralty office, and providing that the Mayor shall fill vacancies on the Board of Supervisors.

Had Mayor Schmitz resigned, the Supervisors, controlled by District Attorney Langdon, would have elected his successor. This would have given the Prosecution the Mayor as well as the Supervisors. On the other hand, had the Supervisors resigned, then Mayor Schmitz would have appointed as their successors men in accord with him and with his policies. Schmitz could then have resigned and the Supervisors of his appointment would have named his successor. This would have permitted the corrupt element to continue the old order in defiance of the Prosecution. Thus, so long as Schmitz held the office of Mayor, the Prosecution, laboring for good government, could not permit the bribe-taking Supervisors to resign. On the other hand, those who had furnished the bribe money did not dare permit Schmitz to give up his office.

In this astonishing situation, that bribe-givers might not gain the upper hand, it was necessary that the sixteen confessed bribe-taking Supervisors should continue in the offices which they had betrayed, so long as

Schmitz's power to appoint their successors continued.[236]

There were, too, further complications. The Prosecution could and did secure the discharge from municipal positions of Ruef's satellites who held their places under the Board of Supervisors. Thus, soon after the Supervisors had confessed, Charles Keane,[237] Clerk of the Board, was forced from his position. On the other hand, the old-time Schmitz-Ruef followers who owed their appointments to the Mayor, continued secure in

[236] The Chronicle, in its issue of April 3, in discussing this phase of the situation, said:

"The spectacle of the entire legislative body of a city confessing to the acceptance of great bribes is astonishing. Their continuance in office and consultation with the good citizens as to the best methods of restoring good government is unique. In many parts of the country there is outspoken disapproval of the course which is being taken, and loud declarations that if there were any good citizenship in San Francisco the confessed rogues would be driven out of office and hustled into the penitentiary. It is declared that in granting 'immunity' to these Supervisors the city is again disgraced. Of course, all this is absurd. In the first place, there is no evidence and little probability that immunity has been promised to anybody. Secondly, if the present Supervisors should resign Schmitz would promptly fill their places with men whom he can more implicitly trust but who would not be subject to indictment or in any way amenable to decent influence. As for Schmitz, he will remain Mayor until he is convicted of crime. The public does not know how that conviction is to be got. It is supposed that some Supervisor can give part of the necessary evidence, but no Supervisor can be compelled to give any evidence at all, and they probably would give none, if driven out. They are not obliged to criminate themselves. As for Schmitz, he is still defiant. He apparently does not believe that under the legal rules of evidence he can be convicted of what he evidently did. The journals which contrast our slow movement with the swift punishment which befell briber and bribed when the Broadway street railroad franchise was purchased doubtless do not understand that the laws and court procedure in California are designed not to convict criminals, but to aid their escape from justice, and that when Jake Sharp bought the New York Aldermen he did not also buy the authority which filled vacancies in the Board. As the situation in this city is unique, so, also, must be our methods of dealing with it. It may be that every Supervisor ought to be promptly indicted but it is certain that that is the one thing most ardently desired by the innumerable company of grafters outside the board. And it may not be but to help them."

[237] Keane had two champions on the board, however, Supervisors J. J. O'Neil and O. A. Tveitmoe. They resisted Keane's discharge, denouncing it as unwarranted and cowardly. Mayor Schmitz vetoed the resolution removing Keane. The Supervisors, however, adopted the resolution over the Mayor's veto.

their jobs. Thus, former Supervisor Duffey, appointed by Schmitz to head the Board of Public Works, continued in that position, although involved by Gallagher in Gallagher's confession of the bribery transactions.

The Chief of Police held office under the appointment of the Board of Police Commissioners. But Schmitz controlled the commissioners. The chief had been indicted with Schmitz and Ruef. The city was clamoring for his removal. But in spite of protests, Schmitz's influence kept the indicted chief in his place at the head of the police department.[238]

The situation could not but cause confusion. To the average man on the street, the Supervisors had

---

238 The San Francisco Call, in its issue of June 10, 1907, said of Schmitz's continued hold on the Police Department:

"The Call has never attached much importance to the well meant efforts of the various citizens' committees to persuade Mayor Schmitz to reorganize the police force and the governing commission of that body. It is easy to understand that Schmitz might engage in some such transaction or bargain if he could be shown his own advantage therein, but that he would surrender control of his most valuable personal asset at this time or, indeed at any other time, was scarcely conceivable in view of the character of the man. This is said advisedly. It is notorious that Schmitz all through his long session in office has treated his control of the police not as a public trust for the common good, but as so much personal property to be used to the limit for his private advantage. Therefore, when Schmitz, in the first instance, gave a committee some sort of pledge that he would comply with its desire or requests, there was a very natural suspicion that the terms of the bargain as a whole had not been disclosed. There was the insistent inquiry, 'What does Schmitz get by the bargain?'

"That question has never been answered from the inside and probably will not be answered, but the committee very shortly quit in disgust, realizing, doubtless, that Schmitz wanted something it could not grant as a consideration for his abandonment of power.

"A second committee that took up the work now finds that Schmitz is deaf to its requests for a reorganization of the police force. The lack of discipline in that body has become a public scandal. At its head is seen a man under indictment for felony, the associate of criminals and accused of tampering with veniremen called to try Schmitz—an accusation whose truth he admits. Governor Gillett has expressed the common knowledge that the Chief of Police is incompetent. He might have used a harsher word. But Dinan suits Schmitz. He is the ready and unscrupulous tool. An honest man in the same place would be of no use to Schmitz!"

confessed to bribery. Why, then, were they permitted to remain an hour in office? Why were they not indicted, placed on their defense and sent to the penitentiary?

The graft defense naturally took advantage of this sentiment. "Government by the big stick," as the hold of the District Attorney's office over the Supervisors was called, was condemned and ridiculed. One heard, however, little reference to the hold of the beneficiaries of the Ruef administration upon the Mayor's office. From all sides the Prosecution was importuned to oust the "boodle Supervisors." But the fact that a "boodle Mayor" would then appoint their successors was not given such wide publicity.

In addition to the complications in the municipal government, due to the Schmitz faction's dogged resistance to the Prosecution, combined with the unqualified yielding of the Supervisors and the partial confession of Ruef, San Francisco was in a condition of confusion and discord.

At the time Ruef entered his plea of guilty to extortion, a year had passed since the great fire of 1906. Thousands were still living in shacks erected in the ruins of the old city. The principal business streets were littered with building materials. There had come the depression following the activity of rehabilitation and the pouring into San Francisco of millions of insurance money. Titles to real property were confused if not in doubt, much of the records having been destroyed in the fire. Thousands found themselves forced into court to establish their titles. A little later, the community was to suffer a visitation of bubonic plague. There were many authentic plague cases and some deaths. For months the city was in dread of quarantine.

There were labor disturbances which for weeks at a time paralyzed industry. At one period between 7,000 and 10,000 iron-trades workers were out on strike. At the time Schmitz was finally convicted of extortion the telephone girls had been on strike since May 3rd. This alone threw the complex organization of a modern city into extraordinary confusion. The linemen struck. On June 21, telegraph operators in San Francisco and Oakland left their keys.

But by far the most serious labor disturbance was the strike of the street-car conductors and motormen. For weeks the entire street-car system was paralyzed. The first attempt to move a car resulted in riot in which one man was killed outright and twenty-six wounded. A number of the wounded died.

President Calhoun of the United Railroads rejected all offers to compromise, announcing his intention to break the Street Carmen's Union. He succeeded; in the end the union was broken and scattered, but at frightful cost to Mr. Calhoun's company and to San Francisco.

During the strike of the carmen the city was filled with gunfighters and thugs admittedly in the employ of the United Railroads. Indeed, there was no attempt made to disguise the fact that the United Railroads had brought them into the city. Clashes between the two factions were of daily occurrence.

Aside from horse-drawn vehicles which had been pressed into service, street transportation was, for a considerable period, practically at an end. The inability of the people to go from place to place paralyzed industry and business. Merchants, hotel keepers, manufacturers, all suffered. There were many failures. Citizens in all walks of life implored Mr. Calhoun to arbitrate his difference with his men. He refused absolutely.[239] Henry T. Scott, president of the Pacific States Telephone and Telegraph Company, as doggedly refused to submit to arbitration the questions involved in the telephone girls' strike.

---

[239] When, through the good offices of a committee of citizens, the difficulties of the iron trades were finally adjusted, The Call took occasion to urge an ending of the stiff-necked policy which kept other employers and employees apart.

"In the car strike," said The Call in its issue of June 1st, "in the telephone strike, in the laundry strike, there is nothing that cannot be disposed of by the same method and through the same agency as those that ended the iron trades controversy. There is no reason why all those disputes cannot be settled reasonably. The conciliation committee stands for public opinion. It voices the demand of the public for peace. No employer can afford to refuse its offices, nor can any representative of the employed afford to decline its offers of mediation. And if that committee, standing as it does for public opinion, could speak with convinction to the iron masters and their striking workmen, it should be able to deal even more effectively with the car strike and with the telephone strike. Those disputes concern public utilities. Street-cars are run and telephones are operated under and by virtue of grants and privileges made by the people, wherefore the people have the right to intervene when the grantees of those privileges are at war with their employes. The people have the right, at least, to mediate for peace. Mr. Cornelius and Mr. Calhoun, Mr. Scott and the leader of the telephone strikers may refuse to listen to the pacific overtures of the conciliation committee, but if they do they must understand that the price of refusal is the loss of public sympathy and support—elements without which ultimate victory is impossible.

"San Francisco has had about enough industrial warfare. The city wants peace, lasting peace. No sane man wants a fight to a finish between labor and capital, or if he does he is San Francisco's enemy. The adjustment of the iron-workers' strike is a hopeful sign. It points the way to an end of all bitterness and contention. It augurs an early return to the harmonious relations of those who earn and those who pay wages, relations which are essential to the progress and prosperity of any community. It is the best news of this stormy, stressful month."

The police seemed utterly unable to deal with the situation. Governor Gillett threatened to call out the militia, and companies at Los Angeles were actually directed to be in readiness to enter San Francisco. But this move was finally abandoned. And through it all, President Calhoun refusing to arbitrate or to compromise, issued numerous proclamations [240] in which he

240 The following, issued on May 17, is a fair sample of the statements which Mr. Calhoun gave out during the period of confusion in San Francisco, in the spring and summer of 1907:

"To the American People—The newspapers of this city published yesterday afternoon and this morning contain sensational statements purporting to give the testimony of Mr. Abraham Ruef before the Grand Jury yesterday afternoon. It is alleged that he confessed that the United Railroads, through some of its officials, bribed the Supervisors to grant the permit for the overhead trolley over certain of its roads. I do not know if Mr. Ruef made any such statements. If he did, they are untrue. I repeat with renewed emphasis my former declaration that no official of this company ever bribed any one, authorized Mr. Ruef or any one else to bribe anybody, knew of any bribery, or approved of any bribery.

"I charge the prosecution with having prostituted the great office of the District Attorney to further the plans of private malice in the interest of a man who organized the Municipal Street Railways of San Francisco on the 17th day of April, 1906, the day before the earthquake and fire, with a capital stock of $14,000,000, of which $4,500,000 were subscribed for as follows: Claus Spreckels subscribed $1,900,000, James D. Phelan subscribed $1,000,000, George Whittell subscribed $500,000, Rudolph Spreckels subscribed $1,000,000, Charles S. Wheeler subscribed $100,000. Ten per cent of the amount subscribed, or $450,000, was paid in cash, as shown by the affidavit of the treasurer of the company, James K. Moffitt, duly filed in the County Clerk's office.

"I charge that, in furtherance of the plans of the private prosecutor to assure evidence that would involve the United Railroads, the District Attorney has been willing to purchase testimony with immunity contracts, purporting to grant immunity to self-confessed criminals, which contracts I am informed were placed in escrow with the private prosecutor, and through which he controls a majority of the Board of Supervisors, who, as a member of the prosecution has declared, are 'dogs' to do his bidding.

"I charge that the District Attorney was in consultation with the members of the self-confessed criminals on the Board of Supervisors in regard to the passage of the resolution holding up the Geary street railroad company, and providing for the forfeiture of its license, unless it yielded to the demands of its striking employes.

"I charge that while the best element in this community was seeking to preserve law and order, the District Attorney was in secret conference with self-confessed criminals, giving aid and comfort to the strikers. Shall his great office be prostituted to the support of lawlessness?

"The officials of this company are ready to meet their enemies in the open, and before they are through, they expect to show to the

intimated that the Graft Prosecution had brought on the trouble which confronted San Francisco. The Prosecution's object, Mr. Calhoun held, was to injure him and his railroad company. In this connection, it may be said, that during the searching investigation of the graft trials, not one word of testimony · was produced to indicate basis for Mr. Calhoun's insinuations and open charges that the carmen's strike was part of a plot to injure him and his company.[241] On the con-

---

whole country the infamy of the methods of the prosecution, the baseness of the motives of the private prosecutor, his readiness to grant immunity to self-confessed criminals, and the willingness of the prosecution to aid the strikers, even if it involved this community in disorder and bloodshed, provided it furthered the private prosecutor's personal ends.

"The organization of the Municipal Street Railways of San Francisco, the attacks upon the officials of the United Railroads, the immunity granted to self-confessed criminals, the strike of the carmen, the hold-up of the Geary-street Railroad Company, the forfeiture of its license to operate, all seek one common end, the injury of the United Railroads and its officials, and the advancement of the personal schemes of the private prosecutor.

"I ask from the American people fair play, and a patient consideration. I ask them to withhold their judgment, freed from the bias naturally created by sensational charges. The contest in which I am engaged is grave, and I cannot afford now to disclose the whole strength of my hand, but before this contest is over, I confidently expect to defeat alike the machinations of Rudolph Spreckels, the private prosecutor, with his corps of hired detectives, and Mr. Cornelius, president of the Carmen's Union, the leader of anarchy and lawlessness, and to see firmly established in this community the principles of American liberty, and the triumph of truth and justice."

On May 21 Calhoun issued a statement directly charging the lawlessness in San Francisco to the Prosecution. He said:

"The drama is now unfolding itself and the citizens of this city will have an opportunity to fix the responsibility for existing conditions. The prosecution has said that the Supervisors would be 'good dogs' and do its bidding. The resolutions concerning the Geary-street line and the United Railroads are on a par with the neglect of the board to see that order is preserved. The prosecution is now responsible for the government of the city; therefore it is responsible for existing conditions, including the failure to suppress violence and to protect life and property."

241 Although representatives of the Defense had intimated repeatedly that the supporters of the Graft Prosecution had brought on the strike for the purpose of injuring the United Railroads, when the Prosecution attempted to introduce evidence to the contrary, Calhoun's attorneys resisted.

trary, the strike might have been averted had the United Railroads adopted a more tactful policy in dealing with its men. And, in addition to this, a more conciliatory attitude on the part of President Calhoun would, during the progress of the strike, have brought it to a close at any time. The fact remains, too, that during the 1907 municipal campaign, which opened even while the United Railroads was crushing the carmen's union, the support of the United Railroads went to the Union Labor party candidate for District Attorney. Heading the Union Labor party ticket was P. H. McCarthy, one of the strongest opponents of the Graft Prosecution, and at the same time ardent backer of the striking carmen.

The efforts of the United Railroads to crush the carmen's union, while at the same time exerting itself to elect the Union Labor party candidate for District Attorney, indicates the confusion that existed in San Francisco following the confessions of the Supervisors and the revelations made by Ruef. And the efforts of the various factions to seize the municipal government increased this confusion materially.

The day following Ruef's confession, a committee of businessmen, representing the Merchants' Association, the Board of Trade, the Chamber of Commerce, the Manufacturers' and Producers' Association and the Merchants' Exchange waited upon Spreckels and Heney to enlist the co-operation of the Prosecution in restoring normal conditions. The committee—called the Committee of Seven because of its numbers—[242] already

---

[242] The seven members of the committee were: F. B. Anderson, manager of the Bank of California; Percy T. Morgan, president of

had the endorsement of Mayor Schmitz. The Chronicle, which acted from the start in the capacity of special pleader for this committee, announced in startling headlines in its issue of May 18, that "Mayor Schmitz practically turns reins of government over to citizens. Committee of Seven may run this city."[243]

"With the exception of the administration of merely routine affairs," said the Chronicle of that date, "the committee, by Mayor Schmitz's written agreement, is to all intents and purposes, the Mayor of San Francisco."

Governor James N. Gillett [244] was reported to be heartily in accord with the committee's purposes. Finally, in an editorial article, the Chronicle announced that "the public looks to this committee to restore the good

---

the California Wine Association and a director in the Pacific States Telephone and Telegraph Company; F. W. Van Sicklen, president of Dodge Sweeney & Co.; F. W. Dohrmann, president of Nathan, Dohrmann & Co.; Henry Rosenfeld, a shipping and commission merchant; C. H. Bentley, president of the Chamber of Commerce, and Judge Charles W. Slack, who, in 1909, was to be one of the principal supporters of the opposition to the prosecution candidate for District Attorney. Illness compelled Mr. Dohrmann to sever his connection with the committee. Mr. William A. Magee served in his stead.

243 The Chronicle, in its issue of May 19, printed the following as the committee's declaration of principles:

"Declaration of principles by the Committee of Seven and what it intends to do:

"We propose to carry out our duty, irrespective of who is affected.

"We have adopted the Constitution of the United States as the fundamental basis for our final action.

"We intend to bring about a clean condition of affairs in this community and make it safe for habitation by human beings and for the investment of capital.

"We shall do nothing in the nature of class legislation and recognize that every element in the community has a right to representation in the government."

244 In a published statement printed May 19, 1906, Governor Gillett said: "The good citizens of San Francisco are for preserving order and the good name of this city, and protecting the constitutional rights of its people. The Committee of Seven, as I understand it, were appointed for this purpose, and every law-abiding citizen and every loyal paper in this city, the Bulletin with the rest, are expected to strengthen their hands and encourage them in their work."

name of the city, and to the prosecuting authorities to stand solidly behind them while they do it."

But in spite of the Chronicle's insistence, the public gave no evidence of spontaneous outburst in favor of the committee. Instead, there was a general turning to the leaders of the Prosecution to note their attitude. The Prosecution gave no evidence of enthusiastic support; quite the contrary. "The District Attorney," announced Langdon, "will not act with any committee that is named by Mayor Schmitz to take charge of the government of San Francisco."

After several conferences with the committee, Rudolph Spreckels refused to join with it on the ground that it had placed itself in a position "to directly or indirectly accomplish results very much desired by Calhoun, Herrin and the coterie who are inimical to the Prosecution." Mr. Spreckels also expressed his belief that a majority of the committee were sincere men who went on the committee with proper motives, but, Spreckels suggested, "if this committee really has its origin in an honest motive, I do not see why it cannot act on its own volition. I do not see the necessity of this committee demanding that I co-operate with it. If its members want to have a change in the municipal offices and the members of the various municipal commissions, let them go ahead and outline their own programme. I have no desire to dictate who shall constitute the membership of the various city offices. I started out in this graft prosecution to bring all guilty municipal officials to the bar of justice and have them punished. That is my single motive. I have no ulterior designs in this matter regardless of whatever anyone may say to the contrary."[245]

In spite of the Chronicle's statement that the public looked to the Prosecution to stand solidly behind the committee, and the protestations of Governor Gillett, the public was content to accept the judgment of Mr. Langdon, Mr. Spreckels and Mr. Heney as final. Without popular demand for it, there was nothing for the committee to do but resign. And it did resign.[246]

The resignation of the Committee of Seven brought from Governor Gillett a statement urging the appoint-

---

[245] The failure to enlist Spreckels with the Committee of Seven brought down upon him the condemnation of leaders of the State machine. "My surprise at this attitude of Mr. Spreckels," said Governor Gillett in an interview printed in The Examiner, May 21, 1907, "is great. It means a bad moral effect on the local industrial disturbance. If a banker like Mr. Spreckels will not act in harmony with the committee from the leading commercial organizations of this city, then I can readily account for the friction all down the line in this city. There ought to be unity of action to get the city out of its present plight, but evidently the leading business men of the town, for reasons I certainly cannot understand, are not in a mood to act in harmony."

[246] When the Committee of Seven retired, May 20, Committeeman Slack issued the following statement:

"The Committee of Seven yesterday decided that nothing could be accomplished by it, in view of the attitude of Mr. Spreckels and Mr. Heney. We met those gentlemen for the fourth time yesterday morning and were informed that they could not act with us. Mr. Spreckels declared, in spite of assurances to the contrary from every member of the committee, that he believed Herrin and Calhoun to be behind us. We had agreed, in the first place, that nothing should be done which would interfere in any way with the work of Mr. Spreckels and Mr. Heney. When we went to them and asked their co-operation they declined to co-operate. Under the circumstances we felt that the committee could not be of any further value and asked to be discharged.

"I think Mr. Spreckels was sincere in his belief that we represented interests opposed to him, and I have nothing but the kindest feelings toward him, although I believe that he was mistaken. I believe the other members of the committee are with me in this.

"My acquaintance with Mr. Herrin is only of the most casual sort, and I should be more likely to act against rather than for him. I do not know Mr. Calhoun at all.

"It is with great regret that the committee has abandoned the work which it felt called upon to undertake, and only the belief that without the assistance of Mr. Spreckels its work would be valueless led it to take this step."

ment of "a strong governing body to take charge of affairs."[247] Acting upon the Governor's suggested plan, the five commercial bodies decided upon the appointment of a committee of seventy-five, or, as the Chronicle, mouthpiece for the advocates of this course, put it, "Seventy-five prominent citizens are to be appointed to

[247] Governor Gillett's suggestions were contained in a statement published in the San Francisco papers on May 25th. It was as follows:

"Mr. Cornelius, as president of the Carmen's Union, and the other labor leaders of San Francisco can bring an end to the acts of violence that are committed daily in this city if they will, and in the event that they don't they will be held morally responsible for what happens in the future, if anything of a serious nature does happen.

"San Francisco does not want to see the State troops enter the city. It is better for the labor unions, the citizens, the city and the State that they should not take charge of affairs, but I will say, if this violence continues and increases the militia will be brought in and will take charge of affairs. Nothing along that line has been planned as yet and the State will wait a reasonable length of time for conditions to be adjusted.

"Something must be done. There must be a strong governing body to take charge of affairs, and along this line I have one suggestion to make. Let the various civic bodies of San Francisco get together and appoint a committee of twenty-five or fifty from their members, a committee of strong-minded men who will not allow politics to enter into the question, and who will fight for San Francisco as plain citizens interested in the welfare of the city.

"Such a committee could accomplish much. The first step to be taken would be to demand the appointment of a new police commission, the removal of officers in charge of districts who are incompetent, and the substitution of competent, firm men.

"Mayor Schmitz would not dare to refuse to accede to the demands of such a committee, and if the body acted with a firm hand the citizens would soon see an improvement in conditions.

"The executive committee, which appointed the Committee of Seven can bring about the organization of such a body as I suggest. It was noticeable that when the Committee of Seven took hold of affairs there was less violence for a couple of days, but as soon as the body tendered its resignation there was an increase in these acts of violence.

"Acts of violence must cease. No self-respecting community will permit a reign of crime day after day, the throwing of bricks and other missiles, the use of vile and abusive language, and the beating of men walking along the streets peaceably. Then, too, we have our wives and daughters to think of. Conditions are certainly deplorable when they cannot go upon the streets of a great city like San Francisco without being compelled to hear obscene language and witness acts of violence such as have been committed within the last three weeks.

"There are strong men here, and if they set about the matter in the right way there will be no occasion for the entrance of the State troops into the city."

restore order." The Chronicle went on to say that "It is understood that Mayor Schmitz is ready to agree to act in accordance with the recommendations of the new committee as he did when the Committee of Seven was formed. He would be glad, it is believed, to have the assistance of such a body of men in meeting some of the conditions which he has to face."[248]

At the time (May 29) of the publication of the Chronicle's belief that Mayor Schmitz would be glad to have the assistance of such a body of men as had been proposed, the Mayor's trial was drawing to its close. A fortnight later he was convicted of one of the gravest felonies that can be charged against an executive. Mayor Schmitz's conviction brought complete change in the situation. It made possible the ousting of the entire corrupt administration. In the ousting, the commercial bodies, as well as the representative labor union organizations, were given opportunity to co-operate. The refusal of the majority of them to participate threw the obligation upon the District Attorney's office.

When the Jury returned its verdict finding Mayor Schmitz guilty of felony, District Attorney Langdon found himself in an extraordinary position. Upon him, as District Attorney, fell the responsibility of naming the chief executive of San Francisco to succeed the discredited Mayor.

There was no question about a vacancy existing in the Mayor's office. Under the California laws, a vacancy in office exists upon conviction of the incumbent

---

[248] See footnote 229, page 206.

of felony. The courts had held repeatedly that a jury's verdict of guilty in a felony case carries conviction.

A vacancy, therefore, existed in the Mayor's office. Under the municipal charter the Supervisors alone were empowered to fill it. But sixteen of the Supervisors, having confessed to felonies, were taking no steps without the approval of the District Attorney. They would name for Mayor, him whom the District Attorney approved and no other. Naturally, Langdon consulted those associated with him in the Graft Prosecution. No better earnest of the sincerity and disinterestedness of Langdon and those who were assisting him is furnished than in this crisis. They had it within their power to select first Mayor and then Supervisors who would be utterly subservient to them. Instead, they proposed a plan by which representative associations were given opportunity to reorganize the municipal government by naming Mayor Schmitz's successor.

Nor was there any hasty action. The office of Mayor was not declared vacant until after Schmitz had been sentenced to the penitentiary. But Schmitz was in the county jail and incompetent to act. It was of immediate necessity that a temporary successor be substituted. Until this were done, San Francisco would be without a chief executive. To meet the emergency, the Supervisors named Supervisor Gallagher to be acting Mayor.[249]

---

[249] Of the eighteen Supervisors, two, O'Neil and Tveitmoe, had been appointed by Mayor Schmitz to fill vacancies after the bribery transactions. They were in no way involved in the briberies. They were, therefore, independent of the District Attorney. O'Neil put Tveitmoe in nomination against Gallagher. "What is the difference," demanded O'Neil, "between Eugene E. Schmitz and James L. Gallagher?" Gallagher's face went red with rage, but there was no way of silencing the critic.

After the sentencing of Schmitz the rapidly developing situation made it necessary that the convicted official's office be declared vacant and his successor appointed. But the successor had not been named, nor had plans for the change in administration been formulated.[250] In this further emergency, it was decided to name one of the Supervisors to be Mayor to serve until a permanent successor of Mayor Schmitz could be named. The unhappy Boxton [251] was decided upon.

---

250 This tardiness of appointment was not due to any lack of candidates. Practically every faction in San Francisco had its choice for Schmitz's successor.

251 The election of Boxton to be Mayor may be called the refinement of cruelty. His elevation to high executive office but emphasized the shame of his position. From taking his oath of office he was rushed to the witness stand to testify against Louis Glass on trial for participation in bribing him to oppose the granting of the Home Telephone Company franchise. D. M. Delmas was conducting the case for the defense. Delmas suavely turned Boxton's elevation to account. He scrupulously addressed Boxton as the "Mayor." And, in comparison, he wrung from the new Mayor's lips: "I took bribes and was a spy for Halsey."
Nor did Delmas confine his refined ridicule to the unhappy Mayor Boxton. Heney had, for example, asked the court to take judicial notice of the fact that while Schmitz was in Europe, Gallagher had served as acting Mayor.
"I don't think," interrupted Delmas, "your honor will extend your judicial knowledge that far, because that would be to keep track of the change of Mayors here, and it would keep you too busy to discharge your duties."
A grim party surrounded Boxton while he took his oath of office. Boxton gave no evidence of pride of his new station.
"When I think," he said during a lull in the proceedings, "of the things that have come into my life in the last ten years, I realize how few of them were of my own planning. When we came back from Manila, I had no idea of politics, but they insisted in making heroes of us, and I had to run for Supervisor. Now I wish I had not done it."
Later on he gave out the following interview:
"This has come to me as a great surprise. I very much regret the circumstances which have led up to this appointment. I hope the people will bear with me for the few weeks that I am in office. As to my official policy, I cannot discuss that at present.
"You know, it is with a feeling of sadness I take the office. I am glad it is a temporary appointment and will last only a short time. I didn't know when I told you this morning that I was willing to do whatever was thought best, either to remain in office or to resign from the board, that this would be put upon me. I am sorry they have asked me to take the office, and will be glad when it is

The Supervisors, by resolution, definitely declared the office of Mayor vacant and elected Supervisor Boxton to be Mayor.

On the day that Boxton was named Mayor of San Francisco, District Attorney Langdon made public a plan for a convention to select a Mayor to serve until the successor of Mayor Schmitz could be elected and qualified. Mr. Langdon proposed that the convention should be made up of thirty members, fifteen to be appointed by organized labor and fifteen by the organized commercial bodies. On the side of Labor were apportioned eight delegates to the Labor Council and seven to the Building Trades Council. The five commercial bodies, the Chamber of Commerce, Merchants' Association, Board of Trade, Real Estate Board and Merchants' Exchange, were allowed three delegates each. That the convention might proceed in its choice unhampered, the District Attorney pledged that he and his associates would wholly refrain from participation after the convention had assembled.[252]

But this did not suit the several factions at all. Admittedly, the Prosecution could name the Mayor. Each faction wanted its man named, and while there remained a chance for its man to be named, did not care to see the extraordinary power in the hands of

---

over. The only thing I can say is that I believe during the short time I will hold the office the people will have no cause to——"

Boxton halted for his words—"Again find fault with me."

The Examiner commenting upon Boxton's elevation, said "Having put our brike-taking Mayor in jail, and having put in his place a taker of smaller bribes, we have now substituted for Gallagher, Boxton, who differs from Gallagher principally in having sold his vote for still less of the bribing corporations' money."

252 The District Attorney's statement of his plan to the various organizations concerned will be found in full on page xxii of the Appendix.

the District Attorney delegated to the uncertainties of a convention.

In the scramble for advantage, the self-control and self-forgetting attitude of the members of the Prosecution, instead of exciting admiration, was condemned. The Examiner, referring to Langdon's associates, for example, announced: "Their failure to agree on anyone has led to some alarm for fear their divergent political ambitions are making each of them endeavor to secure a place for his personal puppet." Had the Prosecution named the Examiner's "personal puppet," this particular source of criticism would undoubtedly have been silenced and the Examiner's vilification and abuse of the Prosecution during the years that followed averted. What is true of the Examiner in this regard is true of the other institutions and interests which, in this crisis of the city's history, were clamoring for "recognition."[253] District Attorney Langdon's plan, on the whole, was not received in the spirit in which it was offered.

The Building Trades Council, under the influence of P. H. McCarthy and O. A. Tveitmoe, promptly rejected the District Attorney's proposal and refused to name delegates.[254] This action influenced the Labor

---

253 The Chronicle, however, endorsed Langdon's plan, and urged the several labor and industrial bodies to participate. "As the matter appears at present," said The Chronicle, "the prosecution has resorted to the only safe and reasonable plan of restoring good government, and fault-finding with the method adopted will be confined to the hyper-critical and those who imagine that they would find profit in a continuance of unsettled conditions."

254 The resolutions adopted by the Building Trades Council rejecting Langdon's plan for reorganization of the municipal government, were as follows:

"Whereas, An invitation has been received by this council from the District Attorney of this city and county, requesting this

Council, which, on the ground that in the absence of delegates from the Building Trades Council the Labor Council representatives might be outvoted, refused to participate.

Of the five commercial bodies, the Real Estate Board alone promptly accepted the District Attorney's invitation. The board named its three delegates and so notified the District Attorney.

The Merchants' Exchange demanded that the number of delegates be increased from thirty to forty-five by the addition of fifteen professional men, and proposed that the convention name a new Board of Supervisors as well as Mayor.[255]

---

council appoint seven delegates to participate in a convention composed of thirty delegates, made up of fifteen representatives from the labor organizations of this city and fifteen representatives from the civic organizations outside of the labor organizations; and whereas, said convention is to be called for the purpose of selecting a person to be appointed Mayor of the City and County of San Francisco; and whereas, at this time this council is not possessed of sufficient information upon the subject to determine whether or not the action proposed to be taken by the convention would be legal, and whether or not such action, if taken, would not lead to a multiplicity of suits by reason of the appointment to an office where a doubt as to the vacancy in said office exists, and as a result lead to endless litigation and regrettable confusion; and whereas, those who have arrogated to themselves the duty of guiding the destinies of the entire municipality of San Francisco only last Tuesday, by the exercise of assumed power, through the Board of Supervisors, placed in the Mayor's chair one who is to their own knowledge legally disqualified, to the exclusion of one or the other of two gentlemen who are members of that board in the personnel of O. A. Tveitmoe and J. J. O'Neil, whose characters, both public and private, are above reproach; and whereas, the Building Trades Council was organized and is maintained for the purpose of directing, protecting and conducting the building industry from the standpoint of the journeymen with justice alike to the owner, contractor and artisan, and not for the purpose of making mayors through the instrumentality of star chamber conventions, thereby usurping the rights and prerogatives of the people; therefore, be it

"Resolved, That this Building Trades Council, in regular meeting assembled, instruct its secretary to acknowledge the receipt of the said invitation, and decline to act thereon for the reasons herein stated."

[255] Langdon's reply to the objections of the Merchants' Exchange was as follows:

"We cannot entertain any such proposition at this date. We

The Board of Trade refused to co-operate unless the delegates be increased in number by the addition of "professional men and others."

The Chamber of Commerce and the Merchants' Association finally accepted, but stipulated that a two-thirds vote of the thirty delegates should be required for a choice.

The failure of the several organizations to join in the selection of a Mayor, made it necessary for Langdon himself to proceed with the reorganization. All that Langdon and his associates required was that the new executive should be independent of political control and free of the influence of those public-service corporations that had been trapped in bribe-giving. It was also the aim of the Prosecutor to name as Mayor one whose standing was such that none could be so unfair as to charge him with being in the slightest degree under the influence of the Prosecution.

Langdon and his associates agreed that Dr. John Gallwey was independent of corrupting influences and

---

have already had submitted to us, and have considered at least one hundred plans for calling an electoral convention, and after carefully deliberating on all these plans, decided upon the plan which we have announced. This plan gives the opposing factions of labor and capital each an equal representation in the electoral body. The responsibility of deciding who shall be the Mayor is distinctly imposed on the two most important factions in the community, and as far as giving a square deal to everybody, we do not see how our announced plan can be improved upon. Certainly the addition of fifteen delegates appointed by any special committee cannot improve the plan. In our announcement it has been clearly stated that all the commercial and labor organizations called have until Saturday to name their delegates, and these delegates will assemble next Monday to nominate the new Mayor. The plan announced will not be modified in any way. It places the issue squarely before the people and if they do not wish to act upon it we cannot help it.

"In regard to the proposition to permit the electoral convention to name sixteen new Supervisors, I will say that while there is no objection to it, we do not think it is wise to incorporate it in our present plan."

to Dr. Gallwey the appointment was offered. But Dr. Gallwey declined to accept the responsibilities of the Mayor's office on the ground that he could not afford to devote his time to the duties of the office to the extent that would be required in order to conduct it properly, and on the further ground that he could be of more service to humanity in the practice of medicine than in the discharge of the duties of Mayor.

The place was then offered to Ralph Harrison, a former member of the Supreme Bench. But Judge Harrison declined on the ground that he thought the duties of the office, under the conditions existing [256]

---

[256] Schmitz's resistance of the elevation of Gallagher no doubt influenced the aged Justice in his refusal. From the county jail Schmitz continued to insist that he was still the de facto Mayor of San Francisco. The Chief of Police, himself under indictment, sided with Schmitz. Gallagher during his eventful term blocked by the police, was not permitted to enter the Mayor's office. When Boxton was made Mayor, Langdon went with him to the Mayor's office and seized the furniture. Schmitz's partisans boasted that the Mayor would be released on bail, march with his followers to the meeting place of the Supervisors, and, with the aid of the police, oust Gallagher by force. Schmitz's resistance made itself felt in many ways. For example, an athletic club had arranged for a boxing match, for which a permit signed by the Mayor had to be issued. Gallagher had signed the permit. Chief of Police Dinan, however, refused to recognize it unless it were signed by Schmitz. The manager of the affair was compelled to go to the county jail for Schmitz's signature. Schmitz notified the bondsmen of City Treasurer Charles A. Bantel that he would hold them responsible for any moneys paid out by Bantel without his (Schmitz's) signature. The bondsmen notified Bantel that as a matter of precaution he must have the signature of Schmitz as well as that of Gallagher as authorization for paying out funds. This precautionary course was followed to its logical conclusion. On July 12, a contractor by the name of J. J. Dowling cashed a municipal warrant which bore the signatures of no less than three Mayors, Schmitz, Gallagher and Boxton.

Late in June, Schmitz sent to the auditor warrants signed by himself for June salaries for himself, his secretary, his stenographer and his usher. The auditor decided to allow these warrants for that part of the month up to the date of Schmitz's conviction. San Francisco allows its Mayor $300 a month for contingent expenses. Both Schmitz and Gallagher claimed this $300 for July. The auditor decided to recognize neither claim. In answer to Schmitz's demand that Gallagher be ignored as Mayor, the auditor sent the imprisoned executive a soothing or grimly humorous letter, as one may view it, in which he recognized Schmitz as the de jure Mayor, pos-

would be too onerous for him to undertake at his time of life.

Dr. Edward R. Taylor,[257] dean of the Hastings College of Law, was then consulted. Dr. Taylor agreed to accept the position. In tendering Dr. Taylor the mayoralty, the Prosecution left him entirely free to conduct the office according to his own judgment. He was assured that no one connected with the Prosecution would expect or ask him to be guided or controlled or influenced in any way by all or any of them.

sessing "the honor and the title," and Gallagher "simply as a de facto Mayor," possessing the office.

When the bribe-taking Supervisors resigned, Schmitz, from the county jail, appointed their successors. Seven of these Schmitz appointees actually took the oath of office. On the night of Taylor's election to succeed Boxton as Mayor, one of Schmitz's appointees, Samuel T. Sawyer, appeared before the board and demanded that he be sworn in as Supervisor. Gallagher, who was presiding refused to recognize Schmitz as Mayor and refused Sawyer a seat.

Even after Taylor had been elected, Chief of Police Dinan continued to recognize Schmitz as Mayor. Dinan, for example, placed the automobile maintained by the city for the use of the Mayor, under guard of a policeman and for several days prevented Mayor Taylor securing it.

Mayor Taylor gave effective check to this harassing opposition by refusing to sign warrants upon the treasury which bore Schmitz's signature. Gradually Schmitz's resistance to the new order died out.

Schmitz contented himself with issuing a statement through the Associated Press that he would be a candidate for re-election. He said:

"You may announce that I will be a candidate for re-election this fall, and that I expect to win. I have already begun my campaign in a preliminary way, and shall carry it forward steadily from this time. I have no fear of the race. I am willing to make it without the aid of the Ruef organization, whose support I had in each of the three campaigns since 1901. Presumably that organization no longer exists, but its component parts, though scattered, are as much in existence as ever. It is up to me to gather them together and cement them into an organization of my own—a task I am prepared to undertake."

257 Dr. Edward Robeson Taylor was born at Springfield, Ill., Sept. 24, 1838. He came to California in 1862. In 1865 he graduated from the Toland Medical College. In 1872, he was admitted to the California bar. He served as dean of the Hastings College of Law. For thirty years he was Vice-President and President of the Cooper Medical College. He was one of the freeholders who framed the present San Francisco municipal charter, and at the time of his selection as Mayor, had served San Francisco and the State in many important public capacities.

Boxton, after Taylor had agreed to serve, resigned his office. The Supervisors then elected Dr. Taylor to fill the vacancy.[258]

The next step in the reorganization of the municipal government was the resignation of the sixteen Supervisors who had confessed to bribery and the appointment of their successors. When Mayor Taylor [259] had

---

258 Dr. Taylor's selection gave general satisfaction. "My belief is," said Governor Gillett in a published interview, "that he will make an able and trustworthy executive. It is particularly fortunate that he is identified with no factional politics and can work for a clean reorganized administration of the city government."

"The most important feature connected with the selection," said the Chronicle, "is the doctor's absolute freedom from alliances with any particular interest. He is free from all entanglements, and his ability and firmness of character give assurance that his efforts will be wholly directed to bettering the condition and restoring the confidence of the community. We repeat that San Francisco owes the doctor a debt of gratitude for sinking considerations of personal comfort and devoting himself to the general welfare, and that the prosecution has acted wisely in selecting and inducing him to act."

On the other hand, The Examiner ridiculed the selection. Labor Union party leaders of the type of P. H. McCarthy were loud in expressions of their disapproval.

259 Mayor Taylor, the day of his election, issued the following statement:

"I accepted this office with much reluctance, and only because I believed that any man who was requested to serve the city in this capacity in the hour of her need should heed the request, no matter what the personal sacrifice might be.

"Had any pledges been exacted of me by those who tendered the office, I would not have considered the tender for one-thousandth part of a second.

"I would not submit to any dictation in the administration of the office, nor do I believe that any one who knows me would attempt to dictate to me.

"If I am called upon to appoint a Board of Supervisors, I will select the very best men who can be induced to accept the offices, and I shall exercise my own judgment as to who are the best men.

"I am going to do the best I can for the city without regard to partisan politics, and, so far as I am concerned, there will be no partisan politics.

"As Mayor of this city, every man looks just as tall to me as every other man.

"The first essential to good government is perfect order, and I shall employ every arm of the law to the end that such order shall prevail.

"I believe in autonomy in every department of the city government, and I believe that commissioners should be permitted to administer the affairs of their respective departments, free from dictation, as long as they demonstrate by their acts that they are honest and competent."

found sixteen representative citizens willing to serve, the change was made. One by one the discredited officials resigned their positions. After each resignation had been accepted Mayor Taylor named the resigning member's successor.[260]

The scene was as painful as it was extraordinary. When it was over, the Schmitz-Ruef administration, so far as the legislative and executive branches were concerned, had passed.

---

[260] The citizens named by Dr. Taylor to act as Supervisors were: Dr. A. A. D'Ancona, dean of the Medical Faculty of the University of California; Harry U. Brandenstein, attorney and former Supervisor; Gustave Brenner, capitalist and retired merchant; James P. Booth, newspaperman and former Supervisor; A. Comte, Jr., attorney and former Supervisor; George L. Center, real estate; Bernard Faymonville, vice-president Firemen's Fund Insurance Company; E. J. Molera, civil engineer and president of the Academy of Science; W. G. Stafford, president of the W. G. Stafford & Co., coal merchants; Henry Payot, retired merchant and former Supervisor; Matt I. Sullivan, attorney; Thomas Magee, real estate; Lippman Sachs, capitalist and retired merchant; L. P. Rixford, architect; C. A. Murdock, printing and bookbinding; D. C. Murphy, attorney.

A. Comte, Jr., successor of Supervisor McGushin, did not take office until several days after his associates on the new board. This was due to McGushin's hesitation about resigning. Mr. McGushin finally resigned, however, and Comte was named in his stead.

Of the Taylor Board of Supervisors, The Chronicle, in its issue of July 27th, said:

"Mayor Taylor's choice of men for the new Board of Supervisors will fortunately not meet universal approval. It will satisfy all honest men who regard public office as a public trust and not as a private snap, but it will not satisfy those who are accustomed either to actually corrupt public servants or to use a secret pull to obtain private and undue advantage. It will not satisfy the criminal element who thrive by the wide-open town, and who abhor a Board of Supervisors who will back up an honest and capable Mayor.

"The board which the Mayor has selected may be safely accepted as the leaders of the people. All interests are recognized except that of the boodlers. The city has many knotty problems to solve. Somebody must work them out. Probably no two capable and honest men would resolve the various doubts which will arise in precisely the same way, and yet out of all the possible ways in each case some particular way must be chosen. And it will be the duty of the Mayor and Supervisors, in the light of much more information than the majority of us can obtain, to select that way. And when it has been determined all patriotic citizens must get behind them."

CHAPTER XVIII.

The Real Fight Begins.

Nine months after Heney assumed his duties as Assistant District Attorney, Mayor Taylor named the successors of the Ruef-Schmitz Board of Supervisors.

In those nine months much had been accomplished. Ruef had plead guilty to extortion and had made partial confession of his relations with the public-service corporations. The Schmitz-Ruef Supervisors had made full and free confession, and had been removed from office. Mayor Schmitz had been convicted of extortion, ousted from office, and pending his appeal to the upper courts was confined in the county jail. The back of the Schmitz-Ruef political organization was broken, and its forces scattered.

Had the Prosecution stopped here, the men whose devotion and self-sacrifice had made the undoing of the corrupt administration possible, would have retired with nothing more serious confronting them than the condemnation of the impotent puppets of large interests whom they had brought to grief. But those behind the Prosecution were not content to leave their work at a point where the regeneration of San Francisco had scarcely begun. They proposed to go to the bottom of the graft scandal. It was not sufficient, they held, to punish poor men who were without friends or influence, while their rich and powerful associates went unpunished. The bribe-taking Supervisors might be put in the penitentiary, but other bribe-taking Supervisors would eventually take their places. Ruef, punished by imprisonment, would serve as an example for political bosses that would cause them to hesitate for long before embarking in corrupt enterprises such as had brought the discredited boss to grief. This would make it hard for bribe-giving corporations to secure agents for bribe-passing, and make bribe-giving correspondingly difficult. But the conviction of high corporation officials, responsible for the bribe-giving of public-service corporations, was regarded as more important than all, for this would demonstrate bribe-giving to be unsafe, and check the practice at its very fountain-head. Such conviction, the Prosecution held, would have greater deterrent effect against bribery of public officials than the confinement of 500 bribe-taking Supervisors in the penitentiary.[261]

---

261 Heney's attitude toward the bribe-givers is expressed in an affidavit filed in the case of The People vs. Calhoun et als., No. 823. Heney in setting forth a statement made to Rabbi Nieto says:

"I consider that the greatest benefit which we will have done this city and this country by these prosecutions will be the insight which we will have given them into the causes of corruption in all large cities, and into the methods by which this corruption is maintained. The testimony of the members of the Board of Supervisors throws great light on this question, and Ruef could aid considerably in making it an object lesson to the world, if he would do so. The only way we can stop this kind of corruption is by enlightening the people as to its causes and by thereafter endeavoring to remove the temptation which causes evil by proper remedial legislation, and in order to impress this object lesson on the people strongly enough to accomplish much good we must punish the principal men who have been involved in it. Do not imagine this is a pleasant task to me. It is far from being so. It involves men like Frank Drum, whom I liked and respected as a friend for years, and who has quite recently paid me a good attorney's fee for services performed for a company represented by him. I have met Patrick Calhoun socially, and greatly admire his ability and found him to be a man of very agreeable, attractive manners. I wish there was some other way to secure a proper deterrent effect without causing these men and their innocent families to suffer, but unless the laws are enforced, Doctor, our republican form of government cannot continue very long. It is not sufficient to punish the poor man who has no friends or influence. The people

"I would be willing," Rudolph Spreckels testified at the Calhoun trial, "to grant immunity to any man who would bring to bar a man of great wealth who would debauch a city government, and who would use his wealth to corrupt individuals and tempt men of no means to commit crime in order that he might make more money."

Such was the stand taken by District Attorney Langdon and his associates. The announced policy of the Prosecution, therefore, included the prosecution of the bribe-giver to the end. In pursuing this policy, Mr. Langdon and his associates aroused the astonishingly effective opposition of interests representing hundreds of millions of capital. Every indictment of capitalist charged with bribe-giving was signal for a new group of financial leaders, their satellites, beneficiaries and dependents, to array themselves on the side of the graft defense.[262]

---

will lose respect for the courts and for the law unless the rich and powerful can be made to obey the laws. It has a greater deterrent effect, in my opinion, to put one rich and influential man in prison than to put a thousand poor ones there. It would do no good to send a few miserable, ignorant Supervisors to the penitentiary. Others of the same kind would soon take their places, and the carnival of crime would continue as before. If we can put Ruef in the penitentiary it will have a wholesome effect upon other political bosses for the next decade at least. And if we can put a few captains of industry there with him, and particularly a few of the head officials of public service corporations, it will have a greater deterrent effect against bribery of public officials than putting five hundred of such officials in the penitentiary."

262 "I subscribed to the Graft Prosecution fund," said one capitalist whose own skirts were clean of the graft scandal, "but before the investigation was over I had to exert myself to prevent my own attorney going to jail."

The manner in which every indictment increased the circle of opposition to the prosecution is well illustrated by the following selection from the San Francisco Chronicle of March 25, 1907:

"The indictment of Louis Glass, former vice-president of the Pacific States Telephone Company, for bribery, on testimony given to the Grand Jury by E. J. Zimmer, who was the auditor of the company under Glass, and is now vice-president of the reorganized

With every indictment came a new group of attorneys to raise technical objections to the proceedings, all of which the attorneys for the Prosecution were obliged to meet.

The first attack was upon the validity of the Grand Jury. The attorneys for Ruef and Schmitz had apparently exhausted every point that could be raised for the disqualification of the Grand Jurors, but this did not prevent the heads of corporations who found themselves under indictment making similar attacks. And between them, in this new move to quash the indictments, the defendants enlisted the ablest members of the California bar.[263]

In this new opposition an astonishing number of technical points were raised by one or the other of the groups of defending lawyers. Nothing was overlooked.

corporation, has caused consternation in certain fashionable circles, in which Glass was one of the most popular men.

"At the clubs of which the indicted telephone magnate was a member, much sympathy is expressed for him. He was extremely popular because of his affability and good-fellowship, and he has a host of friends, who are loth to believe that he has committed a crime which may put him behind the bars of San Quentin for fourteen years.

"Attorney George Knight, who, it is expected, will be retained as counsel for Glass, voiced the sentiment of many of his friends, yesterday, when he said:

" 'Louis Glass is one of the best fellows in a social way that ever lived. He is proud, high-spirited and in all his personal relations with others he has always been most particular. I cannot imagine what has led him into doing what he is said to have done in the telephone bribery, and I am sure that in spite of the indictment, when the truth is known, he will not appear in such a discreditable light.' "

263 Among those who challenged the validity of the Grand Jury were: Patrick Calhoun, Thornwell Mullally, Tirey L. Ford and William Abbott of the United Railroads, represented by A. A. Moore and Stanley Moore; Louis Glass of the Pacific States Telephone Company, represented by Delmas and Coogan; John Martin, Eugene de Sabla and Frank Drum of the San Francisco Gas and Electric Company, represented by Garret McEnerney; T. V. Halsey, represented by Bert Schlesinger, William P. Humphries and D. M. Delmas. The several attorneys represented the best legal ability obtainable in San Francisco. No less than fifty-two attorneys, all working to the same end, were employed by the several graft defendants.

Just before the principal indictments were brought, for example, the San Francisco merchants had given a banquet to celebrate the progress which San Francisco had made during the first year following the fire.[264] Langdon and Heney were given places of honor. They were the heroes of the occasion. Every reference to their work was signal for tremendous demonstration. There was no suggestion then that the pursuit of criminals would "hurt business."

"A severe earthquake," observed Frank J. Symmes, president of the Merchants' Association, "is a serious misfortune, and a great conflagration a great trial, and each awake the sympathy of the Nation, but a corrupt government is at once a crime and a disgrace and brings no sympathy."

"We foresee," said Bishop William Ford Nichols, another of the speakers of the evening, "the greater San Francisco. We mean to make it fairer to the eye. But how about making it better? Size and sin may go together. Rehabilitated buildings may house debilitated character."

A month later, after indictments had been brought against some of the most prominent business men of the city, word went out that steps would be taken to disqualify every member of the Grand Jury who had attended that merchants' banquet.

The Grand Jurors were again called to the witness stand and put through a grilling to determine whether or not they were biased. Rudolph Spreckels was under

---

[264] The Merchants' Association banquet, April 18, 1907, the first anniversary of the great earthquake and fire.

examination for hours in efforts to show that his motives in backing the Prosecution were bad.[265]

Every step of the proceedings at the organization of the Grand Jury was scrutinized. The question of the method of employing the stenographer to the Grand Jury was made subject of hours of argument. If she were irregularly employed, it was held, she was an unauthorized person in the Grand Jury room and her unwarranted presence sufficient to invalidate the indictments. Garret McEnerney, representing Eugene de Sabla, Jr., Frank Drum and John Martin, whose indictments grew out of the bribery of the Supervisors to fix the gas rate at 85 cents per 1000 cubic feet instead of 75 cents, was the first to raise this question. But attorneys for other defendants took it up and seriously considered it as valid objection to the sufficiency of the indictments. A further point was raised by several of the defendants that the stenographer had not been properly sworn. The question was seriously debated, whether she had looked at Prosecutor Heney or Fore-

---

[265] At one of the examinations of Spreckels, Attorney A. A. Moore, representing the United Railroads, is reported as demanding:

"Can it be that we have got to a point where a private prosecution, hiring a lawyer, hiring an attorney, hiring a detective—and then when indictments are found that you cannot set them aside? That is the line of testimony I intend to pursue."

"In addition," said Attorney Stanley Moore, A. A. Moore's associate in the defense, "we expect to show that Mr. Spreckels is the head and shoulders of a large street railroad company, organized by himself for the purpose of putting the United Railroads out of business.'

"I will say this again," went on Moore, "we will prove the statement that we have made, to wit: that Mr. Heney was an unauthorized person before the Grand Jury by reason of the fact that he was during all that time privately employed by Rudolph Spreckels, who was entertaining a plan to destroy the property of the United Railroads, and to carry out that plan they gave immunity to the Board of Supervisors to carry out their bidding."

man Oliver at the moment she was sworn to secrecy.[266]

---

[266] The Chronicle, in its issue of June 7, 1907, in discussing the
delaying tactics of the defendants, said:

"It cannot be too often repeated that in connection with the
boodle cases there are but two questions which are of importance,
and those are, first: Did the accused commit bribery within the
meaning of the statute? and secondly, If not, did they commit
bribery in such a way that the law cannot reach them?   Both
these questions will be settled by the evidence in the trials.   If
the verdict is that the accused committed bribery within the meaning of the statute, they will go to State's prison.   If the evidence
shows that they committed bribery so skilfully that it cannot be
legally proved, they will not go to the penitentiary, but they will
stand disgraced men and unconvicted felons.   In either case all that
an honest man prizes most highly is at stake, and as all claim to
be as innocent as unborn babes, one would expect the band to be
tumbling over each other in their eagerness to be first to face a
jury and rehabilitate their damaged reputations by a public demonstration of their untarnished character.

"Quite the contrary.   So far from their taking this obvious
course to secure justification the aid of a shining and costly array
of legal talent is invoked to prevent, if it may be possible, any
show-down whatever of the evidence in any court.   They object to
even coming into court and pleading whether they are guilty or not.
It is declared that it will be alleged that the purported Grand Jury,
which went through the form of indicting them, is an illegal body,
with no standing whatever in court, and that, therefore, there is no
indictment at all.   It will not, apparently, be claimed that the members of the alleged Grand Jury were not discreet citizens, legally
competent to serve as Grand Jurors; that they were not regularly
appointed as such according to law; that they were not duly sworn
into office, or that, having listened to sworn evidence delivered
under the forms of law, these reputable citizens, upon that evidence, accuse them of felony.   None of these things, it is supposed,
will be alleged.   What is to be alleged, it is said, is that the number
of names from which the Grand Jury was drawn was 113, instead
of 125, which, by the way, is promptly denied.   What earthly
bearing could that have, if it were true, on the guilt or innocence
of the men accused of felony?   Can it be conceived as possible,
even if that were proved, that our laws are drawn so completely
in the interest of criminals as to enable men accused of felony to
escape trial?

"The personal character and qualifications of the Grand Jurors
were fully brought out in the Ruef case.   For weeks they were subjected to a grilling which it was a disgrace to our laws to permit.
That was not repeated in the Schmitz case.   In that the counsel
of the accused have seemed to be relying for overturning a conviction on the alleged over-zealousness of the prosecuting officer.
Again, what has that to do with the guilt or innocence of the
accused, even if it has occurred?   A District Attorney is in possession of all the evidence, and if that is such as to arouse his indignation, shall the people thereby be deprived of all remedy?   Obvious
misconduct of an attorney is more likely to injure the people than
the accused.   It could hardly have any other influence on the verdict of a jury.   If no crimes are to be punished in which there is
energetic prosecution, which may occasionally involve expressions
which the law discountenances, we may about as well shut up our
criminal courts.   Almost any attorney may be baited into making
uncourteous remarks.   Happily the Supreme Court has recently
decided that no matter what the District Attorney does, a felon
duly convicted upon sufficient evidence shall not thereby be turned
loose.   And that is as it should be."

Another point was brought up by the defendants in the United Railroads bribery case, that inasmuch as the defendants Calhoun, Mullally and Ford, had been called to the Grand Jury room and compelled to fall back upon their constitutional rights to avoid testifying, that they had been placed in a prejudicial position before the Grand Jury, which constituted reversible error.[267] Another objection was that the Grand Jury box had been

---

[267] Heney in court made caustic answer to this argument: "After the Supervisors had confessed," he began, "and sixteen of them had testified that they had been paid $4,000 apiece to vote for the trolley franchise, these defendants thought in their own minds that they were so connected with the crime that Patrick Calhoun, Thornwell Mullally and Tirey L. Ford each made a public explanation in the press, denying that they had bribed a city official. A crime had been committed, and the first question to be asked was, Who had the motive? The Supervisors had testified that they received the money from Gallagher, and Gallagher had testified that he received it from Ruef. Did Abraham Ruef own the trolley lines? The question arose as to who had the motive? Ford and Mullally came to me personally and told me they had not bribed a city official. Wasn't that an explanation? Will it not be an explanation when these defendants are put on trial that they will say it was an attorney's fee? If, under these circumstances, the Grand Jury cannot call the officers of the company to learn who authorized the giving of the bribe money, what would an investigation be worth? If we had not called them, then you would have heard the other cry, that this was a conspiracy to destroy the good name of Patrick Calhoun.

"If it had been a poor, ignorant man, or a helpless woman—if the Grand Jury had dragged her from the jail and compelled her to testify against herself, and she had not known what her constitutional right was, it would have been a different picture. But these four gentlemen are learned in the law. One of them had been Attorney-General of this State, another had been his assistant in that office for four years. Mullally is an attorney and Patrick Calhoun is an attorney whose mind is equal to that of any man's in California.

"Advised of their rights! Why, they came in there on a subpoena which General Ford has declared in his own affidavit was faulty and ineffective. They came on a defective process, which they knew to be defective. They refused to be sworn, and they were not sworn, and they left the Grand Jury room without having answered a question, for the purpose of coming solemnly here to get these indictments set aside on the grounds that their constitutional rights have been invaded. That's trifling with the law. Laws weren't made to juggle with. Laws were made for the protection of the innocent.

"They knew they didn't have to go, but they went, and they refused to testify; and now they want the indictments set aside because their great constitutional rights have been tampered with.

"They say he could have waived the point and testified, but because he refused and walked out he has been deprived of his constitutional right."

destroyed in the great fire of 1906, and that no order had come from any department of the Superior Court ordering its restoration. Again, it was asserted, that Grand Juror James E. Gordan was a member of the Grand Jury panel of 1906, while the other Grand Jurors were chosen from the 1907 list. Indictments brought by a Grand Jury thus constituted were claimed to be without effect.

Had any one of these and many other similar objections been sustained, all indictments against the graft defendants would have been invalidated. Every objection had to be met. Days and weeks were spent by the District Attorney's office in meeting, or preparing to meet objections which to the layman appear trifling and ridiculous.

In the midst of this technical fight to have the indictments against them set aside, the graft defendants received aid from an unlooked-for source. Sympathizers with the United Railroads conductors and motormen, then on strike, whose union Patrick Calhoun was at the time endeavoring to crush—and finally did crush—started an independent attack upon the Grand Jury.

Four union sympathizers had been indicted in connection with street riots. Their attorneys, before Superior Judge Cook, raised the point that as the Oliver Grand Jury had continued in service after a new panel had been drawn in the office of the clerk and put on file, the term of the Grand Jury's service had expired. It was, therefore, no longer part of the machinery of the Court and had no power as an inquisitorial body. Under this interpretation, not only would the indictments against the strikers be invalidated, but those against the alleged bribe-givers also.[268] Thus four of Mr. Calhoun's striking carmen, in their efforts to evade trial on charges growing out of opposition to the United Railroads, were making stronger fight to release Mr. Calhoun from indictment than Mr. Calhoun, although enjoying the ablest legal counsel that money could secure, had been able to make for himself.

Eventually, these technical objections were decided adversely to the defense; the validity of the Oliver Grand Jury was never successfully attacked. But the technical objections raised caused delays which the defense was able to put to good account. While the prosecution was battling to force the graft cases to trial on their merits, the graft defense was conducting a publicity campaign to misrepresent and undermine the prosecution. The astonishing success of these efforts were to appear later. By 1909, for example, in the city which when the graft prosecution opened, the practically universal sentiment was for the crushing out of corruption, there was strong opinion that the prosecution of influential offenders had gone too far, had been injudiciously conducted, was "hurting business,"

---

[268] In commenting upon the point raised by the indicted carmen, the Chronicle, in its issue of July 30, 1907, said:

"In attacking the legality of the Grand Jury the attorneys of the carmen indicted for making assaults with deadly weapons and throwing bricks at street cars may have played into the hands of their arch enemy, the president of the United Railroads. If the Supreme Court should hold that the Oliver Grand Jury passed out of legal existence when the 144 new names were selected by the twelve Superior Judges, the indictments against those connected with the telephone, gas, trolley and Parkside briberies would be set aside and all the work of the prosecution would have to be done over. It would be a curious outcome to the efforts of an attorney to free men charged with crimes which the unions condemn, but it would not be the first instance of a miscarriage of the purposes of organized labor."

and that for the good of the community the graft cases should be dropped.[269]

The evident policy of the defense was to undermine the prosecution and create public opinion against it, until both prosecution and community should be worn out, and made to quit.

The principal attack was through the newspapers. The prosecution had not been long at work before the weekly papers, with few exceptions, were devoting the bulk of their space to ridiculing and vilifying all who were in any way responsible for the graft exposures and impuning their motives.

What these publications received for their work is indicated by the subsidies paid one of the least of San Francisco weekly papers—a publication since suspended —the Mission Times.

In January, 1907, a man by the name of Williams purchased the Times for seventy-five dollars, giving his unsecured note for that amount. In less than a month the new proprietor had received $500 from an agent of the United Railroads. Later on, he received a regular subsidy of $250 a week, something more than $1,000 a month, which continued for thirteen weeks. The subsidy was later reduced to fifty dollars a week. But during the interim between the weekly subsidy contracts, lump sums were paid. It is estimated that in little over a year, Williams received from agents of the United Railroads upwards of $7,000. The Times at first covertly, and later openly, opposed the prosecution. If the unimportant Mission Times, which at the open-

---

[269] Some went so far when examined for jury service at the later graft trials as to say they would not vote to convict.

ing of the year 1907 had changed hands for seventy-five dollars, received upwards of $7,000 from agents of the defense, the not unreasonable question may be asked, what did more important weekly papers, whose graft prosecution policy was practically the same as that of the Times, receive? In this connection it is pertinent to say that the majority of these publications gave evidence during 1907, of a prosperity that was quite as mysterious, if not as suggestive, as had been the prosperity of the Schmitz-Ruef Supervisors during 1906.

As has been seen, the entire daily press of San Francisco was, in the beginning, heartily in accord with the prosecution. Gradually, however, The Examiner and The Chronicle [270] shifted their policy. Even while The Chronicle was backing the prosecution in its editorial columns, its reports of the proceedings at the various

---

270 The graft investigation uncovered something of the curious ethics governing this sort of publicity. For example, Mark L. Gerstle of the law firm of Thomas, Gerstle and Frick, who acted as attorneys for the Home Telephone Company, testified before the Grand Jury that the company paid the San Francisco Chronicle $10,000 to educate the people to the idea of a competing telephone system. The testimony was as follows:

"Q. During that time in 1905, were any newspapers paid to help the good cause? A. Yes.

"Q. What papers? A. Only one.

"Q. What paper was that? A. Chronicle.

"Q. How much was paid to it? A. $10,000.

"Q. What were the terms of that employment? A. The object of paying that money was to educate the people to the idea of a competitive telephone system. There seemed to be a prejudice among everybody, or a great many people, as to the value or necessity of another telephone system, and we could not obtain the assistance of any newspaper in that work without paying for it. Some required it in the shape of advertising which we did not need—don't do any good—others wouldn't take it in that way; the Chronicle wouldn't take it that way and we were forced in order to have some newspaper assist us in that work, to pay the price which was $10,000.

"Q. Did they give editorial work for that? A. No. They were supposed when the matters came up before the Board of Supervisors to write it up favorably, that is to say, talk about the advantage of a competitive telephone system in the way of keeping out a monopoly, and doing away with the poor system of the Pacific States."

hearings were colored in a way well-calculated to undermine Langdon and his associates.[271]   Gradually the covert opposition of its news columns became the open editorial policy of the paper.

But the most effective opposition came from The Examiner.   The Examiner supported the prosecution until the conviction of Schmitz and the change in the municipal administration.   Failure to dictate the selection of Mayor and Supervisors may have had more or less influence in the change of policy.   At any rate, the invention of The Examiner's writers and artists was tortured to make the prosecution appear to disadvantage.

The most tawdrily clever of The Examiner's efforts were the so-called "Mutt cartoons."   The cartoons appeared from day to day, a continuous burlesque of the work of the prosecutors, and of the graft trials.

Heney was pictured as "Beaney;" Detective Burns, as Detective "Tobasco;" James D. Phelan as "J. Tired Feeling;" Rudolph Spreckels, as "Pickles;" Superior Judges Dunne and Lawlor, before whom the graft cases were heard, as Judge "Finished" and Judge "Crawler," respectively.   In these "Mutt cartoons" every

---

271 The Chronicle's reports of the work of the Graft Prosecution are models of the journalism which strikes in the dark.   When, for example, the defense called Rudolph Spreckels to the stand in its efforts to disqualify the Grand Jury, The Chronicle, while in its editorial columns condemning such proceedings, reported the incident in its news columns as follows:

"Spreckels, who had been keeping in the background, came forward, glancing furtively at Heney, whose lips were moving nervously."   In the column from which this quotation is taken, Heney is represented as replying "nervously" to charges made by attorneys for the defense, and Spreckels, when a question was put to him as looking "appealingly" to the attorney representing the prosecution.   But observers of the proceedings recall no perceptible nervousness on Heney's part, nor "furtive" nor "appealing" glances from Spreckels.

phase of the prosecution was ridiculed. For example, when the excitement over the graft trials was at its height, there were rumors that the assassination of Heney or Langdon would be attempted. In ridiculing this, The Examiner pictured "Beaney" with a cross on his neck where the bullet was to strike. A few weeks later, during the progress of one of the graft trials, Heney was shot down in open court, the bullet taking practically the same course which in the "Mutt" cartoon The Examiner had pictured. After the shooting of Heney, The Examiner discontinued the anti-prosecution "Mutt cartoons."

Mr. William Randolph Hearst's San Francisco Examiner did effective service in discrediting the graft prosecution. But Mr. Hearst, with curious inconsistency, outside California, gave the prosecution his personal endorsement.

In his Labor Day address at the Jamestown Exposition, September 3, 1907, for example, Mr. Hearst among other pleasing observations on the work of the San Francisco Graft Prosecution, said: "You hear much today of how a Mayor of San Francisco has fallen, but you hear little of how powerful public service corporations tempted a wretched human being with great wealth and brought a once respected man to ruin and disgrace. You hear much of how a Mayor elected on a Union Labor ticket is in jail, but little of the fact that it was an honest District Attorney, elected on the same Union Labor ticket, who put him there, an honest District Attorney, who is doing his best to put beside the Mayor the men really responsible for all this debauchery and dishonor. While it is the fashion to criticise

San Francisco just now, I venture to assert that the
only difference between San Francisco and some other
cities is that San Francisco is punishing her corruptionists. There is many an official elsewhere who has
stolen office or dealt in public properties who would fare
like Schmitz if there were more honest and fearless
District Attorneys like Union Labor Langdon."

Later on, after Ruef had been sent to the penitentiary, an article on the San Francisco Graft Prosecution appeared in one of Mr. Hearst's magazines.[272] The
article was printed under the signature of Mr. Edward
H. Hamilton, one of the ablest of Mr. Hearst's employees. Mr. Hamilton gave the credit for the work
of the graft prosecution to Mr. Hearst and The Examiner. The men whose steadfastness of purposes and
high integrity had made even approach to the prosecution of influential offenders possible, upon whom Mr.
Hearst's Examiner had poured ridicule and abuse, were
more or less favorably mentioned in the article, but Mr.
Hearst was given the bulk of the credit for what the
prosecution had accomplished. In California, where
The Examiner's treatment of the prosecution was well
known, Mr. Hamilton's article was received with some
amusement and not a little resentment.[273]

---

272 The Cosmopolitan, issue of July, 1911.

273 The Sacramento Bee, in an editorial article, "Laureling the
Brow of a Harlequin 'Reformer'," said of Mr. Hamilton's claims for
Hearst:
    "The San Francisco Examiner is advertising an article by Ed-
ward H. Hamilton in the July Cosmopolitan—an article which is a
tissue of the most shameless misrepresentations from beginning to
end—an article which falsely and most mendaciously credits the
conviction and imprisonment of Abraham Ruef to William Randolph
Hearst.
    "The Cosmopolitan is a Hearst magazine; Hamilton, a Hearst
writer. Undoubtedly in New York many will believe Hamilton has
written the truth. Every man in California knows otherwise.
    "It is strange that a writer with the ability and the reputation

Although, with few exceptions, the policy of the San Francisco press was adverse to the prosecution, the principal interior papers gave Langdon and his associates loyal support. But eventually a chain of papers covering the greater part of the interior of northern and central California was enlisted on the side of the de-

---

of Edward H. Hamilton would for any consideration write an article so brazenly false that one marvels at the audacity alike of the eulogist and the laureled.

"For Hearst had no more to do with the fate of Ruef than Ruef's own lawyers. He labored on the same side—to make the graft prosecution so unpopular that no conviction of the guilty could result. Day in and day out the Examiner reeked with slanders aimed at the men who were endeavoring to place Ruef behind the bars.

"Day in and day out, the most malicious cartoons were published against Spreckels, Heney, Phelan, Burns and all who were battling for the punishment of public and semi-public scoundrels. Day in and day out in the Examiner Judge Wm. P. Lawlor was referred to as 'Crawler.'

"Day in and day out the reports of the trials were so colored, so exaggerated in favor of the defense and so emasculated when the prosecution scored a point, that the Examiner was ranked with the gutter weeklies as a friend, champion and defender of the indicted, and a most venomous traitor to good government and to public honor.

"The Examiner knew the feeling against it in San Francisco. For, when Heney was shot and there was danger of mob violence, the editorial rooms of the Examiner were barricaded and the Examiner men were supplied with rifles.

"And their fears were to a certain extent justified. One of the vilest cartoons against Heney pictured 'Beany' in danger of his life from imaginary assassins. On 'Beany's' neck was a mark to show where the bullet was to strike. By an extraordinary coincidence, the bullet that struck Heney down at the Ruef trial found almost the identical spot that a few days before had been marked on 'Beany's' neck in Hearst's humorous cartoon.

"On the night of the day that Heney was shot, indignant San Francisco in an immense mass meeting thundered its denunciation of Hearst and the Examiner. And graft-prosecution leaders found it necessary to plead with an inflamed populace to attempt no violence.

"No more 'Beany' cartoons made their appearance. The Examiner wrote of all connected with the graft prosecution in terms of respect. But this repentance born of fear did not prevent Californians by the thousands stopping the Examiner.

"The Cosmopolitan eulogy of Hearst in the graft-prosecution matter is a long line of known misstatements from beginning to end.

"It is humiliating to have to record that a man of Ned Hamilton's talents could so debase them as to present in the light of a militant Paul of the graft prosecution one who was its most contemptible Judas Iscariot.

"Regrettable indeed is it that
"Poor Ned 'must torture his invention
To flatter rogues or lose his pension.' "

fense. The papers were started or purchased by a news-paper publishing company known as the Calkins Syndicate.

The Calkins people had for several years been identified with a number of unimportant papers, printed in the interior. Suddenly, from publishing obscure weeklies and dailies, the Calkins Syndicate became one of the most important, if not the most important, publishing concern in California. A modern printing plant, one of the finest on the Pacific Coast, was installed at San Francisco. The establishment took over much of the printing of the Southern Pacific Railroad Company, including the printing of the railroad corporation's monthly, The Sunset Magazine. The Sacramento Union, the most important California morning newspaper printed north of San Francisco, and the Fresno Herald, an afternoon daily, were purchased outright. A bid was made for the San Francisco Post,[274] but terms could not be made. The Calkins people accordingly started the San Francisco Globe, an afternoon daily newspaper. Less important papers were established at various points. In an incredibly short period, the Calkins Syndicate had a chain of newspapers covering the greater part of northern and central California.

The distinctive feature of these publications was their opposition to the San Francisco graft prosecution. But the abuse of the Calkins newspapers was not so cleverly presented as in the Examiner, nor so adroitly handled as in the Chronicle. So violent were the Calkins papers'

---

[274] After the failure of the Calkins syndicate its successors to the ownership of "The Globe," purchased the Post and combined the two in one publication under the name of Post-Globe. The policy of the paper was not changed.

attacks, in fact, that they injured rather than assisted the defendants' cause. This was generally recognized. The Calkins Syndicate, after losing whatever effectiveness it may have had, eventually went into bankruptcy.[275]

---

[275] The astonishing business conditions under which the Calkins Syndicate was conducted were brought out during the proceedings in bankruptcy. For example: The Union Trust Company, closely connected financially with the Southern Pacific Company, and the United Railroads, advanced the syndicate $175,000.

To secure this loan, the Syndicate gave the Union Trust Company as collateral 1251 shares of the 2500 shares of the capital stock of the Sacramento Publishing Company, 150,100 shares of the 300,000 shares of the capital stock of the Calkins Publishing House, the majority of the capital stock of the Fresno Publishing Company, which published the Fresno "Herald" and bonds of the company publishing the San Francisco "Globe," valued at $30,000.

This loan remained unpaid at the time of the Syndicate's failure. The stock of the Fresno Publishing Company sold under the hammer for $4,850. The 1251 shares of the Sacramento Publishing Company were estimated to be worth $51,000. The stock of the Calkins Publishing House was of doubtful value. The Union Trust Company, before the failure, released the Globe bonds without payment of the note or consideration of other security. This left the stock of the Sacramento Publishing Company, valued at perhaps $51,000, as sure security for the $175,000 loan.

But this stock was curiously involved. The entire stock of the company consisted of 2500 shares of a par value of $100 a share. The corporation's property consisted of the Sacramento Union newspaper and the real property where the paper was published.

Soon after purchasing the Sacramento stock, the Calkins Syndicate organized a second Sacramento Publishing Company. The first company—that of the 2500 shares—was organized as The Sacramento Publishing Company. The Calkins people in organizing the second company dropped the "The," calling it "Sacramento Publishing Company." The second company was organized with a capital stock of 300,000 shares,—175,000 shares common stock and 125,000 shares preferred.

The Syndicate took 100,000 shares of this preferred stock to the London, Paris and American Bank, and used it with certain stock of the Nevada County Publishing Company, another Calkins concern, as collateral to secure a loan of $30,000. Of the 25,000 (preferred) shares remaining, the Calkins people sold 10,000 shares for money. The 15,000 shares remaining, Mr. Willard P. Calkins, head of the Calkins Syndicate, took to compensate him for his peculiar labors in the transaction. This disposed of the 125,000 shares of preferred stock in the second company.

The 175,000 shares of common stock still remained to be disposed of. Mr. Calkins, as president of the Calkins Syndicate, wanting more money, took the 175,000 shares to the London, Paris and American Bank, and pledged them as part collateral for a second loan. He did more—he pledged the "Union's" Associated Press franchise as further security for this second loan.

Eventually, the second loan was paid off, but the London, Paris and American Bank continued to hold the 175,000 shares of common stock and the Associated Press franchise, under an alleged collateral agreement, as further security for the first loan of $30,000. The first loan was eventually reduced to $16,085.02. When the

Almost as effective as the newspaper publicity against the prosecution, was the opposition of fashionable social circles and of the clubs. The graft defendants became much in evidence at the best clubs in the city. To be sure, their persistent appearance all but disrupted some of the clubs, members in sympathy with the enforcement of the law openly objecting to their presence.[276]

crash came, two Sacramento Publishing Companies, one with a "The" and one without a "The," claimed ownership of the Sacramento "Union." A majority of the stock of the first company was pledged to the Union Trust Company as part collateral for a loan of $175,000; 175,000 shares of the common stock of the second company and 100,000 shares of its preferred stock, together with the paper's Associated Press franchise, were in the hands of the successor of the London, Paris and American Bank, the Anglo & London, Paris National Bank, to secure a balance of $16,085.02 due on an original loan of $30,000.

But there were further complications. The first Sacramento Publishing Company, the directors and officers of which were the directors and officers of the second company, transferred the corporation's office building to the second corporation. The second corporation thereupon mortgaged this real estate to the People's Bank of Sacramento to secure a second loan of $20,000.

When Mr. I. W. Hellman, Jr., manager of the Union Trust Company—also one of the prominent managers of the Hellman movement in local politics—was on the witness stand, at the time of the Calkins investigation, he was asked to whom he looked for the payment of the $175,000.

"To the Calkins Syndicate," replied Mr. Hellman.

276 The presence of President Calhoun at an Olympic Club dinner in July, 1907, met with strong objection. Calhoun was not a member of the club. He had, it was charged, been brought there by one of the employees of the Southern Pacific Company, who was a member. His appearance led to open protest. It was finally arranged that objection should not be made to him, on condition that he would not attempt to make an address. But the defense claque had evidently planned otherwise. A demonstration was started for Calhoun. He began a speech which brought members to their feet in protest.

"I object," said Dr. Charles A. Clinton, one of the oldest members of the club, "to the presence here of Mr. Calhoun and I protest against his making a speech on the ground that the gentleman has been indicted by the Grand Jury for a most heinous offense; that he has been charged with bribing and debauching public officials, and should not be a guest of the club until he can come with clean hands. I do not pass upon this man's innocence or guilt, but feel that until his hands are clean he should not come to the club."

The outcome was that, by action of the Board of Directors, Dr. Clinton was expelled from the club. The course was generally denounced. "The Olympic Club of San Francisco," said the Sacramento Bee, "has shamed itself in the eyes of every decent, honest, manly, self-respecting citizen in this State by its recent act, through its Board of Directors, in expelling Dr. Charles A. Clinton

The Real Fight Begins 259

But in the end, the defendants prevailed and were loudly apparent at the principal clubs of the city even while under the inconvenience of indictment.

San Francisco's so-called fashionable society was, during the graft trials, practically organized as an adjunct of the defense. Those in accord with the prosecution were cut off visiting lists. Some of the non-resident indicted ones brought their families to San Francisco. Their wives and daughters at once became prominent in social matters. It was the refinement of the custom of bringing in "the wife and innocent children" of the defendant at a criminal trial.

This character of defense was most effective. The

---

from membership. The offense of Dr. Clinton was merely that he protested, as every other honorable member of the Olympic Club should have protested, not so much against the plotted appearance in that club at a banquet, of Patrick Calhoun, indicted for high crimes, as against the subsequent effort on the part of some members of the Olympic Club to force Calhoun to make a speech and become the hero of the affair."

When the American battleship fleet visited San Francisco in 1908, much opposition developed over the efforts of upholders of the defense to have Calhoun invited to the banquet given in honor of the visitors. Calhoun's representatives finally overcame the resistance, and Calhoun was invited.

Calhoun's social and other activities during this period resulted in much newspaper discussion. "The action of Patrick Calhoun," said the Examiner, "in appointing himself, Thornwell Mullally and William Abbott, all under indictment on bribery charges, as delegates to the Industrial Peace Conference caused such indignation and protest on the part of the other delegates that a committee on arrangements last evening demanded that Calhoun withdraw the names of himself and his two subordinates and substitute others." Mrs. Eleanor Martin gave a dinner in honor of Congressman and Mrs. Nicholas Longworth on the occasion of the visit of President Roosevelt's daughter to San Francisco. Mrs. Martin ranked as highest of San Francisco's so-called social leaders. The alleged fact that neither Calhoun nor Mullally was present on that important occasion was made subject of much curious newspaper comment. The "social side" of the graft defense not infrequently furnished saving comedy for an overstrained situation. It was, however, most effective in breaking down the prosecution. "Socially" the defense had decidedly the better of the situation. Calhoun, for example, became a member of the Olympic Club. There was a deal of newspaper protest at the club's action in admitting him, and defense of the club and other comedy. But Calhoun wore the "winged O" emblem of the Olympic Club on his automobile, nevertheless.

charming entertainment of those wives and daughters of indicted magnates who engaged in the social publicity campaign in the interests of their troubled male relations, went far toward building up public opinion against their prosecutors. The supporters of the prosecutors were treated with scant ceremony. To be a supporter of the prosecution was not regarded as "good form." All in all, the social side was one of the cleverest and most effective features of the publicity campaign carried on by the graft defense.[277]

The boycott of those in sympathy with the prosecution extended to the larger business world as well as to exclusive social circles. When, for example, the American battleship fleet visited San Francisco on its tour around the world in 1908, the committee appointed by the Mayor to arrange fitting reception and entertainment of its visitors, organized by making James D. Phelan, prominently associated with Mr. Spreckels in the Graft Prosecution, chairman.

That Mr. Phelan should be made head of the committee, or even identified with it, gave serious offense to the large business and financial interests that did not approve the prosecution.[278]   The large interests thus

277 One of the most amusing experiences which the writer had during this period was in listening to a woman, prominent in Episcopalian Church affairs, as she voiced her indignation because of a slight put upon her at an important social event of her church, at which daughters of one of the graft defendants had place in the receiving line.

278 Some of the letters of refusal to contribute are of curious interest.   For example, Timothy Hopkins, a capitalist of large affairs, wrote curtly: "Yours of the 4th in reference to contributions for the entertainment of the United States Fleet has been received. I am not contributing. Yours truly,   TIMOTHY HOPKINS."

E. E. Calvin, for the Southern Pacific, wrote "that under present conditions we cannot afford to contribute money to any purpose other than charity or a pressing public necessity."

A. H. Payson, for the Santa Fe, wrote that under his instructions he "was not able to make a subscription for this purpose in behalf of the Atchison Company."

offended refused to contribute to the reception fund. William C. Ralston, United States Sub-Treasurer at San Francisco, and treasurer of the Fleet Reception Committee, reported to the committee that several large banks and public service corporations would not contribute to the reception of the fleet unless Mr. Phelan left the reception committee.[279]

The committee, refusing to submit to this arrogant dictation, accordingly proceeded to the entertainment of the fleet without assistance from the anti-prosecution financiers and institutions. The smaller merchants, assisted by those banks and enterprises which had not been offended by the proceedings against the corrupters of the municipal government, contributed upwards of $75,000. The reception to the fleet was thus carried to successful conclusion without the assistance of the graft defense element.

---

[279] Mr. Ralston, in an interview printed in the San Francisco Examiner, September 26, 1908, said of this incident:

"The true facts of the case are that when P. N. Lilienthal and myself called on many of the banks and all of the public utility corporations they came out boldly and stated that they would not give one dollar while Phelan was Chairman of the Executive Committee, or connected with the reception of the fleet.

"Some of the banks that refused are the Crocker National Bank and the Wells-Fargo National. Some of the other banks only gave $100 when they would have given much larger amounts. They disliked Phelan. Among the corporations were the Telephone Company, the Spring Valley Water Company, and the Gas and Electric Light Company. The Southern Pacific and Santa Fe refused to subscribe and it is presumed their reasons were the same as the other corporations.

"When I learned the true situation," Mr. Ralston went on, as he widened the mouth of the bag for the certain escape of the cat, "I went before the Executive Committee, at a meeting at which Mr. Phelan was present, and guaranteed the sum of $25,000 more if Mr. Phelan resign or step out. I even went further and said that besides guaranteeing $25,000, I felt assured that the sum of $50,000 could be easily collected if Mr. Phelan would drop out. This Mr. Phelan refused to do. These matters all came up in executive meetings."

In this connection it is interesting to note that at the 1914 election in California, Mr. Phelan was elected to represent the State in the United States Senate, while Mr. Ralston was defeated at the Republican primaries for nomination for Governor.

In the work of undermining the prosecution, the humbler circles of municipal life were not neglected. The claquer in labor union, and wherever groups of laboring men and women met, was quite as active as his prototype at club and exclusive function. In labor circles the prosecution was described as a movement to discredit labor and to disrupt the unions. Here, Rudolph Spreckels was described as the unrelenting foe of labor organizations. At club and function, on the other hand, the prosecution was condemned as agent of "labor organization and anarchy," and Mr. Spreckels denounced as a man who had "gone back on his class." In all quarters stories were circulated, questioning Spreckels' motives. The most persistent charge against him was that he had started a street-car system of his own, and had instituted the graft prosecution to drive the United Railroads out of business. This story was told and retold, although the purposes for which Mr. Spreckels had contemplated engaging in the street-car business were well known.[280] It was quite as well known, too, that the briberies alleged against officials of the United Railroads were committed long after the graft prosecution had been inaugurated.

Heney [281] was also made target for criticisms. His

---

[280] See Chapter III.

[281] President Calhoun's denunciation of Heney was scarcely consistent with the high regard in which Heney was at the opening of the prosecution, held by the United Railroads' executives So well did they think of Heney that they selected him to sit on the Board of Arbitration which met late in 1906 to adjust differences between the United Railroads and its employees. This fact was given by Acting Mayor Gallagher as one of the reasons for removing Langdon from office, in October, 1906, when the Graft Prosecution opened. Specification 7 of Gallagher's order removing Langdon because of the appointment of Heney reads: "Specification 7, That said Francis J. Heney at and prior to the time of his appointment as assistant district attorney was the representative of the corporation controlling the street-car system of said city and county (The United

whole life was gone over in the search for flaws. It was discovered that in self-defense he had, years before, shot a man in Arizona.[282] This was made basis of a charge that Heney had committed murder. The new version of the Arizona incident was fairly shouted from San Francisco housetops.

Heney was denounced as a "special prosecutor, a human bloodhound, engaged in hounding of men to the penitentiary." It was charged against him that he had received excessive fees from corporations; that he had accepted fees from the Federal government while acting as deputy to the San Francisco District Attorney, and that therefore his San Francisco employment was illegal;[283] that he had been a drunkard.

Railroads), in a certain dispute between said corporation and its employees. That the appointment of said Heney to said office will, in regard to the enforcement of law against said corporation, be prejudicial and detrimental to the interests of said city and county."

Heney resigned his position as arbitrator in the United Railroads controversy soon after the prosecution opened.

[282] The graft defendants sent men to Arizona to have Heney indicted, charging murder of a Dr. Handy. Years before, Heney had taken the case of Handy's wife in divorce proceedings, after other attorneys had declined it because of fear of Handy. Handy had boasted that he would kill the man who took his wife's case. After Heney had agreed to represent Mrs. Handy, Handy announced that he would kill Heney with Heney's own gun. He actually attempted this, and Heney, in self-defense, shot him. Heney was exonerated at the time. When the graft trials opened, first representatives of Ruef, and then representatives of the United Railroads went to Arizona for the purpose of working up this case against Heney, and if possible secure his indictment for murder. Ruef's representatives even went so far as to attempt to secure the services of Handy's son to get Heney indicted. Young Handy went to Heney, told him what was going on, and offered to go to Arizona to protect Heney. But Heney declined to permit this sacrifice. Young Handy expressed gratitude for what Heney had done for his mother. Heney's brother, Ben Heney, with full knowledge of what was going on, watched the efforts of those who were endeavoring to make this case, long since disposed of, a matter of embarrassment to the prosecutor. As the graft defense investigators found nothing upon which to base a charge, this move against the graft prosecution failed.

[283] Dean John H. Wigmore of the Northwestern School of Law at Chicago, author of Wigmore on Evidence, made sharp reply to

A most effective attack consisted in charging connection of the graft prosecution with the California Safe Deposit and Trust Company.

This institution closed its doors during the 1907 panic. It had carried an enormous volume of deposits. Thousands of homes were affected. The California Safe Deposit and Trust Company was, as a result, very unpopular. Stories were circulated that the company had backed the prosecution, and had contributed funds for its work. J. Dalzell Brown, one of the leading spirits of the company, was also described as one of

---

this contention. In a letter to President Calhoun, dated August 10, 1909. Dean Wigmore said:

"Chicago, 87 Lake Street, 10 August, 1909.
"Mr. Patrick Calhoun, San Francisco.
"Sir:—Recently there arrived in my hands by mail, with no sender's address, a pamphlet of ninety pages, entitled 'Some Facts Regarding Francis J. Heney.' On page 12 your name appears as a printed signature. I am assuming that you caused the contents to be prepared and mailed.

"The pamphlet contains assertions reflecting on the conduct of Francis J. Heney and the Federal Department of Justice, in taking part in the prosecution of a criminal charge of bribery in the State Court of California against yourself. The pamphlet contains no defense of yourself; it does not even mention your name, except as its signer and in the title of exhibits; much less does it allege or attempt to show your innocence. It merely asks an answer to 'three important constitutional and moral questions' affecting Mr. Heney and the Department of Justice.

"Before answering those questions, let me say that this does not appear to be the method of an innocent man. The public press has made notorious the charge against you and its prosecution by Mr. Heney. Thoughtful citizens everywhere have discussed it. Many (not including myself) had assumed that you were guilty. You now appear to have spent a large sum to print and circulate widely a pamphlet concerning the case. Anyone would expect to find the pamphlet devoted to showing your innocence; and thus to removing unfavorable opinions based on casual press dispatches. An honest man, desiring to stand well with honest fellow-citizens, and possessing means to print, would naturally take that course. You do not. Your pamphlet merely attacks the technical authority of one of the attorneys for the prosecution, incidentally abusing two judges. This is not the course of an innocent man. It is the course of a guilty man who desires to divert the attention of the tribunal of public opinion. The tradition is here fulfilled of the attorney's instructions to the barrister acting for his guilty client, 'No case; abuse the opposing counsel.' I am compelled now to assume that you have no case, because all that your expensive

the prosecution's backers. It was shown at the Cal-

---

pamphlet does is to abuse one of the counsel for the prosecution. Until now I have supposed it proper to suspend judgment. I do so no longer.

"And what are your three 'constitutional and moral' questions, —since you have sent me a pamphlet asking an answer to them? I will answer them frankly.

"1. Was Mr. Heney's payment by the Department of Justice covertly for the California prosecution but nominally for other and Federal services?

"Answer: I do not know. But I and other honest citizens will presume in favor of the honesty, in this act, of a President, an Attorney-General, and an Assistant Attorney-General who proved in all other public acts that they were honest and courageous beyond example, especially as against a man like yourself who publishes a pamphlet based throughout on anonymous assertions.

"2. Can a Federal Assistant Attorney-General, under Federal salary, lawfully act at the same time as State Assistant District Attorney?

"Answer: As to this 'constitutional' question, I leave this to the courts, as you should. As to this 'moral' question, I say that it is moral for any Federal officer to help any State officer in the pursuit of crime, and that only guilty lawbreakers could be imagined to desire the contrary.

"3. Can a private citizen contribute money to help the State's prosecuting officers in the investigation and trial of a criminal charge?

"Answer: He can; and it is stupid even to put the question. Under the original English jury-system (of which you received the benefit) and until the last century, the private citizen was usually obliged to pay the prosecuting expenses; for the State did not, and crime went unpunished otherwise. If nowadays, in any community, crime is again likely to go unpunished without the help of private citizens, there is no reason why we should not revert to the old system. As for Mr. Spreckels (the private citizen here named by you), his name should be held in honor, and will ever be, as against anything your pamphlet can say. As for Mr. Heney and his receipt of $47,500 officially and 'large sums of money additionally' from Mr. Spreckels, it may be presumed that he spent most of it on trial expenses, and did not keep it as a personal reward. But even if he did so keep it, let me register the view that he is welcome to all this—and to more—if anybody will give it; that no money compensation is too high for such rare courage; that the moral courage displayed by him is as much entitled to high money compensation as the unprincipled commercial skill displayed by yourself—and this solely by the economic test of money value,—viz., demand and supply.

"Apart from this, the high sums said to have been paid by you to Abraham Ruef solely for his legal skill estop you from questioning the propriety of lesser sums said to have been paid to Francis J. Heney for his legal skill.

"Just twenty-five years ago I sat in an upper room on Kearny street, with five other young men, and helped to organize a Municipal Reform League. Two or three others, still living, will recall the occasion. Abraham Ruef was one of them.

"Fate separated all of us within a short time. Ruef went his own way,—the way we all know. It is the memory of those earlier days, in contrast with the recent course of events in my old home, that has interested me to give you these answers to the questions asked in the pamphlet you purport to have sent me.

"JOHN H. WIGMORE."

houn [284] trial that neither Brown nor his company had contributed a dollar toward the prosecution fund. Nevertheless, persistent reports that the prosecution had had this support, unquestionably had its effect upon the losing depositors. Hiram W. Johnson had acted as Brown's attorney. Johnson had appeared as assistant to the District Attorney at a number of the graft trials. Johnson was condemned for taking the case of a criminal guilty of the offenses charged against Brown. Mr. Johnson's critics did not, however, condemn the attorneys who had taken the cases of the alleged bribe-givers.

Another charge was that the prosecution was hurting business; that the material prosperity of California demanded that the proceedings be stopped; that capital would not seek investment in California until the disturbance caused by the prosecution had subsided.

Every move of the prosecution was made subject of criticism. Announcement, for example, that immunity had been given the Supervisors was received by the anti-prosecution press with a storm of protest, and used by the pro-defense claque most effectively.

The treatment accorded Ruef was subject of constant objection and criticism. During the period of Ruef's apparent co-operation with the prosecution, when he was in custody of the elisor, the pro-defense press harped on the uselessness of the expense of keeping Ruef in the luxury of a private jail.[285] The Chronicle

---

[284] See Rudolph Spreckels' testimony in The People, etc., vs. Patrick Calhoun.

[285] As early as April 20, 1907, the Chronicle began its objection to Ruef's confinement. The Chronicle on that date said, in an editorial article:

"It appears that it is costing the city about $70 a day to keep

even went so far as to say it would be well if Ruef
forfeited his bail, provided the bail were set high enough.
Ruef was, at the time, thought to be a willing witness
for the prosecution. That the case of The People
would be weakened were he to leave the State did not
seem to appeal to the Chronicle. Later on, when it
became evident that Ruef was not assisting the prosecution, there were outcries against the alleged cruel
treatment that had been imposed upon him during his
confinement in the custody of the elisor.

But this potent and far-reaching opposition did not
cause a moment's hesitation on the part of the prosecution. The work of bringing influential offenders before trial juries went steadily on. As soon as the

---

Ruef in jail. That expense should be shut off and shut off now.
There is no reason why Ruef should be treated differently from
any other criminal who jumped his bail. Incidentally the public is
getting impatient to hear that the $50,000 bail already forfeited has
been collected. If that were in the treasury we should be more
willing to incur this large expense. The public will very sharply
criticise authorities who incur such expense for the care of Ruef
without promptly collecting the forfeited bail or beginning suit for
it. Perhaps it has already been collected and the public has not
heard of it.

"The city has provided a jail and a jailer. Let him have Ruef.
Of course, he will 'connubiate' with him, but what of it? The
Sheriff will be under the direction of the Court and if, when otherwise ordered, he grants Ruef privileges not proper, he can himself
be put in jail, we suppose. We trust the trial judges will not be
discouraged in their efforts to enforce respect to their courts. They
will find the people behind them who are already sitting in critical
judgment on the legal refinements of the higher courts.

"We suppose that a criminal who has once jumped his bail may
be kept in jail when caught. But we see no use of it. By once
running away he has warranted the Court in fixing new bail at such
a rate that the public would gladly have it forfeited. We could
afford to pay something handsome to clear Ruef entirely out of the
country and into Honduras, and if we could extort from him a few
hundred thousand dollars for the privilege it would be the best trade
we ever made. But we do not believe he would run away if the bail
were made right. But if he is not to be bailed, let him go to jail,
where the total cost of his keep will not exceed 25 or 30 cents a day
or whatever it is. And if the Sheriff is not trustworthy—as, of
course, he is not—let Elisor Biggy have a key to a separate lock on
his dungeon. But there is no sense in spending $70 a day for the
keep of only one of our municipal reprobates."

Schmitz extortion case had been disposed of, Louis Glass of the Pacific States Telephone and Telegraph Company, the first of the indicted capitalists to face a jury, was brought to trial.

CHAPTER XIX.

The Glass Trials and Conviction.

On the day that Mayor Schmitz was sentenced to serve five years in the penitentiary for extortion, six jurors were secured to try Louis Glass, for bribery.

Mr. Glass had been indicted with T. V. Halsey for alleged bribery transactions growing out of the opposition of the Pacific States Telephone and Telegraph Company to competition in the San Francisco field. Mr. Halsey's business was to watch, and, so far as lay in his power, to block, such opposition telephone companies as might seek entrance into San Francisco.

Mr. Glass was Mr. Halsey's superior. To Glass, Halsey reported, and from Glass, Halsey took his orders. Eleven Supervisors had confessed that Halsey had paid them large sums to oppose the granting of a franchise to the Home Telephone Company. Testimony given before the Grand Jury had brought the source of the bribe money close to Halsey's superior, Glass.

Glass was indicted. The specific charge on which he was brought to trial was that he had given Supervisor Charles Boxton a bribe of $5000.

As in all the graft cases, there had been in Mr. Glass's defense technical attack upon the validity of the Grand Jury, demurrers, and other delaying moves. But point by point the prosecution had beaten down opposition, and by the time the Schmitz extortion case had been disposed of, District Attorney Langdon and his associates were able to proceed with the trial of Glass.[286]

The District Attorney's office was represented by Heney. D. M. Delmas and T. C. Coogan appeared for Mr. Glass.

There were none of the difficulties in securing the jury, as were experienced in the later graft trials. The Glass jury was sworn two days after the trial opened.

Dr. Boxton took the stand and testified, with a minutia of detail, how the bribe had been paid to him. Dr. Boxton was the first of the Supervisors to testify before trial jury and public, of his corruption. During the next year and a half San Francisco was to hear the story repeated time after time from the lips of sixteen men who had occupied the supervisorial office. But Boxton was the first. The spectacle of a man testifying that he had taken bribes and betrayed the city was new; it was astonishing, thrilling with sensation.

Boxton's position was emphasized by his elevation, on the day of the beginning of his testimony, to the mayoralty office. He was spared by neither prosecution nor defense. He was kept on the witness stand for hours. The prosecution treated him with coldness, making no attempt to palliate or excuse his conduct. The defense harassed him with subtle ridicule.

During the greater part of Boxton's examination,

---

[286] Glass's attorneys contended to the last moment that the trial judge had no jurisdiction to hear the case. After the District Attorney's opening statement had been made, but before the taking of testimony had begun, Mr. Delmas for the defense, stated that in the opinion of the counsel for the defendant the court had no jurisdiction to try the case on the ground that the Grand Jury which returned the purported indictment was an illegal body, having no power to sit as a grand jury at the time it returned the indictment.

the Board of Supervisors was in session. As Mayor of San Francisco, Boxton was supposed to preside over the Board. He was repeatedly dragged from presiding desk to witness stand, and hustled back from witness stand to presiding desk, the whole city watching every move.

"You were elected Mayor of this city?" inquired Delmas after one of the witness' shameful admissions.

"Through no fault of mine," replied Boxton wearily.

But in spite of the ridicule and the hammering, Boxton testified positively to receiving money from Halsey to influence him against casting his supervisorial vote to give the Home Telephone Company a franchise. That Halsey paid the money was not seriously disputed. The question raised by the defense was, did the bribe money necessarily come through Halsey's superior, Glass?

This question the prosecution attempted to meet. Halsey, it was shown, was employed under Glass in an inferior position and had neither authority nor power to use the corporation's funds without authorization.

Mr. Glass's position in the company was an important one. He had long been vice-president and general manager. After the death of John I. Sabin, president of the company, in October, 1905, Glass became acting president, a position which he held until Henry T. Scott assumed the duties of that office late in February, or early in March, 1906. The evidence went to show that at the time of the alleged bribery transactions, Glass was serving as general manager and acting president. Officials of the company testified that during Sabin's administration checks had been signed by "John I.

Sabin by Zimmer," or "E. J. Zimmer for the president," and countersigned by the treasurer. Zimmer was Sabin's confidential clerk.

During Mr. Glass's administration, after Mr. Sabin's death, up to the time that Mr. Scott took hold, the checks were signed by Mr. Glass, or Mr. Zimmer for Mr. Glass, bearing as well the treasurer's signature.

Zimmer had testified before the Grand Jury that at the direction of Mr. Glass, he had drawn large sums in currency from the banks, and given the money to Halsey. Halsey [287] gave no vouchers for this money which he received from Zimmer. The amounts were accounted .for at the company's office by tags in the cash drawer.

The testimony which Zimmer had given before the Grand Jury connected Glass directly with the large amounts which Halsey, without giving vouchers, had received from the telephone company's treasury at the time of the bribery transactions. The prosecution depended upon Zimmer's testimony to solidify their case. But when Zimmer was called to the stand, he refused to testify.

Zimmer based his refusal upon the ground that in his opinion the Grand Jury had indicted a number of gentlemen upon evidence which Mr. Zimmer regarded as insufficient, and that he would not, to protect his own interests, testify.[288]

---

[287] See Chapter XIV and footnotes 189 and 190, page 171.

[288] Mr. Zimmer's statement to the court was as follows: "As previously stated, the Grand Jury has heretofore charged and indicted a number of gentlemen on evidence which I have read, and which seems to be insufficient, for which reason I have taken this stand to protect my own interests; the stand I refer to is not to testify in the case which I had intended and not knowing my

The court instructed Mr. Zimmer that his position was untenable. The witness continued obdurate. The court sentenced him to serve five days in the county jail for contempt.

After his five-days' term had expired, Zimmer was again called to the stand, and again did he refuse to testify; again was he sentenced to serve in the county jail, this time for one day. Upon the expiration of this second sentence, Zimmer was for the third time called to the stand, for the third time refused to testify. For the third time was he adjudged guilty of contempt. His third sentence was to serve five days in the county jail and pay a fine of $500. Before he had served his time, the Glass trial had been concluded. Zimmer, therefore, escaped testifying against his associate, Glass. But for his refusal, he served eleven days in the county jail and paid a fine of $500. The maximum penalty for the crime of bribery alleged against Glass was fourteen years penal servitude. Mr. Zimmer thus served fewer days than Mr. Glass might have been sentenced to serve years had he been convicted. The testimony which Zimmer [289] gave before the Grand Jury, was not presented to the trial jury.

Nevertheless, the prosecution considered that it had made out a strong case, but Mr. Heney and his associates had reckoned without D. M. Delmas, Glass's chief counsel. The defense introduced no evidence, but

---

rights in the matter. I was sworn, though my intention was not to be sworn." Zimmer positively refused to place his declination on the ground that his testimony might tend to subject him to prosecution.

[289] Zimmer was later tried before a Justice of Peace for contempt, found guilty and sentenced to three months in the county jail. He appealed to the higher courts.

Delmas, in a masterful argument, raised the question of reasonable doubt. He insisted that Glass had not necessarily given the money to Halsey. He argued that several others of the officials of the company could have authorized the transaction. By an elaborate chain of reasoning, for example, Delmas insisted that if the money had been given Halsey at all, President Henry T. Scott [290] could have provided for it.

---

[290] Scott had been elected President before the alleged bribery transactions, but had left soon after for the East. The Prosecution held that Scott did not assume his duties as president until after his return from the East, when the alleged briberies had been completed. Delmas concluded his argument on Scott's possible responsibility as follows:

"And then you are called again further on in this same process of elimination. 'We expect to prove to you that Halsey had no power to expend moneys without a voucher, and that no person at that time in the Telephone Company had any power to expend money without the approval of the executive Board of Directors, except Glass, and Scott, who was away.' Scott had gone, we were told, on the 18th or 19th. These transactions took place on the 22d, 23d and 24th. Scott could not have authorized them from the simple fact that Scott was then in the East, and he was not here in San Francisco to direct or authorize the management of the affairs of this corporation. A true elimination, gentlemen, if the facts were true, but the facts are not true. Mr. Scott did not leave for the East—bear this in mind—Mr. Scott did not leave for the East until all these transactions were closed; he did not leave until the 27th of February when the last of these checks had been paid. Who drew it? Scott himself. I challenge contradiction. The Assistant District Attorney told you on the first day that he addressed you that Scott left on the 18th or 19th. Did he know that Scott did not leave until the 27th? Did he? If he did, then there are no words that would apply to the deception that was sought to be practiced upon you, and I do not charge any such deception. Had Mr. Scott informed the District Attorney that he left on the 18th or 19th? I do not know. There is no evidence before you that he had. How, then, did he get the idea which he made to you under the oath of his office as District Attorney that Scott left on the 18th or 19th, when in point of fact Scott did not leave until the 27th? He came back from Portland on Monday or Tuesday of the preceding week. He was here during the whole of these transactions; he remained until the last check had been paid. He remained until the ordinance had been passed on the 26th of February, and left the defeated camp on the next day. How, then, upon that evidence, is Scott eliminated from this transaction? And I do not want you to understand that I am charging Mr. Scott with crime. That is no part of my business. It is no part of my office. I am assuming, upon the theory of this prosecution, that a crime was committed, and I say you, yourselves, Mr. District Attorney and your attendants, have undertaken by the process of elimination which you have selected, to show us that Mr. Scott could not have committed this crime. It is sufficient for us to show you that he could without charging that he did."

The jury, after being out forty-seven hours, failed to agree. At the final ballot it stood seven for conviction and five for acquittal. That Delmas's argument had strong influence upon those who voted for acquittal was indicated by their published interviews. If these statements are to be credited, Glass escaped conviction because a number of the jurors held to the opinion that some telephone company official other than Glass could have authorized the passing of the bribe money.[291]

As soon as the prosecution could bring Glass to second trial, impaneling of the jury began.[292] Glass, at this second trial, was tried for the alleged bribery of

---

[291] The following are taken from interviews with the several jurors which appeared in the Examiner of July 29, 1907:

Juror Jacob Wertheimer—"I voted as I did (for acquittal) because there was a reasonable doubt in my mind as to whether or not Glass had authorized the giving of the money. There were too many others that might have been the ones."

Juror Charles P. Fonda—"I voted not guilty. It was simply a question of whether Glass paid over this money as charged. Five of us did not believe that the Prosecution produced sufficiently convincing evidence to find the defendant guilty."

Juror Michael C. Samuels—"The evidence did not link Glass up. So far as the bribery went, it might have been done by another official of the company than Glass."

Juror Hugo Schnessel—"There was always something lacking in the evidence to convince me beyond a reasonable doubt of the defendant's guilt. It seemed to me that possibly some one else other than Glass might have paid over the money."

[292] Of the delaying tactics in the Glass case, The San Francisco Call in its issue of August 14, 1907, said:

"Anything to delay trial and judgment is the policy of the accused bribe givers. Every day's proceedings in the retrial of Glass provides ample proof to convince the most skeptical citizen that the last thing desired by the men charged with debauching the boodle Board of Supervisors is prompt determination of the issues on their merits, and every pettifogging move for delay, every cunning attempt to betray the court into technical error is confession of a case too weak to be given to a fair jury on a plain showing of the facts. The attitude of the lawyers for Glass is sufficient to indicate that he needs lawyers of their peculiar expertness—'distinguished attorneys,' Heney calls them—'distinguished for their ability to defeat justice.'

"Judge Lawlor's unhesitating denial of a motion to permit the

Supervisor Lonergan. The trial was in many particulars a repetition of the first. Again, there was no seriout attempt to dispute that Halsey had paid Lonergan the bribe money. Zimmer again refused to testify against his superior, and was again committed for contempt. But the prosecution was careful at the second trial to show beyond the possibility of the question of a doubt that neither President Henry T. Scott, nor any other official of the Pacific States Telephone Company, other than Glass, could have authorized the payment of the bribe money.

By the minute books of the corporation, the prosecution showed that checks drawn by the corporation on San Francisco banks were to be signed "by the assistant treasurer or his deputy, and by the president, or his private secretary, E. J. Zimmer, for him, or by the general manager." As for Mr. Scott, the prosecution

lawyers for Glass to shift their ground in the midst of the impaneling of the jury and hark back to an attack on the validity of the indictments, and his sharp reprimand to Attorney Coogan for his method of misleading talesmen by adroitly framed questions, ought to expedite this trial. Lawlor has a reputation for dealing sternly with legal tricksters and for compelling counsel in the cases that he hears to get down to business and keep at it. At the same time his record on the bench is that of a just judge and always impartial. It is because he is impartial and stern that crooked lawyers, with crooked clients, deem it 'hard luck' when their cases are assigned to Lawlor.

"Now Judge Lawlor has a rare opportunity to prove anew his worth as a jurist. He will please a patient and long suffering public and will satisfy the ends of the justice which he administers when he makes the lawyers quit trifling and forces them to let the trial go on. We may expect to see the trial made as tedious and as costly in time and money as high priced counselors can arrange. It is all part of the game—tire out the public, the jury and the prosecution; delay is the safest course for the man accused against whom the people's case is strong. But we may also expect to see Judge Lawlor trimming the matter of technicalities and pressing it to a conclusion. It was because the people had come to expect such things from Judge Lawlor that they re-elected him, when all the machines of municipal corruption were grinding against him."

showed by the testimony of Assistant Treasurer Eaton [293] of the telephone company that the corporation did not notify the banks to honor President Scott's signature until February 27, which was after the alleged bribery of Supervisor Lonergan had been consummated.

The jury, after being out less than a half hour, brought in a verdict of guilty.

Pending his appeal to the Appellate Court, Glass was confined in the county jail.

Of the Pacific States Telephone bribing charges, those against T. V. Halsey remained to be disposed of.

Even while the second Glass trial was under way, Halsey's trial for the bribery of Supervisor Lonergan was begun. There had been the same delaying tactics to ward off appearance before a jury which had characterized the other graft cases. The impaneling of the trial jury was, however, finally undertaken. But the proceedings were suddenly brought to a close. Halsey, after eight jurors had been secured to try him, was stricken with appendicitis.

On this showing, his trial was postponed. Later on, Mr. Halsey was threatened with tuberculosis, which

---

[293] Eaton testified at the second Glass trial as follows: "Mr. Scott did not sign any checks between February 8, 1906, and the latter part of March, 1906, for the company; not to my knowledge. Notices were sent out by me to the different banks in regard to the signatures that could be accepted upon checks after Mr. Scott was elected president. They were sent on the 27th of February, 1906, to all the San Francisco banks that we had an account with."

Eaton testified further that the day the banks were notified, Mr. Scott went East. Mr. Scott could, Eaton said, previous to that date, have signed checks, but up to that time they would not have been honored at the banks. Halsey, in the Mills Building, gave the Supervisors, of whom Lonergan was one, their bribe money not later than February 26. Supervisor Lonergan testified that to the best of his recollection he had been paid by Halsey some time between February 14 and February 20.

further delayed proceedings against him.   Until after
the defeat of the Graft Prosecution in 1909, Mr. Halsey's health did not permit of his being tried.   His
trials under the new administration of the District Attorney's office, resulted in acquittals.

Mr. Halsey, in August, 1913, still survives both the
appendicitis attack and the threatened tuberculosis.

CHAPTER XX.

THE FORD TRIALS AND ACQUITTALS.

The conviction of Glass, following immediately upon the overthrow of the Schmitz-Ruef municipal administration, and coupled with the pitiful position in which, all recognized, Halsey would find himself before a jury, stirred the graft defense to astonishing activity. Although it developed later that the defendants had had their agents at work even before the bringing of indictments,[294] little was suspected of the extent of their labors until after the Glass trials. During the trials of General Tirey L. Ford, who followed Glass before trial jurors, however, the work of the defendants' agents and their methods became notorious. From the opening of the Ford trials, the representatives of the various graft defendants who congregated in the courtroom ranged in social and professional standing from the highest priced lawyers of the character of Alexander King, President Calhoun's law partner, down

---

[294] John Helms, a detective, testified at the trial of Patrick Calhoun that he had been employed by the United Railroads as early as May 3, 1907; that his duties consisted of "mostly shadow work, watching out for things being done by the prosecution"; that Patrick Calhoun had himself authorized him (Helms) to employ men to follow Burns on motorcycles. Later on automobiles were substituted for the motorcycles.

If Helms's employment began on May 3, as he testified, the United Railroads was preparing for its defense at least three weeks before indictments were brought against its officials. The extent of that corporation's defense, or the details of it, are not known to those outside the corporation. At the Calhoun trial the Prosecution accounted for every dollar spent in the operations against the Schmitz-Ruef regime. The attorneys representing the United Railroads were invited to make as frank statement of the expenditures made by the defense, but they declined.

through layers of the typical, criminal lawyer of the Earl Rogers-Porter Ashe [295] grade, to characters of the type of Harry Lorenstzen,[296] notoriously known throughout Central California as the "Banjo-Eyed Kid," and Dave Nagle, the gun-fighter, who numbered among his accomplishments the slaying of Judge Terry. Nor were the defending corporations alone represented. The Southern Pacific, although none of its officials were under indictment, had men at work in the interest of the defense.[297]

With such motley array of attorneys, detectives, gun-fighters and agents, District Attorney Langdon and his associates contended until, what was practically the ending of the graft prosecution, the defeat of Heney for District Attorney at the municipal election of 1909.

Ford had been indicted for his alleged part in the

[295] Ashe participated in the first Ford trials. At the time of the later trials he was involved in the scandal of the alleged kidnaping of Fremont Older.

[296] In referring to the men and women employed by the graft defense, The Call, in an editorial article, in its issue of September 26, said:

"The retinue of the trolley magnates, as exhibited in the Ford case, makes a remarkable picture. Behind the expert lawyers of last resort troops a motley train of gun fighters, professional plug-uglies, decoys, disreputable 'detectives,' thugs, women of the half world and the wolfish pack of gutter journalism. It must be, indeed, a hard case that needs such bolstering.

"How will Mr. Calhoun square with his protestations of high-mindedness the presence and the efforts in his behalf of such creatures of the slums and stews as 'Bogie' O'Donnell and 'The Banjo Eyed Kid'? Are these and the others of their kidney laboring in the same behalf as friends and sympathizers of Mr. Calhoun or merely as his hired men?"

[297] At the Ford trial, Supervisor Lonergan had testified that he had been followed during a recess of the court. The following testimony followed:

"Q. Was that Mr. Melrose, a detective of the Southern Pacific, who is sitting there? A. I don't know Mr. Melrose.

"Q. Is he the gentleman sitting immediately back of Mr. Ford? A. That is the gentleman; that is him.

"Q. He was following you around during the noon hour? A. Yes, sir.

"Q. Don't you know he is a detective of the Southern Pacific? A. I don't know anything about the gentleman."

bribery of the Supervisors by the United Railroads to secure its over-head trolley permit. At his first trial, Ford answered to the charge of bribing former Supervisor Lonergan. Lonergan had not been long on the stand before the defense demonstrated the astonishing effectiveness of the work of its agents.

Earl Rogers, for the defendant, on cross-examination, presented a paper signed by Lonergan within the month, in which Lonergan set forth that when he voted for the trolley permit he had not been promised, nor did he understand, there would be any monetary consideration allowed him—nor any other member of the board—for voting in favor of the measure.

Lonergan had testified on direct examination that some time prior to the granting of the permit, Supervisor Wilson had brought word to him there would be $8000 for him in the passing of the trolley ordinance. Later Wilson had told him that the amount would be $4000 only. This amount, Lonergan testified, Gallagher had paid him. Lonergan's statement, signed a few days before the opening of the trial, to the effect that when he voted to grant the United Railroads its trolley permit no monetary consideration had been promised him, came as a surprise to the prosecution.

The story of the manner in which the paper came to be in Rogers's possession, however, was quite as sensational as the statement itself. Lonergan, the driver of a bakery wagon, confronted by the keenest practitioners at the California bar, harassed and confused, stammered out explanation of the manner in which he had been induced to sign the paper in Rogers's hands.

Long before he had signed it, one Dorland had secured introduction to him. Dorland had represented
himself to be a magazine writer, who held that the
ousted Supervisors had been misused. Dorland stated
that his purpose was to set the Supervisors right in
the East. He represented that he was to prepare an
article on the San Francisco graft situation from an
independent, unbiased standpoint. Dorland made himself very agreeable to Lonergan. He took the unhappy
fellow to lunch. He gave him and members of his
family automobile trips and expensive dinners. Lonergan finally signed the statement which the agreeable
"magazine writer" was to use in his behalf, and with
which the graft defense [298] confronted him on the witness stand.

The statement which Lonergan had signed was a
rambling account of conditions in San Francisco, the
one pertinent paragraph touching upon the United
Railroads graft being buried in a multitude of words.

"And you intended to say to all the readers of the
magazine what you set forth over your signature
there?" demanded General Ford's attorney.

"Yes," replied Lonergan, weakly, "but when I made
that statement I was not under oath."

---

[298] The Call, in its issue of September 26, 1907, stated in explanation of how the graft defense had come by the statement Lonergan
had made to Dorland that: "After court adjourned (September 25)
Attorney Rogers offered an explanation for Walter Dorland, the man
who was charged by the prosecution with having attempted to kidnap Lonergan. Rogers's story differed from that told by Dorland.
Rogers stated that Dorland was not a detective, but was in charge
of a hospital in Chicago. He came to San Francisco, where he met
Luther Brown, an associate of Rogers. Brown and Dorland were
old friends and the former induced Dorland to get statements from
the Supervisors for him. Dorland did this. Rogers says he has
statements from all the Supervisors with the exception of Gallagher."

Then Lonergan was confronted with the affidavit which he had signed at the opening of the Graft Prosecution when Langdon was fighting against Ruef, Acting Mayor Gallagher and the Schmitz-Ruef Supervisors to keep himself in the office of District Attorney and Ruef out. In that affidavit Lonergan set forth that he had "never committed a felony of any kind or character," and had "never been a party thereto."[299]

"I didn't read that paper at the time I signed it," faltered the miserable witness. "I did not consider I was committing a crime when I signed that document."

"If it be a crime to have me sign that," he continued in answer to General Ford's attorney's merciless hammering, "then I must have (committed a felony)."

Then on re-direct examination Lonergan testified as to how he had come to sign the affidavit. George B. Keane, clerk of the Board of Supervisors, Ruef's right-hand man, secretary of the Sunday-night caucuses, had, Lonergan testified, said to him, "Tom, there is a document across the street there for you to go over and sign. All the boys are signing it." Lonergan testified that he had gone over and signed it. "I am almost sure," Lonergan continued, "that some of them said to

---

299 Heney states in an affidavit filed in the case of The People vs. Patrick Calhoun et als., No. 823, that he had been informed that the reason given by Ruef for securing the signatures of the Supervisors to this affidavit was to find out which, if any of them, had confessed, upon the theory that any one of them who had confessed would refuse to sign an affidavit, and upon the further theory that if such a confessing member did sign the affidavit, he would thus be making a contradictory statement under oath, which could thus be further used against him by Ruef or Gallagher, upon the trial of either of them.

But whatever Ruef's far-seeing motive, this affidavit which he, through Keane, induced the Supervisors to sign, was used by the attorneys for the defense at the graft trials to show contradictory statements of the confessing Supervisors.

me that it was a matter of form, merely eulogizing the board."

"When proper inducements or circumstances occur," sneered General Ford's attorney, "you will testify falsely concerning your offenses."

"I will not testify falsely on this stand," replied the unhappy witness, "to whatever has happened during my term as Supervisor."

But complicated as the position in which the prosecution found its principal witness, it might have been more complicated had all the plans of the agents for the defense been carried out.

On the night before Lonergan was to take the stand against Ford, Dorland, the alleged magazine writer, called him up by telephone and invited him "to make a night of it." Dorland stated two women would accompany them. Before accepting the invitation, Lonergan notified Detective Burns. Burns instructed him not to go on the trip, but to meet Dorland and to take Mrs. Lonergan with him. Lonergan, with his wife, accordingly met Dorland and the two women at the appointed place. Dorland expressed his chagrin when he found Lonergan not alone.

"He said," Lonergan testified, "he was sorry I was not alone; two nice young ladies were there."

Lonergan's testimony of Dorland's dismay when the detective found that Mrs. Lonergan accompanied her husband, was received with amusement. The one-time Supervisor went on no automobile ride that evening. Thus tamely ended what the prosecution insisted was a plot to kidnap, or at least compromise, Lonergan on the eve of his appearance as a witness against General Ford.[300]

Out of this attempt to involve Lonergan, grew the scarcely less astonishing kidnaping of Fremont Older, managing editor of the San Francisco Bulletin.

Among those alleged to have participated in the Lonergan affair was an employe of the graft defense by the name of Brown. The defense had at the time two employes of that name, "Luther" and "J. C.," the latter of whom is alleged to have been the one who cooperated with Dorland in his attempt upon Lonergan. The Bulletin, in its account of the affair, confounded Luther with J. C. Brown. Based on the Bulletin's allegations against Luther Brown, warrants were sworn out at Los Angeles, charging Managing Editor Older with criminal libel. The manner of serving these Los Angeles warrants was characteristic of the times.

Late in the afternoon of September 27, Older, while at Heney's office, received a telephone message that he was wanted at a prominent hotel. As he approached the hotel in response to the message, he was stopped by a number of men who claimed to be peace officers from Los Angeles. These displayed the warrant, and

---

[300] The San Francisco Call, in its issue of September 25, 1907, in commenting on Lonergan's testimony, says: "While Lonergan's narrative tells a portion of the story, it is not all. In another automobile were Detective Luther Brown and the 'Banjo-Eyed Kid' of the United Railroads. They followed close on the heels of the auto occupied by Detective Dorland. Both machines sped to a resort near the park, where a meeting place had been arranged and where Lonergan was to be turned over to the custody of the 'Banjo-Eyed Kid.' The rest was to be left to the Kid. If the plan had carried there would have been no Lonergan at the trial yesterday, the defense would have flashed the statement secured by Dorland and set up the cry that the entire prosecution of the United Railroads was a plot set on foot by Rudolph Spreckels."

hustled Older into an automobile. Older demanded that he be taken before a local court. His captors promised him he should be. But instead they headed the machine for Redwood City, a town some twenty miles south of San Francisco on the line of the Southern Pacific. When Older protested a revolver was pressed against his side, and he was ordered to keep silent.

At Redwood City, Older was put on board a Los Angeles train. On the train were R. Porter Ashe and Luther Brown. Older was not permitted to communicate with his friends nor with the passengers, but was confined in a stateroom which his captors had secured.[301]

In the meantime, the entire police force of San Francisco was scouring the city for the missing man. There had been rumors that those prominent in the prosecution, Older among them, were to be made away with. Older's unaccountable disappearance tended to confirm these rumors. His alarmed friends were prepared to act promptly when word finally reached them that Older was on the southbound train.

The train was due to reach Santa Barbara early the following morning. Arrangements were accordingly made to rescue Older at that point. When the train arrived there, deputy sheriffs were awaiting its arrival. Older was taken into court under habeas corpus proceedings. His release followed,[301] another sensation of the graft defense thereby coming to sorry ending.[302]

301 Several who participated in this affair were later indicted for kidnaping. There were no convictions.

302 Burns in an affidavit filed in the case of The People vs. Patrick Calhoun et als., 832, refers to a plot hatched about the time of the Ford trials to kidnap Ruef. Burns charges that Ruef was to

There were other surprises for the representatives of the prosecution at the Ford trials well calculated to confuse them. Alex. Latham, chauffeur for Ruef, whose testimony connected Ruef and Ford, during the period of the alleged bribery transactions was, when his name was called as a witness, found to be missing. He was alleged to be in Colorado.

George Starr, treasurer of the United Railroads, whose testimony was needed in the tracing of the exact amount of the bribe money paid Ruef in the overhead trolley deal, $200,000, that had been placed in Ford's hands under somewhat peculiar circumstances, went East about the date the trial opened. The United Railroads' cash book was sent East about the same time, and could not be produced at the trial.[303]

have been taken into a mountain county and held there until the United Railroads cases had been disposed of. He states his belief that Ruef was party to the plot.

303 The disinclination of the United Railroads to produce its books continues to cause that corporation inconvenience and trouble. In 1913, for example, the corporation applied to the California State Board of Railroad Commissioners for permission to issue promissory notes to the amount of $2,350,000. That the Commission might determine the necessity of such an issue, request was made for the corporation's books. This request was denied. The Commission withheld authorization of the note issue. In commenting upon its refusal, the Commission said:

"It should be understood that the conclusions hereinbefore set out have been reached on the partial information which has been submitted to the Commission, and that if an examination of the original books which the company has refused to supply should reveal a different condition, the responsibility for these conclusions, which we contend inevitably must be drawn from what evidence is before us, lies with the applicant because of its failure to submit its books for examination by the Commission.

"It is an axiom that evidence suppressed is deemed to be adverse, and having in mind this axiom certainly the Commission is justified in concluding that the books which the applicant refuses to produce at least would not better its showing."

Following the defeat of the graft prosecution in November, 1909, peculiar transactions are recorded against the United Railroads. For example, the Railroad Commission found, and has so reported, that "in the minutes (of the United Railroads) of May 25, 1910, it appears that four years' 'back salary' was voted to Patrick Calhoun, president of the United Railroads of San Francisco, in the

Then again, witnesses who had testified freely before the Grand Jury became forgetful. Supervisor Wilson, who had conveyed word to Lonergan from Gallagher that there would be $4000 in the trolley deal for Lonergan, could, when brought to the witness stand, remember nothing of the incident. Supervisor Coffey also proved equally forgetful.[304]

In the midst of these extraordinary happenings, General Ford's trial went on, marked by repeated attacks by attorneys for the defense upon those who had been instrumental in bringing about the Graft Prosecution. Rudolph Spreckels in particular, was made object of vicious denunciation. It was recognized from the beginning that the defense was battling not for General Ford alone, but for President Calhoun, and the other officials of the United Railroads under indictment.

The State's attorneys, target for constant abuse and ridicule at the hands of the defense, proceeded, however, to present the case of The People. In spite of sensations, the disappearance of witnesses and the forgetfulness of witnesses, the prosecution brought out testimony to show that the Supervisors had received $85,000 for their votes granting the trolley permit. By

sum of $75,000 a year, or a total of $300,000. No explanation is made of this item, but it at once suggests the necessity of a thorough investigation in order to determine the items claimed by applicant as operating expenses of the United Railroads over a series of years." See Decision No. 439, Railroad Commission of California, in the matter of the application of the United Railroads, etc., February 4, 1913.

304 Both Wilson and Coffey were indicted for bribe-taking. Wilson later on found his memory. At other graft trials he explained that his testimony at the first Ford trial had been given after he had undergone an operation that had involved the use of large quantities of cocaine. He insisted that he did not know to what he was testifying. Coffey was tried for bribe-taking and convicted. The Supreme Court, however, set aside the verdict on technicalities.

the testimony of officials of the United States Mint it was shown that Patrick Calhoun had, after the fire, but before the opening of the San Francisco banks, created a fund of $200,000 at the Mint.

None of the directors of the United Railroads who could be dragged to the stand knew anything about this $200,000. Other amounts, which the United Railroads, during the days of stress following the fire, had received at the Mint from the East, could be accounted for by the books and vouchers, but not this $200,000.[305] United Railroads employes who could be made to testify could throw no light upon its final disposition.

But the prosecution did show by the Mint officials that President Calhoun had ordered the $200,000 paid to General Ford and that it was paid to General Ford.

The following dates, brought out by the testimony, showed the receipt and suggested the disposition of the money:

May 21—Overhead trolley franchise granted by the Board of Supervisors.

---

[305] It was shown at the Ford trial that about $175,000 in addition to the unaccounted-for $200,000 was received by the United Railroads through the United States mint. Every dollar of this $175,-000 except $3,000 loaned to Ruef by Mullally, was taken out by the treasurer of the company, and carried to the United Railroads' office and there put in its safe and used as needed, that it was taken in gold and was paid out to its employees in gold. It was further shown that not one dollar of currency was ever put in any of the safes at the United Railroads' office by any person during that period of time covered by Ford's withdrawal of money from the mint, and that no currency was deposited to the credit of the company in any of its bank accounts nor to the credit of Ford or Mullally or Abbott, and that no currency was turned over to the treasurer of the company during that time. Thus by a process of exclusion this $200,000 was left in the hands of Ford absolutely unaccounted for upon any theory consistent with an honest use of it. Add these facts to the further facts that Ruef was traced to Ford's office on two of the days on which Ford got the money, and that Ruef on each occasion, within a day or two, paid the same kind of money to Gallagher, that currency was not generally in circulation at all in San Francisco.

May 22—$200,000 placed in the Mint to the credit of Patrick Calhoun.

May 25—General Ford drew $50,000 from the Mint which he exchanged for currency of small denominations.

July 31—General Ford drew $50,000 from the Mint, which he exchanged for currency.

August 1—The Supervisors received from Gallagher their first payment for voting to grant the overhead trolley permit. Gallagher testified that he had received the money from Ruef. The payments were in currency, the bills being of small denominations.

August 23—General Ford drew $100,000 from the Mint, which he exchanged for currency, receiving bills of large denominations.

August 24-30—The Supervisors received their final payments from Gallagher for their votes on the trolley permit. These last payments were made in bills of large denominations. Gallagher testified that he had received the money from Ruef.

The withdrawals from the Mint had been made by General Ford, on Mr. Calhoun's instructions to the Mint officials that the payments should be made to the General.

The testimony of the Mint officials and employes was to the point and at times sensational. Nathan Selig, a clerk at the Mint, for example, assisted Eugene D. Hawkins as assistant cashier,[306] in making up a pack-

---

[306] The two men were at the time detailed to handle the money of the relief fund. The mint officials could not accommodate Ford with the currency he wanted. They gave him gold. The gold which Ford secured at the mint was trucked across the hall to relief headquarters, where it was exchanged for the currency. Selig and Hawkins counted out the bills.

age of $50,000 in bills which were turned over to Ford. Selig fixed the time of the occurrence at "shortly after the Mayor signed the franchise bill for the overhead wire."

"What impressed that upon your mind?" was asked him. "Because I made the remark to Mr. Hawkins, as he was going out," replied Selig, "that that was—I though it was, the Supervisors' 'bit'."

Having traced this $200,000 from Calhoun to the Mint and from the Mint to Ford, the prosecution proved by Charles Hagerty, Ruef's office boy, that during the weeks after the fire General Ford and Mr. Mullally of the United Railroads, had had conference with Ruef at Ruef's office. Ruef was traced to Ford's office. Ford's stenographer testified, reluctantly, to Ruef's presence there. Ford was shown to have sent warning, through his assistant Abbott, to Ruef, at the opening of the graft investigation, that the Grand Jury was taking up the matter of the United Railroads trolley privilege, that the prosecution had not made any headway, that it was thought the next step would be to lay some trap for the Supervisors.[307] That Ruef and Ford had more or less intimate relations during this period was fully established.[308] The question raised was: Did the $85,-000 in currency which Ruef gave Gallagher to be paid to the Supervisors for their votes on the overhead trolley permit pass from Ford to Ruef? Did the money paid the Supervisors come out of the unaccounted-for

---

[307] See transcript of testimony, trial of The People vs. Tirey L. Ford, No. 817, taken September 25, 1907, page 270.

[308] Mr. Mullally, assistant to Mr. Calhoun, and also Mr. Calhoun were known to have enjoyed friendly relations with Mr. Ruef during this period.

$200,000 which had disappeared into General Ford's possession? [309]

A word from Abe Ruef would have lifted the case out of the plane of circumstantial to that of positive evidence.

A word from General Ford would have shown the manner in which the money had been disposed.

Those who took seriously Ruef's protestations at the time of his plea of guilty to extortion, that his life would thereafter be devoted to undoing the wrong he had wrought, looked to see the prosecution put Ruef on the stand.

The many supporters of General Ford—he was one of the most likable and popular men in the State— who still held belief in his innocence, looked to see him take the stand to clear his name by accounting for the disposition of that $200,000 which he had received, at the order of President Calhoun, from the Mint officials.

But neither Ruef nor Ford took the stand.

Later developments in the graft cases showed why the prosecution did not call upon Ruef to testify.

But no satisfactory showing has been made why General Ford did not take the stand to tell, under oath, of the disposition of that $200,000 last seen in his possession.

---

[309] The facts brought out at General Ford's trial are interesting in connection with General Ford's interview in the San Francisco Examiner of October 28, 1906, soon after the Graft Prosecution opened. See Footnote 92.

Ruef, in "The Road I Traveled," printed in the San Francisco Bulletin, states that he gave Schmitz $50,000 and kept $50,000 for himself out of the $200,000 which was given to him by Tirey L. Ford from Patrick Calhoun to pay for the granting of the trolley permit.

Heney, in an affidavit [310] acknowledged March 10, 1908, tells why Ruef was not called upon to testify.

Some ten days before the taking of testimony in the first Ford trial began, according to this affidavit, Heney had Gallagher and Ruef at his office. The two men had told stories of the passage of the ordinance granting the trolley permit, which conflicted slightly. Heney's purpose in confronting them, he tells us in the affidavit, was that he might determine in his own mind which was right. Heney had not seen Ruef, except as he had passed him in court or corridor, since he had proved that Ruef had made misrepresentations to him in the French Restaurant cases.[311] The conversation between Ruef and Gallagher did not tend to change Heney's opinion of the broken boss. Indeed, Heney became more firmly convinced than ever that Ruef was not acting in good faith, that he was not telling the whole truth. A few days after this meeting, Burns brought Heney word that Ruef would not testify at the Ford trial at all, unless the prosecution allowed him to withdraw his plea of guilty in the extortion case, and dismissed all the indictments against him. Heney refused to be coerced. He sent word back to Ruef that the prosecution had had sufficient evidence to convict Ford before Ruef had told anything; that if Ruef were called to the witness-stand it would be without further talk with him; that none of the cases against him would be dismissed, and that if called to the stand he could testify or not testify, as he saw fit.

---

310 This affidavit deals with the Graft Prosecution from its beginning down to the spring of 1908. This document was filed in the case of The People vs. Patrick Calhoun et als., No. 823.

311 See Chapter XVI, page 211, and footnote 119, page 111.

That night, according to Heney, Rabbis Nieto and Kaplan, with Ruef's attorney, Henry Ach,[312] appeared at Heney's office. Ach announced in substance, according to Heney's affidavit, that inasmuch as Heney and Langdon had promised to permit Ruef to withdraw his plea of guilty to the extortion charge, and then dismiss the case, as a condition upon which Ruef signed the immunity contract,[313] the time had arrived when, in justice to Ruef, this ought to be done.[314]

Heney let Ach finish.

"We might as well understand each other," Heney then announced. "You know perfectly well that I did not at any time make any such promise to Ruef or to you, or to any one present, or to any one else on earth."

Heney then recited the exact terms of his promise.[315]

---

[312] This is the same Ach who dramatically left the Ruef defense at the time of Ruef's plea of guilty to extortion. See Chapter XV, page 204.

[313] For immunity contract see page xix of the Appendix. For the negotiations upon which Ach's claim was based see Chapter XV.

[314] Heney sets forth in his affidavit that Ach's claim did not surprise him. He says of Ach's statement: "I was not very much surprised by its substance as I had long before commenced to suspect that Ruef, Ach, Dr. Kaplan and Dr. Nieto would claim eventually that such agreement existed in regard to case number 305 (the extortion case) if it became necessary to do so in order to keep Ruef out of the penitentiary. In fact I would not have been greatly surprised by anything that Ach might have claimed, as I have learned to know him pretty well and am sometimes at a loss to decide whether he or Ruef is entitled to first place as an artistic and imaginative 'equivocator,' to use Ruef's language."

[315] See Chapter XV, pages 190-7. Heney states in his affidavit that both Nieto and Kaplan agreed that Heney's statement of the arrangement was correct. "Yes, you are right, Mr. Heney," the affidavit sets forth Nieto said. "I understand it that way, and consequently I never told Ruef anything about that. He never got that from me." The affidavit sets forth that Kaplan said in substance: "Yes, that is what you said, Mr. Heney, but I always understood that Mr. Ruef would be allowed to withdraw his plea of guilty in the French Restaurant cases and would not receive any punishment."

Heney replied in substance: "You may have so understood, Doctor, but you had no right so to understand from anything which I said."

Both Kaplan and Nieto agreed with him that his statement was correct, but Kaplan insisted that he had understood that Ruef was to be allowed to withdraw his plea, arguing that he had told the truth and that his evidence was very important.

"Ruef lied to us," answered Heney emphatically, "in the French Restaurant case, and I proved it to him in this very room, and he simply laughed in my face. He also lied to us in all the other cases. He is not entitled to immunity in any case, and I not only will not permit him to withdraw his plea of guilty in case number 305, but on the contrary it is my present intention to ask the court in that case to give him no leniency whatever, but to sentence him for the maximum term which is prescribed by law."

Heney suggested that Ruef's representatives take this word back to their principal.

"Ruef," Heney concluded, "tried to job the prosecution and he has only succeeded in jobbing himself into the penitentiary."

Ten days later, when Heney made his opening statement before the first Ford jury, he carefully refrained from stating that the prosecution expected to prove any fact that necessarily depended in whole or in part upon Ruef's testimony. And with all San Francisco on tiptoe of expectancy,[316] Heney closed the

---

316 Heney, in his closing argument, told the jury that Ruef had not been put on the stand because the prosecution did not trust him. Heney said: "Nobody except Mr. Ford and Mr. Ruef could tell about it (the passing of the $200,000). They did not complain about my asking why they did not put Mr. Ruef on the stand. They asked why we didn't put him on the stand and vouch for his veracity and enable them to put words in his mouth, and I will answer now, because we DID NOT TRUST HIM."

case of The People without putting Ruef on the stand.[317]

The defense offered no evidence. The case went to the jury on the evidence which the prosecution had presented. The jury failed to agree, eight standing for acquittal, and four for conviction.

General Ford was immediately brought to trial for the second time. The case selected was for the bribery of Supervisor Jennings Phillips.

Heney, in his opening statement, announced that he did not intend to put Ruef on the stand. The second case presented was, if anything, stronger than the first,

---

[317] Heney, in his affidavit, describes the disappointment of Ruef, Ach and Nieto when the case was closed without Ruef being called. Heney says: "I rested the case on behalf of the prosecution in the first Ford trial in this department of this Court on the 2nd day of October, 1907, and the attorneys for the defendant asked for time to consider what they would do about putting in evidence, and Court adjourned for the purpose of giving them such time. I had noticed Henry Ach and Ruef sitting together next to the aisle, which was directly in front of where I sat, and could see that up to the time I closed the case they were anxiously waiting for me to call Ruef as a witness. When Court adjourned they remained sitting and as I passed them Ach stopped me and said in substance, 'Why didn't you put Ruef on the stand as a witness? Are you not going to dismiss these cases against him?' I replied in substance, "There are a lot more cases to be tried. There will be plenty of opportunities to dismiss these cases if I want to do it.' Ruef said, with one of his most winning smiles, in substance, 'I guess he is going to put me on in rebuttal just as he did in the Schmitz case.' I replied in substance, 'Oh, I don't know about that, Ruef. I don't like to try all my cases the same way.' I started to leave and Ach stopped me as I had taken only a couple of steps, and said in substance, 'There isn't any change in the situation, is there in regard to Ruef?' I smilingly and meaningly replied, in substance, 'Not a particle, Henry, since our last talk,' meaning thereby the talk which Ach and myself had on or about the 19th or 20th day of September, 1907, at night in my office in the presence of Dr. Nieto, Dr. Kaplan, William J. Burns and Charles W. Cobb, as hereinbefore set forth. As I made this statement I walked on out of the courtroom and someone stopped me somewhere between there and the entrance door of the building and Dr. Nieto came up to me, all smiles, and said in substance, 'You didn't put Ruef on the stand, did you?' I replied, 'No, I did not, Doctor.' Dr. Nieto then said in substance, 'There isn't any change in the situation, is there?' And I replied with a smile in substance, 'None whatever since our last talk, Doctor,' meaning the talk at my office just hereinbefore referred to, at which Dr. Nieto, Dr. Kaplan and Ach were present. The manner of Ach and the manner of Dr. Nieto when I made this reply to each of them indicated plainly that each understood exactly what I meant."

but the jury brought in a verdict of "not guilty." General Ford was tried on a third of the indictments against him, and again was the verdict of the jury "not guilty."

Long after, the prosecution discovered that agents for the United Railroads had systematically corrupted members of its detective force. On the evidence in the hands of the prosecution, a search warrant was secured, and the offices of the United Railroads raided in a search for stolen documents. Copies of over 2400 documents belonging to the prosecution were found. It developed that men in the employ of the prosecution were receiving regular monthly salaries from agents of the United Railroads to turn these reports over to agents of the defense for copying. The defense was in this way kept informed of all that had been reported to the prosecution regarding jurors, etc., by Burns's own agents.[318]

---

[318] Calhoun protested vigorously against the raiding of his offices. Concerning the raid and Mr. Calhoun's protests, the interior press expressed general approval of the first and condemnation of the latter.

"It is not a question," said the Oroville Register, "alone of graft in San Francisco now. It is rather a question as to whether in America, where 'all men are free and equal,' there is a law for the rich and another law for the poor, and whether a little money can put our whole penal system at naught and make monkeys of judicial officers. Unluckily in the Calhoun case we can not in America resort to the czar-like methods which should be resorted to, but must fight it out by the long and slow process of law. Luckily for the honor of America Mr. Heney and his associates are gifted with the courage, ability and tenacity to fight it out on this line even if it takes this summer and the whole of the next so to do."

"The 'private sanctity' of Calhoun's offices," said the Santa Barbara Independent, "was violated, his defenders say, when the police entered to search for stolen goods. The fact that the goods were concealed in the offices—that the police unearthed there a 'fence' for the reception of stolen goods—doesn't seem to have destroyed the sanctity of the place.

"Recently the police in Los Angeles raided a cigar store, where they found concealed some of the money that three months ago had been stolen from the Monrovia bank. The cigar dealer's lawyers

At the time of the third Ford trial, for example, Heney was engaged with Ruef's trial in the Parkside case. The Ford trial was conducted for the State by John O'Gara. One of Burns's men, Platt by name, was appointed to assist O'Gara by advising him of the character of the men drawn for jury service. O'Gara repeatedly discovered Platt's advice and suggestions to be unreliable. Long after it was discovered that Platt was at the time in the employ of agents for the United Railroads. The reason for the character of his advice and suggestions was then apparent.

At none of the Ford trials did the defense attempt to meet the evidence which the prosecution presented. At the third trial, the prosecution called President Calhoun and Abe Ruef [319] to the stand. But both declined to answer. The disposition of the $50,000 in currency in small bills, and of the $150,000 in currency in large bills, which passed into General Ford's hands, at the time that currency of this exact amount and description passed into the hands of Abe Ruef, $85,000 of which Ruef distributed among the Supervisors for voting for the United Railroads trolley permit, continues as great a mystery as it was on the day that the first Ford trial opened. Ruef at the time of his plea of

---

should go into court and protest against violation of the 'private sanctity' of the thief's hiding place.

"It is beyond understanding how men can view a similar circumstance in different lights. To an unprejudiced mind a thief is a thief, whether he has stolen an old pair of shoes or robbed the public through a municipal or other government. And the honest man rejoices in his capture, the recovery of the stolen goods and apprehension and punishment of persons who receive and conceal the fruits of theft."

[319] Calhoun and Ruef were placed on the stand April 29, 1908. Their refusal to answer will be found in the transcript of testimony taken that day. Complete records of all the graft cases were in 1912, when this review was written, in the possession of A. A. Moore, prominently connected with the graft defense.

guilty to the extortion charge, and five years later in the story of his career published in the San Francisco Bulletin, admitted that the $200,000 that on Calhoun's order was turned over to Ford was soon after paid to him (Ruef) because of the granting of the trolley permit. The $85,000 that Gallagher divided among the Supervisors on account of their granting this permit, Ruef has stated in his several confessions, came out of this Calhoun-to-Ford, Ford-to-Ruef· $200,000.

And in California there are many who hold that in this instance, at least, Ruef is telling the truth.

CHAPTER XXI.

The San Francisco Election of 1907.

Scarcely had the prosecution overcome the delaying tactics of the defense, and forced graft cases to trial, than District Attorney Langdon had to defend title to his office at the polls.

Langdon had taken office in January, 1906. His term was to expire in January, 1908. The municipal election, at which Mr. Langdon's successor was to be elected, was to be held in November.

At that time was to be elected besides the District Attorney, the Mayor, Supervisors and practically all the other municipal officials.

The old convention system of naming candidates for office still prevailed in San Francisco. However, California had even then entered upon the struggle of throwing off the yoke of machine domination through the convention system of naming candidates. The delegates to the several conventions had, under primary law provisions, to be elected at the polls.

San Francisco was divided upon one issue—that of the Graft Prosecution. The opposition which years of adverse publicity was to develop, did not then confront those who were standing for vigorous prosecution of the corrupters of the municipality. But under the hammering of an adverse press, and the claquer's systematic belittling, the graft defense had made gains sufficient to give it at least a fighting chance at the polls.

On the side of the defense, too, was the solid support of the powerful Southern Pacific Company, and of the various public service corporations, as well as the purchasable press.   On the side of the prosecution stood the people of San Francisco, not yet worn out, nor misled, nor yet alienated from the policy of vigorous prosecution of the corrupters of the municipality. The people recognized that effective continuance of the prosecution required that Mr. Langdon be re-elected.

That the action of the prosecution in making Taylor Mayor, might be endorsed at the polls—thus receiving the stamp of public approval—Mr. Taylor's election became quite as important as that of Mr. Langdon. The same was true of those of the Taylor-appointed Supervisors who became candidates for election.   But the contest waged about the election of Taylor and Langdon.

Such was the issue which confronted San Francisco at the 1907 election.

There was but one issue.   There were, however, three prominent political parties, Union Labor, Republican and Democratic.   None of the three could be called the prosecution party, nor for that matter, the defense party; nor had any faction of any of the parties the temerity to declare against the prosecution of those trapped in corruption, however vigorously opposed to the prosecution this or that faction might be. But each of the three parties did divide on the question of the election of Langdon and Taylor.

Broadly speaking, the supporters of the prosecution in all parties demanded that Taylor and Langdon be nominated.   The opponents of the prosecution, while declaring loudly for the prosecution of all offenders against the law, labored for their defeat. On this issue, not always clearly defined, the intraparty factions met at the primary polls. The prosecution, therefore, had three independent political fights on its hands.

Langdon had been elected by the Union Labor party. Taylor was a Democrat. But in the confusion of the times the principal primary fight was within the Republican party.

The Republican opposition to those roughly described as "pro-prosecution," found expression in the remnants of the old-time machine—generally called Herrin—element. At its head were many of the experienced machine leaders. The Republican pro-prosecution forces were at first without definite leadership. But in this emergency most effective leadership developed.

Daniel A. Ryan, a young "Irish-American," came to the fore as captain of the reform forces within the Republican party.

Ryan is of the highest type of his race, as developed under the advantageous conditions to which the immigrant and his descendants have, in these United States, been admitted. Well educated, forceful, a brilliant speaker, effective as an organizer, a lover of the political game, Ryan was soon the recognized leader of the new movement.

He was trusted implicitly. The selection of candidates for convention places was left largely in his hands. Under Mr. Ryan's leadership the fight for effective continuation of the Graft Prosecution was carried on within the Republican party.

The division in the Union Labor party was scarcely

less pronounced. The party, roughly speaking, divided with P. H. McCarthy heading the anti-prosecution side, and men of the type of Walter Macarthur, one of the founders of the party, leading the forces supporting Langdon and his associates.

But here again there was most confusing division. Thomas F. Eagan, chairman of the Union Labor Party County Committee, for example, was quoted within a week of the primaries, as announcing: "Schmitz is an ideal candidate (for Mayor). If available, he would be nominated by the delegates that will be elected on the regular Union Labor ticket." Nevertheless, Mr. Eagan was unalterably opposed to Mr. McCarthy heading the ticket.

The Democratic division was less pronounced than in either the Republican or Union Labor party. The side favoring Taylor, without much reference to Langdon, went to the primary polls under the regular Democratic leadership, with Thomas W. Hickey, chairman of the Democratic County Central Committee, at its head. Prominent in the opposition was Lewis F. Byington, who had preceded Mr. Langdon as District Attorney. Mr. Byington was brother-in-law of General Tirey L. Ford, even then under trial for bribery, and one of General Ford's attorneys.

In the confusion of these many-sided contests, the defense had its best opportunity for success. But the result, so far as the Democratic and Republican parties were concerned, was overwhelmingly successful for the prosecution.[320]

320 The outcome of the Republican primaries was looked upon as a victory for good government. Said the Call, in discussing the

Of the delegates to the Republican convention the Ryan (pro-prosecution) forces elected 142, the "Herrin" (anti-prosecution) forces 7 only. Of the 164 delegates to the Democratic convention, 161 were elected by the regular (pro-prosecution) element, and 3 by the Byington (anti-prosecution) side. The popular vote within these parties was scarcely less pronounced.[321] On the other hand, within the Union Labor party the anti-prosecution forces were overwhelmingly successful, the McCarthy faction electing 185 delegates and the forces led by Walter Macarthur and his associates 13 only.

Under the alignment, it was expected that the Republicans and Democrats would unite without hesitation upon Taylor and Langdon, leaving the cause of

---

returns: "Two things stand out prominently in the returns of the primary elections yesterday. One is that the Republicans of San Francisco have had enough of Herrin. The other is that they have not had enough of the graft prosecution. The victory for decency and for the independence of the party from the thralldom in which Herrin has so long held it for the use and benefit of the Southern Pacific was complete, with a vote large enough to make it plain to Herrin and to the interests exposed and to be exposed in the debauchery of public servants that they must look elsewhere than to the Republicans of San Francisco for the old corrupt conditions. The Call takes to itself credit for some share in the accomplishment of this good work. It was this paper that spoiled Herrin's infamous apportionment scheme by which he planned to fill the burned district with his dummies and thus control the municipal convention. It was this paper that began and carried on to the last moment a vigorous campaign in behalf of the decent element of the Republican party, whose leadership was in the capable and clean hands of Daniel A. Ryan. The Call has no candidates. It wants only honest, capable independent men. It made this winning fight because it wanted a clean government for San Francisco and because it wanted the graft prosecution carried out to the end."

[321] The primary vote was the largest up to that time cast in San Francisco. It was as follows:

Anti-Herrin (Ryan) Republican.................8,116
Herrin Republicans............................3,207
Irregular Republicans 1,549
Regular Democratic 2,438
Byington, Democratic 1,081
McCarthy, Union Labor 3,655
Macarthur, Union Labor........................2,197

the indicted corporation managers to find expression in the Union Labor party platform and candidates.[322]

But scarcely had the primary returns been made public than the San Francisco Call, generally regarded as stanchly on the side of the prosecution, brought confusion upon the pro-prosecution element, by suggesting the candidacy of Mr. Ryan for Mayor and belittling the candidacy of Mayor Taylor.

"Ryan," said The Call through its political representative, Mr. George Van Smith, "has not sought and is not seeking the Republican nomination for Mayor. He may have it forced upon him and find himself the recipient of similar endorsement of his powers as a boss-buster, from the Democratic organization."

The Call, in the same issue, hinted that the Democrats might not nominate Taylor. Without a Democratic nomination, Taylor could not expect nomination at the hands of the Republicans.

"That the Democrats will nominate Mayor Taylor," said The Call, "is more than doubtful. Mayor Taylor was drafted into the city's service. He has not given any indication of a desire to serve the city as the head of its government after the time when a popularly selected successor could be qualified. If the Democrats

---

322 On the eve of the primary election, P. H. McCarthy, leader of the anti-Prosecution faction of the Union Labor party, issued a warning to union men in which he said: "Too much caution cannot be exercised by you, nor too much diligence displayed in order to protect your rights at the polls today. One of the most cunning, deceptive and vicious attacks ever made on organized labor in this city is now being launched in order that your wages may be cut and your working hours increased to suit the millionaires in this city. To do so, those millionaires have drawn to their side by what force we are unable to say, certain labor men (Walter Macarthur and his associates) with a view to shuffling, confusing and thoroughly misleading the labor union voters and their sympathizers in this city."

do not nominate Dr. Taylor, the Republicans would scarcely be expected to do so. The fact that the men who will make up an almost exclusive majority of the Republican convention seem to be committed to the idea of nominating Ryan appears to preclude the nomination of Taylor by either party."

The source of The Call's information is not apparent. Up to the time of the publication of its article, August 15, there was no sentiment in San Francisco for the election of Mr. Ryan to the Mayoralty. On the contrary, the understanding was that Mr. Ryan had entered the contest from motives of good citizenship only, and that he was in no sense a seeker of office for himself.[323] Such had been the understanding during the primary campaign; such was the sense of the community after the primary vote had been cast.

All recognized, however, that Mr. Ryan was in a position of great power. He had been trusted implicitly. The selection of anti-Herrin candidates for delegates had been left largely in his hands. Few thought, however, that he had selected delegates for the purpose of giving himself the Republican nomination for the Mayoralty. Then, again, aside from the confusion his candidacy would work in the ranks of the anti-Herrin, pro-

---

[323] Many Ryan Republican district tickets contained the following printed statement:

"The candidates on this ticket are pledged to use all their influence in the convention to secure the nomination of a ticket of capable men and hope that they will be indorsed by the conventions of all parties. They do not care who these men may be, but will vote for no man who can be suspected of peddling offices or jobs in return for support. They do not desire nor expect for themselves or for their friends any offices or jobs. No candidate on this ticket has ever sought or held a political office or job. The candidates on this ticket have all accepted the pledge of the Regular Republican League. Daniel A. Ryan, chairman; Perry H. Newberry, secretary."

prosecution element, Mr. Ryan, while a pleasing young man and clever politician, it was generally recognized had few qualities usually looked for in the Mayor of a community of half a million people.

To add to the confusion, The Examiner, which was now in active opposition to the prosecution, came out strongly against Mr. Ryan's candidacy, denouncing it as "a grotesque piece of effrontery." "For the primary leader," said The Examiner, "to appropriate the office to himself, is like the agent of a charity fund determining that he is the most worthy object of the charity, and putting [324] the money in his own pocket."

---

[324] The Examiner, in its issue of September 19, 1907, in discussing Mr. Ryan's proposed candidacy said: "It is generally understood that Mr. Dan Ryan proposes to nominate himself as the Republican candidate for Mayor of San Francisco. That he has the power to do this thing is one of the curiosities of our political system.

"The theory is that the delegates to a convention represent that part of the public which marches under the political banner of a political party. But Mr. Ryan evidently considers that the delegates to the Republican convention were chosen to advance his personal political ambitions.

"The people do not mean that the accidental leaders of a primary fight should put the offices in their own pockets.

"They elect delegates as agents to select candidates from among the people. The delegates are the bearers of a trust and neither they nor the man who happens to captain them in the scramble between factions has a right to appropriate the nominations.

"The trust is not fulfilled if the primary leader assumes that because the people elected his primary ticket they want him in office. They don't want him, for they don't want primary politicians in the Mayor's chair.

"The theory of any convention is that it is assembled to choose the best man in the party for its candidate. The spectacle of Mr. Dan Ryan holding a caucus with himself, and deciding that he is better qualified to be Mayor of San Francisco than any other man in the Republican party, is a grotesque piece of effrontery.

"All sorts of men rise to the top in primary fights, but most of them have a sufficient sense of modesty, if not of the fitness of things, to abstain from making themselves the recipients of what the delegates have to give.

"For the primary leader to appropriate the office to himself is like the agent of a charity fund determining that he is the most worthy object of the charity and putting the money in his own pocket."

But Ryan's candidacy was not to be defeated by adverse criticism. Mr. Ryan had been largely instrumental in selecting the Republican delegates who were to name the candidates. Besides, he had the clever support, in its local columns at least, of the San Francisco Call. He had about him a number of enthusiastic young men who were ambitiously active in urging his candidacy.

"Every time the Taylor boomers gain a man they lose one," announced Perry Newberry, Secretary of Mr. Ryan's organization, and Ryan's right-hand man. "As far as the Republicans are concerned Daniel A. Ryan is as good as named. It will be Ryan, not Taylor, who will sweep the city."

With the advocacy of Ryan's candidacy, came quiet, systematic opposition to the nomination of Langdon.

With Mr. Ryan and his associates in control of the convention that was to nominate, it began to look as though the victory which the pro-prosecution Republicans, under Mr. Ryan's leadership, had won at the primaries, was barren indeed.

Among the Democrats, the opposition to Langdon and Taylor was even more discouraging. Langdon had been candidate for Governor two years before on the Independence League ticket. Theodore A. Bell had had the Democratic and Union Labor nominations. Bell had been defeated by a plurality. Bell ascribed his defeat to Langdon. The so-called Bell Democrats accordingly made this an excuse for objecting to Langdon.[325] As

---

[325] It was anything to defeat Langdon, even though a pro-prosecution attorney be employed against him. Hiram W. Johnson, for example, was suggested as his opponent. But Johnson let it be understood, and with characteristic positiveness, that under no considerations would he be a candidate against Langdon.

to Taylor, with the ability of the forces at work to defeat the prosecution considered, opinion gained daily that the failure of the Republican convention to nominate Taylor, would be followed by a refusal of the Democrats to give him nomination.

Thus with the supporters of the prosecution overwhelmingly successful at the Republican and Democratic primaries, there was grave danger that their purposes would be set aside by political manipulation.

But at this crisis a new element was injected into the situation.

Citizens who stood for enforcement of the law hastily formed a non-partisan organization to uphold the hands of the prosecution.[326] They called their organization the Good Government League. Taking for their motto "CITIZENSHIP ABOVE PARTISANSHIP," they boldly announced their support of Langdon for District Attorney, and of Taylor for Mayor.

The attitude of San Francisco toward the Graft Prosecution was shown by the reception given the new organization. Citizens by the thousands sent in their application for membership. Funds for the purposes of the campaign were forwarded by men in all walks of life.

The Democratic leaders were the first to appreciate the significance of the reception given the new movement. What was practically a combination between the two forces resulted. This insured the nomination of

---

[326] The members of the Good Government League Executive Committee were: E. L. Baldwin, J. E. Cutten, George Renner, Gen. Samuel W. Backus, George R. Fletcher, Sigmund Bauer, B. H. Gurnette, Frank W. Marvin, Frank W. Gale, L. C. McAfee, George Uhl, Rev. Chas. N. Lathrop, Isidor Jacobs, Rudolph Spreckels, Edgar A. Mathews.

Langdon and Taylor by the Democrats. It also assured
the nomination of Langdon by the Republicans, for
after the stand taken by the Good Government League,
for either Republican or Democratic party to have
rejected Langdon would have been an exhibition of
"poor politics."   But Ryan still controlled the Republican convention.   The Republican convention nominated
Mr. Ryan for Mayor.

Mr. Ryan's nomination was not accomplished without protest.   The citizens who attended the convention
as spectators were overwhelmingly for Taylor.   Taylor
received 53 out of the 148 convention votes, 95 being
cast for Mr. Ryan.   The minority charged that in the
nomination of Mr. Ryan, the Republicans of San Francisco had been betrayed, and that they would not be
bound by the nomination nor support the nominee.[327]

The Union Labor party, following out its policy of
opposition to the prosecution, nominated P. H. McCarthy [328] for Mayor, and Frank McGowan for District
Attorney.

The planks of the several parties dealing with the
prosecution were characteristic of the conventions from
which they issued.

The Union Labor plank definitely pledged its candidate for District Attorney to prosecution of the Super-

---

[327] The minority which voted for Taylor, in a memorial to the
convention, charged "that the majority of the delegates to this
convention have betrayed the confidence reposed in them by their
constituents" and gave notice that it would not be bound by the
nomination of the convention for Mayor and would not support
the nominee, but would do all in its power to further the election
of Dr. Edward R. Taylor.

[328] The Union Labor party convention also had its sensations.
Thomas F. Eagan, for example, and his followers bolted the convention because of McCarthy's nomination. The Carmen's Union
refused to accept the Union Labor party ticket because Langdon
had not been nominated for District Attorney.

visors who had confessed to bribe-taking although it had been clearly pointed out that such prosecution would bar effective prosecution of those responsible for the bribe-giving.[329]

___

[329] Heney, on the eve of election, in reply to McGowan's argument that the bribe-takers should be prosecuted, effectively answered this contention. Heney's communication read: "To Frank McGowan, Esq. Sir: You are reported by the newspapers as having stated that you will prosecute the boodling Supervisors and that you will also prosecute Patrick Calhoun and the other rich bribers, and that you will grant immunity to no one. I invite you to answer specifically the following questions either in the newspapers or the next time you make a public speech:

"1. If you prosecute Supervisor Lonergan (or any other Supervisor) for accepting a bribe to influence his vote in the matter of the trolley franchise, what witness, or witnesses, will you call to prove that he accepted the bribe?

"2. Every child in town now knows that if Lonergan received the money at all it was from Supervisor Gallagher. Will you prove the fact by Gallagher? If you call Gallagher as a witness, how do you expect to induce him to testify without granting him immunity?

"3. When you prosecute James L. Gallagher for giving a bribe to Tom Lonergan or to any other Supervisor to influence his vote on the trolley franchise matter, by what witness or witnesses, will you prove that Gallagher paid the money to Lonergan or to any other Supervisor? Will you call Lonergan or any other Supervisor as a witness, and when you call him, how will you induce him to testify without granting him immunity?

"4. By what witness do you expect to convict Gallagher of giving a bribe, or Tom Lonergan, or any other Supervisor of accepting a bribe in the matter of fixing the gas rate, or in the Home Telephone Company franchise matter?

"5. If you prosecute Ruef for giving money to Gallagher to distribute to the Supervisors to influence their vote on the trolley franchise, by what witness, or witnesses, will you prove that Ruef gave the money to Gallagher? Will you put Gallagher on the stand to prove it, and if so, how will you induce him to testify without granting him immunity? Will you put Ford on the stand to prove that he gave the money to Ruef, and if so, how will you get him to testify without giving him immunity? Will you put Pat Calhoun on the stand to prove that he gave the money to Ford to give Ruef to give to the Supervisors, and if so, how will you induce Pat to testify without giving him immunity?

"6. You say that you will prosecute Patrick Calhoun for bribing the Supervisors to influence their votes in the matter of the trolley franchise. By what witnesses will you prove that the money was given to Gallagher or to any of the other Supervisors to influence their votes in this matter? Will you prove by Ford that he gave the money to Ruef, and if so, how will you induce Ford to testify without giving him immunity? Will you prove by Ruef that he gave the money to Gallagher to distribute to the other Supervisors, and if so, how will you prove it by Gallagher without giving him immunity? Will you prove by the other Supervisors that they received money from Gallagher, and if so, how will you induce each of them to testify without giving each of them immunity?

"7. Will you prosecute Frank G. Drum and the other officials

The Republican plank left the reader in doubt as to whether or not the delinquent Supervisors were to be prosecuted. The Democratic plank alone pledged unqualified support to the prosecution "in any effort it may make to convict any guilty person." [330]

---

of the gas company for bribing the Supervisors for fixing the gas rates, and if so, how will you prove that the money was paid without granting immunity to Ruef and to some or all of the Supervisors?

"8. Will you prosecute A. K. Detweiler for bribing the Supervisors in the Home Telephone franchise matter, and if so, how will you prove your case against him without granting immunity to Ruef and to some or all of the members of the Board of Supervisors?

"9. Can jurisdiction be conferred on a court by consent, and if so, how could you proceed with the Ford trial on a legal holiday?

"10. If you found it necessary to grant immunity to either the bribe-taker or the bribe-giver in the trolley franchise matter to prevent an utter failure of justice and the escape of both the bribe-takers and the bribe-givers, to which side will you recommend the granting of immunity by the court? Will you prosecute the friendless, insignificant Supervisors and grant immunity to ex-Attorney-General Tirey L. Ford and his employer, Patrick Calhoun, president of the United Railroads of San Francisco, or will you recommend that the court shall grant immunity to the friendless and insignificant Supervisors in order to convict the rich, powerful and influential Patrick Calhoun and his general counsel, Tirey L. Ford?

"Yours, etc.,   FRANCIS J. HENEY."

330 The Republican convention "pledged its party and its nominees to assist and continue the vigorous prosecution of all persons guilty of crime, in whatever walk of life, high or low, in San Francisco," and "to incessant and energetic war on graft in every form, to the end that this plague may be exterminated from the body politic."

The Union Labor plank on the Graft Prosecution was as follows: "We demand the punishment of all offenders against the law, and we pledge our nominee for District Attorney to prosecute vigorously all bribers, boodlers and grafters without distinction, and particularly do we pledge him to prosecute those public officials, confessed criminals, who have been guilty of the greatest crime in the city's history, but who have been permitted to go unwhipped of justice, and to remain outside the walls of the penitentiary behind which they should now be imprisoned. We further pledge our nominee for District Attorney to abolish private prisons, wholesale 'immunity baths,' and all other institutions created for the benefit and protection of criminals."

The Democratic Graft Prosecution plank read: "We commend the work of the prosecution, which has removed from public office criminals who have dishonored and debauched our city and has secured convictions that must be forever a warning to official wrongdoers and those who participate with them in crime; and we pledge our support to the prosecution in any effort it may make to convict any guilty person."

The new alignment which followed the clearing of the atmosphere by the nomination of candidates, and the adoption of platforms, involved some astonishing changes.

The Examiner, which, on September 19, preceding the nominations, had described Mr. Ryan's candidacy as "a grotesque piece of effrontery," and compared him to the custodian of a trust fund who puts the money in his own pocket, announced its support of Mr. Ryan for Mayor. On October 20, a month and a day after publication of the custodian-of-a-trust-fund editorial article, The Examiner "unhesitatingly recommended to all the voters of San Francisco," Mr. Ryan, "as the man best qualified to be the next Mayor of the city."

On the other hand, The Call, which was the first to suggest Mr. Ryan's candidacy, describing him a heroic young "boss buster," to whom the Democrats could logically turn for a mayoralty candidate, after his nomination, described him as "a cheap politician itching for office," [331] whose candidacy was the one element which threw a doubt upon the election of Mayor Taylor. Following the conventions, The Call supported Taylor as against the field.

---

[331] "There never would have been doubt anywhere about Taylor's successor," said the Call in its issue of November 5, "if it had not been for the grossly selfish and unpatriotic course of Daniel A. Ryan. The one possibility of McCarthy's election was opened to him by Ryan. Failing of other support, Ryan turned renegade to all his party professions and went into an infamous alliance with that arch enemy of Republicanism, Hearst. For four weeks he has been scrambling for votes. . . . Ryan has fully revealed himself as a cheap politician itching for office. He has boasted of his youth, and yet he was the first of the candidates to break down and go to bed. He has declaimed about his own honesty, until his voice is in tatters and has filled the air with promises of what he would do if elected. Never has he explained or attempted to explain the nature of those 'certain concessions' that led him to nominate himself, although he knew that in so doing he was jeopardizing the future of his city."

The Chronicle tactfully refrained from taking sides until after the nominations were announced.[332] Then The Chronicle gave support to Taylor. If the shifting policy of the newspapers had raised a doubt as to where the people of San Francisco stood on the issue, that doubt was dispelled by the opening meeting of the Taylor-Langdon campaign. The largest auditorium in San Francisco was packed to the doors,[333] with citizens

---

[332] Said the Chronicle of Mr. Ryan's candidacy in its issue of October 3, 1907: "The Chronicle has neither apologies nor regrets for urging its readers to support the Regular Republican League movement headed by Daniel A. Ryan. We believed at the time, as others believed, that Mr. Ryan's sole desire was good government for San Francisco and that such desire was unsmirched by personal ambition. General confidence in the sincerity of Mr. Ryan and his associates led to the triumphant election of the delegates to the Republican convention named and approved by Mr. Ryan, which was accepted throughout the country as evidence that the people of San Francisco were sound at heart.

"When we urged the public to support the Ryan primary tickets, we did so, not in the interest of Mr. Ryan, but in the interest of good government. We considered Mr. Ryan in the light of a useful and public-spirited citizen, upon whom, in due time, the people would delight to confer official honors should he be willing to accept them. Those who voted the Ryan ticket at the primaries did not vote for Mr. Ryan, but for the cause which he championed. As for considering him a candidate for Mayor, nobody thought of it. It is no disparagement to a young man like Mr. Ryan to say that as yet he has no such standing in the community as justifies him in aspiring to such an honor."

In its issue of October 5 the Chronicle said: "The moral collapse of Daniel A. Ryan is deeply regretted by every lover of San Francisco. It is not a matter of the rise or fall of one man. It is a question of whether the people will ever again trust any man who appears as a leader of reform. Few men ever get such an opportunity as Mr. Ryan has thrown away. Doubtless the lesson is for the people never again to trust an unknown man. It is not too much to ask of any aspirant to leadership on an important scale that he shall have some record of honorable achievement of some kind as an earnest of what to expect of him should the confidence reposed in him place him in a position of power."

[333] The Call, in speaking of the Taylor-Langdon meeting said: "Young Mr. Ryan ought to have been at that meeting. We have nothing against Mr. Ryan except that he is not the man of the hour. We shall not even reproach him with his youth. That is not his fault and he will get over that. But he is not the man of the hour. The people have said it. Mr. Ryan embodies no principle. To the people of San Francisco he means nothing in particular at this critical time. He might have read that message in the mighty roar that went up from the meeting in welcome of Dr. Taylor. Mayor Taylor stands for something, stands for much. Mr. Ryan has only his own ambition and a certain command of language."

whose one purpose, expressed by approving cheers every time the subject was mentioned, was support of the prosecution which had broken up the Schmitz-Ruef organization, and which bade fair to bring to book the corrupters of the municipal government.

The meeting was thoroughly representative. Labor touched elbows with capital. Among the speakers were representative Labor Union leaders, who had definitely broken with the Union Labor party.

"It is inconceivable to me," said Walter Macarthur, one of the organizers of the Union Labor party, in a ringing address, "that any honest thinking labor man would stand for the proposition that those men who have debauched the officials of our city should go scot free while the victims of their cupidity be sent behind the prison bars alone. I believe that labor will join with all honest people in declaring that if the corrupt bribe-taker is punished the man who is at the head of this corruption must be punished also. That is the issue of this campaign and I believe that election day will prove the virtue of my faith."

That the contest for the District Attorney's office overshadowed in importance the mayoralty fight was fully recognized. The Union Labor party, which had nominated and elected Langdon in 1905, had repudiated him, and named Frank McGowan as Langdon's only serious opponent. The Republicans and Democrats, who had under a fusion arrangement in 1905 opposed Langdon's election; united, in 1907, to fight for his continuance in office. The public service corporations, especially those whose officials were under indictment, generally opposed Mr. Langdon's election, and supported the candidacy of his Union Labor party opponent.

This was particularly astonishing in the case of the United Railroads, whose president, Mr. Patrick Calhoun, was even then posing as a "labor union buster," while the United Railroads was very effectively grinding to pieces the San Francisco Carmen's Union.[334]

Nevertheless, there was certain consistency in the political course taken by the United Railroads. Whatever the differences President Calhoun, in his role as a "union buster," may have had with the labor union, there was much in common between him and the San Francisco Union Labor party as headed by Mr. McCarthy.[335] President Calhoun and his company opposed the prosecution vigorously. Mr. McCarthy and his party went quite as far in this opposition. President Calhoun was most emphatic in his denunciation of those who had made the graft prosecution possible. Mr. McCarthy was scarcely less emphatic in his denunciation. Indeed, Mr. McCarthy opened his campaign with an attack upon the graft prosecution. Inasmuch as the one issue before the people was the continuance of the graft prosecution along the lines that had proved so distasteful to Mr. Calhoun and those in the same predicament as himself, the support of the Union Labor

[334] The San Francisco Call, in its issue of November 5, charged that orders had gone out from the United Railroads to "vote for McCarthy and the Union Labor ticket—straight." In the cars of the United Railroads appeared dodgers which read: "Workingmen. Workingmen—Are you going to put a big stick into Spreckels' hands to club you over the head with?"

[335] The same is true of the Los Angeles Times, which has a national reputation as an opponent of organized labor. The Times, while at issue with Mr. McCarthy on the question of the desirability of unions, was scarcely less vehement than he in denunciation of the San Francisco graft prosecution.

party candidate for District Attorney by a union-labor-busting corporation was not entirely inconsistent.

And yet, Mr. McGowan, the Union Labor party candidate, definitely pledged himself to continue the prosecution, but he promised that the prosecution which he would carry on should not "disturb business," that Heney [336] should no longer be retained as special prosecutor, that the Supervisors who had confessed to bribe-giving should be prosecuted [337] as well as those who had given bribes.

This last was one of the chief arguments advanced in support of Mr. McGowan's candidacy. On the ground that a mistake had been made, if a wrong had not been done, when the Supervisors were granted immunity,[338] it was urged that Mr. Langdon should not be continued in the District Attorney's office.

---

[336] One of the allegations made against Heney was that he would not prosecute Patrick Calhoun, because Heney's brother-in-law was employed by Calhoun as a detective. This argument was intended to weaken Heney and the prosecution with the union element that Calhoun was endeavoring to crush.

[337] In a political advertisement which appeared in the San Francisco Call November 3, 1907, Mr. McGowan said: "If elected District Attorney I will prosecute every man accused of crime, regardless of his position in life. I will continue the present graft prosecution with more vigor, and the District Attorney's office will not be used for politics, nor to disturb business. I will be the District Attorney in law and in fact, and I will never allow any man or set of men to control the office for any purpose. I will honorably enforce the law without the aid of any millionaire's money."

[338] Langdon, at the opening of the Republican campaign, took up the question of the prosecution's policy in granting immunity to the Supervisors. He said:
"In this prosecution we have tried to be practical, to be effective. What would you have said if we had made a scapegoat of a petty criminal and let the giants go? What would you have said if in all this graft and corruption we had arrested and jailed two or three obscure Supervisors you had never heard of before they came to office, and will never hear of them again now that they are retired to private life, and had let escape the giants in crime?
"There have been graft exposures before in the history of American municipalities and the graft has gone on. And it was bound to go on so long as the prosecutions failed to stop the sources

The election returns [339] were conclusive of San Francisco's attitude on the several issues raised. Taylor was elected Mayor, with a clear majority of 415 over all his competitors. Langdon's majority over all competitors, including the Socialist candidate, was 13,510, his plurality over McGowan being 14,808. And with

---

of evil, to gather into the fold of the penitentiary the corrupt men of business and the corrupt political leaders who have dared to use weak men for their own ends. These giants in crime are perfectly willing that the physical life of the weak men they use shall be fed into the jails of the State to appease public wrath exactly as they have been willing to use up the moral life of these men to satisfy their own greedy needs in the Board of Supervisors. Profiting by the mistakes of previous prosecutions, this office has struck straight at the very roots of public graft; at the crooked public service corporations; but which of the criminals were to be allowed to give evidence for the State and enjoy its alluring protection; the giants of crime who have always been most responsible and who have always escaped or the petty, miserable fellows who have entered upon these things through ignorance and weakness?

"Immunity had to be given in order that crime might be punished and it was given to the Supervisors that the very roots of political corruption might be torn from the soil in which they thrived. We did it because this prosecution has a moral as well as a legal significance. It is time to stop the cynicism of common men when they view democracy and say it is for the powerful and the rich; that the poor must go to jail for the theft of bread and the rich escape for the theft of privilege, the purchase of men's souls and the degradation of government. It is time to stop the brazen and confident effrontery of the irresponsible criminal rich, who commit crimes and rest back, thinking they can buy judges as they bought legislators and executives, and knowing they can buy legal talent to interpose every technicality in every courtroom until justice is a human travesty tangled in its own web.

"We are after the 'men higher up' because they are the severest menace to our institutions, the enduring factors that program and bribe each Board of Supervisors as they come and go. We are after the 'men higher up' so as to make criminal acquisition unprofitable in terms of human desire. We are after the 'men higher up' so that young men and women growing up in this and other communities will once more believe with ardent fervor not only that dishonesty does not pay, but that of all the goods on this earth the greatest treasure is a straightforward life."

[339] The vote for Mayor and for District Attorney was as follows:

```
For Mayor—
          Taylor .......................28,766
          Ryan .........................  9,255
          McCarthy .....................17,583
          Reguin (Soc.)................. 1,503
For District Attorney—
          Langdon ......................34,923
          McGowan ......................20,115
          Kirk (Soc.)................... 1,298
```

the election of Taylor and Langdon [340] were elected all the Good Government League candidates for Supervisors.

The Graft Prosecution had successfully passed another crisis. It had, too, received overwhelming endorsement of The People at the polls.

---

[340] In commenting upon the outcome of the election, the Examiner, in its issue of November 6, said: "And this revolt of union labor against misrepresentation in office began long ago. Before the primaries, when most of the registering was done, it was observed that the number of Republicans recorded was far in excess of the adherents of union labor. The story was told then. Disgusted with the dishonesty of the men they had placed in office, finding the local Democratic party a mere memory, they registered as Republicans because they were determined to vote against the representatives of Ruef and Schmitz who had captured their organization.

"Langdon's majority will surprise no one. His election was a matter of course, for union labor, like all other decent elements in the community, was determined to sustain the prosecution of the grafters.

"The swing of union labor to Taylor will surprise the gentlemen who have been so fond of assuming that the working people would vote as a class regardless of principle. The fact that they set aside all class feeling, all personal preference, and rolled up a big majority in favor of the man considered most likely to defeat the zebra-striped bandits who had captured their organization proves that government in America is safe in the hands of the plain people.

"It is union labor, and union labor chiefly, which has saved San Francisco from McCarthy and McGowan."

"Yesterday," said the Chronicle the morning after the election, "was a great day for San Francisco. It was the turn of the tide. It was the beginning of the ascent to nobler ideals and better days. The passions of the conflict will soon die away. With an honest government assured, capital will not shun us but seek us. And we can look back on the events of the last six years as we remember a nightmare from which we awake to find ourselves in security and peace."

"The indicted bribe-givers," said the Call, "may as well make up their minds that there is no way of escape for them except through trial and by the verdicts of the juries. The people have spoken and they have said that the clean-up must be thorough. The sweeping success of Langdon means that the prosecution of the grafters will be pressed to its fitting conclusion upon the facts and under the law. There need be no delay now. Soon all the cases should be settled and another chapter added to the history of San Francisco—a chapter in which will have been written the means, the manner and the fullness of our atonement for Schmitz-Ruef chapter just before it, the vindication of the city's good name."

CHAPTER XXII.

Higher Courts Free Schmitz and Ruef.

On January 8, 1908, the municipal officials elected with Mayor Taylor assumed the duties of their office. That day, Ruef was taken from the custody of the elisor and locked up in the county jail. In the jail with him were Schmitz, convicted of the extortion charge to which Ruef had pleaded guilty, and Glass, who had been convicted of bribery.

The following day, January 9, the Appellate Court, for the First District, handed down a decision in the Schmitz extortion case, which, later sustained by the Supreme Court, unlocked the prison doors not only for Schmitz, but for Ruef also.[341]

The decision was the first serious setback in the graft cases that District Attorney Langdon's office had received.

The prosecution had prevented Ruef seizing the District Attorney's office; had defeated the efforts of the defense to have the indicting Grand Jury declared an invalid body; had overcome the resistance of the defendants to facing trial jurors; had, after meeting

---

[341] The opinion was written by Justice Cooper and concurred in by Justices Hall and Kerrigan. This is the same Kerrigan who appears in the Santa Cruz banquet scene picture, in which Ruef occupies the position of honor with the Republican nominee for Governor, J. M. Gillett, standing at his back with hand resting on Ruef's shoulder. (See Chapter IV.)

Supreme Justice Henshaw, whose sensational action in Ruef's favor will appear in another chapter, is also one of the Santa Cruz banquet group.

the clever opposition of the best legal talent obtainable for money, forced trials before juries and secured convictions; and finally, the prosecution had met the defense before the larger jury of The People, and, at the polls, had won again. But, with a stroke of the pen, the Appellate Court swept aside the greater part of the accomplishment of fifteen-months struggle against corruption. The court found the indictment under which Schmitz had been convicted of extortion to be insufficient and ordered the defendant to be discharged as to the indictment.

In as much as Ruef, Schmitz's co-defendant, indicted jointly with him for extortion, had plead guilty to the same indictment as that under which Schmitz had been convicted, the effect of the decision was to free Ruef as well as Schmitz.

Before passing upon the sufficiency of the indictment, the court took occasion to deal with the points of error as raised by the defense. On five principal points the court found that error had been committed.[342] On this showing, the case could have been sent back to the Superior Court for re-trial. In that event, Ruef's status would not have been affected. But the

---

[342] The Appellate Court enumerated the following errors at the trial:

(1) That the trial court erred in allowing the peremptory challenge of a juror after he had been sworn to try the case; and the removal, after he had been sworn, of a second juror without cause.

(2) That error was committed in the appointment of the elisor that had charge of the jury.

(3) That the court erred in admitting hearsay evidence of witnesses, Loupe, Blanco, Malfanti, Debret and Rosenthal.

(4) That error was committed when Schmitz was required, under cross-examination, to answer question as to whether he had received from Ruef part of the money extorted from the French restaurant keepers.

(5) That Ruef's testimony that he had divided the money with Schmitz was not proper rebuttal evidence.

court went back of the trial to the indictment, on points raised in the defendant's demurrer, found for the defendant, and held the indictment to be insufficient.

In the discussion of the decision which followed, criticism was confined almost exclusively to the court's rulings on the sufficiency of the indictment. The point raised was that the indictment did not state facts sufficient to show that any public offense had been committed.

The court held in effect that the facts presented did not, under the definitions of the California codes, constitute the crime of extortion.

In the California Penal Code [343] extortion is defined as "the obtaining of property from another, with his consent, induced by a wrongful use of force, or fear or under color of official right." The section following [344] defines "Fear such as will constitute extortion may be induced by a threat either: (1) to do an unlawful injury to the person or property of the individual threatened, or to any relative of his, or member of his family."

The court found that the threat which induced the fear in the Schmitz-Ruef extortion cases, was a threat to prevent the parties from obtaining a liquor license, and thus to prevent them from carrying on the business of selling wines and liquors at retail. A license to sell liquor, the court showed, is not property in the ordinary sense of the word,[345] but a mere permission,

---

[343] California Penal Code, Sec. 518.

[344] California Penal Code, Sec. 519.

[345] The general feeling regarding the Schmitz decision was well expressed by Attorney J. C. Hutchinson, in a letter to Justice Cooper. The letter follows:
"Hon. James A. Cooper, Presiding Justice of the District Court

and the license is but the evidence that the permission has been given by the proper authorities. "There is grave doubt," [346] the court held, "as to whether a threat to prevent a party from obtaining a permission or license by one who has no authority in the premises, is a threat to injure property within the meaning of the sections quoted."

But the court found it unnecessary to decide this question, for the reason it held the indictment insufficient "because it does not allege nor show that the specific injury threatened was an unlawful injury." [347]

---

of Appeals, First District, 1420 Sutter street, city. Dear Sir: Yours of the 15th inst. received. I did not expect you to reply to mine of the 13th inst., which was more in the nature of an ejaculatory protest than a letter. Nevertheless, I think you are right to reply, especially as I know you have replied to letters complimenting you on the same decision.

"I have never before written a letter to a judge commenting upon a decision in which he had taken part, and I ordinarily would consider such a course highly unprofessional. During twenty-five years' practice, I have always remained silent in the face of decisions, however adverse, even in some cases where I was perfectly well aware that improper influences behind the scenes had prevented me from obtaining justice. But in this case the situation is different from anything I have ever experienced. The very air seems to be full of revolutionary feeling. At the universities, clubs, in the trains, on the streets and in the home, I find no one (except the friends, connections and lawyers of the grafters) speak with anything but emphatic protest against this decision so far as it relates to the validity of the indictment.

"I have cast no personal reflection upon yourself. The attack is upon the atmospheric environment of a statement which could lead a man of your integrity and intelligence honestly to believe that such a decision could be correct; and if the Supreme Court should unanimously hold the same, that would, according to my view, only make the matter so much the worse.

"Very respectfully yours, J. C. HUTCHINSON."

[346] See 7 Cal. App. Reports, page 330.

[347] The Court, in discussing this point, said: "The indictment does use the words 'unlawful injury' in the first part of it; but when the facts are specifically set forth as to what the defendants threatened to do we find that the threat was that defendants 'would prevent the said Joseph Malfanti, Charles Kelb and William Lafrenz from receiving said license or obtaining the same.' There is no allegation that any unlawful act was threatened, and the attorneys for the prosecution frankly admit that they rely upon the fact that the defendants obtained the money by threatening to do an injury, which they claim was unlawful solely for the

To the man on the street, the reading of the opinion conveyed the impression at least, that according to the Appellate Court, when Schmitz had shown his power to prevent the French Restaurants getting their licenses, thus endangering investments valued as high as $400,-000, and Ruef because of the fear engendered by this showing, acting with Schmitz, had secured large sums of money from the enterprises thus threatened, the crime of extortion had not been committed.

---

reason that the threats were made with intent to extort money. In other words, it is claimed that even though the French-restaurant proprietors were violating the law, and conducting immoral places used as resorts by lewd women, and thus not legally entitled to a license to sell liquor, a threat to prevent the issuance of licenses to such places by laying the facts before the Board of Police Commissioners in a legal manner, constitutes a crime if such threat was made with the intent to extort money. Such, in our opinion, is not the law. The statute uses the words that the threat must be to do 'an unlawful injury'; and in order to charge a crime the indictment must aver in some way that the threat was to do an unlawful injury. It is apparent from the language of the statute which we have hereinbefore quoted, that it is not every kind of fear that will support a charge of extortion because of property obtained thereby. The fear must be induced by one of the threats enumerated in the statute. The Legislature has seen fit to provide that the threatened injury to property upon which a charge of extortion may be predicated must be an unlawful injury to property. That is, the injury threatened must be, in itself, unlawful, irrespective of the purpose with which the threat is made. As the word 'unlawful' is used in the statute it qualifies the 'injury' and not the 'threat.' Unlawful means contrary to law. It is true that from a high standard of ethics it could not be claimed that one could extort money by a threat to do a lawful act, if the intent was to get money by the use of the threat, but every wrong is not made a crime. There are many wrongs done every day that are not enumerated in the category of crimes contained in the Penal Code that are of much more serious consequence in their nature than others which are defined therein; but we must look to the statute to find whether or not an act is a public offense for which a prosecution will lie. To procure property from others by a mere threat to do a lawful act is not a crime. The object of the statute—or at least one of its objects—is to protect the party from whom the property is extorted; and if such party pays the money in order to secure protection in violating the law he cannot be heard to complain. He in such case would be a party to the violation of the law. In this case, if the parties as a fact paid the money in order to prevent the evidence as to the character of places they kept from being exposed to the Board of Police Commissioners, they are not in a position to complain."

The decision was received with protest[348] and denunciation. The Call dubbed it "bad law, bad logic and bad morals." "Any ordinary intelligence," said The Examiner, "would construe the threat to take away a license to sell liquor from a restaurant unless a certain sum of money was paid as the plainest kind of extor· tion."

"When," said Dr. William Rader of Calvary Presbyterian church, in a sermon preached on the evening of the Sunday after the decision was made public, January 12, 1908, "extortion is not a crime, when bribery is not even a wrong, when a confessed felon can learn that he is really righteous, and that his trial, confession and conviction have all been nothing but a mistake—

---

[348] The Examiner, in its issue of January 11, 1908, said of the decision:

"The District Court of Appeal has overturned the conviction of Mayor Schmitz on the ground that threatening to prevent the French-restaurant keepers from getting a license to sell liquor does not constitute the crime of extortion, with which he is charged. This is one of the decisions that will aggravate the dissatisfaction of the public with the courts.

"Abe Ruef, once political boss of San Francisco, testified that he had divided with the Mayor the 'fees' for getting the licenses which Schmitz had held up until the money was paid. 'A license to sell liquor is not property in the ordinary sense of the word,' declares the court, making the point that the indictment 'does not allege any threat to injure property.'

"Any ordinary intelligence would construe the threat to take away a license to sell liquor from a restaurant unless a certain sum of money was paid as the plainest kind of extortion, particularly when the Mayor was shown to have shared in the money thus exacted, and the fact that the contrary ruling of a court acts as a release of a man whose guilt was clearly established, will not change that view."

"Even the lay mind," said the Call, "is competent to reach the conclusion that this decision is bad law, bad logic and bad morals."

The decision was generally condemned by the interior press. The Sacramento Bee denounced it as a "palpable evasion of justice." The Oakland Enquirer stated that it came as a "shock and a surprise to the law-respecting people of California and of the entire country." "San Francisco in particular," said the Los Angeles Evening News, "California in general and the republic at large have suffered great wrong by reason of this reprehensible decision."

a slight mistake—I repeat that however correct this may be legally and ethically, it has the effect of making us stand amazed at the rapid revolutions of the legal wheels. Perhaps tomorrow we shall learn that this last decision has been a mistake, too. I hope so; I believe so."

"We of this city," said Rev. Dr. Evans at Grace Episcopal Cathedral, "are dumfounded by a judicial pronouncement which enables the high officials of our city to rob and plunder without any technical breaking of the law. It is enough—such an audacious mockery of the first principles of common sense—to justify the appointment of a lunacy commission to inquire into the sanity of men who could formulate such a judgment and it ought to provoke an explosion of righteous indignation from one end of the State to the other. We need not hesitate to declare that such an opinion as this has its inspiration in that place where public sentiment without a single dissenting note would give it its unanimous approval."

The decision did not immediately release Ruef and Schmitz. The prosecution had still an appeal to the Supreme Court for a re-hearing and, pending such an appeal, the defendants remained behind the bars. This delay annoyed those interested in seeing the graft defendants go free. Stories were circulated that the prosecution would not appeal. But the prosecution did appeal. Three months later, the Supreme Court rendered its decision.[349]

The decision was against the prosecution.

---

[349] See California Appellate Reports, in which the Supreme Court decision is printed, Vol. No. 7, Page 369.

"The (Supreme) court is unanimous in the opinion," the decision read, "that the District Court of Appeal was correct in its conclusion that the indictment was insufficient, in that it did not show that the specific injury to the property of the restaurant-keepers threatened by the defendant was an 'unlawful injury.'"

The Supreme Court went a step further than the Appellate Court had done and attacked the indictment on the ground that it had not set forth that Schmitz was Mayor at the time of the alleged extortion, nor that Ruef was a political boss practically in control of the municipal government.

The prosecution in its application for a rehearing had set forth that "it will be found and decided by this court that levying blackmail upon licensed businesses by the Mayor and the political boss of a metropolitan community is a crime under the law of California and should not go unwhipped of justice."

This observation was denounced in the Supreme Court's decision as "a gross misstatement of the case and of the question to be decided as presented by the indictment."

"We again emphasize the fact," reads the opinion, "that the indictment does not aver that Schmitz was Mayor, or that Ruef was a political boss, or that either of them had any power, or influence, or control over the Police Commissioners, or that they threatened to use such power, influence or control in preventing the issuance of a license."

The storm of protest with which this opinion was received was even greater than that which followed the Appellate Court decision. Once more did press, pulpit and public, from one end of the State to the other, join in expression of indignation.

The court in return insisted that it was misrepresented and misunderstood. Chief Justice W. H. Beatty essayed the task of writing an explanation of the ruling, that "the man on the street" might understand.

The Chief Justice's article appeared in the Sacramento Bee of April 29, 1908.[350] Again was the omission from the indictment of the fact that Schmitz was Mayor and Ruef a boss, emphasized.[351] And again, it

---

[350] The Bee prefaced the Chief Justice's article with the following statement: "The decision of the Supreme Court of California in the case of Eugene Schmitz is one not only of State but even of national importance. It has been the fruitful topic of varied comment throughout the Union. And yet, after all the discussion, there remains a prevailing ignorance as to WHAT WAS DECIDED; and even among those laymen who had a fair idea upon that point, there is certainly little if any knowledge as to WHY IT WAS SO DECIDED.

"Having a very high idea of the granitic probity of Chief Justice Beatty of the Supreme Court, and believing it to be the duty of that Court to answer when citizens respectfully ask for light, the editor of this paper on March 31st last wrote to Chief Justice Beatty and asked him to publicly explain just what the Court had decided and just why it had so decided; to explain it so that the man in the street might easily understand. In that quite lengthy letter to the Chief Justice, the editor of The Bee wrote:

" 'The ignorance of the general public as to what was decided and exactly why it was decided has undoubtedly given rise to considerable of a public suspicion that all is not as it should be—that injustice has triumphed where justice should have prevailed—that the good work of almost two years has been practically wiped out by a judicial obeisance to technicalities—that the guilty have been saved by the interposition of a judicial hand that could with more propriety and equally as much regard for the law have turned the scales to record the verdict of the highest tribunal on the side of good government.'

"Justice Beatty answers the questions at length, but with such clearness that the 'man in the street' can understand. His explanation should be read by everybody, so that hereafter those who discuss the matter can do so with a full and thorough understanding of exactly what the Supreme Court decided in the Schmitz case, and exactly why it considered it had so to decide."

[351] "I repeat," said the Chief Justice in his Bee article, "that the only question presented for decision was the question of statutory construction here stated, for it was never seriously contended before the Supreme Court by the Attorney General, or by the District Attorney of San Francisco, or by any of his assistants or deputies, or by the learned counsel, whose names are signed to the petition for a rehearing, that the indictment did allege a

may be added, did the stupid man on the street fail to understand. In fact, disapproval of the decision continued. Heney attacked it respectfully in tone, but with sharp criticism.[352]

James M. Kerr,[353] in his Cyclopedia Penal Code of

---

threat to do an unlawful injury of the character indicated. What it did allege on this point, and all that it alleged, was that one E. E. Schmitz (without showing that he was Mayor of the city, or that he had any official or other influence over the Board of Police Commissioners greater than, or different from, that of the humblest private citizen), and one Abraham Ruef (without showing that he had any such power or influence) had told certain keepers of a restaurant that they could, and had threatened that they would, prevent them from obtaining a renewal of their license to sell liquors, etc. The indictment, in other words, had no more force in legal contemplation than if it had been directed against Jack Stiles and Richard Noakes, for though the facts that Schmitz was Mayor and Ruef the political boss of the city may have been as notorious in San Francisco as the fire or earthquake, no lawyer would contend for a moment that they were facts of which a court could take judicial notice in passing upon the sufficiency of the indictment."

[352] Heney's reply to Chief Justice Beatty was published in The Sacramento Bee. Section 961 of the California Penal Code expressly provides that no fact of which a court may take judicial notice, need be alleged in any indictment. The Codes enumerate certain matters of which the courts are required to take judicial notice. Among the matters are "State offices and their incumbents." The Political Code defines who are "State officers," and among them are included "Mayors of Cities." Heney, in his reply, held Chief Justice Beatty and the court to be wrong, even on the face of the statute. No lawyer in the State attempted to answer Heney's reply, although many of them would have been glad to have earned recognition from the Supreme Court by doing so.

[353] James M. Kerr is author of Kerr's California Cyclopedic Codes. These works are accepted as standards throughout the country.
"It is thought," says Kerr in California Cyclopedic Codes for 1908, "that . . . the [Schmitz] case cannot be safely relied upon as an authority outside of California. It is a flagrant violation of the spirit if not the letter of Section 4 ante, and the old rule that it is the duty of the court, where it is possible, so to construe the statute as to uphold the indictment and promote justice, instead of effecting a miscarriage of justice. Several things occur in connection with a consideration of the foregoing quotation from the Supreme Court.
"1. If an indictment can lawfully be upheld, the court, as the judicial voice of the State, is bound so to uphold it. It is not the province of the court to seek some strained view of the law by which an indictment of one accused of crime can be quashed.
"2. The construction of the code provision on extortion is to be made, not technically, but according to the fair import of its terms, with a view to its object and to promote justice.
"3. It is not charged, and the statute does not require it to be

California, published in 1908, declared in effect that in the Schmitz decision the Supreme Court of California formulated bad law and advocated bad pleading.

As for Ruef's position as a political boss, Kerr contended, it was merely a matter of evidence, and not a matter to be pleaded. "The Supreme Court," concludes the law writer, "seems to lose sight of the fact that the crime of extortion in this State is not confined to persons in office and exercising official influence."

Dean John H. Wigmore of the Northwestern University School of Law, and author of the standard work, Wigmore on Evidence, in a crushing criticism of

---

charged, that the threat was made by Schmitz, acting in his official capacity. The crime of extortion, under our statute, is not the old common-law crime of extortion, which could be committed only by an official acting in his official capacity. Under our statute it is immaterial whether Schmitz held any official position, or whether Schmitz and Ruef had any power or influence to carry out the threat; the only thing to be considered is, Did the accused extort money by means of a threat? Official position or power to carry out the threat is neither material nor proper.

"4. It is entirely immaterial by what means Schmitz and Ruef intended to accomplish their threat to have the liquor license withheld; whether by fair persuasion of the Board of Supervisors, or by menace, duress, fraud, or undue influence. The crime charged did not consist in the dealings with the Board of Supervisors, but in the threat made to the French restaurateurs, by means of which the fears of the latter were aroused, and were forced to pay to Schmitz and Ruef money to which the latter were not entitled, as a means of preventing Schmitz and Ruef from carrying out the threat. To require the indictment to contain an allegation of the means intended to be used by Schmitz and Ruef to accomplish their unlawful purpose—the means to be used with, or to influence, or to menace, or duress, or fraud in dealing with, the Board of Supervisors—is indubitably bad law and bad pleading.

"5. The declaration that the case 'is not one which is sufficient to charge an offense in the language of the statute defining it,' made by the court, needs some reason and good authorities to make it good law outside of this State, and also in this State under the system of criminal pleading provided for by the code—which should be the law by which criminal pleading is to be measured.

"6. It does not seem to have been suggested to the court, and it does not seem to have occurred to the learned judges thereof, that the trial court was required to take judicial notice of the head of department of a co-ordinate department of the government of the City and County of San Francisco, and to take judicial notice of the fact that Schmitz was at least de facto Mayor. See Kerr's Cyc. Code Civ. Proc., Sec. 1875, Subd. 5.

"7. The position and practical control of Ruef, as the 'political

the decision and the various documents in the case, charged the Chief Justice with being "plainly inconsistent."

"The truth is," said Dean Wigmore, "that the learned Chief Justice in endeavoring to support his decision weaves a logical web and then entangles himself in it." [354] The moral of the Schmitz decision is,

---

boss' of San Francisco (a position unrecognized by law), and his undue influence over the Board of Supervisors (the exercise of which is contrary to public policy), was merely matter of evidence, and not a matter to be pleaded; the only thing that is important is, Was the threat made? and did the defendants, Schmitz and Ruef, through such threat, extort money, and by means of the fear raised thereby? If they did, it is utterly immaterial whether Schmitz was Mayor, or Ruef was a 'political boss,' and had or had not any influence with the Board of Supervisors. The Supreme Court seems to lose sight of the fact that the crime of extortion in this State is not confined to persons in office, and exercising official influence.

"8. A threat to do a lawful act, if made for the purpose of putting a person in fear, and thereby securing money or property which the person was not in law entitled to have and receive, renders such person guilty of extortion, under the weight of decision and the better doctrine; and taking the case in that view, the indictment is amply sufficient, and should have been upheld by the court. The case of Boyson vs. Thorn, 98 Cal., 578; 33 Pac. Rep., 492, has no application, and its citation by the court only tends to befog the issue."

[354] Dean Wigmore's criticism of the decisions in the Schmitz case, and of the articles written in defense of them was as follows: "I have read the letter of Mr. Heney, and the letter of the Chief Justice, and have re-read the opinion of the Court in People vs. Schmitz, 94 Pac. Rep. 419. The Chief Justice's letter and Mr. Heney's reply turn largely on the legal rule of judicial notice. The learned Chief Justice finds himself iron-bound by the rules of that subject. But the whole spirit of the rules is misconceived by him. Their essential and sole purpose is to relieve the party from proof,—that is, from proof of facts which are so notorious as not to need proof. When a party has not averred or evidenced a fact which later turns out, in the Supreme Court's opinion, to be vital, the rule of judicial notice helps out the judge by permitting him to take the fact as true, where it is one so notorious that evidence of it would have been superfluous. Now these helping rules are not intended to bind him, but the contrary, i. e., to make him free to take the fact as proved where he knows the proof was not needed. Moreover, it follows that, since these rules cannot foresee every case that new times and new conditions will create, they can always receive new applications. The precedents of former judges, in noticing specific facts, do not restrict present judges from noticing new facts, provided only that the new fact is notorious to all the community. For example, the unquestioned election of William H. Taft as President of the United

Dean Wigmore concludes, "that our profession must be educated out of such vicious habits of thought."

The extravagance of the criticism of the decision was more than equaled by the claims made by the opposition to the prosecution, of its effect upon the status of Schmitz and Ruef.

"Schmitz," said a writer in The Chronicle, "is now

States is notorious; but no man named William H. Taft has ever been elected President, and no judicial precedent has noticed the fact. But no court would hesitate to notice this new notorious fact.

"If, then, a man named Schmitz was notoriously Mayor of San Francisco and a man named Ruef was notoriously its political boss, at the time in question, that is all that any court needs; and the doctrine of judicial notice gives it all the liberty it needs. It is conceivable that a trial judge might sometimes hesitate in applying this doctrine of notoriety, because the trial court might fear that the Supreme Court would not perceive the notoriety. But there never need be any such hesitation in a Supreme Court, if that court does see the notoriety.

"And this is just where the learned Chief Justice is to be criticised. He does not for a moment ask or answer the question, 'Did we actually, as men and officers, believe these facts to be notoriously so?' but refers to certain mechanical rules, external to his mind. What that Supreme Court should have done was to decide whether they under the circumstances did actually believe the facts about the status of Schmitz and Ruef to be notorious. In not so doing, they erred against the whole spirit and principle of judicial notice.

"And Mr. Heney's demonstration that there is nothing in the codes to forbid them is complete; for, of course, the Code of Procedure, in telling them (Section 1875) that 'the courts take judicial notice of the following facts,' simply gave them a liberty of belief as to those specified facts, and did not take away their liberty as to other unspecified facts.

"But there is a deeper error than this in the learned Chief Justice's letter, and in the court's opinion. The letter says: 'If by means of these allegations or otherwise it had been made to appear that the defendants had caused the applicants to believe that they could and would influence the Police Commissioners to reject their application regardless of its merits I have never doubted that the indictment would have been sufficient.' He stakes his decision on this point. The point is that, in determining the fear caused by the threat, which constituted extortion, the belief of the restaurant-keeper as to Schmitz's and Ruef's power, and not their actual power, was the essential thing. If that is so, then of what consequence was it whether one or the other was Mayor or boss? And of what consequence was it whether those facts were averred or judicially noticed. None at all. The indictment alleged that the threats were made to use influence or power over the Commissioners, and that their purpose was to obtain money by means of (i. e., through fear of) such threats. Obviously, then, the actual power or influence was immaterial; and the belief of

thoroughly exonerated of the charge of having squeezed money from Malfanti, the French-restaurant man."

However this may have been, the practical result of the decision was that both Schmitz and Ruef, with

---

the restaurant-keeper, the only material fact, was a question of the evidence on the trial, and not of the legal sufficiency of the indictment. All the lucubrations about judicial notice were therefore beside the point.

"The inconsistency of the learned Chief Justice, in thus taking as essential the actual status of Schmitz and Ruef, is further seen in his next paragraph. There he declares 'it could not be assumed that such private persons could prevent the issuance of the license otherwise than by adducing good reasons.' But why does he assume that, on the contrary, a threat by a Mayor or a boss could prevent the issuance of the license otherwise than by adducing good reasons? He says that if it had appeared that the threats were made by a Mayor and a boss, then this would have sufficed, because, in his own words, their influence to reject the application would have been used 'regardless of its merits.' See what this means. Suppose that two persons, a Mayor and a private citizen, tell a restaurant-keeper that they will do all they can to induce a Commissioner to revoke the license unless money is paid; for one of these persons, the learned Chief Justice immediately assumes that he can and will do this 'regardless of its merits'; for the other he says 'it cannot be assumed.' Why not for one as much or as little as the other? He does not say that the private person could not possibly succeed in influencing the Commissioner corruptly—he merely says that 'it cannot be assumed.' On the other hand, why assume it for the Mayor? Surely a Mayor might fail in trying to influence an honest Commissioner by a corrupt threat to remove him. In short, either assume that on the facts of the trial a private person might have power to influence corruptly the license; in which case an allegation of his Mayoralty would be superfluous. Or else refuse to assume that a Mayor, merely as such, could and would inevitably influence a Commissioner corruptly; in which case the mere allegation of his being Mayor would not be enough, and judicial notice would not cure. But the Chief Justice says it would be enough! He is plainly inconsistent.

"The truth is that the learned Chief Justice, in endeavoring to support his decision, weaves a logical web, and then entangles himself in it.

"Such disputations were the life of scholarship and of the law six hundrd years ago. They are out of place today. There are enough rules of law to sustain them, if the court wants to do so. And there are enough rules of law to brush them away, if the court wants to do that.

"All the rules in the world will not get us substantial justice if the judges have not the correct living moral attitude toward substantial justice.

"We do not doubt that there are dozens of other Supreme Justices who would decide, and are today deciding, in obscure cases, just such points in just the same way as the California case. And we do not doubt there are hundreds of lawyers whose professional habit of mind would make them decide just that way if they were elevated to the bench tomorrow in place of those other anachronistic jurists who are now there. The moral is that our profession

no convictions against them, by furnishing bonds in the bribery cases, were able to walk out of prison.

Schmitz did not return as a prisoner. Ruef enjoyed his liberty until November, 1908.

---

must be educated out of such vicious habits of thought. One way to do this is to let the newer ideas be dinned into their professional consciousness by public criticism and private conversation.

"The Schmitz-Ruef case will at least have been an ill-wind blowing good to somebody if it helps to achieve that result.

"December 7, 1908.   JOHN H. WIGMORE."

CHAPTER XXIII.

THE DEFENSE BECOMES ARROGANT.

The prosecution's reverses in the Appellate and the Supreme Courts were followed by startling changes of policy on the part of the defendants.

The officials of public service corporations, who by every technical device within the ingenuity of the best legal talent that could be purchased, had for months resisted trial, suddenly became clamorous for their trials to begin. Abe Ruef, who had been counted, by the public at least, as friendly to the prosecution, openly broke with the District Attorney and his associates.

President Calhoun of the United Railroads, who had been in the East, returned to San Francisco demanding trial. The San Francisco Examiner, now openly opposing the prosecution, announced this new move to be a bomb-shell thrown in the prosecution's camp. Nevertheless, The Examiner could not entirely conceal the astonishment caused by the defense's new policy.

"Just what has brought about this change in Calhoun's attitude," said the Examiner in its issue of January 28, 1908, "was not explained yesterday. Tactics of evasion, motions of obstruction, and every other artifice known to legal legerdemain to stay proceedings have heretofore been the accepted etiquette of the graft defendants, and conspicuously that of Patrick Calhoun."

The Call, supporting the prosecution, boldly charged that the graft defendants were in treaty with Ruef.[356] And this view the District Attorney's office was finally forced to accept.

No sooner had the decision of the Appellate Court been made public than Ruef clamored for dismissal of the extortion charge to which he had plead guilty, but which the higher court had decided in the Schmitz case did not constitute a public offense. In this Ruef was backed by Rabbis Nieto and Kaplan.

Ruef, after the Schmitz-Ruef officials had been swept out of office, had been confined in the county jail. From the day of his jail imprisonment the two

---

[356] When Calhoun returned to San Francisco demanding immediate trial, the Examiner announced that he "threw a bombshell into the camp of the prosecution." The Call, however, dealt with the incident as follows:

"Patrick Calhoun has come back in a hurry, shouting for an immediate trial. He is certain that he has the prosecution on the hip. His men are in treaty with Ruef. His organs in the press, the Examiner, the Chronicle and the gutter weeklies, begin to see Ruef in a wholly new light. Three weeks ago Ruef was the vilest criminal. No immunity for him. Indeed, immunity, in the lexicon of the Calhoun press, was then a worse crime than bribery or graft. It is very different now that the new alliance between Ruef and the bribe givers is in process of negotiation. Ruef has at once become the persecuted sufferer, the victim of a heartless cabal, pushing one more unfortunate to his ruin and positively 'rushing' him to trial with indecent haste, with no lawyers but Henry Ach to hire. It is too bad.

"Why this astonishing and sudden change of front? It is simply that Calhoun has made up his mind that this is the time for grafters and boodlers and bribe givers to stand together. He has persuaded himself that the prosecution is dazed by the extraordinary decision of the Court of Appeals, and that the same has put Ruef in a receptive mood for a treaty of alliance, offensive and defensive, among all varieties of boodlers, franchise grabbers, bribe givers and bribe takers. Calhoun knows that Ruef on trial or before trial is a very different person from Ruef after conviction. He wants to keep Ruef in his present state of mind. Of course, he knows that he can not trust Ruef. No man who has had dealings with the shifty boss knows on what side he will turn up next. At present Ruef lends a responsive ear to Calhoun's overtures. Consultations are held without disguise between Calhoun's lawyers and Ruef. It is time for Ruef and Calhoun to stand together. The association is suggestive but natural."

Rabbis besought the District Attorney day and night[357] not to force the broken boss to remain behind the bars.[358]

Langdon, not having decided at the time to appeal from the Appellate Court decision to the Supreme Court, finally yielded to the importunities of the two clergymen and stated to Judge Dunne that Ruef wanted to make a motion to withdraw his plea of guilty in the extortion case. Judge Dunne replied that he would not consider such motion.[359]

This closed the incident so far as dismissal of the case before the Supreme Court could pass upon it, was concerned. But it did not stop Ruef's insistence that not only should he be allowed to withdraw his plea of guilty, but that he be given complete immunity from prosecution of all the charges against him.

Langdon, even before he had spoken to Judge Dunne about permitting Ruef to withdraw his plea, had become convinced, as Heney had become convinced long before, that Ruef was not playing fair with the prosecution. Ruef, when confronted with charges of holding

---

[357] The graft prisoners unquestionably suffered greatly from their confinement.

"No matter," said Ruef, in an interview printed in The Examiner January 11, 1908, "how much effort is made, the place cannot be kept clean. Filth accumulates and no running water has been provided. The gases from the drain pipes permeate the cells and are always present. No prisoner can keep himself clean, and it is no wonder that clothing and everything is uncleanly."

Schmitz, long of body, complained that he needed a long cell. "I would like a longer cell," he is reported as saying. "My legs are too long and I cannot stretch them out. The hole is beastly and no place for a clean man."

Louis Glass declared that he would be dead in a few days if not permitted to remain outside his cell.

[358] See affidavit filed by District Attorney Langdon in The People vs. Patrick Calhoun et al., No. 823.

[359] See affidavits filed by District Attorney Langdon, and by Judge Dunne, in the case of Patrick Calhoun et al., No. 823.

back evidence, shifted and evaded, until Langdon, losing patience, charged him with falsehood.

About the middle of January, evidence came into Langdon's possession [360] which convinced him beyond a shadow of a doubt that Ruef, instead of observing the immunity contract, was, as a matter of fact, dealing with and assisting his co-defendants, advising them of every move.

Langdon [361] at once called Ruef before him and notified him that the immunity contract was canceled.[362]

The abrogation of the immunity contract brought open break between Ruef and the prosecution. Ruef

---

[360] Langdon does not state in his affidavit what this evidence was. But at the trial of Ruef for offerng bribes to Jennings Phillips to grant the Parkside Railroad franchise, former Supervisor Wilson testified that at the first Ford trial Ruef had asked him to bury his memory of the money transactions and discussions with Ruef. Ruef at the time was pretending to be assisting the Prosecution in conformity with the terms of his immunity contract.

[361] District Attorney Langdon, in an affidavit filed in the case of The People vs. Patrick Calhoun et al., No. 823, states his attitude toward Ruef. Mr. Langdon says:

"Affiant further avers and declares that if affiant believed that the defendant Ruef had fully and fairly performed his part of the agreement, and had honestly rendered such service to the State as would have entitled him to the consideration set forth in the immunity contract, this affiant would have moved in open court to dismiss the indictments against defendant Ruef, and if said motion were denied and affiant was directed by the Court or any other official to proceed with the trial of said defendant, this affiant would have declined to do so, and after exhausting every resource at his command to carry out the terms and conditions of said immunity agreement, would have resigned his official position of District Attorney of the City and County of San Francisco, rather than prosecute the defendant Ruef.

"This affiant avers that it was only when he became convinced that the defendant Ruef was still traitorous to the State he had debauched, and whose laws he had defied, and that instead of trying to make reparation for the wrong he had done, was endeavoring not only to save himself from the punishment he so richly deserved, but also was endeavoring to make certain the escape from punishment of his co-defendants, that affiant determined the immunity contract to have been broken by Ruef, and no longer in force and effect."

[362] The Examiner in its issue of January 19, 1908, stated that the abrogation of the immunity contract, "means among other things that Ruef will now have aligned in his defense, the massed influence of interests represented by the prosecution to command $600,000,000 in wealth."

set up claim that under his immunity contract all the graft cases were to be dismissed against him, including that under which he had plead guilty to extortion. He insisted that he had lived up to his part of the agreement and charged that the prosecution was breaking faith.

In this position, Ruef was backed up by Rabbis Kaplan and Nieto, who for months had been clamorously active in his behalf. Indeed, long before the open breach had come, so persistent had the Rabbis become in their insistence that Ruef be released, that Heney had found it necessary to request Kaplan to remain away from his office.[363] When Ruef finally broke with the prosecution, the two Rabbis were to the fore backing up his contention that the prosecution was not keeping faith with him.[364]

Kaplan soon after filed an affidavit setting forth that under the agreement with the prosecution, Ruef was to

---

[363] Heney, in an affidavit filed in the case of The People vs. Patrick Calhoun et al., No. 823, states that he finally said to Kaplan, "You only annoy and irritate me by coming here, Doctor, and I wish you would stay away. I don't want to get mad at you, because I respect you and am satisfied that you are sincere, but Ruef is making a fool of you, and I have wasted more time than I can spare in talking with you about these things. You will do me a great favor if you will stay away from my office."

In spite of this suggestion, Kaplan, a few days later, called Heney up on the telephone. Of the incident, Heney says in his affidavit: "A few days later, however, he called me on the telephone. I was at my office at the time, and do not know where he was. He said over the telephone in substance, 'Mr. Heney, I don't like to trouble you any more, but I had a talk with Mr. Burns and I have since had another talk with Mr. Ruef, and I am sure that Mr. Ruef's testimony will now satisfy you. He says that when he is on the witness stand and you ask him'—I interrupted him at about this point and said in a very severe tone of voice, 'Dr. Kaplan, I don't want you talking such stuff to me over the phone, or anywhere else. I have asked you not to talk to me about this matter any more and not to come to my office, and I will now have to ask you not to call me any more on the telephone. I don't want to hear anything more about Ruef's testimony."

[364] See affidavits filed by Rabbis Nieto and Kaplan in the case of The People vs. Patrick Calhoun et al.

have had complete immunity, and be allowed to withdraw his plea of guilty in the extortion case. Later
on, Nieto, "Ruef's diplomatic middle man," as he was
called, filed an affidavit to the same effect. Ruef, on his
part, filed a voluminous affidavit, purporting to cover
all his transactions with the prosecution, in which he
not only set up the claim that he was to have been
given complete immunity but alleged that Langdon,
Heney and Burns, were guilty of subornation of perjury in having endeavored to get him to swear falsely
against Schmitz and Ford.

Rabbis Kaplan and Nieto, in their affidavits gave
versions of the meetings with Judges Dunne and Lawlor, when the Judges stated their confidence in the District Attorney and his assistants, which differed from
the accounts contained in the affidavit of Heney and
the judges.[365] This brought the trial judges as well
as the assistant prosecuting attorney into the controversy.

The members of the Grand Jury that had indicted
the graft defendants had already had their trials in
open court;[366] petit jurors and witnesses had, in effect,
been on trial also. And now District Attorney and trial
judges were placed on their defense.[367]

Other graft defendants joined in the upholding of

---

[365] See Chapter XV.

[366] See Chapter XV.

[367] A letter from W. H. Payson, a leader of the San Francisco
bar, to Rabbi Nieto fairly expressed the public attitude on the
Rabbi's stand. Mr. Payson's letter read: "Rabbi Jacob Nieto.
Dear Sir:—As you have written a letter to the public explaining
your connection with the Ruef case, it may not be out of place
for one of the public to reply.

"When Mr. Ruef made his apparently frank statement admitting that he had betrayed his city into the hands of the spoilers,

Ruef and the denunciation of the prosecution. Adverse
newspapers joined in the cry of unfairness and hinted

---

but promised to do all in his power to right the wrong, whatever
the consequences might be to himself, the public believed him and
believed that he was going to do right because it was right and
for his own self-respect, and not at the price of saving his own
skin. Acting on this assumption many of us congratulated Mr.
Ruef and assured him that he had gone far toward recovering his
position in the public esteem. It now turns out from your letter
of explanation that Mr. Ruef's public statement of his high and
noble purpose was a mockery and hollow sham; that he had
rejected any proposition to act the man, but like his contemptible
associates, sought only to escape his just deserts.

"We recognize the unfortunate necessity the prosecution was
under of granting immunity in order to secure the evidence to
convict the greater felons, but surely the officers of the law were
fully qualified to attend to that miserable business. If you could
have influenced Mr. Ruef to stand on the higher plane of honor
and decency of which you are the advocate and representative,
you would indeed have done a great public service and you might
have saved him for better things, but it would seem that your
services were directed chiefly to saving him from the just penalty
of his crimes and that the arrangement with him was on the same
sordid level as the immunity contracts with the Supervisors, for
which no ministerial services were necessary. From your position
and religious heritage we had a right to expect that your distinguished services would have been put to a better use. I am
still sufficiently credulous as to believe that with proper influence
Mr. Ruef might have been induced to take the course we were
led to believe he had taken.

"Your letter even leaves it to be inferred that Mr. Ruef is justified in his present attitude, and that the judges, who, from your
statement, were ready to go to the extreme of mercy and consideration, are now to be censured for not carrying out an immunity
contract which has been flagrantly broken by the other party to it.

"The serious features of this unfortunate situation are not that
officials should receive bribes, or that men of wealth and standing
should bribe them, or that attorneys of reputation should engineer
the filthy operation, but that not one of the army of bribed and
bribers has been found of sufficient manliness or moral stamina
to make a frank statement of the facts and give aid in the cause
of justice, and that so many people are willing to shield the influential criminals for commercial motives, and that there is so low
a state of public morals as to make these things possible.

"The great body of the public is heart and soul back of this
prosecution, because we believe it is an honest attempt, not merely
to convict certain criminals, but to elevate the standard of public
morality, and whatever may be the outcome and even though,
through successive miscarriages of justice, every guilty man escape
his legal punishment, the graft prosecution has, nevertheless, succeeded beyond our fondest hopes; nine-tenths of its work has been
accomplished, and in the teeth of the most determined and desperate opposition perhaps ever known.

"Be assured that every guilty man will be convicted at the bar
of public opinion, and from that conviction there will be no appeal
and no escape; they will be known and branded for life, each and
every one. The public is not a party to the immunity contracts.
"Very truly yours,

"W. H. PAYSON.

"San Francisco, January 30, 1908."

at worse. The story became current that no appeal would be made from the Appellate Court's decision in the Schmitz case to the Supreme Court. Another story had it that the prosecution was breaking down, that the situation had become so complicated that no other trials could be had.[368]

On the other hand, the outcry did not in the least shake the faith of the citizens who were insisting upon the crushing out of corruption at the State's metropolis. Colonel Harris Weinstock, one of the largest merchants of the State, in a ringing address condemned the efforts made to discredit the prosecution.[369] The same position

---

[368] District Attorney Langdon's statement in reply to these criticisms was as follows: "I have no answer at this time to make to the statements given out by Patrick Calhoun and made in behalf of other defendants in the graft cases with the intention of discrediting the prosecution and attempting to lead the public to believe that we have acted unfairly in the conduct of these cases. The time will come when such charges will be answered, but they will be answered only as events shall dirct.

"Nothing that has occurred within the past few weeks has in any way complicated the situation as far as the prosecution is concerned or has tended to weaken our position. The original plans of the prosecution are to be carried out just as we have always intended to carry them out. The Ruef case will be tried immediately, and every other defendant under indictment will be brought to trial just as quickly as the courts are able to dispose of the cases. We shall not falter in our duty. I can promise that while the present District Attorney is in office this battle will be fought out to the end of the last case.

"The fact is that at the present time we have the tactical advantage over all the defendants, who have allied their interests for mutual protection. They know we have this advantage and that is why they are shouting so loudly from the housetops. We do not answer the attacks that are made because we are trying law cases and our every energy is bent to the prosecution of those cases. We are entirely satisfied, however, with the position in which we stand at this time and are prepared to fight our battles in the courts to a finish."

[369] The following are extracts taken from Mr. Weinstock's address:

"After all, the saddest thing is to find men who are rated as decent, law-abiding, intelligent, presumably high minded and moral, condoning the sins of the bribe givers and deploring their indictment and prosecution.

"Both the commercial and political bribe givers committed serious crimes, but by far the more serious was the crime of corrupting public officials, because the tendency of this crime is to under-

was taken in pulpit, club room and street discussion. From all parts of the State resolutions and memorials were sent the prosecution approving and upholding its work.[370] And doggedly the prosecution proceeded to justify the expressions of confidence in its singleness of purpose and in its ability to cope with the tremendous odds brought against it.

The immediate indictments about which the controversy raised by Ruef's claim for immunity centered were those in the United Railroad cases. The prosecution accordingly went before the Grand Jury then sitting—the Oliver Grand Jury which had brought the original indictments had long since adjourned—and secured three indictments against Ruef, Calhoun and Ford for the bribery of three Supervisors, Furey, Nicholas and Coleman.

In these indictments every technical error which the ingenuity of the defense had brought out was

mine the very foundation of the State, thus leading to the ultimate destruction of democracy.

"If the spirit of the respectables, fighting and condemning the graft prosecution, is to become the common spirit, then must we bid farewell to civic virtue, farewell to public morality, farewell to good government and in time farewell to our republican institutions and to civic liberty."

370 A very good example of this is shown in a memorial from Sonoma. The memorial read as follows:

"Sonoma, Cal., March 18, 1908. To William H. Langdon, Francis J. Heney, Rudolph Spreckels and others engaged in the graft prosecution in San Francisco. Gentlemen: It appearing that a portion of the press of this State is engaged in belittling the efforts of those engaged in the prosecution of the graft cases in San Francisco, and is endeavoring to impute improper and unjust motives to all who have such prosecution in charge; and we realizing that it is the duty of all honest people everywhere to uphold the hands of the prosecution, and to encourage them to proceed in all lawful ways to continue in their efforts to bring all law breakers to justice,

"We, the undersigned citizens and residents of Sonoma and vicinity, mindful of the good work you are all doing, wish to show our appreciation of your efforts, and encourage you in continuing to pursue the course you have marked out, to the end that all law breakers shall be punished and the majesty of the law vindicated."

eliminated.   The new indictments were not secured
because the prosecution regarded the objections as having merit, but that the District Attorney's office might
be prepared to meet any emergency which might arise.[371]

The next step was to bring Ruef to trial.   The
prosecution selected the indictment under which Ruef
had been brought to bar for offering a bribe to Supervisor Jennings Phillips to vote for the Parkside street
railway franchise.[372]

---

[371] Heney, in a published statement regarding these indictments, said: "We do not consider for a minute that there is a
particle of merit to any of the claims made by the defendants that
the former indictments were defectively drawn in any detail.   It
is wise, however, to be prepared for anything that might happen
at any subsequent time, and so the present true bills have been
found.   These indictments are so drawn as to eliminate every
technical objection that has been made by any of the defendants
to the former indictments, and the action has been at this time so
that the statute of limitations would not run against the crime
charged.   There is absolutely no significance to the fact that the
name of Abbott and Mullally were omitted, except that we feel
that the cases against the three defendants named are of far
greater importance.   Our sole purpose has been to throw an
anchor to windward to avoid possible trouble in the future."

[372] James D. Phelan, at the mass meeting called after the
attempted assassination of Heney, summed up the Parkside case
tersely: "Take the Parkside case," he said.   "There were some
men who wanted a franchise which we were all willing to concede,
but the boss said it would be advisable to pay for it.   Instead of
making a demand upon the Supervisors and an appeal to the citizens on the justice of their cause and the desirability of giving
them the franchise, they continued their dickering with Ruef, and
for so much money, thirty thousand dollars, I believe, he said he
would give it to them.   Then they 'doctored' their books and went
down to the Crocker National Bank and got the money in green-
backs, handed out to them by the teller of that institution, whose
managers were stockholders in the Parkside, among them a gentleman who told you the other day to vote against the Hetch-
Hetchy proposition, Mr. William H. Crocker.
"Now, finding that they could get so easily a privilege by paying for it, what did they do?   They asked Mr. Ruef to give them
the franchise, not on Twentieth avenue, an ungraded street, which
they first wanted, but in Nineteenth avenue, which had been dedi-
cated as a boulevard for the use of the people, which was substantially paved, and which was the only avenue we had to cross
from the park to Ingleside.   He said to them that that would take
fifteen thousand dollars more, and they said 'It's a bargain.'   And
these gentlemen who sought the least objectionable franchise, tell
you now that they were victims, tell you now that they could not
get their franchise any other way.   They were glad because they
were a part of the system, a part of the 'other fellows' of the
affiliated interests.   They were glad to pay their money, which was

Prospect of immediate trial made a different man of Ruef. He was at once seized with the panic which had come upon him when the jury had been completed to try him on the extortion charge. He begged for time. He insisted that he was without counsel. He asked for three weeks, a week, even two days.[373]

Then came an entirely new technical defense based upon the immunity contract. Ruef alleged that he had been deprived of his constitutional rights as a defendant, by following the set program outlined in the contract. But here Ruef had over-reached himself. He had on January 31 entered a plea of not guilty in the Parkside case, the case on trial. The District Attorney had abrogated the immunity contract thirteen days before, on January 18. Whatever technical advantage Ruef may have had because of the immunity con-

a paltry sum to them, in order to perpetuate the rule of Ruef; that they could go to him on any other occasion to get an extension, or a privilege or a franchise, or anything that they wanted, by simply paying for it. It would be the simplest form of government, my friends, to have somebody sitting in a place of power and pass out to you what you want. It would save you the expense of a campaign, it would save you the advertising in the newspapers, it would save you the cost of mailing a circular to every voter. It is indeed, a most economical and direct method of getting what you want from the government."

373 The Oakland Tribune, in support of Ruef's plea for delay, said: "Now the question arises: Is Ruef now being prosecuted in good faith for the offenses alleged against him or is he being forced to trial without adequate preparation merely to coerce him into giving testimony he has repeatedly told Heney, Langdon and Burns would be false? Is not the summary process of law being invoked to compel Ruef to tell to a trial jury a different story from the one he related under oath to the Oliver Grand Jury? In other words, is not the prosecution now trying either to punish Ruef for refusing to commit or convict himself of perjury or intimidate him into assisting, as a witness under duress, Heney and Langdon to make good the threat they reiterated on the stump last fall that they would send Patrick Calhoun to State prison?

"Admitting Ruef to be guilty of all the crimes of which he stands accused, is he not now being proceeded against in a criminal spirit and with a criminal intent? Having failed to get what they want by compounding the felonies of Ruef and his followers, are not the prosecution resorting to compulsion under the forms of law to compel the commission of perjury?"

tract was forfeited by his plea of not guilty after its annulment.

His attorney gravely contended, however, that Ruef —one of the shrewdest practitioners at the San Francisco bar—was without legal counsel when he had entered his plea, and that he had therefore innocently foregone his constitutional rights. This contention provoked a smile even from Ruef's partisans. The point was not urged further.

Seeing that trial could not be warded off on technicalities, Ruef endeavored to disqualify Judge Dunne, the trial judge. But this move proved premature. Judge Dunne was about to go on his vacation and Judge Dooling,[374] a Superior Court Judge from the interior, was called to sit in Judge Dunne's stead. Ruef thereupon proceeded to disqualify Judge Dooling. He alleged that Judge Dooling, as Grand President of the Native Sons of the Golden West, had signed an order expelling him (Ruef) from the order; he alleged further that Judge Dooling had attacked him in a speech at a banquet.

Judge Dooling, placed on trial as Judges Lawlor and Dunne had been, was forced to make defense. He denied in affidavits that he had ever specially mentioned Ruef's name in any speech, but admitted that he might have said that any man guilty of crime should be expelled from the Native Sons order.

Ruef went to the Appellate Court for a writ of pro-

---

[374] Judge M. T. Dooling was at the time Superior Judge of San Benito, one of the smaller of the interior counties. He had, however, already a State-wide reputation for integrity and ability. He left the San Benito County bench to accept the appointment of President Wilson as United States District Judge.

hibition to prevent Judge Dooling trying the case. The Appellate Court denied his petition. Then Ruef went to the Supreme Court. Here again his prayer was denied. Thus, protesting as vigorously as a cat pulled over a carpet by the tail, was Ruef for a second time dragged to trial. The work of securing a jury to try him began.

Gradually, the jury box filled. But before it was completed there occurred an incident of the prosecution even more startling than the sending of cash books out of the State, the trailing of members of the prosecution by agents of the defense,[375] the disappearance of witnesses, the larceny of the prosecution's records, or the attempted kidnaping of Witness Lonergan and Editor Older.

On the eve of taking testimony in the Ruef case an attempt was made to murder James L. Gallagher by dynamiting his residence. Gallagher was the pivotal witness against Ruef, as well as against Ford, then on trial.

In the Ruef case, Gallagher had taken word from Ruef to the Supervisors that there would be $750—later increased to $1000—for each of them if they granted the Parkside franchise. Without Gallagher's testimony the case against Ruef would fall flat.

General Ford's third trial was then in progress and well advanced. Here again, Gallagher was the pivotal witness. He had taken the trolley bribe money from

---

[375] Some of these trailers were arrested and forced into court. On one day four men, Frank Shaw, alias Harry Nelson, Harry Smith, alias Harry Zobler, J. R. Johnson, alias J. R. Hayes, and Cliff Middlemiss were placed under arrest for following Detective Burns.

Ruef to the Supervisors. He supplied the link between those who had been bribed, and Ruef. His testimony was indispensable if Ruef and Ford—then on trial— were to be convicted. His testimony was equally necessary in the cases against Calhoun, Drum, in fact all the graft defendants, except those who had dealt directly with the Supervisors.

The evening of the day following Gallagher's testimony in the Ford case, but before he appeared at the Ruef trial, dynamite was exploded at the front doors of the house in which he was residing. The dynamite had been placed next to the dining room. Gallagher was at the time living at the home of W. H. H. Schenck at Oakland.

So violent was the explosion that the house, a frame building, was split in twain. A pillar from the porch was thrown 150 feet. In the building on the adjoining premises, every window was broken. The family had just completed the evening meal and a number of them were still seated around the table. The table was split from end to end. At the moment of the explosion, one of those in the house was showing a curious watch guard and had the watch in his hand. The watch stopped, thus fixing the exact time of the explosion, 7:30 P. M.

There were in the house at the time of the explosion, W. H. H. Schenck and wife, and three children, the youngest seven years old; Lieutenant Guy Brown of the National Guard; and Gallagher and his wife. Every one in the building was thrown down by the force of the explosion, but extraordinary to say, none of them was seriously injured. Gallagher and his wife were in an upper room of the building. The stairway was demolished, and Gallagher was obliged to lower his wife to the ground, getting down himself the best way he could.

A month later three buildings in Oakland belonging to Gallagher were destroyed by dynamite. Soon after this second explosion a young Greek, John Claudianes, was arrested and charged with the outrage.

Claudianes made full confession, involving his brother Peter as principal. Peter Claudianes was finally captured at Chicago. On his return to San Francisco he confessed,[376] stating that he had been employed by

---

[376] According to Peter Claudianes' confession to Burns, he had been summoned from Chico to San Francisco by Felix Pauduveris early in March. Pauduveris told him he had a hard piece of work for Claudianes to do, namely, kill Gallagher, the chief witness in the graft prosecution. Pauduveris had told him there was $1000 apiece and three dollars a day for expenses in the job for them. The first proposition, according to Claudianes' confession, was for Claudianes to shoot poisoned glass into Gallagher's face by means of an ordinary sling-shot. But this plan was abandoned on the ground that Claudianes' capture would be sure to follow. A plan to poison Gallagher was also abandoned. Destruction by means of dynamite was finally decided upon. Pauduveris had taken Claudianes over to Oakland and showed him where Gallagher resided. After the failure of the dynamite plot, Claudianes had arranged to secure apartments in the same building with Gallagher and put poison into Gallagher's milk. Before this plot could be carried out, John Claudianes had confessed and Peter had become a fugitive from justice.

In his confession to Burns, Peter Claudianes stated: "Pauduveris said the prosecution with Heney, Langdon, Burns and Spreckels had put about 50,000 men out of work. We must get rid of Gallagher as he is their principal witness. If he is put out of the way the Prosecution will end. There is about $2000 in it for us and about $1000 in it for your brother John. Felix Pauduveris was very angry because no one was killed in the explosion at the Schenck house. He said it was not a clean job."

In his confession, Claudianes stated further:
"I thought I was working for Ruef, as I knew Felix was a very intimate friend of his. When Felix told me I had got to shadow Gallagher I knew the word came from Ruef. Felix said that Ruef would never go across the bay, as he had them all buffaloed. Ruef was too smart for those fellows, Felix said, and the gang was all behind Ruef. The prosecution had no grudge against Gallagher, but it had a grudge against Ruef."

a Greek, one Felix Pauduveris,[377] to murder Gallagher. Felix Pauduveris fled the city and the police of the world have been unable to locate him. Peter Claudianes was convicted of the attempt upon Gallagher's life, was sentenced to prison for life, and at present writing is confined in San Quentin prison.[378]

Quite as extraordinary as the attempted assassination of Gallagher was the indifference with which the outrage was received by the press that was supporting the graft defense.[379] The Chronicle condemned the outrage, but took occasion to denounce Gallagher.[380]

377 Pauduveris had been employed by the United Railroads as a "spotter." At the time of the explosion he was still in that corporation's employ. He was at the same time a political follower of Ruef.

378 The attempt upon Gallagher's life led the prosecution to take steps to secure his testimony in a form in which it could be used before a trial jury in the event of Gallagher's death. Under the California law, testimony taken at a preliminary hearing can, in the event of the death or disability of a witness, be used at the trial of the case. After the Parkside case trial, Ruef was arrested on a charge of bribery and given a preliminary examination at which Gallagher testified against him. Gallagher's testimony was thus made secure against poison or dynamite.

379 The Examiner following the explosion printed a series of ridiculing cartoons picturing the dynamiting of a bird cage and describing at length the escape of the parrot that had occupied it.

380 The Chronicle took advantage of the dynamite outrage to voice its condemnation of Gallagher. "There is," said that paper in its issue of April 24, "no more undesirable citizen on earth than the contemptible boodler James L. Gallagher, who is living on the profits of the shame which he brazenly flaunts in the face of mankind, but the effort to discover the miscreant who dynamited the house where he was living should be pushed as vigorously as if the intended victim was the most estimable citizen of California. Society despises such boodlers as Gallagher, but it does not seek their destruction by dynamite. The dynamiter is a coward who is even more contemptible than a boodler. He sneaks up in the dark, fires his explosive and runs, because in his craven soul he dare not stand up and meet his enemy. The punishment of the dynamiter—successful or unsuccessful—should be severe, but it should be solemnly inflicted after due process of law.

"It is, of course, possible that some of the wretches with whom he was associated during his career of crime have taken that method of getting rid of his testimony, but it is not probable. Among those against whom he has not yet given the testimony which he will give are the only persons who can be conceived of as having a motive to get Gallagher out of the way, but no one that

The weekly press, however, treated the affair as something of a joke on the confessed bribe-taker.[381]

In the face of the ridicule of the graft-defense press, the dynamiting of witnesses, and the continent-wide hunt for the dynamiters, the Ruef trial went steadily on.

One incident of the beginning of the trial, because of the event that grew out of it, eventually proved even more important than the trial itself.

During the examination of jurors, an ex-convict, one Morris Haas, was discovered to have been sworn to try the case. Heney exposed him and he was ex-

---

we hear of suspects any of them of having resorted to that atrocious method of defense, in which six persons besides Gallagher himself came near being murdered. In the absence of any conceivable sufficient motive the dastardly act must be assumed the work of a wicked man gone crazy."

381 The following from the San Francisco Argonaut of May 2, 1908, is fairly expressive of the attitude of the San Francisco weekly press on the attempt on Gallagher's life: "Mr. Heney in so far as it lay in him to do it, 'placed' the 'crime' upon the 'minions' of Calhoun. The other independent and all-seeing minds of the prosecution's staff fell in with this theory of the case. So far as the so-called graft prosecutors are concerned there is no mystery about the matter—the explosion in Gallagher's house was nothing less than an attempt to assassinate that eminent worthy for the sake of 'getting him out of the way.' This theory has to face several embarrassing considerations. In the first place, Gallagher's testimony has been given again and again, and stands as an official record in a half-dozen instances. Getting Gallagher out of the way would not, therefore, do away with his testimony. Furthermore, there are other witnesses competent to testify to every vital fact in the Gallagher story. So far as the immediate case is concerned, Gallagher has already given his testimony and the effect of 'getting him out of the way' would be only to emphasize his statements. Furthermore, if there had been any wish to get Gallagher out of the way there has been plenty of chances to do it any time this year and a half past. If assassination has been part of the scheme of the defense, there have been ten thousand opportunities since the striking of that famous bargain between Spreckels and Gallagher inside the Presidio gate. The thing might have been done, too, without hazarding the lives of half a dozen women and children."

In view of the inability of Mr. Langdon's successor in the District Attorney's office to make effective prosecution of the graft cases, on the ground that Gallagher, who had left California, was absent from the State, and that his testimony was necessary to secure convictions, the Argonaut article makes interesting reading.

cused from service.[382]   The incident, compared with
the other tremendous happenings of the time, was of
small importance, but it was destined to lead to the
greatest outrage of all the history of the prosecution,
the shooting down of Assistant District Attorney Heney
in open court.   But for the time, Haas passed out of
the graft cases and was forgotten.

The Ruef trial was not unlike the Ford trials.   The
courtroom was packed with detectives, agents and
thugs employed by the various graft defendants.[383]
There was the same hesitancy on the part of witnesses.
At one stage of the proceedings Ach, Ruef's chief of
counsel, sneered that the State was having trouble with
its own witness.

"Yes," replied Heney, "The People have no witness—no volunteer witnesses.   We merely produce
them."

When J. E. Green, president of the Parkside Company, who had authorized the payments to Ruef, refused to testify on the ground that he might incriminate himself, it looked as though the case was going
against the prosecution.   But Heney met this objection.
He promptly moved the dismissal of the fourteen indictments pending against Green.[384]   Ach objected, but
the motion was granted.   Green was left free to testify.

---

[382] Heney's exposure of Haas was unquestionably warranted and
necessary.   The incident, however, has been made subject of much
misrepresentation and attacks upon Heney.

[383] Heney in a speech made before Mayor and Supervisors
showed how the prosecution was harassed by thugs.

[384] See transcript in The People vs. Ruef (Parkside case) for
dismissal of these indictments and of other indictments against
Parkside officials.

Green testified how he had sent his attorney,[385] Judge Walter C. Cope, to Ruef to find out what Ruef was after. Ruef wanted $50,000 to put the franchise through. Green testified that Ruef finally agreed to take $30,000, and was actually paid $15,000 on account.

G. H. Umbsen testified to having received $30,000 from the Parkside Company for Ruef and had paid Ruef $15,000, the balance being held until the deal should be consummated. In addition to this, the sorry manner [386] in which the company's books had been juggled to cover up the transaction was shown by witnesses connected with the Parkside Company.

Ruef's intimation through his attorney that the money had been paid as a fee was offset by testimony that the books had been juggled to cover up the payment to Ruef because Ruef was the political boss of the city, and it was believed that it would do the company no good if the fact of his employment were known.

Gallagher testified that he had been Ruef's representative on the board; that Ruef had told him that the Parkside franchise was to be held up and delayed; that later Ruef had stated that each Supervisor would receive $750 because of the Parkside deal; that finally, after the fire, Ruef had told witness that the Parkside people wanted the franchise in a new form, and that the $750 to each Supervisor would be increased to $1,000; that he (Gallagher) had conveyed this information to the Supervisors. Supervisors testified to having been given the information by Gallagher.

---

[385] For additional data regarding this case, see Chapter XIV, footnotes 180, 181, 198, 199, 200, 201.

[386] See footnote 199.

Ruef offered no testimony. The jury was out forty-three hours. By a vote of 6 to 6 the jury failed to agree. Again a graft trial had ended in discouraging failure for the prosecution.[387]

After the disagreement of the jury in the Ruef Parkside case, to judge from most of the San Francisco public prints of the time, the prosecution was utterly discredited in San Francisco. But there is a surer means of estimating public opinion—namely, by the votes of the people.

Much of the graft defense's abuse and vilification was heaped upon Judges Lawlor and Dunne, who had stood firmly for enforcement of the law regardless of who might be affected. Judge Dunne's term as Superior Judge was to expire in 1909. He was, at the November election of 1908, a candidate for re-election.

Judge Dunne was frankly fought by the graft defense, and supported by those who approved the work of the prosecution. The Republican county convention refused to nominate him, and hissed his name. The Union Labor party convention received his name with a turmoil of hoots and jeers. A letter to the last-named convention from the Good Government League urging his nomination was thrown into the waste-paper basket.

---

[387] Months after, when men had been indicted for endeavoring to influence jurors to vote for Ruef's acquittal in the United Railroads case, Isaac Penny, who had acted as foreman of the jury that failed to agree in the Parkside case, in a public statement denounced that jury as not honest. "Had I known then," said Penny in an interview printed in the San Francisco Call, September 30, 1908, "what I have since learned about jury tampering, I would have sprung a sensation in Judge Dooling's court that would have resulted in the haling of numerous men before the court. * * * I have been turning this over again and again in my mind, and there is but one answer—that jury was not an honest one."

Later, Penny gave sensational testimony along this line in Judge Lawlor's court.

On the other hand, when given opportunity for expression The People gave Judge Dunne encouraging endorsement. The Good Government League proceeded to have his name put on the ballot by petition. For the petition 1,765 signatures were required. Over 3,000 persons signed it the first day. The press—outside San Francisco—following the graft trials closely, was practically a unit in urging Judge Dunne's return to the bench.[388] And in spite of the costly contest of his election, The People of San Francisco re-elected Judge Dunne.

Thus again were the contentions of the graft defense repudiated at the polls.

Another important endorsement of the prosecution came from the Board of Supervisors. The Supervisors provided in their annual budget $70,000 to meet the extraordinary expenditures because of the graft cases. Burns and the men who had theretofore been paid out of the fund controlled by Rudolph Spreckels, became regular municipal employees operating under the District Attorney.

---

[388] From one end of the State to the other, Judge Dunne was warmly commended as a jurist and a man. "The name of Judge Dunne," said the Pasadena News, "stands in California honored among honest men because of the enemies he has made. Every politician and every newspaper that has defended bribery and sought to embarrass the graft prosecution is against Judge Dunne. They stocked a political convention against him. Judge Dunne's defeat in San Francisco would be a disgrace to that city and a reflection on the honor and intelligence of the people of California."

"The corrupt corporation organs," said the Sacramento Bee, "and the servile journalistic tools of the predatory rich—such as the Argonaut, for instance—are barking in unison at the heels of Judge Dunne in San Francisco and declaring he is unfit to sit on the bench. Dunne's crime in their eyes is that he did his simple, plain duty in the graft prosecution cases. If he had neglected that duty, to tip the scales of Justice over to favor the 'higher ups,' the same gang, with the Argonaut in the lead, would be praising him to the skies as a most just judge, a righteous judge, and would be clamoring for his re-election."

The criticism of the defense had been that it was shameful that a privately-financed prosecution should be tolerated. Their cry now was at the shame of wasting the public funds on Burns and his staff. Action was instituted, through William H. Metson, to prevent the municipal officials paying Burns and his associates out of this fund. For months the salaries of those affected were held up. Although eventually the opposition to the prosecution lost in the contest, and the men were paid the amounts due them, the suit was an annoyance and a handicap.

But in spite of the tremendous opposition which the graft defense was working up, the prosecution went steadily on with its work. Ruef was put to trial for offering a bribe to Supervisor Furey to vote for the permit giving the United Railroads its overhead trolley franchise.

CHAPTER XXIV.

Jury-Fixing Uncovered.

From the beginning of the graft trials rumors of efforts to tamper with the trial jurors had been current. The failures of juries to agree in the face of what to the man on the street appeared to be conclusive evidence, lent more or less color to these reports. But it was not until Ruef's trial [389] for offering a bribe in the over-head trolley transaction opened, that the jury-fixing scandal took definite shape. Then, came sensational exposures, involving indictments and trials for jury-fixing which for a time over-shadowed in interest the graft trials themselves.

Ruef's trial for offering a bribe to Supervisor Furey to vote for the over-head trolley franchise, began Au-

---

[389] Of the "fixing of juries," The Chronicle in its issue of September 19, 1908, said: "Every move made in the Ruef trials gives moral evidence that systematic bribery of juries is being practiced which is as convincing to the public as were the signs of corruption during the entire Schmitz regime, but before the explosion. Nobody doubted then that the Mayor, the Supervisors and all officials appointed by Schmitz were thieves. Nobody doubts now that all through these graft trials there has been systematic corruption of juries. In private conversation it is treated as a matter of course. Nobody, of course, could 'prove' it. Nobody needs legal proof to be convinced."

Of the incident, The Call said in its issue of September 19, 1908: "For a long time there has been every reason to believe that veniremen summoned to try Ruef were being bribed or promised bribes to vote for acquittal. The dubious character of Ruef's attorneys, or some of them, and their known affiliations were wholly consistent with this theory. Circumstances not amounting to absolute proof, but giving cause for strong suspicion, came to the surface from time to time. The jury fixers grew bolder with impunity, and, in fine, the pitcher went to the well once too often."

gust 27, 1908.[390]   But nearly a month before, on July 31, District Attorney Langdon had been given definite information that an attempt had been made to bribe one of the talesmen who had been called for jury service at the Ruef trial.   The talesman in question was John Martin Kelly, a real estate salesman.

The list of prospective jurors had been made public in July.   Late on the afternoon of July 31, Mr. Langdon received a telephone message from Kelly requesting an interview, which was granted immediately.

Kelly told Langdon [391] that that afternoon he had

---

[390] The trial had been delayed by Ruef's preliminary hearing. The hearing was held in order that Gallagher's testimony might become of record in a way that would permit of its being used at Ruef's trial, in the event of Gallagher's assassination.

Ruef's attorneys by lengthy cross-examinations and other delaying tactics, succeeded in dragging the case along for sixty-nine days.   Further delays were caused by the usual efforts made to disqualify Judge Lawlor as trial judge.   In this way, the defense managed to keep the attorneys for the State engaged until late in August.   Then Ruef was made to face another jury.

[391] Kelly claimed to have telephoned Langdon within a few minutes after Blake had left him.   In this he was borne out by his employer, Samuel M. Snyder.   Snyder testified that on his return to his office on the afternoon of July 31, he met Blake leaving.   Kelly had followed him into his private office.   Of the interview which followed Snyder testified at the hearing of the case as follows:

"I said (to Kelly) 'Well, what is the matter now?'   And he said that Mr. Blake was just in and wanted to give him $500.   I said, 'What for?'   'Well,' he said, 'to do the right thing on the jury.' He had been called on a jury case, the Ruef case.   He said, 'I had a notion to punch his head.'   That is just the remark Mr. Kelly used.   I said, 'Oh, I would not get excited like that; that is foolishness.'   He said, 'What do you advise doing?   If I go out and do anything rash I am liable to get into trouble, ain't I?'   I said, 'Yes, you better not do that.'   I said, 'If I were you'—this is the language I used to Mr. Kelly, I said, 'I would telephone to Mr. Langdon and tell him.'   He said, 'Well, that might hurt your business.'   I said, 'Well, I don't believe that would hurt my business any.   I firmly believe that jurors should not be tampered with by anyone to try any case, no matter what it is.'   And from there he did telephone to Mr. Langdon.

The Court: "When was this, Mr. Snyder?"

"A.   That was on the 31st of July, pretty close to 5 o'clock in the afternoon.

"Q.   Did Mr. Kelly call up a telephone number from the office at that time?

"A.   He called up Mr. Langdon from the office at that time. I was sitting right by the side of him."

been approached by a building contractor, E. A. S. Blake, and offered $500 if he would qualify on the Ruef jury and vote for acquittal.[392]

Langdon called in Burns. Burns advised Kelly to pretend to listen to Blake's overtures, to insist that $500 was too little, and to demand $1000, to the end that Blake might be trapped and the jury-fixing, which all believed to be going on, be uncovered.

Kelly, co-operating with Burns, followed these instructions. In his dealings with Blake, Kelly insisted upon $1000 as the price of his services in Ruef's behalf, which Blake finally consented should be paid him. The negotiations were carried on during August. Finally on September 3, Burns directed Kelly to step up to the bar of Judge Lawlor's court where Ruef's trial was proceeding, and tell his story.

As Kelly on that day approached the bar, during a lull in the proceedings, Ach, it is alleged, was heard to ejaculate to the little group about Ruef, "There she goes."

---

[392] Of Blake's negotiations Kelly testified: "Mr. Blake began about this way: He said, 'Now, John, I have got a proposition to make to you, and I don't know how you will take it. If you like it, all right, if you don't, just keep it quiet.' He says, 'There is a chance for you to make a little money.' He said, 'You are drawn to serve on the Ruef jury.' I was surprised to hear that. I told him, 'I know I am on some panel in Judge Lawlor's Court, but didn't know it was the Ruef jury.' I said, 'How did you find out?' 'Oh,' he said—I think he said a friend of his told him, or something like that; but anyhow he said, 'Now, it is this way; there is $500 in it for you if you will get on that jury and vote to acquit Mr. Ruef.' I says, 'Well, Mr. Blake, I have never done anything like that, and it is a pretty big chance to take. I don't want anything like that'; and he began to urge it on me. I said, 'Now, give me a chance to think it over.' "

Kelly testified that his first impulse was to denounce Blake. But instantly he reflected that the denunciation would do no good. Besides, he reflected, it was possible that Blake might be trapped. As soon as Blake left the office, Kelly told what had occurred to his employer, Snyder, and within an hour was in consultation with District Attorney Langdon and Burns.

Frank J. Murphy, one of Ruef's attorneys, immediately jumped to his feet, and claimed the court's attention.

"If your honor please," said Murphy, "if that completes the examination of this panel and it is necessary to draw further from the box, there is a statement I desire to make to this Court which is based upon some reflection and upon the advice of the Presiding Judge of this court. Some several weeks ago, or about two weeks ago I should say, one of the jurors upon this panel sent to me indirectly and offered to accept money for his vote. Charges of bribery, of course, have been numerous in connection with this case, but this is the first instance that I have ever heard of in connection with this case or in connection with any other case that any juror has solicited a bribe, or has been offered a bribe. I consulted with Judge Sturtevant [393] about the matter on the 1st of September. I stated to him the facts in the case and he advised me that whenever the time became ripe for the juror to be called into the box that it was my duty to present it to this court. Now, the juror's name is John Martin Kelly, and I was informed indirectly that Mr. Kelly solicited $1000 for his vote in this case, and the matter is of so much importance, your Honor, that I think an investigation should

---

[393] Judge Sturtevant, at the investigation which followed, showed himself not at all clear as to details. Finally Murphy asked him:

"Q. Judge, do you remember that I said to you that I had information that one of the jurors was willing to sell his vote for $1,000 and someone had come to me with that?

"A. I remember, Mr. Murphy, you mentioned the amount of $1,000 regarding one of his statements, but I would not go further than that; I don't remember what this man had agreed to do for the thousand dollars. That is my general recollection that that is about the substance of the statement you made to me."

be had by this court before this case proceeds further, and if necessary the Grand Jury should look into this matter and give it a thorough and exhaustive examination. Now, if your Honor please, I don't want to do Mr. Kelly an injustice. I would hesitate, if the Court please, to make a charge of that kind, but my informant is a man whom I have known but a very short time, and after a thorough examination by me of him, after eliciting from him every fact I could in connection with the case, I am induced to believe that he came with authority from Mr. Kelly to make this proposition to myself and one of the attorneys who was connected with one of the other cases. Now, if the Court please, under the advice of Judge Sturtevant, whom I consulted on the subject twice, I deem it my duty to call that to the attention of your Honor and if it is necessary to file any affidavit to set the machinery of this court in motion I am willing and ready to procure an affidavit to file so that a complete investigation may be had of this matter."

Murphy's statement created a sensation, which was more than duplicated by the statement made by Heney the moment after.

"If the Court please," said Heney, "before Mr. Murphy takes the stand I have a statement to make. Mr. Murphy says that he discussed this subject on the 1st. I have in my pocket a statement dictated by Mr. Kelly —this is one of the most audacious pieces of business I have yet met with—I have a statement made by this juror on August 28, 1908, that is before Mr. Murphy bethought him to go and see Judge Sturtevant, in which this juror sets forth fully the fact that a man was sent to him to bribe him in this case, and this juror not only made that statement on August 28th, but this juror went to the District Attorney's office, to Mr. Langdon, the other day, on July 31st, the day it was made, it is a long time now and he has been acting under the District Attorney's advice ever since, and Mr. Murphy never saw fit to call your Honor's attention to it until he saw Mr. Kelly come in the door there and anticipated from the fact that Mr. Blake was traced to Mr. Ach's office yesterday that Mr. Kelly was about to state to your Honor that he wanted this matter investigated, and that an attempt had been made to bribe him, and that under the District Attorney's advice he was going on to permit them to pay the money, if necessary, so that we might catch them in this act, and it is only because they have had occasion to suspect we knew it, that Mr. Murphy has the audacity to come in here and ask for an investigation. Now, we ask that Mr. Kelly take the stand and make the statement to your Honor that he came here for the purpose of making, and that Mr. Murphy didn't say anything about until he saw him standing there ready to make it to your Honor. He jumped up as soon as he saw Mr. Kelly walk in here."

After Heney had made his statement, Murphy took the stand and swore that Kelly, through Blake, had solicited a bribe of $1000 from Murphy to vote for Ruef's acquittal. Nevertheless, Mr. Murphy, as well as Mr. A. S. Newburgh, another of Ruef's attorneys, admitted under oath that they had suggested to Blake that he interview Kelly.[394]

---

[394] Murphy's testimony on this point was as follows: "On a day between the 20th of July and the 1st day of August, I went

Kelly took the stand and testified in a straightforward manner that he had been approached by Blake, that he had consulted with the District Attorney, and that a trap had been set to catch the alleged jury-fixer.

Detectives were sent out to notify Blake that he was wanted in court. But Blake could not be found. Later he was arrested as he was about to board an outgoing train.

Blake was found to be a poor man on the brink of bankruptcy. He had neither money, nor property. Nevertheless, attorneys [395] came forward to defend him;

to the office of Mr. Newburgh. Mr. Newburgh was then engaged in defending Mr. Ruef on a preliminary examination had in one of the Parkside cases. We were discussing generally the Ruef cases and the graft prosecution, and a man came into the office who was introduced to me by Mr. Newburgh as E. A. S. Blake. This present jury panel had been drawn, and we were discussing the Ruef cases generally, and finally I made a remark that the trial of Mr. Ruef in one of these cases—referring to 1436, 1437 and 1438, would proceed as soon as the Police Court examination was finished, and I stated that a jury had been impaneled, or a jury had been drawn, I had a list of the jury in my pocket, and I pulled it out and said to both Mr. Newburgh and to Mr. Blake: 'Perhaps you might know some of these people.' Mr. Blake glanced at the list, and he came down to the name of Mr. Kelly, and he said, 'I know Mr. Kelly; I have known him for a number of years; I used to work at Shreve's jewelry store with him; and he is an intimate acquaintance of mine.' Then I said, having in mind the decision of your Honor in the contempt case of W. J. Burns and others—"

The Court: (interruption): "Did this occur after that decision?"

"A. Yes—no, your Honor—I don't know—no, no. But having in mind—I will state what I had in mind—a statement your Honor had made at some previous time, that either side had the right to find out how the jury stood; that is, if they used legitimate means. I said to Mr. Blake, I said, 'How do you think Mr. Kelly stands on the graft prosecution?' 'Well,' he said, 'Mr. Kelly is a very liberal-minded fellow and I think he would give Ruef a square deal.' So I then said, 'Well, I would like to find out whether any of Mr. Burns' gumshoe men have interviewed him, or whether he belongs to the Good Government League or the League of Justice or any kindred organizations.' He said he would find out the next time he met Mr. Kelly."

See printed transcript on appeal The People vs. Abraham Ruef, Part II, Vol. II, p. 878. For Newburgh's statement see same transcript, part and volume, pages 943 and 944.

[395] In this there was remarkable similarity to the legal assistance given thugs who were from time to time arrested for interfering with the work of the Prosecution.

bonds were furnished him. The most powerful and wealthy defendant in the graft cases was not better served. But the best of legal service could not save Blake from indictment. Later, both Newburgh and Murphy,[396] Mr. Ruef's attorneys, were indicted also, charged with corruptly attempting to influence a juror.[397]

Kelly, at Blake's trial, told the same straightforward story which he had given at the original investigation. He was corroborated by his employer, and others. His testimony was most sensational. He stated, for example, that Blake had told him that it would be easy for him to qualify as a juror; that Ruef's attorneys would try to make it appear that they did not want him, and that their examination would be so thorough that the prosecution would not ask a question. Blake had also told him, Kelly testified, that he need not worry; that some jurors had taken money for their votes in the former Ruef trial and had not been caught.

---

[396] Murphy had figured in the Ruef trials, somewhat sensationally, from the beginning. When, for instance, Ruef, early in March, 1907, was a fugitive from justice, Murphy was acting as one of his attorneys. He was placed on the stand in Judge Dunne's court. The Chronicle, in its issue of March 7, 1907, contained the following account of his testimony:

"Frank J. Murphy, one of Ruef's lawyers, testified that he had last seen Ruef just outside Hebbard's courtroom on Monday.

"'Have you been doing any business with him since?'

"Murphy declined to answer this under his privilege as an attorney. 'We are looking for an absconding and hostile defendant, and the witness should not be allowed to draw conclusions as to whether the business he is doing for him is privileged,' declared Hiram Johnson.

"Heney suggested that it was the request to do this business rather than the business itself, that was sought by the Prosecution.

"A compromise was effected on an answer by the witness that he had not communicated directly or indirectly with Ruef during the past forty-eight hours."

[397] About the same time, Captain John J. West became involved in a charge of being connected with an alleged attempt to corruptly influence a talesman named John R. Foley to vote to acquit Ruef. But the West case was so overshadowed in importance by the Blake-Murphy-Newburgh proceedings that the public paid comparatively little attention to it.

Blake was convicted. He was later sentenced to serve four years in the penitentiary. After Blake's conviction, but before sentence was passed upon him, he sought out Attorney Matt I. Sullivan, one of the few prominent San Francisco attorneys who had kept free from entangling alliances with the graft defense. To Sullivan, Blake made confession [398] of his participation in the jury-fixing transaction. In his confession he involved Attorneys Murphy and Newburgh. Later, in open court, he made public statement of his participation.[399]

Blake in his statement in court set forth that he had become acquainted with Newburgh through having

[398] "Confessing his crimes," said The Call in its issue of October 30, 1908, "Blake, the jury briber, lays bare the ulcer that eats away the vitals of popular government. He explains why the San Francisco Graft Prosecution has not yet put anybody in the penitentiary. He makes it clear why Ruef is not in stripes. He shows why it is next to impossible to convict a rich man. He answers the familiar question, 'What's the matter with San Francisco?'

"On his way to prison Blake pauses for a moment and gives the people of San Francisco the most convincing argument in favor of the Graft Prosecution that they have had since the boodled Supervisors told their story of shame, and Ruef, in tears, delivered his confession, since recanted. Blake's revelation is of inestimable value to the cause of decency. Opportunely he tears away curtain and scenery and lets the people see what goes on behind the showy pretense of the graft defense. In the nick of time he exposes some of the actors in that satirical comedy which might very well be called 'To Hell with the Law—Money is Above It.' "

[399] Members of the faculty of Stanford University sent the following communication to Rudolph Spreckels, William H. Langdon, Francis J. Heney, William J. Burns and their associates:

"We, the undersigned citizens of the State of California, realizing the far reaching significance of the sworn confession, as a jury briber, of E. A. S. Blake, extend to you our earnest and sincere congratulations on having successfully demonstrated the nature of some of the obstacles blocking the way of the conviction of powerful criminals in our commonwealth.

"Believing that no stability of social relations, including normal business conditions, can be established on a less firm basis than incorruptible courts and honest juries, leading to the prompt and sure administration of justice, we wish to assure you of our continued confidence and moral support in the great work upon which you are engaged."

The letter was signed by President David Starr Jordan and practically all the members of the faculty.

offices in the same building with him. He had, he said, met Murphy in Newburgh's office. Newburgh had introduced them. Murphy, he stated, had shown him a list of prospective jurors, and had asked him if he knew any of them. He had told the lawyers that he knew John Martin Kelly. They had, Blake stated, got him to make an offer to Kelly, which he did. He had offered Kelly $500 and finally $1000. Kelly (acting under instructions from District Attorney Langdon and Burns) had finally agreed to take $1000. Blake testified that he had reported back to Murphy that Kelly would accept the money.

Following his arrest, Blake testified, his lawyers had come to him without his solicitation,[400] with the statement in explanation that they had come from a mutual friend. Blake stated that he had heard afterward that the "mutual friend" was Murphy and Newburgh. His bonds had been furnished without his stir, through his attorneys. Murphy and Newburgh, he claimed, had assured him they would do everything they could for him; that he need not worry; that they would provide for him and provide for his wife in case he were convicted.[401]

Continuing, Blake stated that after his conviction he had had a talk with Murphy. The general nature of the interview was that he had good ground for a new trial. "They said," Blake testified, " 'when we get up

---

[400] Similar testimony was given at Murphy's trial.

[401] It developed later that the Blakes had been living together under a contract marriage. Later they went through the marriage ceremony. This phase of the case was made much of by the defense. Mrs. Blake, however, stood devotedly by her husband through all the trying events that followed his arrest and imprisonment.

to the higher court, it will be thrown out,' or something of that kind."

According to Blake's statement, a fund of $10,000 was promised him and an agreement was made that his wife should be paid $100 a month during his imprisonment. Murphy, he said, showed him what purported to be promissory notes [402] aggregating $7500. The notes, he alleged, were made to Murphy and signed with

---

402 Of these promissory notes Blake, in his statement to the court as published at the time, testified as follows:

"Q. How much money were you to get? A. I was to get $10,000.

"Q. For what? What were you to get that $10,000 for? A. Well, I was to say nothing about this matter, and that my wife would—

"Q. In other words—. A. She was to be provided for. She was to get $100 a month. The Court. How? A. To be taken care of when I was convicted, you know.

"Q. During your incarceration? A. Yes, and I was to have the $10,000.

Mr. Langdon: "Q. Who told you he would give you $10,000? A. Mr. Murphy.

"Q. What did he say? Just tell us what he said about that. A. The money was to be placed in the hands of a third party, who I would select, provided the one I selected would be satisfactory to them and they felt they could always have confidence in, or something of that kind. That $10,000 was to be turned over to me immediately upon my sentence—just as soon as my sentence was passed the money was to be turned over.

"Q. As soon as the court sentenced you you would receive the $10,000 that Murphy put into the hands of this third person? A. Yes.

"Q. Did he tell you what kind of money it was, or what representative value it was. Did he show you any of that? Did Murphy show you anything? A. Yes, he showed me $7,500, but he did not show me the $10,000 that was put into the hands of the party that I selected. He told me that he had it.

"Q. What was this $7,500 that Murphy showed you? In what form or shape? A. In notes.

"Q. Promissory notes? A. Yes.

"Q. Signed by who? A. Signed by Mr. Ruef.

"Q. Abraham Ruef? A. Yes.

"Q. Who else signed them, if any one? A. They were indorsed by his father and sister.

"Q. His father?

"The Court—promissory notes to you from Abraham Ruef, and indorsed? A. The promissory notes, your honor, were made out to Mr. Murphy, and he was to turn these over to the third party, indorsed, I presume, to the third party, who I might select. The notes read, "One year after date I promise to pay to Frank J. Murphy,' that is the way the notes read.

"Q. And signed? A. And signed by Mr. Ruef, and then they were countersigned or indorsed by his father and sister."

Ruef's name with the endorsement of Ruef's sister and father. Blake was requested to select a representative to hold the notes. It was alleged that Blake named Martin Stevens, an attorney, as such representative.[403]

After Blake's confession came the trials of Murphy and Newburgh. They did not differ to any great extent from the principal graft trials. There were the delaying tactics that had been characteristic of the graft cases; failure of jurors to agree; acquittals.

Murphy's trial came first. There was against him the testimony of Blake and Kelly, corroborated at many points by other witnesses. Murphy made denial. In his defense, too, many witnesses took the stand to testify to his good character.[404] Murphy was acquitted.

Newburgh's trial followed. The first jury failed to agree. It was stated at the time that the jury stood six

---

[403] Stevens denied this. Stevens was called before the Grand Jury and questioned. He declined to answer on the ground that the relations of attorney toward client cannot be violated. Blake exonerated Stevens from this obligation. But Stevens held that he acted for Murphy as well as Blake. The court held, however, that the communications were not privileged. Stevens in his testimony which followed, denied everything that tended to implicate himself and Murphy in any way with the attempted jury fixing, or with the alleged $10,000 fund.

[404] Among those who testified to Murphy's good character was Rev. H. H. Wyman, at that time the head of the Paulist Order at San Francisco. Another Paulist priest, Rev. Stark, showed great interest in Murphy's welfare.

After Murphy's acquittal a story was current in San Francisco to the effect that at a dinner given soon after Murphy's acquittal, Murphy had promised a present to the Paulist Church, St. Mary's, and that Father Stark had announced that a plate bearing Murphy's name and the date of his acquittal should be placed upon the gift.

However unjustified the story may have been, Murphy did give St. Mary's a present—a pulpit. On the pulpit was put a plate bearing Murphy's name and a date. The incident so incensed priests of the Paulist order who were not in sympathy with the course of Fathers Wyman and Stark at Murphy's trial, that they entered the church with a screw-driver, removed the plate, and threw it into San Francisco bay. Later a second plate was put upon the pulpit. So far as the writer knows, the second plate is still in its place.

for conviction and six for acquittal. At his second trial, Newburgh was acquitted.

But Blake was in jail under a four years' sentence to the penitentiary. Astonishing as the revelations in the Blake jury-fixing case had been, they were to be overshadowed by the events of Ruef's trial. Even as the city stood aghast at the evidence of jury tampering, Assistant District Attorney Heney was, during the progress of the trial, shot down in open court.

CHAPTER XXV.

The Shooting of Heney.

In spite of the sensational events following the trapping of Blake, the work of impaneling a jury to try Ruef went steadily on. After months of effort,[405] a jury was finally sworn to try the case.

Again the telling of the sordid story of the city's betrayal commenced.

Gallagher, the pivotal witness, had begun his sorry recital. In the midst of it occurred what those who had followed the methods of the graft defense had long predicted.

Assistant District Attorney Heney was shot down.[406] The shooting occurred in open court during a brief recess.

Heney was seated at his place at the attorneys' table

---

[405] Seventy-two days were required to impanel the jury before which Ruef was tried, fifty days being devoted to actual court work. There were summoned 1,450 talesmen, of whom 446 were examined. Six jurors were denied their freedom for forty-two days before the jury was completed. Blake, arrested for jury-fixing, was trapped, tried and convicted before the jury was completed. Two of Ruef's attorneys were, during the impaneling of the jury, indicted for alleged connection with Blake's attempt to influence the jury in Ruef's favor.

[406] There is, so far as the writer can find, no evidence that the Graft Defense or its agents employed Haas to kill Heney any more than there is evidence that the Graft Defense or its agents employed Pauduveris to murder the pivotal witness, Gallagher. But that Haas was urged to kill Heney because of the exposure of Haas's previous record at the first Ruef trial is well established.

"I was urged frequently," said Haas in a confession made to Langdon and Burns, "to kill Heney by certain persons whose names I will not tell you, and I also talked to other people about killing Heney and was advised by them not to do it. In addition to that, certain persons approached me several times and referred to the

talking with an assistant. The jury had left the court-room. Gallagher had for the moment left the witness box and was standing a few feet from Heney waiting opportunity to speak with him. A few feet further away was Heney's body guard. In the room were something more than 200 citizens waiting for the trial to be re-sumed. There was the usual confusion which attends a five-minute court recess. Court attaches, officials, at-torneys, citizens were passing to and fro without hin-drance.

The man who shot Heney had no difficulty in gain-ing access to the courtroom. He walked deliberately to the attorneys' table, and before he was even noticed,

---

time I was thrown off the Ruef jury, saying: 'I'd never stand that sort of a roast,' and 'I'd kill a man who did that to me,' and sim-ilar things.''

Who urged Haas to do this thing, and what was their motive? Haas alone could have answered the first question. But the bullet that ended his life sealed his lips forever.

Of Haas's purpose in getting on the first Ruef jury we have some testimony. Joseph Brachman, a close associate of Ruef, who had known Haas for nearly a quarter of a century, said in an inter-view published in the San Francisco Call, November 15, 1908:

"When Ruef was on trial in the Parkside case, on the bribery charge, I heard that Haas had been called on the jury panel. At that time I was frequently in consultation with Ruef, every day, in fact. But I was afraid to go to Ruef with what I knew of Haas. so I went to one of his lawyers—I won't say which one—and told him of the record of Haas. I told him that Haas was a bad man and an ex-convict. I said that Ruef should challenge him.

"I was in court the day that Haas qualified and passed into the jury. Again I told his attorney that Haas was a bad man, to get rid of him, but nothing was done. When Heney produced the evidence showing that Haas was an ex-convict I was in court, also. I met Haas after he had been disqualified. Haas told me the rea-son why he stayed on the jury and why his record was not made public by the defense of Ruef. He told me that he expected $4,000 from Ruef for his services on the Parkside case jury. He said that he was hard up, that he was in debt, that he owed money on his saloon and that if he had been permitted to stay on the jury he would have been able, with the $4,000 to be paid him by Ruef, to clear himself of debt.

"He also told me, Haas did, on the day that he was disquali-fied, that he was going to 'kill one of the prosecutors.' He did not say which one, but he frequently repeated to me, that he was 'going to get one of the prosecutors.' I met him many times and often, frequently he told me that he was 'going to get one of the prosecutors.' "

had fired deliberately at the Assistant Prosecutor. The gun was held not more than six inches from Heney's head. In an instant, Heney's bodyguard was upon the assassin. But the bodyguard's efforts came late. Heney, apparently mortally wounded, was lying unconscious on the floor, the blood gushing from a ragged hole in front of the right ear, just under the temple.[407]

Heney's assailant was found to be one Morris Haas, an ex-convict, who had succeeded in securing a place on the jury at the former Ruef trial. Heney had exposed him.[408] When it was demanded of him why he had attempted to kill Heney, he murmured incoherently, that it was "for humanity's sake." Although closely questioned Haas would tell little of value to those who were seeking to get at the real motive behind the assault. He was thoroughly searched both by Detective Burns and Captain of Police Thomas Duke, and then taken to the county jail where he was closely guarded.

A short time before the shooting of Heney, Judge Lawlor had had attorneys of both sides before him to state that in his judgment, he should remand Ruef, who was out of jail under heavy bonds, to the custody of the Sheriff for the remainder of the trial. Shortly after this conference Heney had been shot down.

When the court had re-convened, and the jury had been dismissed for the day, Judge Lawlor carried out his intention and ordered the Sheriff to take charge of Ruef. The shooting had occurred on Friday afternoon,

---

407 Physicians state that Heney's escape from death was by a hair's breadth. Had the bullet, striking as it did, taken any other course death would have been inevitable.

408 See Chapter XXIII.

November 13. The court adjourned until the following Monday.[409]

Heney in the meantime had been taken to a hospital. There it was found that the wound was not necessarily fatal. The rumors current that Heney had been killed were denied. This tended to calm the excitement.

Nevertheless, San Francisco and all California were aroused as never before in the State's history. In a twinkling, the results of months of misrepresentation, ridicule and abuse of the Prosecution were swept away. Haas' bullet had not killed Heney,[410] but it had awakened the community to tardy realization of its responsibility.[411] Men who had laughed at the Examiner's "Mutt

[409] "Will they," demanded The Call the morning after Heney had been shot down, "stop at nothing? Are not stealing, perjury, bribery, dynamiting, murder, enough? Must the course of justice in this community run the gamut of violence, as well as of slander and pettifogging obstruction?

"Apparently it must. But there is at least no longer any reason to doubt where the responsibility lies. A bare chance, the momentary tremor of an assassin's hand, may have saved the life of Francis J. Heney to this community. There will be no tremor in the finger of scorn that points past the miserable wretch that did the shooting to the men that inspired it. A worthless crank, of course. It always is. Dirty hands for dirty work. But softer hands and keener brains plan it. And the community will waste no wrath on the miserable tool, now cowering in jail. It was not he who has dogged the steps of Francis J. Heney these two years with hired thugs. It was not he who has filled the courtrooms with professional ruffians. It was not he who dynamited Gallagher—or hired it done. Least of all was it he who made a joke of that crime and sought to make a joke and a byword of the heroic Heney—'poor Beany.' "

[410] While Heney lay wounded at San Francisco, and Haas lay dead, another tragedy growing out of the Graft Prosecution was being enacted on the other side of the globe. John Krause, who had been T. V. Halsey's assistant at the time of the Pacific States Telephone briberies, killed himself on the steamer Adriatic as it plied from Cherbourg, France, to Queenstown, Ireland. Krause had disappeared from San Francisco in December, 1907. It was never charged that Krause was a principal to the bribery transactions, or that he had even guilty knowledge of them. His only possible connection with the graft cases was as a witness against the Pacific States Telephone and Telegraph Company officials.

[411] "A great work," said Hiram W. Johnson, in an interview printed in the San Francisco Call, November 14, 1908, "undertaken and accomplished, though not yet wholly completed, has been

cartoons" ridiculing the Prosecution, now threatened to mob The Examiner office. Patrons of the defense-supporting Chronicle now voiced their utter condemnation of that paper. Thousands withdrew their subscriptions from the two publications. The time was ripe for the demagogue. An unpolitic word from the defense just then, an incendiary speech from some unwise partisan of the Prosecution, would have been sufficient to have sent a mob marching upon the jail in which Haas and Ruef were confined, or upon the residences of the indicted bribe-givers, or against the newspaper offices which for months had labored to make the Graft Prosecution unpopular.

There was a feeling that the criminal element was too powerfully intrenched to be reached through the ordinary legal channels. The feeling, which had subsided when the Graft Prosecution opened,[412] that the

---

retarded for a day by an assassin's bullet. When Frank Heney fell today while in the performance of his duty, decency and the right were stricken. For two years this one man has persevered in the right, for right's sake alone. Without compensation, sacrificing a great legal practice, giving without complaint the best years of his life, Francis J. Heney, facing all the combined forces of evil in this community and State, has stood unflinchingly at his post, making the fight that is the fight of all of us. Daily abuse and vilification have been his portion and reward. In spite of it, where a weaker man would have faltered, Heney has persevered. He has done in seeking to make equality before the law an assurance in this State, all that a strong and a brave man could do. Were he to pass away tonight he'd need no other monument than the work he has done. For generations his expose of rottenness in San Francisco, his prosecutions of the criminal rich will live and make this city and State better. He has been shot simply because he was fighting for the right. Not alone has he been wounded; but the community and the commonwealth have suffered the injury.

"We who were with him in the early days of the struggle, and knew his every mood; who saw him at his work day and night, and loved the qualities that made it possible for him to accomplish what he has, can not express our horror and indignation and anger at his attempted assassination. May God speed his recovery."

412 See Chapter IV.

graft evil could not be corrected except by extra-legal means, was to some degree revived.

In this emergency, the leaders of the Graft Prosecution, by counseling moderation and observance of the law, did yeoman service in the keeping of good order in San Francisco.

The Citizens' League of Justice [413] called a mass meeting for the Saturday evening following the shooting. Even in the call, the League urged there be no breach of the peace.

"Francis J. Heney," the League's call read, "has fallen by the hand of an assassin, shot from behind while fighting at his post in the cause of justice for the people of this city. He would be the first man to appeal to the calm reason of the citizens to preserve order and proceed only by the processes of law; to look not for vengeance, but to demand swift justice through the courts. We make the same appeal."

Mayor Taylor presided at the meeting. Long before the hour set for the opening, the auditorium was packed to the doors, with thousands on the outside clamoring

---

[413] The Citizens' League of Justice was organized immediately after the attempted assassination of Witness Gallagher by means of dynamite. Those immediately connected with the prosecution, it had been amply demonstrated, were risking their lives. In the Citizens' League of Justice was proposed an organization, entirely separate and apart from the graft prosecution, to back the prosecution. The idea originated with Bruce Porter, the artist. Rev. Charles N. Lathrop, of the Church of the Advent, became interested. The initial meeting was held at Father Lathrop's house. While the League had, no connection with the prosecution, it became most effective in support of the prosecution group. Professor George H. Boke, of the University of California Law School, accepted the hazardous position of the League's executive officer. In spite of the fact that he was jeopardizing his position at the State University by his course, Professor Boke did much effective work in bringing the conditions which confronted San Francisco squarely before the public. Matt I. Sullivan, who afterwards became Chief Justice of the State Supreme Court, served as the League's president.

for entrance. Those in charge of the meeting were compelled to call it to order several minutes before they had intended.

Professor George H. Boke of the University of California Law School, and manager of the Citizens' League of Justice, was to introduce Mayor Taylor. Several minutes before the time set for the meeting, the crowd started a cheer for Heney. The demonstration lasted for fully five minutes. Then some one started the cry, "Throw the Examiner out." Hundreds half rose from their seats, their eyes bent upon the press table where representatives of The Examiner were seated.

Professor Boke at once grasped the significance of the movement, and acted on the instant. Stepping to the fore, he made a brief address introducing Mayor Taylor, thereby checking the threatened demonstration.

Mayor Taylor was quick to sound the keynote of the meeting. "Let us," he said in introducing the first speaker, "see to it that no matter who else breaks the law, that we shall not break it." [414]

---

[414] Dr. Taylor's observations on this point were as follows: "Let us see to it that no matter who else breaks the law, that we shall not break it. In this crisis, we must, above all things, keep our heads. We must, above all things, while resolute and determined, be self-restrained.

"San Francisco has had many afflictions. She now has this additional affliction of the assassination of one who stood for the people's rights; of one who was fearlessly engaged in the important and priceless business of civic regeneration, and who, while in the act of performing the greatest of all duties as a citizen, was laid low by the bullets of an assassin.

"But let us not add to the affliction the affliction of breaking the peace. Let us, above all things, as I have said, keep ourselves restrained. Let us not add to the afflictions that are upon us the affliction of mob law. Let us go about our business, whatever we may do in this matter, in a peaceful way, but in a resolute way, in a determined way. I am satisfied that the officers of the law will do their duty. I am satisfied that the judges will do their duty, and that our juries will do their duty. And if they, each one of them, perform faithfully the functions upon his part, we have nothing to fear, and we shall see that those who are guilty are punished and are rightfully punished."

Every speaker who followed the Mayor emphasized this. "Let us," said the Rev. William Rader, "have heads which are cool and minds which are rational."

"We stand in this fight," said District Attorney Langdon, "for law and order. And I want to say to you and ask you to pass it on to your neighbors, that, as crimes have been committed, those crimes must be punished, but punished within the law. And I want to say further, that as the law officers of this city and county, we shall consider any man who expresses an opinion or sentiment that we ought to resort to measures extra-judicial, as an enemy of good government."

"Why," demanded James D. Phelan, "should we take violent steps? Is not San Francisco a great, civilized community? Are not our American institutions still intact? They are. And although in the early days of San Francisco the Vigilance Committee, an extra-legal tribunal, was resorted to for the purpose of correcting such abuses, we must remember that at that time we were a border State, at that time we were a mining camp. Only such a strenuous method would then have succeeded, because judges who were on the bench were elected by ballot-box stuffers, a council was elected in the same way. Crime was rampant, nobody was punished. Then the men of San Francisco organized a tribunal and gave an orderly trial to every offender whom they apprehended, and as a result this city was cleansed of crime and remained a model community for twenty years.

"But conditions now are different. It is true that within the last year there has been a feeling in this community that the criminal law had broken down, and that we could not, under the law, punish the offenders; and that the courts, the highest courts, abetted and aided criminals by the rankest interpretations, technical interpretations of the statutes. They refused to lean on the side of order and justice, and they have brought disgrace upon the judiciary of California, all over the world.

"But our civilization and our institutions are safe. That vote the other day, and the election of Judge Dunne, the election two years ago of Judge Coffey and Judge Lawlor, give us courage and confidence to believe that, under the constitution and the laws, we can win our battle if you only give us time, without any resort to violence; and we are willing, though one hundred days have passed, to pursue that work, because that is the only way we can do it under the constitution and the laws."

When Rudolph Spreckels entered the building he was greeted with demonstration. He, too, while expressing great sympathy for his friend who had been stricken down, joined in counseling that nothing be done outside the law.

With the urging that no exhibition of mob-violence be added to the burden of the afflicted community, was given assurance that the Graft Prosecution should go on; that the laws should be upheld; that those responsible for the conditions which had been forced upon San Francisco should be brought to justice. Whatever danger there was of violence to members of the graft defense, vanished at that Citizens' League of Justice mass meeting. At its conclusion, resolutions were adopted condemning the methods of the defense, declaring unwavering allegiance of those present to law, and pledging support in the cleansing of the city of grafters and boodlers.[415]

---

415 The following resolutions were adopted at the meeting:
"Whereas, following unparalleled disaster from the elements our unfortunate city fell upon times of unprecedented civic corruption, necessitating the tearing down of the wreckage of government, and the rebuilding of our civic structure on foundations of law and justice; and

"Whereas, the first labor necessary was the prosecution of criminals, bribe givers, bribe takers and brokers in corruption; and

"Whereas, the prosecution, beset with many difficulties, obtained its evidence in the only way that such evidence could be obtained; and

"Whereas, in the subsequent attempt to convict the guilty there was developed a vast conspiracy to thwart the ends of justice, which conspiracy has involved social boycott and unjust and coercive business pressure, has openly employed thugs to terrorize the officers of the law, has employed lawyers to browbeat and insult witnesses, prosecutors and the judges on the bench, and to waste the time and money and to exhaust the patience of the people by useless and technical delays, and which conspiracy has moreover involved so large a part of our public press that many of our people have been deprived of the truth and have been fed upon poisoned lies; and

"Whereas, up to the present time the law as administered has proved inadequate to secure that prompt and certain application of justice, which must be the basis of social order; and

"Whereas, out of this conspiracy grew plots to kidnap, and actual kidnaping; plots to bribe juries, and actual jury bribing; plots to assassinate witnesses and an attempt to assassinate a witness by dynamite; and out of it also grew plots to assassinate the prosecutors, and the attempted assassination of the bravest friend that San Francisco has known, Francis J. Heney;

"Therefore be it resolved, that here and now we declare our unwavering allegiance to law, and that if the criminal law be found to be so framed as to permit the escape of civic malefactors we shall see to it that the law be amended; that if the lax administration of the criminal law be due to misinterpretation by judges, we shall see to it that men be placed upon the bench capable of construing the law.

"Be it further resolved, that we call upon the Supervisors to provide adequate funds for the District Attorney's office to secure the detection, prosecution and conviction of criminals, high or low, and the full protection of officers in the discharge of their duties;

"Be it further resolved, that we demand the truth from our public press, and shall see to it that our people are informed of the facts that they may judge of those who by lying and misrepresentation are perverting public opinion.

"Be it further resolved, that we solemnly assert our utmost confidence in the law-abiding character of our people; that we here declare our gratitude for the inestimable service rendered us by the office of the District Attorney in the restoration of reputable and responsible government; and that we stand firm in our determination to indorse and to aid that office to the end that all persons accused of crime shall be fairly tried and their guilt or inno-

Another crisis had passed in San Francisco. The situation was not unlike that of two years before, when the clamor that drastic means be taken to free the city of Ruef's domination, was silenced by announcement that Rudolph Spreckels had guaranteed a fund for the investigation of municipal conditions, and to prosecute those found to be guilty of corruption.[416]

But even as the citizens met in mass meeting another tragedy of the Graft Prosecution was enacted. Haas, under the eyes of policemen specially detailed to watch him, killed himself or was killed. With him died all hope of discovering who had urged him to avenge himself upon Heney.

Haas' suicide, if it were suicide; or his murder, if it were murder; is one of the mysteries of the graft cases. He was shot with a derringer. The weapon was an inch through at the butt and 5-8 wide at the muzzle— certainly an easily discovered weapon by officers practiced in searching men. And yet, Haas had, before he was put in his cell, been thoroughly searched both by Captain Duke[417] of the police force and Detective

---

cence be finally established in accordance with the provisions of law.
   "To these ends we pledge ourselves, that our beloved city may be purged of boodlers and grafters and be a better home for ourselves and our children.
   "Be it further resolved, that we send word to our wounded champion, that his labors for us are appreciated and that his sufferings for our sake are not in vain."

416 See Chapter IV.

417 Captain Duke, at an investigation which followed, testified: "At Mr. Burns's suggestion, we took Haas into the room off the courtroom occupied by the stenographers. First we made a slight search, and then I said to Mr. Burns: 'Are you sure we searched him thoroughly?' and we went over him again. I felt down to his shoes. I always search a man that way, for when I first went on the police force I had an experience with a Chinaman, whom Policeman Helms, who was recently killed, and myself had arrested. We found a dagger in his shoe, and since then I have always

Burns. The two officers are certain that Haas had no weapon upon him. And yet, one theory advanced by his keepers is that Haas had the derringer all the time concealed in his shoe. Another theory is that the derringer was smuggled in to him. But, with Haas under watchful eyes of special guards, by whom? Another theory, popular at the time, was that Haas had been murdered in his cell. But if murdered—or even if the derringer were smuggled in to him—what was the motive behind it? These are questions which, short of some death-bed confession, perhaps, are not likely to be answered.

Those who hurried to his cell at the report of the derringer found Haas dead. Whether he had shot himself or whether he had been shot, his lips were sealed forever.

On the Sunday following the shooting of Heney, most of the Protestant pastors of San Francisco made the attempted assassination the subject of their sermons. The same course was taken throughout the State generally. In the afternoon mass meetings were held in all parts of the State, at which resolutions were adopted

---

examined a man's feet. I will state that I felt the man's shoes the other day after they had been put on the corpse and the derringer placed in them, and from the bulge I noticed then I am sure that I would have felt the weapon had it been in his shoe at the time of the arrest. We were looking for anything that we could find. From something the man said—that he didn't care if he lived or not—I thought that he might make an attempt to commit suicide.

"It would have been an utter impossibility for the derringer to have been anywhere else than in the man's shoe," Duke continued. "If it was in his shoe it would have been under the stocking and the man would have had it there 29 hours before he killed himself. It would have made a mark on the flesh or interfered with his walking, and he did not even limp. If the cartridges had been in the shoe they could have got under the foot and the man could not have walked."

condemning the methods of the defense, [418] and pledging support to the prosecution.

Telegrams [419] of condolence and of encouragement poured in from all parts of the country.

---

[418] Neither press nor defending lawyers were spared in the criticism. "We have," said Rev. Bradford Leavitt of the First Unitarian Church at San Francisco, "dreamed that we were living under the government of laws, whereas we were living under the government of newspapers hired by corrupt corporations, and the enemies of civic decency."

"The lawyers who are paid to thwart this Graft Prosecution," said Charles S. Wheeler, "have proceeded with deliberate plan to destroy the effectiveness of the prosecution by withdrawing the support of the people. In this way they have reached the home of every individual. They have brought cunningly into the home their hireling periodicals, and a press misguided or worse, has been largely instrumental in aiding their desire."

[419] President Roosevelt's telegram to Mr. Spreckels was as follows:

"White House, Nov. 14, 1908.

"To Rudolph Spreckels, San Francisco.

"Am inexpressibly shocked at the attempted assassination of Heney and most earnestly hope he will recover. The infamous character of the would-be assassin no less than the infamous character of the deed call attention in a striking way to the true character of the forces against which Heney and you and your associates have been struggling. Every decent American who has the honor and interest of the country at heart should join not only in putting a stop to the cause of violent crime of which this man's act is but one of the symptoms, but also in stamping out the hideous corruption in which men like this would-be assassin are bred and flourish, and that can only be done by warring as Heney has warred relentlessly against every man who is guilty of corrupt practices without any regard to his social standing and his prominence in the world of politics or the world of business. I earnestly hope that Heney will recover, and I give utterance to what I know would be Heney's wish when I say that I earnestly hope that whether he recovers or not there be no faltering in the work in which Heney has been so gallant and efficient a leader.

"9:10 A. M.

"THEODORE ROOSEVELT."

President Roosevelt telegraphed Mrs. Heney as follows:

"White House, Nov. 14, 1908.

"Mrs. Francis J. Heney:—Am inexpressibly shocked at news of the attempted assassination of Mr. Heney and am greatly relieved at the news this morning that he is doing well and will probably recover. I hope you will accept my deepest sympathy. Like all good American citizens, I hold your husband in peculiar regard for the absolutely fearless way in which he has attacked and exposed corruption without any regard to the political or social prominence of the offenders or to the dangerous character of the work. Your husband has taken his life in his hands in doing this great task for our people and is entitled to the credit and esteem, and above all, to the heartiest support of all good citizens. The infamous character of the man who has assassinated him should add not only to the horror and detestation felt for the deed, but also to

But in spite of this popular expression of sympathy, there were astonishing exhibitions on the part of the associates of those who had been indicted or nearly indicted because of the graft revelations, of feeling against Heney. For example, Rev. David J. Evans, of Grace Episcopal Church, on the Sunday following the attempted assassination, offered prayer for the recovery of the stricken prosecutor. Instantly there was commotion in the pews. Members of the congregation, by frown and toss of head, indicated their profound disapproval of their pastor's petition.[420] But frown and head-toss and open disapproval of the pews neither stopped the prayer, nor prevented its answer. The prayer was offered; Heney did not die.

Within an hour after Heney had been shot down, three of the foremost lawyers at the California bar, Hiram W. Johnson, Matt I. Sullivan and Joseph J. Dwyer, volunteered their services to take up the strug-

---

the determination of all decent citizens to stamp out the power of all men of his kind.

"THEODORE ROOSEVELT."

[420] Grace Episcopal Church is attended by many of the most prominent citizens of San Francisco. At the time of the shooting of Heney, several prominent Episcopalians were under indictment. In spite of the intense feeling in his congregation, against the prosecution, Rev. Mr. Evans continued to give the work of the District Attorney's office his approval. An era of petty persecutions for Mr. Evans followed. He was finally brought to resign his pastorate and accept a less important charge at Palo Alto.

In this connection it is interesting to note that in spite of powerful opposition to the prosecution of prominent Episcopalian laymen, the Convocation of the Church held at San Francisco in August, 1907, adopted the following resolutions unanimously:

"Whereas, Our government is imperiled by the criminal use of wealth to influence legislation; and

"Whereas, Existing conditions in San Francisco present a moral issue; therefore be it

"Resolved, That, in the judgment of this convocation, bribery is always a crime deserving punishment, and, furthermore, that duty commands every Christian man to exert himself to foster a public recognition of the quality of the crime."

gle for civic righteousness at the point to which Heney had carried it.

But the attorneys for Ruef, having exhausted every other delaying move, saw in the shooting of Heney opportunity for further delay. They accordingly moved for change of venue. Failing here, a motion was made for thirty days' delay. This being denied, Ruef's attorneys moved that the jury be dismissed. This move failing, an attempt was made to examine the twelve men in the jury box to determine whether the shooting had prejudiced them and unfitted them for jury service. These many motions were backed up with affidavits containing all that had been said at the public meetings, and all that had been printed in San Francisco newspapers, since Heney had been shot. The reading of the voluminous affidavits consumed hours. The prosecution filed answering affidavits which also consumed time. But Judge Lawlor finally denied all the contentions of the defense and ordered the trial to proceed.

During these proceedings, the jury had been locked up in charge of the regular court officials. The jury had not been in the courtroom when Heney was shot, and from the moment of the shooting had been shut away from the public. But lest the jury had learned something of the shooting, and to account for Heney's absence, Judge Lawlor deemed it incumbent upon him to notify them that Heney had been shot, and to admonish them that the transaction so far as the court, the jury, the defendant, the People of the State, the counsel, and all other interests interested or involved in the trial were concerned was to stand as though it had not occurred. This Judge Lawlor did.[421]

The trial itself was not unlike the other graft trials. The Supervisors told the story of their bribery. Gallagher told how Ruef had given him the money, and how he had given it to Supervisor Furey. Furey testified that he had received the money from Gallagher because of his vote to grant the overhead trolley permit to the United Railroads. The story had by this time

---

[421] Judge Lawlor's statement to the jury was as follows: "Gentlemen of the Jury: I have a few words to say to you before this trial is resumed at this time. Since you have been sworn as jurors the Court has on many occasions, with elaborateness and repetition, sought to convey to your minds an understanding of your duties as jurors in this case. It has been pointed out to you that to the charge which is on trial here, the defendant, Abraham Ruef, has interposed a plea of not guilty. That charge, considered in connection with that plea, puts in issue, for the determination of this Court and jury, the allegations of that charge. You have been sworn as jurors to pass upon the facts in the case and to apply those facts, when resolved from the evidence, to the rules of law which the Court shall finally state to you to govern you in the rendition of your verdict. These many admonitions, as it has also been pointed out to you from time to time, are founded upon a provision of the law which makes it the duty of the Court to administer those admonitions.

"The purpose of the law requiring those admonitions to be given is that when a jury is sworn to try an action it shall divest itself of all matters which theretofore might have found lodgment in the minds of the members and to proceed to render a verdict solely upon the matters which shall be brought to the attention of the jury in the due course of judicial proceedings. These constant reminders of that duty are calculated to keep the sense of jurors alive to a full compliance therewith.

"I doubt if anything I could say at this time would tend to amplify what has already been declared from time to time in that behalf, but in view of a transaction that occurred in the courtroom on the afternoon of Friday, November 13, 1908, the Court deems it proper to re-emphasize with all the power that it may command the duty of the jury to proceed to the further discharge of its duty at this time in utter disregard of that transaction. The Court realizes that the jurors may have heard or seen a part of that transaction, or that phases of that transaction may have been communicated to the jury. Now, without regard to what extent that assumption may be justified, the Court desires the jurors to in every manner relieve their minds of any impression or anything that they have heard, or anything that has been said, or anything that has been communicated, or that shall hereafter be communicated concerning that transaction; in other words, we are to resume this trial at this time at precisely the point that had been reached when the recess, during which the transaction occurred, was declared.

"I may state to you generally, that on that occasion Mr. Fran-

become sadly familiar to the people of San Francisco.

The trouble experienced with witnesses at former trials characterized this trial as well.

Alex. Lathem, for example, at one time Ruef's chauffeur, disappeared from the State about the time the trial was to begin. He was brought back from Oregon under extradition, charged with having accepted a bribe to leave the jurisdiction of the court. On the stand,[422] Lathem repudiated important evidence which

---

cis J. Heney, the Assistant District Attorney, was shot by a man bearing the name of Morris Haas; that Mr. Heney was wounded as a result of that assault. Happily the injury was not a serious one, and at this time there is every indication that Mr. Heney will recover from that injury.

"Now, that transaction, so far as this Court and the jury, the defendant at the bar, the People of the State of California, the counsel and all other interests interested or involved in this trial are concerned, is to stand as though it had not occurred; no person is to be charged with any responsibility for that transaction; this is not the place for the consideration of that transaction.

"It may be stated also to you that the assailant afterward took his own life while he was confined in the County Jail upon his arrest in connection with that transaction.

"And neither matter, I repeat, should find any place in your minds. It should not in any manner form anything in the nature of bias or prejudice concerning anyone.

"This Court would despair of having the law administered upon the charge at bar if the jurors did not in every manner comply with the admonition of the Court to exclude that transaction entirely from their minds."

[422] Lathem testified before the Grand Jury that about the time the bribe money had been passed he had driven Ruef to the Hirsch Bros. store, where Ruef had obtained a shirt box. He had then driven Ruef to the offices of the United Railroads. Ruef had entered the offices with the box. He had come out later with the box and a package. With box and package he had gone to his own office, and from there, taking the box and package with him, he had been driven to the safe deposit vaults of the Western National Bank.

Lathem did not testify before the Grand Jury until after Ruef had confessed, and then Lathem testified with Ruef's consent. It is a significant fact that Lathem was sent out of the State the first time not in the interest of Ruef but of Tirey L. Ford, head of the United Railroads law department. Lathem went to Colorado on an automobile trip with the father-in-law of Luther Brown, one of the United Railroad detectives. Lathem's wife was permitted to accompany them in the automobile. They stopped at the best hotels. Lathem was paid $150 a month.

The importance of Lathem's testimony lies in the fact that at the time he took Ruef with the shirt-box to Ford's office, Ford

he had given before the Grand Jury, and to which he had made affidavit. As a minor incident of the graft trials, Lathem, because of this incident, was indicted for perjury.

But in spite of the backwardness of certain of its witnesses, the prosecution succeeded in getting its case before the jury. The jury found Ruef guilty as charged. He was sentenced to fourteen years' penal servitude at San Quentin prison.

---

had just received from the Relief corporation officials $50,000 in small currency, which made two large bundles, which were carried to Ford's office by Abbott and himself and placed in Ford's desk. This was at the noon hour. A little after one o'clock Ruef went to the Western Pacific Safety Deposit vaults where he then had a deposit box. The cubic contents of this box was not sufficient to accommodate those two bundles. Ruef at that time secured two additional boxes. The cubic contents of all three boxes together was just sufficient to nicely accommodate said two bundles.

The theory of the prosecution was that Ruef carried bribe money in box and package.

At the trial, Lathem stated that the story which he had told before the Grand Jury was not true.

CHAPTER XXVI.

THE CALHOUN TRIAL.

The trial of Patrick Calhoun for offering a bribe to Supervisor Fred Nicholas began immediately after the holidays, following the Ruef trials. The trial brought into play all the machinery of the opposition at its worst to the prosecution. At all points the defense was carried on on a larger scale than at the former trials. There were more and better lawyers employed by the defendant; there were more thugs in evidence in the courtroom; there was greater activity on the part of the detectives, spies and agents engaged to meet the efforts of the men working under Detective Burns.

Due largely to the activity of this army of opposition to the prosecution, the weakness of the methods of enforcing the criminal law was emphasized even more than at the other trials, and the defects shown up more glaringly.

To secure a jury to try Ruef, for example, 1450 talesmen were called. This was regarded as a record. But before a jury had been secured to try Calhoun 2370 veniremen had been called into court, and no less than 922 examined. Thus, for every juror who sat at the Calhoun trial, 197 talesmen were called, and seventy-seven were questioned by the attorneys.

The estimated number of words contained in the transcript of the examination of these talesmen was in millions. To conduct this examination three months were required. The securing of a jury to try Ruef occupied the time of the court for two months only. But it must be noted that the securing of the Calhoun and the Ruef juries occupied five months—to try charges contained in two indictments, whereas in all the graft cases 160 indictments had been brought.

The defendants who preceded Calhoun to trial had an army of attorneys to represent them. But Calhoun's line of legal representatives was quite double that of any of his fellow graft defendants who had been caught in the prosecution drag-net.

Prominent in Mr. Calhoun's defense appeared A. A. Moore, Stanley Moore, Lewis F. Byington, Earl Rogers, J. J. Barrett and Alexander King, supported by the giant of the California bar, Garret McEnerney. That the master mind of Garret McEnerney was directing many of the graft defense cases had been intimated from time to time, but there is no question about Mc-Enerney's part in the defense of Calhoun.

And opposed to the strongest men of the California bar, The People had two representatives. One of them, Heney, was serving without pay, was still a sick man not having fully recovered from his wound inflicted but a few months before, and worn out from the continued effort of a three-years' fight to get at the root of municipal corruption in San Francisco. The second, a regularly employed Deputy District Attorney, John J. O'Gara, was receiving $300 a month for his services. It is not unlikely that some of the best of the attorneys for the defense, for defending Mr. Calhoun, received as much in a day. Compared with the army of lawyers for the defense, the representation of The People was pitifully small.

Through the long, grueling contest of the trial, lasting for five months and eight days, [423] Heney and O'Gara were kept under constant strain, while the defendant's attorneys relieved one another when their labors became irksome.

The bulk of the hammering and of the technical quibbling was directed against Heney. Heney, still suffering from the effects of his wound, received at the Ruef trial, worn-out, over-worked, harassed in the public prints, would at times become thoroughly exasperated. Every indication of impatience on his part, or of temper, was made subject of attack in the opposing newspapers. [424] These attacks, long persisted in, did their part in the general campaign to weary the public with the prosecution, and undermine confidence in Heney.

The examination of talesmen for jury service showed the results of this long-continued campaign. Many talesmen announced their sympathy with the defendants, and deplored the prosecution, which they appeared to

---

[423] From January 12, 1909, to June 20, 1909.

[424] Earl Rogers showed himself particularly clever at goading. His ability in this line was shown to advanatge also, at the trial of Clarence Darrow, charged with jury fixing at Los Angeles, whom Rogers defended. The Fresno Republican in comparing the two cases said, in its issue of July 12, 1912: "When Heney tilted, as prosecutor against Earl Rogers as an apologist for crime, he was the 'wild man of Borneo,' to the more staid and polished members of the San Francisco bar. But now that Fredericks and Ford, prosecutors of Los Angeles, lost their tempers under the goadings of this same Rogers in the Darrow case, nothing is said about the wild man of Borneo. Fredericks and Ford, unlike Heney, are recognized as the socially elect of the profession, but Heney in the wildest excitement of the Calhoun trials, never tried to throw an ink bottle at Rogers, as Ford tried to do the other day. Plainly, as a matter of social etiquette, it depends upon whose ox Rogers gores."

believe had brought shame upon and injured the city.
Some went so far as to call the prosecution of Calhoun
an outrage.[425] Others intimated that the giving of
bribe money might have been justifiable.[426] Such expressions, coming from men of average intelligence and
ordinarily law-abiding, showed conclusively that the
persistent efforts of the defense to poison the public
mind against the prosecution was at last bringing results.

But after months of effort a jury was secured to
hear the case and the trial began.

---

[425] See footnote 269.

[426] The Chronicle, as early as July 10, 1907, punctured the theory that the bribing of public servants is justifiable.
    The Chronicle said: "In the examination of a talesman in
Judge Lawlor's court on Monday an attorney for the defendant
charged with the crime of bribing city officials made the statement
that San Francisco is divided on the subject of punishing men
who have committed the offense named. He said: 'You know, of
course, that San Francisco is divided on this graft question. Half
in favor of the prosecution, and, say, half contrary minded.' Possibly he believes that this is true, but there is absolutely no foundation for the assumption. There is no evidence on which to base
such a statement, and it would not have been made if there was
any possibility of determining its truth or falsity by some simple
test.
    "It is doubtless true that there are plenty of men in this com-
munity who regard the crime of bribery lightly, and are ready to
defend it on the ground that laxity in the conduct of municipal
affairs made it necessary to resort to it or abandon all enterprise.
But the great majority of citizens take the sound view that both
briber and bribed are equally guilty and equally deserving of punishment, and utterly refuse to accept the excuse that the corporations which have been systematically debauching city officials were
forced to that course. They know that the eager desire to secure
advantages is at the bottom of the corrupt condition of our
municipal affairs, and they feel that unless examples can be made
of those who have shown a willingness to profit by the greed and
turpitude of those elected to office the practice of bribing will be
again resumed and continued as long as there is anything to be
gained by the pursuit of criminal methods.
    "Even if it were true that the community is evenly divided it
would be outrageous to plead that fact as a justification for the
commission of criminal acts. If San Francisco should be so lost
to shame that nine-tenths of her population regarded bribery with
tolerance, it would be no less a crime, but there would be infinitely more reason for striving to punish offenders of that character to save the city from the moral degradation involved in the
acceptance of the idea that it is excusable to defy the laws by
debauching public officials."
    At the time of Calhoun's trial, however, The Chronicle read
talesmen who sided with the defense no such lecture.

Heney, in his opening statement to the jury, set forth the prosecution expected to prove that Ruef authorized James L. Gallagher to offer the bribe to Supervisor Nicholas; that Ruef afterwards gave the money to Gallagher to pay Nicholas; that Calhoun authorized Ruef, either through Tirey L. Ford, or personally, or both, to make the offer to Gallagher and to authorize Gallagher to make the offer to Nicholas.

The prosecution showed by Gallagher that the offer had been made to Nicholas and to every member of the Board of Supervisors with the exception of Rea. In this, Gallagher was corroborated by the Supervisors. Not only had the offer been made, but the bribe money had been paid.

Gallagher testified that he had received $85,000 from Ruef to be distributed among the Supervisors for their votes which gave the United Railroads its overhead trolley permit, and that, after keeping out $15,000 for himself, he had distributed the money among them, giving to Supervisor Nicholas $4000 of the amount.

Supervisor Nicholas testified that Gallagher had offered him the bribe and had paid him the money.

By the officials of the United States Mint, the prosecution showed that $200,000, about the time of the bribery, had been turned over to General Tirey L. Ford, on order from Mr. Calhoun. The $200,000 could not be accounted for by the available books of the United Railroads. Ruef and Ford were shown to have been in close touch with each other during the period.[427]

But nobody could be found who had seen Ford pass $200,000 to Mr. Ruef.

---

[427] See Chapter XV, "The Ford Trials."

Here was, perhaps, a weak link in the prosecution's chain of evidence.

Mr. Calhoun did not, however, put General Ford on the stand to tell what he did with the money. Neither did Mr. Calhoun put Mr. Ruef on the stand to testify as to the source of the $85,000 which Ruef gave to Gallagher to pay the Supervisors for their votes by which the trolley permit was awarded to the United Railroads.

But, however weak the link between Ford and Ruef, there was no weakness in the link between Calhoun and Ford. By evidence that could not be disputed, the prosecution showed that Ford got $200,000 through Calhoun.

Frank A. Leach, Director of the United States Mint at San Francisco, testified that Calhoun, with General Ford, had called upon him at the Mint sometime between May 22 and May 24, 1906.[428] Calhoun called, Leach testified, to ascertain how $200,000, which had been transferred from the East to his credit,[429]

---

[428] The trolley-permit was granted May 21, 1906.

[429] The letter placing $200,000 to Calhoun's credit read as follows:

"Treasury Department, Washington, May 22, 1906. Superintendent of the United States Mint, San Francisco, Cal. Sir: Confirmation is certified to a telegram sent you this day, in substance as follows:

" 'Pay to Patrick Calhoun, President United Railroads, $200,000; to Lachman and Jacobi, $12,500; to Beech Thompson, $20,000; to Canadian Bank of Commerce, $250,000; on account of original certificates of deposit Nos. 5251, 5252, 5253 and 5267, issued by the Assistant Treasurer of the United States, New York city. In all amounting to $482,500.

" 'Pay to master California Lodge, Number 1, A. F. and A. M., $319.65 on account of original certificate of deposit No. 112, issued by the Assistant Treasurer of the United States, Chicago.' Respectfully,

"CHARLES H. TREAT,
"Treasurer of the United States."

could be drawn out in certain sums in favor of such persons as he might designate.

Leach testified he had furnished Calhoun with the desired information.

Ford afterwards appeared at the Mint with an order from Mr. Calhoun for $50,000,[430] which was paid to him. Later, Calhoun telegraphed to Leach from Cleveland, Ohio, to pay Ford a second $50,000; and still later the $100,000 remaining.[431]

The Mint officials paid Ford the money in accordance with Mr. Calhoun's directions. Mr. Calhoun offered no evidence to show why this considerable sum was paid to General Ford, or what General Ford was supposed to have done with it. Mr. Calhoun, when the last of the $200,000 had been turned over to General Ford, had given Mr. Leach a receipt [432] in full for the amount.

But what was quite as extraordinary as this direct evidence against Mr. Calhoun was the offer of the District Attorney to meet the defense's charges and insinuations against the prosecution. Rudolph Spreck-

---

[430] The telegrams directing the money to be paid Ford read:
"Cleveland, Ohio, July 28, 06. Hon. Frank A. Leach, Superintendent U. S. Mint, San Francisco. Please pay to Tirey L. Ford, or order, fifty thousand dollars and charge same to my account. Patrick Calhoun, President United Railroads of San Francisco."

[431] Calhoun's order placing the $100,000 to Ford's credit read as follows:
"Cleveland, Ohio, August 21, 06. Hon. Frank A. Leach, Superintendent United States Mint, San Francisco. Please pay to General Tirey L. Ford, or order, one hundred thousand dollars, and charge the same to my account. Patrick Calhoun, President United Railroads, San Francisco."

[432] Calhoun's final receipt for the $200,000 was as follows:
"Received from Frank A. Leach, Superintendent U. S. Mint, two hundred thousand dollars ($200,000) on c/d No. 5251, with Asst. Treasurer U. S., New York.   PATRICK CALHOUN,
                                        "President United Railroads."

els was called to the stand. The attorneys for the defense were invited to ask him any questions they saw fit.

"From the time we attempted to impanel this jury," said Heney, in extending this invitation, "the attorneys for the defendant have been attempting to try Rudolph Spreckels, James D. Phelan and God knows who else. By insinuations they have been endeavoring to get into the mind of this jury the idea that Mr. Spreckels was back of this prosecution for malicious purposes and for gain, for profit, to get hold of the United Railroads. I told them when they were making those insinuations that I proposed to throw down the bars to them; that I proposed to force them to the proof; that I would put the witnesses upon the stand and would not object to a single question asked them.

"The witness, Spreckels, is now upon the stand, and we won't object to their asking him anything on earth, from the time he was born down to the present day, to the present minute."

One of the most frequent charges which had been made against the prosecution was that it had expended money wrongfully. Rogers asked for a statement of the prosecution's receipts and disbursements.

Mr. Spreckels announced his willingness to account for every dollar expended, but refused, until he should be directed by the Court, to give the names of the contributors to the fund.[433]

---

[433] "I want to protect those (the contributors) whom I promised to protect in this matter," said Spreckels. "Outside of that, the matter is entirely an open matter; I have no concern in it."— See Spreckels's testimony, Transcript of evidence in the matter of The People vs. Patrick Calhoun, Page 3385.

"Will you," broke in Heney addressing Calhoun's lawyers, "produce an itemized account of moneys expended in the defense of these matters?"

"I beg your pardon?" questioned Rogers.

"I say," said Heney, "will you produce an itemized account of moneys expended in opposition to these prosecutions?"

The defense did not seize this opportunity to clear itself of the not unreasonable suspicion that money had been used to influence jurors to vote for acquittals; to get witnesses out of the State; to corrupt agents of the prosecution; and perhaps to attempt murder. On the contrary, the attorneys for the defense denounced Mr. Heney's·suggestion as "misconduct."

Mr. Spreckels stated his willingness to furnish itemized statement of the prosecution's expenditures. This he did. Furthermore, he submitted himself to rigorous cross-examination regarding the items of his account. But the clever attorneys for the defense uncovered nothing upon which charge of wrongful expenditure or questionable methods could be based.[434]

The charge that Spreckels had engaged in the Graft Prosecution to injure the United Railroads came to as sorry an ending. By competent witnesses it was shown that the prosecution had been planned, and the preliminary work done, before the bribe-money in the trolley deal had passed. Furthermore, it was shown that Spreckels had offered to assist Calhoun to have the time of his franchises extended, if such extension were

---

[434] The statement in full of the expenditures of the prosecution, as shown in the transcript of the Calhoun trial, will be found on page xxxiv of the Appendix.

necessary for practical installation of the conduit electric system, asking only that the unsightly poles and over-head wires be not inflicted upon the city. It was only when Calhoun, dealing with a Board of Supervisors sus-pected of corruption, showed conclusively that he pro-posed to install an over-head trolley system, whether the people wanted it or not, that Spreckels and his asso-ciates organized their traction company. It was shown that the object of the organizers of the company was to demonstrate that the conduit system was practical for San Francisco. And, finally, the articles of in-corporation under which the company proposed to oper-ate, provided for the transfer under equitable arrange-ments of the proposed new lines to the city, should the city wish at any time to take them over. Mr. Spreckels and his associates were shown not to have had desire or inclination to engage in the street-car business. But it was shown that they proposed to fight for what they considered the best interests of the city of their birth and residence.

Another frequently-made charge had been that Heney was the attorney for Rudolph Spreckels, directing a privately-conducted prosecution.[435] As a matter of fact,

---

[435] The charge of private prosecution was raised early. The Chronicle of May 14, 1907, printed as part of Ford's statement why he did not testify before the Grand Jury, the following:

"The private interests that are behind this attack upon the officers of the United Railroads have free access to this juryroom through their chosen counsel who has assumed to exercise all the official authority of the District Attorney of this city and who, by reason of the exercise of such authority, has become the legal counsellor and guide of this Grand Jury.

"The officers of the United Railroads are not unmindful of the tremendous power for harm that lies in this unusual and extraord-inary situation.

"They, therefore, protest against the consideration by this Grand Jury of any evidence whose legality and sufficiency cannot

Langdon, and not Heney, headed the prosecution, and Langdon let it be known at all times that he was the final arbitrator in all questions growing out of the prosecution. And at no time did he fail to assert himself. But at the Calhoun trial, the fishing expeditions in which the defense indulged, brought the facts out convincingly that Heney, far from being in Spreckels' employ, or directly or indirectly receiving money from him for graft-prosecution services, or any other services, was giving his time to the city, without reward or hope of reward.

Thus, point by point, the allegations which the graft defense had for three years been making against the prosecution, were shown to be without foundation in fact. The bars were down, as Heney put it. Rudolph Spreckels and others who had made the prosecution possible, were under oath, and were prepared to answer any question that might be put to them. The ablest

be judicially determined from a full, complete and correct transcript thereof.

"Second—The subpoena by which my attendance here was compelled was not only insufficient in both form and substance, but was served by a privately employed detective who is not a citizen of California and who is employed and paid by private interests notoriously hostile to the United Railroads.

"Third—There is here present a person not permitted by the laws of this State to be present, namely, an attorney nominally representing the office of the District Attorney, while, in fact, representing private interests in no manner connected officially with any of the governmental affairs of this city and State.

"Fourth—I am the general counsel and legal adviser of the United Railroads and its officers, and whatever knowledge I possess of any of the affairs of the United Railroads or of its officers, has come to me in professional confidence and, under the law of this State, every attorney is compelled to keep inviolate, and at every peril to himself, preserve the secrets of his clients.

"Fifth—Under the statement of the representative of the District Attorney's office in attendance before this Grand Jury, I feel it my duty to stand with the officers of the United Railroads upon my constitutional rights, and the District Attorney knows that he cannot in these proceedings compel me to testify, and he also knows that no unfavorable inference is permitted to be drawn from our declination in this regard."

lawyers, cunning in cross-examination, selected, indeed, for their craft and skill in searching out the innermost secrets of witnesses, were there to question.

But not one statement reflecting upon the purposes of the prosecution, nor of its motives, nor of its methods, was brought out. The graft defense, free to question as it would, was unable to justify the insinuations of baseness of purpose and method; nor to justify its loosely-made charges against the prosecution.[436]

Indeed, the attorneys for Mr. Calhoun even resisted full discussion of Mr. Spreckels' motives.

The intimation, so broad as to approach positive declaration, had been made repeatedly that Mr. Spreckels had inaugurated the graft prosecution for the purpose of injuring Mr. Calhoun and the properties which he represented—the United Railroads. On re-direct examination, Mr. Spreckels was asked by the attorney for the State whether, at the time he had first discussed investigation of graft conditions in San Francisco with Mr. Heney, he had had any idea of investigating Mr. Calhoun. Mr. Barrett, representing the defendant, strongly objected to this line of questioning.[437]

After a wrangle between the attorneys as to the matter of the witness's motives, Spreckels was permitted to make a brief statement to the Court.

"My motives," he said, "have been inquired into, and I have indicated to Mr. Rogers (Calhoun's attor-

---

[436] One of the most complete answers to the charges scattered nation-wide by the Graft Defense, came from Dean John H. Wigmore of the Northwestern School of Law at Chicago, author of Wigmore on Evidence. (See footnote 283.)

[437] See transcript of testimony, The People vs. Patrick Calhoun, No. 1436, page 3723.

ney) that as far as I am concerned the bars are absolutely down; I am willing to take the judgment of this community as to motives, as to my purposes and as to the truthfulness of my statements made here."

Mr. Spreckels was finally permitted to answer the question. He answered in the negative.[438]

The defendant placed no witnesses on the stand. The explanation of their peculiar position which the United Railroads officials were looked upon to make when opportunity offered was not made. The denials which they had for three years been indignantly making through the newspapers were not stated under oath.[439]

---

[438] Mr. Spreckels finally testified on this point as follows:

"Mr. Heney. Q. At the time that Mr. Phelan agreed to contribute the $10,000, Mr. Spreckels, what did you say, if anything, about contributing yourself? A. That was in the first meeting, I think, Mr. Heney, and I told him that I was ready and willing to contribute a similar amount; that I believed it would be possible to get others to join and contribute.

"Q. At that time was anything said by any person about prosecuting Mr. Calhoun? A. Absolutely no.

"Q. Or any person connected with the United Railroads Company? A. The discussion was entirely confined to the administration, the corrupt administration as we termed it.

"Q. At that time did you have any purpose or intention of prosecuting Mr. Calhoun? A. I had not.

"Q. Did you have any reason to believe that Mr. Calhoun at that time had committed any crime? A. I had no indication of such a crime.

"Mr. Moore. Was that time fixed, Mr. Heney?

"Mr. Heney. Yes, it was fixed; the first conversation, and he has fixed it as nearly as he could.

"The Court. Have you in mind the testimony on that point, Mr. Moore? There was some reference to it in an earlier part of the examination.

"Mr. Heney. Q. When you had the talk with Mr. Heney in April, 1906, did you say anything about prosecuting Mr. Calhoun, or anybody connected with the United Railroads? A. I did not.

"Q. Did you at any time tell Mr. Heney, that you desired to have him prosecute Mr. Patrick Calhoun? A. I did not, at any time.

"Q. Did you tell him at any time that you desired to have him prosecute any person connected with the United Railroads Company? A. I did not."

[439] The Chronicle in its issue of March 19, 1907, the day after the story of corruption of Supervisors was made public, refers to the denials of United Railroads officials as follows:

"Weeks ago, when the first charges of a corruption fund was

The trial resulted in a disagreement. According to published statements, purporting to come from members of the jury, on the first ballot four jurors stood for conviction, eight for acquittal; on the second, nine for acquittal, three for conviction. On all the other ballots the jurors stood ten for acquittal and two for conviction.[440]

---

published, Patrick Calhoun issued from his New York offices a typewritten statement, equivalent to about three-fourths of a Chronicle column, in which he announced:

" 'I have just seen the San Francisco papers, in which vague charges are made that the United Railroads of San Francisco paid or caused to be paid $700,000 for a permit to use electricity on the roads that it formerly operated with cable. There is no foundation for this rumor. The United Railroads of San Francisco never paid or authorized any one to pay on its behalf a single dollar to the Mayor, Supervisors or any public official of the city of San Francisco or the State of California.'

"Late last night the following additional denial was issued from the office of the United Railroads:

" 'I am authorized to state in the most positive way that neither Mr. Calhoun nor any officer of the United Railroads ever paid or authorized anyone to pay one dollar to any official.

'THORNWELL MULLALLY,
'Assistant to the President United Railroads.' "

440 The following statement was published over the name of Otto T. Hildebrecht, one of the two jurors who had voted to convict:

"As soon as we entered the jury room, I overheard a crowd of the jurors in the rear of the hall shouting 'Acquit! Acquit!' We then proceeded to name a foreman. This matter disposed of, the members began balloting.

"In the first half hour three ballots were cast. On the first vote it stood 8 to 4 for acquittal. On the second ballot Maguire succumbed to the pressure. I called upon him for his reasons for changing his vote and he replied: 'Oh, these corrupt conditions have always prevailed in San Francisco. The Supervisors in this case are no different from the other men, who have filled those offices. It will always be like that.' To combat this attitude on Maguire's part, I stated, 'Well, it is time to stamp out the crimes in this, city. In order that the evil may be corrected we must put a stop to it.' This seemed to have no weight with Maguire.

"The next ballot showed that Anthes had gone over to the others. From him I secured this information: 'Oh, why I always vote with the majority.' I said, 'Why, how can an honest man take that view of the matter?' I have taken an oath and at that time announced that I would try this case solely on the evidence.

"It is plainly pointed out in the testimony of Sanderson that Calhoun was present when Ruef said, 'This thing will go through on Monday. It is all settled.' This produced no impression upon the others, although I argued that such testimony alone proved Calhoun's guilty knowledge of the plan to put the deal through

Immediately after announcement of the verdict,[441] the District Attorney attempted to bring Calhoun to trial for the alleged offering of a bribe to Supervisor

---

when he remarked in answer to Sanderson's query, 'Then you won't need me?' 'I don't think we do.'

"I then asked the other jurors to come into court, they contending that Ruef had carried on the conversation with Sanderson and that Calhoun was an innocent witness. We asked to have this testimony revealed and the jurors filed into court. Upon returning to the jury room we renewed our deliberations.

"The other ten jurors came at Binner and myself and sought to induce me to stretch my imagination to the end that Calhoun had paid the money to Ruef, but only as a fee. They acknowledged right there that Calhoun had paid over the money but they argued that he didn't know that the money was going to be used as a bribe to the Supervisors,—only as a fee to Ruef. After that I knew that these men had purposely taken the wrong view of the whole matter. I had called them to account for the remarks that the testimony throughout the case was all purchased and that Heney had held the whip over the Supervisors. Thereupon they backed down on that stand and made their whole plea on the ground that Calhoun had given the trolley money to Ruef as a fee.

"I disagreed on the ground that Heney, Spreckels and the other members of the prosecution were not on trial as they insisted, and that the other matters, such as the theft of reports and suppression of testimony, had only been touched upon during the trial to prove that Calhoun knew that the bribery deal had been carried through.

" 'Can't you give Calhoun the benefit of the doubt, that he paid this money as a fee?' was the burden of the others' argument. 'I would be willing to extend him every chance,' I replied, 'but why has he not introduced these vouchers of the United Railroads in court, then we might see what was paid to bribe the juries in the Ford trials.' After this they dropped me like a red-hot stove. I seemed to have struck home. It was a terrifying ordeal to stand off these ten men for twelve hours, but I held firmly to my course and voted throughout upon my conscience. I should have been ashamed to have lifted my head in the future had I fallen down and voted for an acquittal. When the deputy, Mr. Coyle, called to convey the word to Judge Lawlor as to the clearness of an agreement being reached, I met him at the door that night. 'We shall never reach an agreement,' I replied, 'unless these men come over to my side. That I fear shall never come to pass.' The claim has been made in the Globe that I asked for a secret ballot. That is an untruth, as is the statement that I am a Socialist. Not that I am opposed to Socialism, but I have never been inclined to their views. Our political outlooks differ. When I told Coyle that there was no chance of a verdict being reached, the other jurors, one of those standing alongside of me, punched me in the ribs in an effort to make me shut up, as they figured that they ought to be able to convince me. I have received letters from all over the 'State; friends and acquaintances, even utter strangers, congratulating me upon my stand in the Calhoun case and my vote for conviction."

441 Calhoun, after the disagreement of the jury that tried him, issued a statement to the press in which he bitterly denounced those who were responsible for the prosecution, and hinted at retaliation. He continued to insist that Heney was a corrupt offi-

John J. Furey. This the defense resisted. The community was filled with the suggestion that the Calhoun jury, having failed to agree, the costly graft trials should be brought to an end.[442]

Nevertheless, Calhoun's second trial was begun. But before a jury could be secured, Francis J. Heney had been defeated for election as District Attorney. This

cial: "There lies in the courtroom," said Calhoun, "forty checks made by Mr. Rudolph Spreckels to Mr. Francis J. Heney since his alleged appointment as Assistant District Attorney. Those checks were deposited in the American National Bank to his private account. They aggregate $23,800. The first of them amounted to $4,900. They are the price of his infamy. He can not escape the fact that he is a corrupt public official by the contention that he has been engaged in a holy crusade. He can not defend the acceptance of money from a private citizen for the express purpose of enabling him to devote himself exclusively to the so-called Graft Prosecution without committing the crime of accepting a bribe. I here make the formal and specific charge that Francis J. Heney stands side by side with James L. Gallagher as a corrupt public official. I charge him with having accepted bribes and I also charge Rudolph Spreckels and James D. Phelan with having given him the bribes; and if we can get a fair District Attorney in the city of San Francisco I propose at the proper time and in the proper way to submit formal charges against Heney for having received bribes and Spreckels and Phelan for having paid them."

Of Calhoun's threat of prosecution, The Call in its issue of June 22, 1909, said:

"In that soiled and motley retinue of strikers and heelers, jury fixers and gaspipe men that the head of the United Railroads has gathered about him were many who made it a business to proclaim that when the indictments came to the test of fact in court the disposition of that $200,000 would be explained as a perfectly innocent matter in the simplest possible manner. How these promises have been fulfilled we know. The mystery of that $200,000 remains as dark as ever. Not even the stockholders of the company are invited into the confidence of its president. It is not now the question, Where did he get it? but What did he do with it?

"As long as that question remains unanswered by or for Calhoun and as long as he refuses to undergo cross examination and the ordinary legal tests of proof, just so long will the whole American public believe him guilty of bribery. As for his threat of some sort of vague legal proceedings against the prosecutors, that will merely provoke a laugh, as men do laugh at a cheap and obvious bluff."

[442] The free press, not only of California but of the entire nation, protested against such a course. "San Francisco," said the Pittsburgh Times-Gazette, "owes it to the nation to continue her fight against the big grafters of that town. If she lets up now the grafters the country over will take heart, and the next time it becomes necessary to go after the tribe, it will be more difficult even than it has been in San Francisco to convict a briber."

meant the breaking down of the graft prosecution. The District Attorney consented to continuance of the case until the new administration should take charge. The case was not pressed by Mr. Langdon's successor, and finally, with the other graft charges, was dismissed.

CHAPTER XXVII.

The San Francisco Election of 1909.

Scarcely had the disagreeing jury in the Calhoun case been discharged than the Graft Prosecution was again called upon to meet the graft defense at the polls. Langdon's second term was to expire the following January. His successor was to be elected in November.

Mr. Langdon refused positively to be a candidate to succeed himself. The supporters of the prosecution turned to Heney as the most available candidate to oppose the elements united against them.

Heney did not want to be a candidate. The grueling contest of the Calhoun trial, coupled with the nerve-shattering effects of the wound in his head, had brought him to the point of physical and nervous breakdown. But it was demonstrated to him that he had the largest personal following in San Francisco; that the public had confidence in him; that he must make the fight.

And Heney, doubtful of his physical ability to continue to the end of the primary and final campaigns, consented to become a candidate.

There followed the most astonishing campaign for municipal office ever held in San Francisco, or probably in any other American city.

California was at the time groping her way from the clutch of the Southern Pacific "machine." The California Legislature of 1909 had adjourned after a session which had ended largely in disappointing failure for the anti-machine element. The anti-machine element had been in slight majority, but it had blunderingly permitted the machine minority to organize both houses. As a result, the "machine" had been able to defeat the passage of many anti-machine—now known as progressive—measures. In other instances progressive measures were before their passage,[443] in the face of the earnest but unavailable protest of the well-intentioned but unorganized anti-machine majority, loaded with hampering amendments.

Two of these measures bore directly upon the San Francisco situation. The first measure provided for the Direct Primary. The second provided for the elimination of the "party circle" from the election ballot.

This last named measure, known as "the Party Circle bill," passed the Senate, but was defeated by one vote in the Assembly. The defeated measure was intended to restore the Australian ballot to its original simplicity and effectiveness.[444]

Under the machine's tinkering of the State's election laws, the Australian ballot had become a device for encouraging partisan voting. The "party circle" was placed at the head of the column of party candidates. A cross placed in the circle registered a vote for every candidate nominated by the party designated by the circle. The question of "distinguishing marks" invali-

---

[443] See "Story of the California Legislature of 1909," Chapters VIII, IX, X, XI.

[444] This reform was accomplished at the Legislative session of 1911. The undesirable provisions were also stricken by amendment from the Direct Primary law. See "Story of the California Legislature of 1911."

dating entire ballots was ruled upon so closely by the State courts, that many voters voted by means of the one cross in the party circle to avoid the risk of having their entire ballot denied counting because of technical defects that might creep in if a divided ticket were voted. Had the "Party Circle bill" become a law it would have eliminated the "party circle" from the ballot, leaving the voter to select individual candidates of his choice. The one Assembly vote that defeated this measure after it had passed the Senate, went far toward bringing the San Francisco Graft Prosecution to an end.

The Direct Primary measure was not defeated, nor did the machine element succeed in amending it into complete ineffectiveness. The anti-machine Republicans and Democrats, by joining in non-partisan caucus on this measure, succeeded in forcing the passage of the Direct Primary bill, but they were not able to keep it free of defects. Harassed by the machine at every turn, the anti-machine Senators and Assemblymen were compelled to accept many undesirable provisions.[445]

---

[445] "Before voting on this matter," (the Direct Primary provisions) said Senator Stetson, an anti-machine leader in explaining his vote, "lest any one in the future may think that I have been passed something and didn't know it, I wish to explain my vote, and wish to say that this permission accorded a candidate to go on record to support that candidate for United States Senate, who shall have the endorsement of the greatest number of districts, comes from nobody and goes to nobody. It means nothing —mere words—idle words. The only way in which a candidate could have been pledged would have been to provide a pledge or instructions to the Legislature. The words 'shall be permitted' mean nothing and get nowhere. I shall vote for this report, not because I want to, but because I have to if we are at this session to have any Direct Primary law at all."

Senator Stetson was referring particularly to the section which denied the people by state-wide vote the right to indicate their preference for United States Senator, but his words would have applied as directly and as truly to other sections of the measure.

Other good government Senators did, as a matter of fact, denounce the very partisan clause which later contributed so largely to Heney's defeat. Senators Campbell, Holohan and Miller, for

One of these provisions bore directly upon the San Francisco election of 1909, and contributed to a large extent to the outcome.

This clause required a primary candidate to make affidavit giving "the name of his party and that of the office for which he desires to be a candidate; that he affiliated with said party at the last preceding general election, and either that he did not vote thereat or voted for a majority of the candidates of said party at said next preceding general election, and intends to so vote at the ensuing election."

At the time this section was under consideration, anti-machine legislators and the unhampered press pointed out that under it, District Attorney Langdon could not, in all probability, have been nominated nor re-elected in 1907; that Mayor Taylor's election of that year would have been impracticable, if not impossible; that Judge Dunne would have been hampered to the point of defeat in 1908; that under it, both in 1907 and 1908, the so-called "higher-up" element in the field of corruption would have been given an advantage which the better citizenship of the community would have had difficulty in overcoming.[446]

But the machine element denounced these not un-

---

example, while voting for the bill, sent to the clerk's desk the following explanation of their vote:

"We voted for the Direct Primary bill because it seems to be the best law that can be obtained under existing political conditions. We are opposed to many of the features of this bill, and believe that the people at the first opportunity will instruct their representatives in the Legislature to radically amend the same in many particulars, notably in regard to the election of United States Senators, and the provisions that prevent the endorsement of a candidate by a political party or organization other than the one that first nominated such candidate."

446 See files of Sacramento Bee for February and March, 1909, and Senate Journal for March 22, 1909, page 1976.

reasonable objectors as "enemies of the Direct Primary bill," and under cover of the denunciation, and the fight for practical expression of popular choice for United States Senators, the objectionable clause was permitted to remain in the bill.

No sooner had the Legislature adjourned than judicial interpretation of the partisan clause of the Direct Primary Act became necessary. The San Francisco primary election was at hand, and the partisan provisions of the new law proved the first snag which the various candidates encountered.

Although the members of the Legislature, machine as well as anti-machine, voted for the bill, believing that the partisan clause restricted primary nominations to members of the party of the candidates' affiliation, the San Francisco Election Commissioners held there was nothing in the law to prevent the name of a Republican appearing on the Democratic ticket, or of a Democrat on the Republican ticket, provided the candidate made affidavit of the party of his affiliation.

Under this ruling it appeared that, in spite of the objectionable partisan provision of the Direct Primary law, the San Francisco election could be held on the non-partisan basis which had resulted in the election of Taylor and Langdon two years before. The one issue before the San Francisco electors was continuance of the Graft Prosecution. The supporters of the prosecution, Republicans as well as Democrats, desired to vote for Heney. McCarthy was the avowed Labor Union party candidate for Mayor. The Union Labor party was considering the nomination for District Attorney of Charles M. Fickert. The prospects were good that Heney would receive the Republican and Democratic nominations, as Langdon had two years before. He was supported by the better element of both parties, and opposed by the anti-prosecution element of both. This opposition found expression in the Republican party in a committee of twenty-five, at the head of which was I. W. Hellman, Jr., of the Union Trust Company.[447] The better element of the party planned the nomination of Heney, as did the better element of Democrats.

On a non-partisan basis, such as had prevailed in 1907, the Union Labor party would have nominated McCarthy for Mayor, and Fickert for District Attorney, while the anti-machine, pro-prosecution Democrats and Republicans would have nominated a strong candidate for Mayor, and Heney for District Attorney.

Conditions were thus shaping themselves admirably for continuance of the non-partisan administration of municipal affairs, which had at least blocked corruption, even though it had not beaten down the barriers of

---

[447] The Union Trust Company loaned $175,000 to the Calkins' Syndicate, which published papers in opposition to the prosecution. For the curious circumstances under which the loan was made, see footnote 275, page 257. The Union Trust Company officials were among the most effective opponents of the prosecution, and most persistent in circulating the story that the prosecution hurt business. The head of the institution, I. W. Hellman, Sr., returning early in August from a trip to Europe, when the 1909 campaign was opening, said in an interview, published in the Chronicle, August 4, 1909: "In New York I found that there is still a great difficulty in securing capital for San Francisco on account of the Graft Prosecution, or the 'graft persecution,' as they call it there. Of course, I do not know what changes have occurred in the situation here since I left six months ago, but I had an interview with certain people in New York and I found that they were unwilling to send capital here as long as this 'graft persecution' was continued."

technicality, which stood between the corruptors of the municipal government and law-provided penalties.

But this developing non-partisan arrangement was suddenly overturned in an opinion rendered by the Supreme Court, reversing the ruling of the Election Commissioners.

The court held that the partisan provisions of the Direct Primary law prohibited the name of a primary candidate appearing upon any primary ticket except that of the party of the candidate's affiliations.

Under this ruling, Fickert's name could not go on the Union Labor party primary ticket, for Fickert had affiliated with the Republican party. The Hellman committee of twenty-five (Republican) immediately took up the Union Labor party candidate for District Attorney, whose name could not go on the Union Labor party primary ticket, Mr. Fickert being apparently quite as satisfactory to Mr. Hellman and his associates as he was to Mr. McCarthy.

Heney, under the Supreme Court's ruling, found himself in a more difficult position. With other California Progressives, Heney had in 1908 supported Taft for the Presidency. His political affiliations were therefore, under the provisions of the Direct Primary law, Republican. His name could be placed on the Republican primary ticket, but not on the Democratic. But it soon became evident that if his name went on the Republican ticket he would be defeated at the primaries.

The registration of voters under their party designation to enable them to vote at the partisan primaries showed an astonishing condition. The machine, anti-prosecution element was discovered to be massing its strength in the Republican party. Two years before, Daniel A. Ryan, the Republican candidate for Mayor, had received only 9255 votes in San Francisco, while Taylor, the Democratic candidate, had received 28,766, and McCarthy, Union Labor, 17,583. But for the 1909 primaries, no less than 47,945 registered as Republicans, a gain of 38,609 over Ryan's vote,[448] while the Democratic registration was 17,632 only, 11,134 less than Taylor's vote, and the Union Labor registration, 10,546, or 7037 less than McCarthy's vote in 1907. Heney's name could not go on the Democratic ballot. If he permitted it to go on the Republican ballot, the tremendous Republican registration indicated that the anti-machine Republicans would be outvoted by "machine" members of all parties who had registered as Republicans.

By another provision of the election laws, Heney, should he be defeated at the primaries, could not become an independent candidate; defeat at the primaries barred him from running at the final election.

Heney was effectively shut out from participating as a primary candidate. And this, in face of the fact that the anti-machine Republicans and the anti-machine Democrats were striving to make him their candidate.

Had the 1909 primary law prevailed in 1907, Langdon's re-election could have been, and almost to a certainty would have been blocked, and the Graft Prosecution brought to an end two years before it was.

---

[448] Ryan did not receive his full party vote (see chapter XXI) while Taylor received the anti-machine vote of all parties. Nevertheless, this does not account for the extent of the astonishing changes in registration.

At the 1909 Primary election, Heney's name, although he was the choice of the anti-machine element of all parties, did not appear on any of the primary ballots.[449] Nevertheless, 4594 Republicans wrote Heney's name on their primary ballots. But this was not sufficient to give him the nomination. Fickert, whose name appeared on the Republican ballot, as a regular candidate, received 12,480 votes, which gave him the Republican nomination.

On neither the Democratic nor Union Labor primary tickets did the name of any candidate for District Attorney appear. The McCarthy element urged that Fickert's name be written in by Union Labor party voters. They carried their point, Fickert being nominated by the Union Labor party by 3308 votes. But even here there was registered protest at what was going on. Union Labor party voters to the number of 617 wrote Heney's name on their ballots.

In the same way, a determined effort was made to give Fickert the Democratic nomination also. He received 2298 votes. But the pro-prosecution Democrats rallied to Heney's support, and nominated him by a vote of 2386. Thus out of a total of 28,967 who voted for nomination of District Attorney, no less than 7597, or more than 25 per cent., wrote Heney's name on their

---

449 It is interesting to note that the politicians responsible for this condition, and who regarded Heney's position at the 1909 primaries with no attempt to conceal their amusement, were in 1912, loudest in their insistence that they had been disfranchised because the names of Taft electors did not appear on the California election ballot at the 1912 election. It is also to be noted that their representations were based on misrepresentation. They could, under the 1911 election laws, had they had any intention of giving Taft genuine support in California, have placed the names on the ballot by petition, as was done in the case of the Roosevelt electors, who, lest their regular nomination be questioned, were also nominated by petition.

ballots, in protest against the partisan conditions which made his regular nomination impractical.

The law was new; the election, the first held in the State under the Direct Primary. It was difficult to make the electors understand they could vote to nominate Heney by writing his name on the ballot. Of the 38,385 who voted at the primaries only 28,967 voted for District Attorney. Unquestionably, a large percentage of those who did not vote at all, would have written Heney's name on the ballot had they known that such a course was permissible. But they did not know, and more than 25 per cent. of those voting did not vote for District Attorney. As the Rev. Charles N. Lathrop put it: "They have Heney sewed up in a bag, and the bag is the partisan features of the Direct Primary." [450]

Out of this confusing primary election, Fickert came with two party nominations, the Union Labor and the Republican, while Heney had one nomination, the Democratic. This meant that Fickert's name would be printed twice on the final ballot under partisan designation, while Heney's would be printed but once. Thus, for every chance Heney had for a "party circle" vote Fickert had two.

The prosecution forces had supported Byron Mauzy

---

[450] The California Legislature of 1911 corrected the features of the election laws which blocked free expression of the will of the electors. San Francisco, by amendment of its charter, has since placed all municipal elections on a strictly non-partisan basis, with provisions under which no candidate can be elected by a plurality vote. It is interesting to note that although opposed by Mayor McCarthy and the group of politicians about him, these amendments correcting the weaknesses of the election laws, were adopted overwhelmingly. McCarthy's vote in 1911 was practically the same as the vote by which he was elected in 1909. Had the election been held under the same conditions in 1911, as in 1909, McCarthy would almost to a certainty have been re-elected.

for Republican nomination for Mayor, but Mr. Mauzy [451] was defeated by William Crocker, who received the Republican nomination. The Democrats nominated Thomas B. W. Leland for the mayoralty office, while the Union Labor party named P. H. McCarthy. The mayoralty-district attorney tickets were, therefore: Republican, Crocker and Fickert; Union Labor, McCarthy and Fickert; Democratic, Leland and Heney. But the issue before San Francisco, continuance of the Graft Prosecution, had no partisan significance at all. It was supported and it was opposed by members of both parties. The whole fight was over the election of Heney. But never had candidate for office opposition which had more at stake. [452]

Men with apparently unlimited means at their disposal, realized that Heney's election would in all probability mean for them a term in the State prison. They were fighting for their liberty. The commercial interests were warned that, in the words of I. W. Hellman, Sr., the banker, the Graft Prosecution was hurting busi-

---

[451] Mr. Mauzy had the active opposition of the anti-prosecution element, which proposed that old sores be forgotten, and the city be kept free of graft in the future.

"If you think," said The Chronicle, on August 17, 1909, "San Francisco is suffering injury from the fruitless effort to obtain convictions in cases in which evidence is lacking, vote the Byron Mauzy ticket. If you believe that the sane thing to do is to cease wasting money over the attempt to accomplish the impossible, vote for candidates who can be depended upon to give the city an administration from which graft will be eliminated in future."

[452] The platform expressions on the Graft Prosecution issue are interesting. The Republican platform made no reference to it at all. There was some talk of providing that "the District Attorney should do his duty," but not even this was provided. The Union Labor party plank on this question read as follows:

"We believe in the principle of the equality of all men before the law; that every guilty person should be prosecuted with vigor, in accordance with the law of the land, and that the administra-

ness.[453]　The anti-Graft Prosecution press insisted day after day that bribery of public officials, while bad, is the most common of crimes and the most difficult to prove; that San Francisco had tried to convict, had failed and might as well give up.　So-called "improvement clubs" went so far as to adopt resolutions not only protesting against further prosecution, but demanding that the Supervisors withdraw support given the District Attorney's

tion of the law should be free from any and all suspicion of private control.　We condemn favoritism or leniency in behalf of any offender before the law, or any compromise with criminals.　We demand that any and all offenders be dealt with alike, and to such end we pledge our nominees."

The Democratic plank alone pledged support to the Graft Prosecution.　It read:

"We pledge the Democratic party absolutely and unequivocally to the support of the Graft Prosecution which for three years has valiantly battled for the principle of the equality of all men before the law, which has secured convictions against disheartening odds and has paved the way for the clean administration of public affairs which we now enjoy.

"The people must declare at this critical election for or against municipal corruption; for the enforcement of the law, or for its abandonment; for or against not only a greater but a better San Francisco.

"Francis J. Heney, our candidate for District Attorney, embodies these issues, and we pledge him the vigorous and loyal support of the Democratic party."

453 The "hurt business" argument was ably combated by businessmen who were free of the graft mire.

"From all the available information at hand," said Colonel Harris Weinstock, of the firm of Weinstock-Lubin & Co., in replying to this argument, "I find that on the whole the volume of business is greater in San Francisco than it ever was before. I am, therefore, unable to see how business has been hurt by the Graft Prosecution.

"The burden of proof on this point properly rests with those making the charge.　They should present facts and figures verifying their statement that business has been hurt by the graft prosecution before they can hope to have it accepted as fact.

"So far as I have been able to find out, the Graft Prosecution has not hurt business, but even if it had seriously crippled business it would still be your duty and my duty and the duty of every lover and well-wisher of our free institutions to hold up the hands of those who are fighting your battle and my battle in an effort to bring public wrongdoers to justice, and thus prevent harm from coming to the republic.　Let the work go on."

The American National Bank of San Francisco, in a financial letter issued August 25, 1909, gave figures which disproved the Hellman idea.

"It is significant of San Francisco's credit standing in the world at large," the letter read, "that the bonds of this city com-

office in its efforts to land bribe-givers behind the bars.[454]
And finally, the large business interests opposed to the
prosecution, threw strength to McCarthy; not that they
liked McCarthy—they united against him two years later
—but because the election of McCarthy would go far
toward the defeat of Heney. Members of the labor
unions were, to a large extent, supporters of the prosecution. Their votes had made Langdon's election sure

---

mand prices that compare favorably with the issues of other large
municipalities, as measured by the low interest return which investors are willing to accept. To illustrate: For every $1,000
put into municipal bonds at present figures, the purchaser would
receive per annum:

"From San Francisco bonds $39.00
"From Philadelphia bonds 37.00
"From Cincinnati bonds 37.50
"From Cleveland bonds 37.50
"From St. Louis bonds 38.80
"From Pittsburg bonds 37.00
"From Chicago bonds 38.50
"From Minneapolis bonds 38.50
"From Milwaukee bonds 39.00
"From New York bonds 39.50

"Considering these facts, and the readiness with which the San
Francisco bonds are being taken, it does not appear that this city
is suffering in reputation, as some people affect to believe, by
reason of certain trials which have engaged the attention of the
criminal courts for two years past."

"I have no patience," said Heney, in discussing the Hellman
argument, "with this talk that we hear from merchants and bankers that the Prosecution is hurting business. They heard the
same talk in Boston when our Revolutionary sires threw tea over-
board. It would hurt business, they said, to have a war with
England. I can see the picture, when Thomas Jefferson was signing the Declaration of Independence, of a large man, who looked
like the cartoonist's representation of a corporation official, coming through the door behind him and shouting, 'Hold on, Tom,
you'll hurt business.' And when Washington was spending that
terrible winter with his army at Valley Forge, the same class
of men who are now crying at us in San Francisco were shouting
for the war to stop. 'Damn principle,' they were crying. 'It's
hurting business. This war must stop.'"

454 "It is," said the Chronicle, commenting upon the adoption
of such resolutions, "a matter of common knowledge that there
is a widespread feeling among those whose good citizenship cannot
be disputed that the city, having done its best for three years,
without success, to find legal proof which would connect officials
of the corporations which profited by the corruption of the Schmitz
administration with the crime of bribery, it is necessary to dis-
continue the effort. Hitherto no one has been willing to formally

14

in 1907. During the 1909 campaign, and down to the very day of election, the sentiment among laboring men was to vote for McCarthy and Heney. But Heney's name did not appear on the Union Labor ticket.

Labor's support of Heney was vigorously opposed. Appeal was made to workingmen to stay by their class; to vote for the labor candidates, McCarthy and Fickert. On the Monday night before the election, the writer, with Professor George H. Boke of the University of California Law School, joined a group of working men who were discussing the merits of the several candidates.

---

approach the authorities in the matter lest he should appear to show sympathy with evildoers. The Richmond Club, however, has formally memorialized the Supervisors to withdraw further support by appropriations on the ground that it has become apparent that success is impossible, and that further effort would be not only a waste of money and energy but serve to keep before the world the memory of a most disgraceful epoch in our history.

"Bribery of public officials is the most dangerous of crimes. It undermines the very foundation of government by the people. And yet it has been in this and all other large American cities the most common of crimes. In the public mind, and in common speech, any person or firm which has habitually done business with our city government has been held to have on himself the burden of proof that he was innocent of bribery. And then came the riot of debauchery under the Schmitz administration, with corruption in all forms permeating every department of the city government. We have had nothing like that before, and yet until the election of the present Board of Supervisors this city has almost never had a Board on which some members were not believed to be corrupt and constantly on the watch for opportunities to 'hold up' those seeking to do business with the city. It is not believed that any franchise now in existence has been obtained without bribery or operated without continuous bribery. It has been generally assumed that whoever undertook to do business with the city must buy his way in by some form of corruption.

"Bribery is a crime for which conviction is almost impossible. Occasionally pro•f can be got through a decoy, as in the case of the Schmitz Supervisors. What was exposed in that way, however, was no legal proof against the higher officials of the beneficiary corporations. For that other proof must be had, and thus far, except in one case, no conviction has been had. And unless the courts reverse themselves that conviction will not stand. The question then arises as to the duty of the city. Shall we continue to expend energy in striving to accomplish what we all see to be impossible, or shall the city, having done its best, turn its energies

Apparently all but one of them were for McCarthy and Heney. The exception was for Leland and Heney. He was defending himself, when the writer joined the group, against the charge that in voting for Leland he was "voting outside his class."

This Leland advocate was a most noticeable young man. He declared himself to be a member of the electricians' union. Well under thirty, clear-eyed and forceful, he was prepared to stand his ground. When his immediate opponent became personal, the electrical worker, without raising his voice, without excitement, or boast, or display, remarked quietly: "Do not resort to

---

into more hopeful channels? As to that there will be differences of opinion, nor is it possible for anyone to know to what extent those differences are founded in reason, and how much on personal hatreds and a desire for notoriety.

"There is doubtless a feeling that the continuance of these prosecutions is now doing great harm, which could only be counterbalanced by conviction based on clear legal proof, for which it is impossible to hope. In the first place, it is enormously costly and has introduced a universal system of spying which is exciting animosity against both sides of these cases. Decent citizens are coming to resent secret efforts to induce them to compromise themselves on the one side or the other. Secondly, the awful exhibitions of perjury in order to escape jury duty are shocking the moral sense of the community as severely as it was shocked by the exposure of the bribery. And the examination of the jurors are resulting in expressions of opinion by prospective jurors which do not do the city any good. Finally, the conduct of these trials is turning into a farce processes which should be the most solemn exhibitions of the authority of the law. We must all recognize that it is common talk that society ought not to seek to imprison one possible criminal at the cost of the imprisonment for months at a time of innocent citizens dragged from their homes and compelled to listen to the interminable quarrels of counsel over matters having no legitimate bearing on the case and injected solely for the purpose of confusing jurymen. Everybody sees that it will be impossible in the case now on trial to get a jury fit to be intrusted with the fate of a dog. Every intelligent citizen has been 'disqualified' by reading the testimony before the Grand Jury.

"It is a most difficult situation. No reputable citizen is willing to seem to impede the course of justice. But, now that an organized body has formally raised before the Supervisors a question which has long been a daily subject of discussion whenever two men have met, it will be necessary to frankly face the situation and decide where duty lies."

personalities, for if it comes to personalities, what chance have you against me?"

There were no more personalities.

Incidentally his argument was fast bringing out the fact that every worker in the crowd was going to vote for Heney. The effect of it was important. Suddenly from somewhere there appeared a new man to do his part in molding public opinion.

The new-comer went through that crowd with the assurance of a practiced football player through an aggregation of amateurs. In less than five minutes he had addressed every man of the group. But he had none of the marks of a worker, and nobody thought to ask for his "card." His was the pasty face and the pudgy neck and the soft, unclean hand of the cadet. His argument was curious and even ridiculous, but it was most effective. It at least scattered the crowd.

"Of course Calhoun is a grafter," he said in effect. "They are all grafters. Spreckels is a grafter. Of course, Fickert is Calhoun's man, just as Heney is Spreckels's man. They are all out for graft. But if we are to have grafting, let's keep the graft in our own class. Why should you vote to let Spreckels's men do the grafting? You have a candidate of your own. Vote for him. It is only a fight between millionaires anyhow, and a toss-up which is right. Let us vote for the man of our class."

The effect of this running fire of words was immediate. The electrician lost the attention of his associates. The discussion came to an end with murmurs of approval of the newcomer's position. That he should have changed a vote with such argument seems incredible. But that he had created a doubt in the minds of those workingmen was apparent to all who saw. He left them well prepared for the anti-prosecution workers who would meet them at the polls the next morning.

But the laboring element was not the only "class" forced into opposition to Heney. At the exclusive clubs, fashionable hotels, social functions, support of Heney was denounced as treason to the exclusive, fashionable, social class. It was quite amusing to hear first generation descendants of honest steerage immigrants decrying the prosecution of rich men trapped in bribe-giving on the theory that to do otherwise "would be treason to our class."

Thus, Mr. Heney was called upon to meet the "class" opposition of the laborer and the magnate. On the other hand, the unafraid, intelligent people of San Francisco, who recognized no "class" issue, rallied to Heney's support. But they were without the concerted plan of action which the other side had perfected. The San Francisco press, with the exception of The Bulletin and Daily News, gave Heney no editorial support, but the country press, which had no circulation in San Francisco, earnestly urged his election.[455]

---

[455] The following from the Fresno Republican is very good example of this excellent but unavailing newspaper support:

"Good people of San Francisco, give heed and take notice, the way it looks in the clearer perspective of an outside view.

"Francis J. Heney is a candidate for District Attorney, and he is the issue. It is stop the Graft Prosecutions, or go on with them. Your votes will determine it.

"You are 'tired of the Graft Prosecutions.' How long did it take you to get tired of the graft? Can you not be patient as long with militant honesty as you were with sneaking crime?

"You may stop these Prosecutions, if you so vote. But remember the whole civilized world is looking on, and will judge

Good citizens throughout the country wrote urging Heney's election. "To rout the forces of the prosecution at this juncture in San Francisco," wrote Rabbi Stephen S. Wise of New York, "is to hoist the red flag of anarchy, to proclaim that law and order are not always enforceable, or that such enforcement is not always profitable."

But Rabbi Wise was in New York. His influence did not, unfortunately, extend, in any important degree, to San Francisco.

On the day of election, the writer visited many voting places in the districts in which the labor vote was

---

you by that vote. It is the good name of San Francisco that you are voting up or down.

"Banker Hellman says not. He has been to New York and he says 'New York' wants the Prosecutions stopped, and 'New York' will not lend any more money until they are stopped.

"What is Banker Hellman's 'New York?' It is certain banks and certain syndicates in New York. And it is the San Francisco officials of precisely these syndicates that you are now prosecuting. Of course, Patrick Calhoun, of New York, wants the prosecution of Patrick Calhoun of San Francisco stopped. It is Banker Hellman's privilege to have a mere pendulum which swings from his San Francisco office to his New York office and thinks it is in New York. But it is not incumbent on you to share that mental deficiency. If Banker Hellman should announce in New York that he was going to discuss the San Francisco situation, his audience would consist of the New York partners of the San Francisco grafters. He thinks that is 'New York.' The real New York would neither know nor care. It never heard of Banker Hellman. But if Francis J. Heney should be announced to discuss the San Francisco situation in New York, there is not a place of assemblage in the city big enough to hold the people who would want to hear and see him. The whole nation knows Heney and it has made up its mind about him. It is waiting to see what you do, before it makes up its mind about you, too.

" 'The prosecutions must stop, some time,' to be sure. But who has earned from San Francisco the right to say when? When Francis J. Heney says it is time to quit, then it is time; not before. He has given his time, his strength, and almost his life for you. He has purified your politics and regulated your government. He has redeemed your city's name in the esteem of the world. He is making for you a fight which no one ever had the courage, the persistence or the ability to make before. He is not tired yet and he has not surrendered yet. Suppose you leave it to him, when it is time to quit.

"People of San Francisco, the world is looking on. It cannot determine your decision. Neither can you determine what it will think of that decision, when it is made."

strong. Working men by the scores were taking less than a minute to mark their ballots. It was evident that they were voting by means of the party circle. Every Labor Union party vote of this kind was a vote against Heney. The last hope that Heney would get this support was gone. One did not need wait for the counting of the ballots. It was plain that Heney was defeated.

The election returns spoke eloquently of the means that had been employed to defeat Heney. For the primary election 47,945 had registered as Republicans, but Crocker, the Republican candidate for Mayor, received only 13,766 votes at the final election. Although but 10,546 had registered for the primaries as members of the Union Labor party, P. H. McCarthy received 29,455 votes, which, wherever voting was done by means of the party circle, carried a vote for Fickert.

Fickert, with the two nominations, received 36,192. Heney, running on the Democratic ticket, received 26,075 votes, 6481 more than Leland, the candidate for Mayor. But the combination against Heney was too great for him or any man to overcome. Fickert was elected.[456]

The Graft Prosecution had been defeated at the polls.

---

[456] Heney on the day after the election issued the following statement:

"The first battle for equality before the law has been fought and lost, but the war against graft will continue to be waged by all true soldiers who have been fighting with me in the great cause of common honesty, common decency, and civic righteousness.

"The fight between the forces of evil and the forces of good is and must be a perpetual one. The first battle of Bull Run cast gloom over the entire earth, but that disaster only inspired the immortal Lincoln and his followers with stern resolution and fresh courage.

"San Francisco has received a sad blow and the cause of equality before the law a great setback, but be of good cheer and take fresh courage, you many thousands of good men and women who have joined in this fight for the maintenance of the purity and protection of our homes and the uplifting of the moral standards of our city!

"We have been defeated in this election, but the sober moral sense of the community will again reassert itself and San Francisco will vindicate herself before the world.

"I retract nothing that I have said during the recent campaign. On the contrary, I reassert the truth of all that I have stated from the public platforms. I have no regrets except that for poor San Francisco and the many thousands of people who fought shoulder to shoulder with me in the good fight.

"Let us all to-night firmly resolve that we will continue the battle for equality before the law with unabated vigor until success has crowned our efforts."

The following statement was issued by Rudolph Spreckels:

"While the defeat at yesterday's election of the principles for which I have fought is regretted by me, it will speedily bring about a truer estimate of my real motives.

"One of the compensations of this defeat is that I have so quickly been given an opportunity to disprove the charges so frequently made that I have been actuated by sordid or vindictive motives. The individuals against whom it is alleged that I have entertained malicious and selfish designs are entirely removed from the possibility of harm at the hands of the so-called Prosecution.

"Attempting to punish was an unpleasant and incidental portion of the public work which I set out to do. I am glad that the people have taken that task off my hands and left me free to do the more important part of my undertaking.

"Feeling that the people will fully realize this, I desire to say that I shall continue the work of civic regeneration with undiminished hope and earnestness."

CHAPTER XXVIII.

Dismissal of the Graft Cases.

At the time of Mr. Fickert's election to the District Attorney's office, the second trial of Patrick Calhoun for offering a bribe was well under way. As at the other graft trials, there had been delays [457] so that after five months the jury was only half complete. That the trial could not be finished before Mr. Fickert assumed the duties of his office became evident. The case was, for that reason, on December 9, continued until January 10, in order that Mr. Fickert might participate in the selection of the trial jurors. But on that date, Mr. Fickert, who had been in office only two days, very frankly admitted himself to be unfamiliar with the facts, and not prepared to go to trial. Further continuance was accordingly granted until January 31, and then until February 7.

In the meantime former Supervisor James L. Gallagher, the pivotal witness in the case, had disappeared. Gallagher was known to have been in San Francisco for some three weeks after Fickert's election. About De-

---

[457] The second trial of Patrick Calhoun (No. 1437) was begun July 19, 1909. Owing to the illness of one of Mr. Calhoun's counsel, the trial was suspended on August 16th, and resumed September 30th. The following day the defendant secured further continuance until November 15th, upon the ground of the pendency of a municipal political campaign. After the election the trial was resumed. On December 9th, it was, by agreement between the parties continued until January 10th, when the new District Attorney should be in office.

cember 1 he dropped out of sight. He was supposed to have gone to Europe.[458]

On February 7, Mr. Fickert moved the dismissal of the case pending against Mr. Calhoun on the ground that there was not sufficient legal and competent evidence to warrant him submitting the case to a jury.[459]

---

[458] The motives which prompted Gallagher to flee the city are among the undetermined elements of the graft cases. Perhaps recollection of his attempted assassination had something to do with it. It may be that the defense, which had done so many extraordinary things during the course of the graft trials, made it worth his while to go. Gallagher is known to have been plentifully supplied with money while he was away. An attempt was made to create the impression that agents of the Prosecution had been instrumental in getting Gallagher out of the State. But the attempt, while it confused the situation somewhat, was not taken seriously. When in August, 1911, Judge Lawlor dismissed the indictments against the alleged bribe-givers in the trolley case, he took occasion to say: "I am more convinced now than I was when these same motions were urged more than a year ago, that James L. Gallagher is remaining out of this jurisdiction for a specific purpose. The future will make that point entirely clear. When his importance as a witness in any of these so-called graft cases has ceased there is no doubt that James L. Gallagher will be again in our midst. If I were able to lay the responsibility for that situation upon any individual or set of individuals I repeat that appropriate proceedings would have been instituted to have the law redressed in that behalf."

Judge Lawlor was right. After the dismissal of the graft cases Mr. Gallagher returned to San Francisco.

To the intimation of District Attorney Fickert that Gallagher left the State to embarrass the District Attorney's administration, Judge Lawlor on one occasion said in an opinion: "That the former administration may have distrusted the official intentions of the District Attorney toward these indictments might be assumed from all the surrounding circumstances. But it does not seem probable that the former administration would induce a material and indispensable witness to leave the State and thereby make it easy for the District Attorney to secure a result which otherwise might entail serious embarrassment. So far as the showing is concerned there is no tangible proof tending to support the charge of the District Attorney, nor is there any proof which would justify such an inference."

[459] Fickert's motion had been prepared in advance and was read to the court. "Since the calling of this case on January 10th," he said, "I have made a thorough and careful examination of the evidence left in the District Attorney's office by my predecessor, Mr. Langdon, and he informed me on my accession to the office, that he had delivered to me all the evidence of every kind and character in his possession or under his control in this case. I have also examined the transcript of testimony given at the former trial of this defendant; besides this, I have made independent search for further evidence. These examinations convince me that there is not suf-

Judge Lawlor denied the motion. In denying it, Judge Lawlor stated that in the view of the court the action should be tried by a jury and a verdict should be rendered by a jury, if that were possible, in the full operation of the law.

Fickert stated in the discussion which followed that he wanted his motion to apply to all the other graft cases of the same class as Calhoun's, with the exception of the defendants Ruef and Schmitz. But here again did the Judge deny the District Attorney's request.

After Judge Lawlor's ruling, Calhoun's attorneys announced themselves ready to proceed with the trial of the case. Fickert stated that he would be ready in a week. Judge Lawlor thereupon questioned Fickert very closely about the absent witness, Gallagher. Fickert gave assurance that diligent hunt was being made for the witness.

The questioning of the District Attorney was continued ten days later when the case again came up. Judge Lawlor asked Fickert to tell definitely whether he proposed to put the issue before a jury in the absence of his material witness.

Fickert replied that Gallagher's absence greatly weakened the State's case, and that in his belief certain facts could not be proved without Gallagher being present. But as for that, Fickert insisted that even with Gallagher present he did not believe that the State could

---

ficient legal and competent evidence to justify me, as a sworn officer of the law, to present this case to a jury.

"My opinion is confirmed by the fact that 42 out of 48 jurors sworn to try this defendant and the defendant, Tirey L. Ford, upon the same state of facts, voted 'Not Guilty.' I, therefore, 'in furtherance of justice,' move the dismissal of this indictment, on the grounds that the evidence is wholly insufficient to warrant another trial of this case."

make out a case.[460]   Nevertheless, he continued to insist
that he was ready to proceed to try the action even in
the absence of the witness Gallagher.

But Judge Lawlor announced that he did not propose to proceed with the trial of the action:

(1) If a material witness were without the jurisdiction of the court.

(2) If the court did not believe that the cause were
to be prosecuted with the vigor and fidelity that the law
contemplates.[461]

---

[460] Judge Lawlor was also careful to make clear that if the
court proceeded with the formation of a jury, jeopardy would at-
tach to the case. He also pointed out that the statute of limitations had run against the alleged crimes. The following is from
the transcript, the questions being directed to Mr. Fickert:
"The Court: You are aware that if you proceed to form a jury
to try this issue, and the witness does not appear, that jeopardy
has nevertheless attached and that the defendant will be entitled
to ask for his deliverance at the hands of that jury, whether that
witness is produced or not.
"Mr. Fickert: Yes, I am aware of that, if your Honor please.
"The Court: And you are aware further that the alleged criminal act set up in the indictment is outlawed within the meaning
of Section 800 of the Penal Code; that is to say, that more than
three years have intervened since it is claimed that that act was
committed.
"Mr. Fickert: That is correct, if your Honor please.
"The Court: The witness, James L. Gallagher, gave testimony
in the trial of case 1436 against this defendant. You are aware
that the testimony relating to an indictment cannot be read to a jury
on a retrial of the action; in other words, that if James L. Gallagher
does not appear in this trial his testimony cannot be presented to
the jury."
Fickert suggested that counsel might stipulate that the evidence
be read. But counsel for Mr. Calhoun hastened to assure Mr. Fickert that counsel would stipulate to nothing of the kind.

[461] "At the present time," said Judge Lawlor in making this
announcement, "it is the intention of the Court to deal with this
matter, so far as the absence of that material witness is concerned, and to suspend judgment as to the ultimate attitude of the
District Attorney in respect to this and other causes before the
Court. I do not intend to sit here and preside over a trial if for
any reason, whether it seems sufficient to the District Attorney
or not, the Court reaches the conclusion that the case is not being
prosecuted in good faith. The Court, in pointing out the duty of
the District Attorney on February 7th, was not inviting a suggestion that we should proceed to trial without regard to the outcome
of that trial or to its particular features or the manner in which it
should be tried. The Court will try no case, it will not consume
its own time, it will not consume the time of others, it will not

Fickert also stated his position. He insisted that he did not believe that any evidence had ever existed against the trolley-graft defendants Abbott and Mullally, and did not believe it to be his duty as District Attorney to prosecute men against whom there was no evidence. Fickert even attempted to commit Judge Lawlor to this proposition, by stating that the Judge in chambers had confessed as much. This Judge Lawlor denied. Mr. Fickert's assistant, Mr. Berry, had been present during the discussion in chambers between Mr. Fickert and

---

allow the expenditure of public money for the mere purpose of going through the forms of a trial. The Court must feel in the end that the people are represented. Now, what its final view shall be as to the District Attorney will be announced when the Court deems that anouncement pertinent and proper. The Court has its own views as to what may be done within the exercise of its prerogative in the event that it does not feel that the people are represented, and will act upon its own judgment when that time arrives. At this time the witness being absent from the jurisdiction of the Court, the Court points out to the District Attorney his duty under Section 1052 of the Penal Code, to move for a proper continuance of this action until the Court can be advised as to whether or not that witness can be produced."

Later, when Fickert suggested that all criminal causes be transferred to some other department where the judge might be of a different opinion, Judge Lawlor said:

"I have had no occasion to find fault with your acts in respect to any other causes that have been brought before this Court. I am endeavoring to have your mind concentrated upon one thing, and that is the matters which are before this Court, and for the prosecution of which you, under your sworn oath of office are required to give your full attention to. Your own statement in support of your motion to dismiss this case evinces in my judgment a disposition not to do your duty. However, I still say that this matter I bring to your attention, and ask you to give full reflection upon the matter. I have no desire in any manner to hamper you. The process of this Court is at your disposal at all times, in all causes, and if any person or set of persons be found to be interfering with the due administration of Justice you will have a full hearing before this Court in order that you shall not be so hampered. Your statement concerning these cases is calculated not alone to affect the fortune of these undetermined cases, but it is well calculated to affect the disposition of the other causes and other charges wherein convictions were had against other persons growing out of this alleged transaction, and which cases are now on their way for a determination to the courts of appeal in this State."

Judge Lawlor, but Mr. Berry failed to sustain his chief's contention.[462]

"In these cases, the cases against Mr. Abbott and Mr. Mullally," said Fickert, "I shall never proceed in them because there is absolutely no evidence which at all gives even a suspicion."

In respect to the other cases, Mr. Fickert announced that he intended to take the same course that he had in those under discussion, and stated that if the Judge so desired he would advise him before hand as to which of the cases he intended to make a motion for dismissal.

"In view of the statement you made on February 7," [463] replied Judge Lawlor, "the Court will not feel called upon to grant any application looking to a dismissal of any of those cases. The Court will finally deal with them in the manner prescribed by the law. And if that situation is not reached so that the Court can proceed with the trial, the Court will be under the

---

[462] "I think your Honor well knows," Fickert had said, "that certain defendants in this particular class of cases, that there have not been produced here in Court, and I do not think ever existed, any evidence against them. I allude to Mr. Abbott and Mr. Mullally. And I so informed you in your chambers, and you in words confessed that proposition."

Judge Lawlor took this statement up. The following is from the transcript:

"The Court: Now, before you pass to those other cases, in regard to these two cases do you make the statement that I made any statement to you, in the presence of Mr. Berry, that I said there was not sufficient evidence?

"Mr. Fickert: I so informed you, and you, in effect, so stated.

"The Court: Did you so understand it, Mr. Berry?

"Mr. Fickert: That there was no evidence against those men?

"Mr. Berry: I remember Mr. Fickert saying he did not consider there was any evidence against those men, but I do not remember the Court's reply: I do not remember that the Court did reply.

"The Court: I did not. It is not the province of the Court to pass upon the facts in a criminal case. The facts are placed before a jury, and the jury pass on the facts.

"Mr. Fickert: I am certainly not mistaken in that matter.

"The Court: You are certainly mistaken in that matter; I was careful not to make any such statement."

[463] See footnote 459, page 426.

solemn obligation of setting down in its minutes the reason why a trial has not been had in any particular instance, and why cases are dismissed or disposed of without the trial of the general issue. The Court cannot escape its responsibilities. I have pointed out that under the law it is for the Court to say finally what shall become of cases that are not pressed to conclusion, and when the Court does that it must give its reasons—the law says so. In this State, since the formation of the government therein, the power has not for any considerable length of time lodged in the District Attorney to dispose of actions; that matter is confided to the Court. Counsel will be doing injustice to his own position if he assumes that the Court has any other attitude than to finally dispose of these matters according to the law without doing injustice to any person, either to the District Attorney or any person who is unfortunate enough to be involved. But when the Court comes to write down its action it will be based upon what it believes to be the fact and upon nothing else."

Fickert replied that he was ready to proceed with the matter. To this Judge Lawlor reiterated that the Court was not going to permit the District Attorney to proceed in the absence of a witness, who, according to the District Attorney's own statement, was material.[464]

---

[464] "In dealing with the attitude of the District Attorney," said Judge Lawlor, "as is manifested by all that I have said upon that subject, I have endeavored to deal justly with him, to reach no conclusion myself definitely as to the attitude of the District Attorney. I sincerely hope that in these cases, as in all cases that may come before the Court, the District Attorney will do his full duty. I desire it equally understood, however, that if the District Attorney in any case fails of his duty the Court is not going to be recreant and it is not going to sit here as a minister of justice and permit a travesty in any form, for any purpose, whatever the views of the District Attorney may be. Now, I have endeavored to make it

Nor did the earnest plea of attorneys for the defense for dismissal move Judge Lawlor. In the absence of the material witness, Gallagher, he continued the case, on the Court's own motion, until April 25.[465]

On that date, Calhoun's attorneys moved for dismissal of all the indictments pending against their client upon the ground that his trial had been postponed and continued for more than sixty days without his consent and over his objection and exception.

Fickert submitted the motion, fortifying it with a statement that he did not believe that the District Attorney's office would be justified in asking continuance until Gallagher's return.

Judge Lawlor postponed determination of the motion

---

clear that there are two considerations that will affect the Court in the final disposition of this business: First, that it will not proceed with the trial of any action where material testimony is not forthcoming. That would be the disposition of the Court in any case, but it is especially its attitude in this case in view of the sweeping statement of the District Attorney made on February 7th that there is no sufficient evidence upon which to proceed to trial against any of these four defendants."

[465] The statement was made repeatedly that Gallagher was not under subpoena when he left the State. The statement was even contained in the opinion of the Appellate Court, granting the writ of mandate that preceded the dismissal of the graft cases. Judge Lawlor at the proceedings when the cases were finally dismissed, touched upon this feature as follows:

"The Court: The statement has been made in the opinion that I am not able to account for its appearance in the showing. This statement was made that no service had been made upon James L. Gallagher or that he was not under the order of the Court. That is a proposition of fact which has never been resolved by this Court and I am unable to determine how it could be determined elsewhere, how it could be declared elsewhere, in the absence of such testimony as I might be able to give on the subject. I expressly refrained, on an occasion when I made an extended statement covering these cases, from making any final word on that subject. I am not prepared now to say so, because I don't know.

"Mr. Berry: I will state to the Court that I have made a very careful inquiry in the District Attorney's office, and of the records, and of the officials in that office in the previous administration, and I have been unable to secure or to get any definite information on that point."

until July 14.[466]   His ruling was announced on August 3.

Judge Lawlor went exhaustively into the situation

[466] Judge Lawlor, in announcing this decision, said in part: "Section 13 of Article I of the Constitution provides in part: 'In criminal prosecutions in any court whatever the party accused shall have the right to a speedy and public trial. * * *.' Section 1382 of the Penal Code declares in part: 'The court, unless good cause to the contrary is shown, must order the prosecution to be dismissed in the following cases: * * *. 2. If a defendant, whose trial has not been postponed upon his application, is not brought to trial within sixty days after the finding of the indictment, or filing of the information.'

"This provision has repeatedly been declared to be a statutory expression with reference to the section of the constitution to which the Court has referred. It has been held to mark the period within which a party accused of crime is to be brought to trial, unless good cause to the contrary is shown. About the general proposition of law involved in the determination of the present motion there can be little ground for contention. The perplexity usually arises in the determination of what the reserve language of Subdivision 2 of Section 1382 of the Penal Code may be included to cover. An application of this character must be determined according to the peculiar circumstances surrounding the application." * * *

"The Court is of the view that so far as the determination of the motion itself is concerned the onus is on the People to show good cause, which would take the case out of the operation of the constitutional provision and the statute referred to. The Court, in that view of the matter, has addressed the District Attorney as to what his attitude is with respect to the motion, and the District Attorney has made it plain that it is not his intention to take any step toward meeting the application of the defendant to have the causes dismissed. In the view which the Court takes of the general attitude of the District Attorney toward the four defendants at bar, the Court feels it is a case where it must act, and to the extent that it may be needed, to protect the public interests. The Court has judicial knowledge of the history of the charges against these four defendants. It knows judicially that a material, and, it is claimed, an indispensable witness to the prosecution of these charges is without the jurisdiction of the State. It is not prepared, on any evidence before it, to charge the responsibility of the absence of that witness either to the former administration or to the present administration in the District Attorney's office. The fact, however, that the witness is absent from the State and not within reach of the process of the Court, is a fact established before the Court at this time.

"It is not the intention of the Court to disregard the rights of this or any other defendant, that may be urged before this Court, but, it is likewise the disposition of the Court, to see that the public interests are safeguarded, and that no arrangement between the defendants and the sworn officer of the law shall be suffered to direct and control the action of this Court. And in that view of the matter the Court has reached the conclusion that it is its duty to continue these causes further, in order to see whether or not the missing witness can be secured, and if he cannot be secured within such time as this Court may deem to be proper and which would take the case out of the exception contained in the provision

presented.[467]   He pointed out that a material and indispensable witness was absent from the State; he
stated that the Court was called upon to intervene "because the District Attorney has at practically every turn
followed the lead of these defendants"; he held that
through the influence of unusual agencies, so far as the
graft cases were concerned, the law had broken down,
and that the crimes charged are of the most serious
nature, "because such criminal activity tends to sap the
very foundations of government"; he insisted that before the indictments should be finally disposed of every
reasonable effort should be made to get at the truth of
the situation.

"The disposition of grave charges other than on
their merits," he concluded, "is not to be encouraged
and should not be allowed, except in the face of a strict
legal necessity."   He continued the cases until August 29.

Stanley Moore, one of Calhoun's attorneys, when
Judge Lawlor had concluded, demanded that he be permitted to reply.   This demand was refused.

There followed one of the most extraordinary scenes
ever recorded of a court of justice.   The defendant's
attorneys, the District Attorney, and even the prisoner
at bar, openly and contemptuously defied the Judge on
the bench.

Stanley Moore charged him with "doing politics

---

of the statute, and the constitutional provision, then to deal with
this motion.
"It is therefore ordered that the determination of the pending
motion in the causes against the four defendants named be continued for further hearing until 10 a. m., Thursday, July 14, 1910."

[467] Judge Lawlor's decision will be found in full in the Appendix,
page i.

from the bench that you stultify in your occupancy."
A. A. Moore, another of Calhoun's lawyers, accused
him of being "a partisan, a bitter partisan, and doing
dirty politics."

"And," Stanley Moore hastened to add, "have been
before these indictments were ever filed in this court,
as the events of that midnight deal in which you participated on April 29 amply demonstrate." [468]

District Attorney Fickert, in the face of the Court's
direction that he take his seat, denounced "the statements and aspersions you have tried to cast upon me"
as "false in each and every particular."

A third of Mr. Calhoun's attorneys added his denunciation. Mr. John Barrett decried the proceedings
as "infamous."

Judge Lawlor sentenced Calhoun's three attorneys
to serve five days each in the county jail for contempt
and ordered the Sheriff to take charge of them.

But the extraordinary scene was not concluded. The
prisoner at the bar had not yet been heard. Calhoun
took the floor to tell the Judge on the bench that should
the Judge send him (Calhoun) to jail for contempt "it
will be heralded all over this country as an honor." [469]

---

468 See Chapter XV.

469 Calhoun's denunciation of Judge Lawlor was as follows:
"Mr. Calhoun: May it please your Honor: I have been educated,
sir, to have respect for the courts. I have sat in your court under
circumstances that would have tried the patience of any American.
Throughout these trials I have sought, sir, to give you under most
trying circumstances that respect to which your office entitles you.
But, sir, I cannot sit quiet and listen to the vile insinuations which
you yourself have stated there was no evidence before you to
justify. There have been periods, sir, when the greatest honor
that could come to a man was to go to jail; and as an American
citizen I say to you that if you should send me for contempt it will
be heralded all over this country as an honor. You have seen fit,
sir, to send three of the most distinguished counsel of this State

The Court attempted to interrupt the angry defendant. The interruption was ignored. The prisoner at the bar was exhibiting himself as more powerful in San Francisco than the Judge on the bench. When he had said his say, he took his seat.

The trolley-graft cases dragged along for more than a year after this astonishing scene in Judge Lawlor's courtroom.[470]   The defendants applied to the Supreme Court in habeas corpus proceedings, but failed to secure interference. They then went to the State District Court of Appeal, where they secured a writ of mandate directing Judge Lawlor to dismiss the indictments in the cases of the trolley-graft defendants.[471]   The District Attorney's office announced to Judge Lawlor that the District Attorney had no intention of prosecuting an appeal from the judgment and order of the District Court.

---

to jail. Why? Because they have sought to express in terms of respect, and yet in terms of strength, their protest against injustice——

"The Court: Mr. Calhoun——

"Mr. Calhoun: There is a time—pardon me, your Honor—when every man has a right to be heard——

"The Court: Mr. Calhoun——

"Mr. Calhoun: Now, before I take my seat, I desire further to say this, that any insinuation that implies either that I was a party to any obstruction of justice, or that I was a party to the absence of this witness, or that I have sought to control the District Attorney's office of this city is untrue. There is no evidence before this Court. You yourself know it."

[470] Judge Lawlor's term of office expired in January, 1913. At the 1912 November elections he was a candidate for re-election. The force of the influence of the graft defense was thrown against him. Nevertheless, he was re-elected to serve as Superior Judge of the City and County of San Francisco until January, 1919. In November, 1914, however, he was elected to the Supreme Bench of the State, his term of office beginning in January, 1915, and ending in January, 1927.

[471] Of the three Appellate Judges who granted this writ, one of them, Kerrigan, was prominent in the flash-light picture taken at Santa Cruz during the 1906 State Convention, in which Ruef occupied the center position of honor. See Chapter IV.

Judge Lawlor thereupon dismissed the cases as directed. He also included the cases against Frank G. Drum, Eugene de Sabla and John Martin, which were governed by much the same considerations as the trolley cases. Four years and a half had passed since the indictments had been brought. Little by little, the influence of those of the community who were for law and order and impartial law enforcement had been sapped and broken down. The prosecution had been worn out; the community had been worn out. The defense had shown greater staying qualities than either peace officers or community. It had been pretty thoroughly demonstrated that convictions could not be had.[472]

The dismissal of the trolley-graft and gas-graft cases was the final breaking down of San Francisco's efforts to have the cases tried upon their merits. To be sure, the indictments against the telephone-graft defendants and the prizefight-graft defendants, and against Schmitz and Ruef still stood. Glass, a telephone-graft defendant, had been convicted, but the Supreme Court had reversed the decision on technicalities.[473] The absent

---

[472] Assistant District Attorney Berry on the occasion of the dismissal of the indictments said on this point: "If the men who are involved in this transaction have transgressed the laws they are sowing the wind possibly which may reap the whirlwind by breaking down the institutions of the land. I regret exceedingly, if these men are guilty of the offense with which they have stood charged here, that they cannot be convicted. I assure the Court and I state here that it would be my purpose to follow these cases, if these defendants are guilty and the evidence were had, to the uttermost in order to bring about the ends of justice. It is no doubt in the minds of the community that where men of prominence and where men of wealth are concerned, and are brought before the bar of justice and justice is not had, that those who are less fortunate in influence and means are thereby made to feel and believe that this is not a government for those who stand before the law equal with those who stand with the tremendous power of influence behind them."

[473] The seven Justices of the Supreme Court took no less than four views of the points raised in the Glass case. The majority

witness, Gallagher, was not a material witness in the Glass case. But when along in August, 1912, a year after the dismissal of the gas and trolley-graft cases, Glass's case was called, it was found that important witnesses had disappeared. The incident was taken by the papers, not as a reflection upon the community, but as a joke on Judge Lawlor.[474] The Glass cases were finally dismissed.

Former Mayor Schmitz in February, 1912, was brought to trial. Ruef was brought over from San

---

opinion was written by Justice Henshaw, and concurred in by Justices Melvin and Lorigan. Chief Justice Beatty concurred in the judgment, but not in all the particulars of the opinion. In signing the decision, the Chief Justice adds: "I concur in the judgment of reversal and in most particulars in the opinion of Justice Henshaw. I shall, if other pressing duties permit, present my views in a separate opinion." (See 112 Pacific Reporter, page 297.) The dissenting opinion was written by Justice Shaw and concurred in by Justice Angellotti. A third opinion was written by Justice Sloss. Justice Sloss, after defending the single point in the majority opinion in which he concurs, concludes: "On each of the other points discussed in the opinion of Justice Henshaw, I agree with the dissenting members of the court (Shaw and Angellotti) that no prejudicial error was committed."
The fourth opinion, which the Chief Justice intimated he might file, was not filed.

474 The following from the San Francisco Call of August 2, 1912, indicates the completeness of the triumph of the defense campaign:
"Mrs. Theodore Halsey, wife of Theodore V. Halsey, appeared before Superior Judge Lawlor yesterday morning on a bench warrant in the case of Louis Glass, indicted for bribery in the telephone cases growing out of the so-called Graft Prosecution. She was in court to explain the absence of her husband from the State, whose appearance is wanted if Lawlor orders Glass to trial.
"Attorney Bert Schlesinger appeared with Mrs. Halsey, explaining the bench warrant was void inasmuch as Mrs. Halsey was not a fugitive. He said he did not wish to impede the trial in any way and would allow her to answer any questions propounded by the Court.
"Lawlor asked Mrs. Halsey, through her attorney, where her husband was. Mrs. Halsey was not compelled to take the stand. She said Halsey left San Francisco six weeks ago because of ill health, going to Nevada, and that she has not heard from him in a week.
"Assistant District Attorney Berry said a motion was before the Court to dismiss the indictments pending against Glass and he wished to know the Court's intention. Lawlor said he believed Halsey and Emil J. Zimmer, who is said to be in Europe, were competent witnesses against Glass, and it was his duty to try Glass again. He said the result of the former Glass trials showed

Quentin prison to testify against him. But Ruef refused to testify unless the Ruef indictments were dismissed. This, Judge Dunne,[475] before whom many Ruef indictments were pending, refused to do. Ruef did not testify. Schmitz was acquitted. The other indictments against Schmitz were eventually dismissed.

The same course followed in the cases of the other graft defendants. The graft defense had beaten San Francisco; its record of shameful success was complete.

Halsey had knowledge of the source of the bribe money and who paid it to the Supervisors.

"Lawlor continued the cases of Glass until August 12th, to learn from the District Attorney if the Prosecution has exhausted all its resources in the matter.

"Schlesinger and Mrs. Halsey were about to leave the courtroom when Lawlor said, 'I trust, Mr. Schlesinger, you will inform the Court of the whereabouts of Mr. Halsey, if you learn in the meantime.'

"'I will assist the Court in any way possible,' replied Schlesinger. 'But I regard all these Graft Prosecutions as corpses and the mourners have long since ceased to mourn.'

"The Judge said nothing in the record showed such a condition. Detective Sergeant Prool took the stand and said he had learned nothing more of the whereabouts of either Halsey or Zimmer."

[475] Judge Dunne, until the last, stood as staunchly for effective prosecution of the graft cases as had Judge Lawlor.

CHAPTER XXIX.

Ruef's Last Refuge Fails.

That a jury of twelve men had found Ruef guilty of bribe-giving did not mean necessarily that the broken boss would be confined at San Quentin, the prison to which he had been sentenced to serve his fourteen-year term. Indeed, the probabilities were very much against his suffering any such indignity. Ruef had, at the test, continued "true to his class"; he had not assisted the State in bringing the bribe-givers to account. Men, powerful in financial, social and political circles were unquestionably under the greatest obligation to him. He had not "gone back on his class." His "class" owed it to him to save him from stripes, as Ruef by his course had beyond question saved many of his "class" from stripes.

Having been convicted by a jury, the first move was for Ruef to appeal to the trial judge for a new trial. This appeal was denied him. Ruef then appealed from the judgment of the trial court to the District Court of Appeal. The three justices of the District Court of Appeal found nothing in Ruef's contention to warrant the granting of a new trial.[476] Thus four judges found that Ruef's trial had been fair, even technically fair. But Ruef's possibilities were not exhausted.

The Supreme Court could, if four of the seven

---

[476] See Cal. App. Rpts., vol. 14, page 576.

members were so inclined, grant him a rehearing, and to the Supreme Court Ruef applied.

The California State Constitution provides that "the Supreme Court shall have power to order any cause pending . . . . before a district court of appeal to be heard and determined by the Supreme Court. The order last mentioned may be made before judgment has been pronounced by a district court of appeal, or within thirty days after such judgment shall have become final therein."

The District Court of Appeal found against Ruef on November 23, 1910; this action became final thirty days later, or on December 23, 1910. The Supreme Court had thirty days after December 23, that is to say, until January 22, 1911, to grant Ruef a rehearing, if a majority of the seven Supreme Justices so decided. If the Supreme Court failed to act before the close of January 22, Ruef, unless pardoned or parolled, would have to go to State prison.

Ruef, on December 31, 1910, petitioned the Supreme Court for a rehearing. On January 23, announcement was made that the Supreme Court, by a four to three decision, had decided to grant Ruef's petition. The decision was received with protest from one end of the State to the other.[478] The Legislature

---

478 Said the Sacramento Bee in an editorial article discussing this order, the day after it was made public, January 24, 1911:

"It cannot be denied that this order, by a bare majority of the Supreme Court and—with the single exception of the Chief Justice, by the three of its members least esteemed and respected by the public—has excited disgust and exasperation throughout California. There is a strong popular feeling and belief that the Supreme Court should not thus have interposed to save from punishment the most notorious scoundrel and corruptionist in California, a man known to everybody as having enriched himself by systematic grafting and by the bribery of public servants in the interests of corpora-

was in session at the time. Senator George W. Cartwright of Fresno introduced a resolution [479] requesting the Assembly—where impeachment proceedings must originate—to take such steps as might be deemed necessary for investigation of the Supreme Court's conduct.

And finally there came the rumor—at first not generally believed, but later confirmed by the Supreme Justices themselves—that one of the Justices at least had signed the order granting Ruef his rehearing before the Attorney-General had filed his brief in answer to Ruef's petition. The Justice who had thus acted

tions, a man with many indictments resting against him, but convicted only on one.

"What adds to this general disgust and indignation over the Supreme Court's order is apprehension that the rehearing before that tribunal may result in the grant of a new trial for Ruef, a reversal which in all probability would be equivalent to a final discharge. Such changes have taken place in San Francisco in the last two years, especially in the office of the District Attorney, that a new trial would have small chance of ending in conviction.

"No reasons are given by the Supreme Court for its order for a rehearing, but presumably they are of a purely technical sort, for the fact of Ruef's guilt was abundantly proved on the trial."

[479] The Cartwright resolution was in full as follows:

"Whereas, The Supreme Court of this State on or about the 23rd of January, 1911, rendered a decision in the case of the People of the State of California vs. Abraham Ruef, in which the defendant is granted a rehearing; and

"Whereas, Various newspapers have published criticisms condemning said decision, and intimating that the Justices participating therein were controlled by corrupt and unworthy motives; and

"Whereas, The integrity of our courts has been frequently assailed by public speakers and by many of our citizens, all of which tends to destroy the confidence of The People in the purity and integrity of our courts of justice; be it

"Resolved, by the Senate, That the Assembly be requested to appoint a committee of the Assembly, such committee to be authorized, empowered and instructed to investigate the whole subject matter and particularly to investigate said decision, the grounds upon which the decision is based and the conduct of the Justices of the Supreme Court in relation to said decision, and that the committee report to the Assembly the results of such investigation, with such recommendations as to the committee may seem meet and proper in the premises; be it further

"Resolved, That said committee shall have power to summon witnesses, and to send for persons and papers and to issue subpoenaes and compel attendance of witnesses when necessary."

was Justice Henshaw, the same Supreme Court Justice who occupied prominent position in the picture of the banquet scene at the 1906 Santa Cruz convention, in which Ruef appears in the central position of honor.[480]

The facts later brought out involved the following dates:

December 31, 1910—Ruef's petition for rehearing was filed in Supreme Court.

January 10—W. H. Metson was granted permission to file a brief in the case as *Amicus Curiae*.

January 10—Justice Henshaw signed the order granting Ruef a rehearing.

January 11—Justice Henshaw left the State and was absent until after the order granting Ruef a rehearing had been filed.

January 12—Metson filed his brief as *Amicus Curiae*.

January 12—The Attorney-General filed his reply to Ruef's petition for a rehearing.

January 19—Justice Melvin signed the order granting Ruef's petition.

January 20—Attorney-General filed reply to Metson's brief.

January 21—Chief Justice Beatty, and Justices Shaw, Angellotti, Lorigan and Sloss met in the chambers of the Chief Justice for consultation regarding Ruef's petition. Justice Lorigan signed the order granting the petition. Justices Shaw, Angellotti and Sloss declined to concur in such order, and Chief Justice

---

[480] See Chapter IV.

Beatty reserved his decision in the matter until January 22, 1911.

January 22, 1911—(Sunday, the last day on which the order could be signed) Chief Justice Beatty signed the order, his being the fourth name on the document, four signatures being necessary to make it effective.

January 23—A typewritten copy of the order was filed with the Clerk of the Court, the original being retained in the office of the secretaries to the Justices.

Up to this time, eleven judges had passed upon Ruef's case. Seven of them—one Superior Judge, three Judges of the District Court of Appeal and three Justices of the Supreme Court—had decided that Ruef had had a fair trial, that no technicality could be invoked to save him. Four of the eleven judges, in a way which, to the lay mind at least, was somewhat irregular, had decided to grant a rehearing. The public was not at all backward in expressing the opinion that this would mean a new trial; and that under conditions as they were at San Francisco, Ruef would not for a second time be convicted.[481] As is usual in such cases, the public was dissatisfied, suspicious, indignant, but without plan or remedy. Some demanded investiga-

---

481 This view was entirely justified by the outcome in the Coffey case. Coffey was one of the boodle Supervisors who had at the test refused "to go back on his class." He was tried for bribe-taking and convicted. In the Court of Appeal practically the same points were raised in his favor as were raised in the Ruef case. The Appellate Court refused to interfere. The Supreme Court, by a three to four decision, granted Coffey a rehearing and later a new trial. The line-up of the eleven judges was the same in Coffey's case as in Ruef's—seven found Coffey had had a fair trial; four found that he had not. The four—under the rules of the legal game—were more potent than the seven. The jury verdict was nullified. The indictments against Coffey were finally dismissed. Had the Supreme Court's order for a rehearing of the Ruef case stood, the outcome would have unquestionably been the same.

tion at the hands of the Legislature; others wanted impeachment [482] proceedings instituted. Mr. William Denman, a leader of the California bar, urged before the Senate Judiciary Committee that the Legislature owed it to the Supreme Court, as well as to itself and to the public, to make thorough investigation, and demanded of the committee if the Legislature on proper showing would declare the office of a Supreme Justice vacant.

Senator Shanahan, a member of the committee, was quick to reply that under such a showing the Legislature would certainly act. "But," added Shanahan—and here he touched the weak point of impeachment proceedings—"it would take months if not years. That is why impeachment proceedings will not be instituted. Impeachment proceedings from the trial of Warren

---

[482] Some of the ablest men in the State urged impeachment proceedings. "If the charges," said United States Senator John D. Works in a letter to State Senator Hewitt, "made against Judge Henshaw by the Attorney-General of this State, under oath, are true, why is it the Legislature of this State before this has not commenced impeachment proceedings against him?

"The legislature has no right to shrink from this duty and responsibility and relieve itself from taking such a step by relegating that duty and responsibility to The People of the State by the enactment of recall legislation. If Judge Henshaw, or any other judge, has violated his duty to the State and betrayed his office as the charges made against him indicate, the duty of the legislature is imperative, and that duty should be performed without hesitation and without delay."

Justice Henshaw, in discussing Judge Works' letter, in an interview in the San Francisco Examiner, February 15, 1911, is quoted as saying: "All the charges made by Attorney General Webb in his affidavit attacking the Ruef rehearing order of January 30th are true. The orders were signed in the manner stated and I told him so when he visited my office. There was nothing unusual about it. It was done in accordance with the usual practice of this court.

"We seldom meet in session to sign the orders. There may be twenty cases to be passed on in one week. Each Justice looks them over at his leisure and signs what orders he agrees to.

"I was out of the State, as Mr. Webb says, and at the time that he says. I did not even imagine that there was a legal point involved. The practice never has been questioned before."

Hastings to the present time have proved unsatisfactory."

But, however individuals differed on the question of impeachment proceedings, the general attitude was that the Attorney-General should take steps, if such course were practical, to have the order granting Ruef a rehearing set aside. This the Attorney-General did. He attacked the order before the tribunal which had made it, the highest tribunal in the State, the only one to which appeal could be made.

And the Supreme Court set the order aside, declaring it to be "ineffectual for any purpose and void."

But the Supreme Court did not set the order aside because Justice Henshaw had signed the document before the argument of the prosecution had been heard. The order was set aside on the ground that Henshaw, being absent from the State when the signature of the fourth Justice was attached thereto, was at the time, being absent from the State, unable to exercise any judicial function as a Justice of the Supreme Court. Without Henshaw's signature, the signatures of but three of the Supreme Justices appeared on the order. As the signatures of four of the Justices were required to make the order effective the Court declared it to be worthless.[483]

---

[483] The following is from the Supreme Court decision revoking the Ruef order for a rehearing (see California App. Reports, Vol. 14, page 576): "The moment Justice Henshaw left the State, in view of the authorities already referred to, he became unable to exercise any judicial function as a Justice of the Supreme Court, in this State or out of it, and this disability continued during the whole period of his absence. During that time his situation was the same as if he had absolutely ceased to be a member of this court. It is true that there was a suspension, only, of his judicial power, instead of a final abrogation thereof, but the suspension, while it continued, was as absolute in its effect on his judicial power as would have

Thirty days from the time the judgment of the District Court of Appeal became final having expired, the Supreme Court could not interfere further. Ruef had lost his last technical play on a technicality. He went to State prison.

But Ruef did not go to State prison because a jury of twelve men had found him guilty of offering a bribe to a Supervisor; he did not go to State prison because seven out of eleven judges who passed upon the questions involved had found that he had had a fair trial. Ruef went to State prison when he did because a member of the Supreme Court of California was absent from the State at a time inopportune for Ruef.

Ordinarily, after his failure in the Supreme Court, Ruef would have had two more chances for escaping the full penalty of his bribe-giving, namely, parole at the hands of the State Board of Prison Directors, and pardon from the Governor.

But again was Ruef unfortunate. Hiram W. Johnson, as Governor of California, sat at Sacramento.

---

been a complete vacancy in his office. Assent to or concurrence in a decision or order of the court being the exercise of a purely judicial function, his previous proposal to concur in a proposed order, one that had not yet been made and one that had not yet received the assent of other justices making it an accomplished decision, temporarily ceased to be effectual for any purpose, and so continued ineffectual for any purpose during the whole period of his absence. Such previously indicated willingness to concur could not accomplish that which the absent justice himself could not accomplish. The time having expired before he returned it follows that he never concurred with even a single other justice in the purported order. (1) Admittedly this order, if it ever did become effectual, did not become so until January 22, 1911, when the fourth justice appended his name. At that time, however, Justice Henshaw could not effectually join therein, because of his absence from the State, and his previously indicated willingness to join therein could have no legal effect. The result is that only three justices of this court concurred in the purported order, and as such order could be made only by the concurrence of four justices, it was ineffectual for any purpose and void."

He had gone into office pledged "to kick the Southern Pacific machine out of the State government." He was keeping his pledge. There was no pressure which men of Mr. Ruef's "class" could bring upon Governor Johnson to move him to grant Ruef freedom.

The possibility of parole was as remote, although the State Board of Prison Directors—who in California are appointed for ten-year terms—continued for a time under the old order.

One of the five directors was Tirey L. Ford [484] of the United Railroads. Ruef went to prison convicted of a charge of bribing a Supervisor to vote to give the United Railroads its overhead trolley permit. The evidence indicated, if it did not show, and Mr. Ruef has since confessed, that this money came to him from General Ford. Ruef, because of the crime, found himself confined in a prison of which General Ford was

---

484 Ford's term as prison director expired January 12, 1914. He continued in office until his term had expired and his successor had been appointed. After Ruef had confessed that the trolley bribe money had come to him through Ford, the Sacramento Bee of August 30, 1912, after reciting the allegations of Ruef's confession, said:

"There, in brief, is the tale which Abraham Ruef tells with much particularity. It is now in order for the Board of Prison Directors to ask the resignation of Prison Director Ford.

"Undoubtedly, Governor Johnson would make a demand to that effect were he in the State.

"Much sorrow, if not sympathy, has been felt for Tirey L. Ford all over California. The Bee has expressed some itself. The feeling has been that a man of naturally fine principles and honorable sentiments had been warped by his environments, and had done under instructions that at which his better nature rebelled.

"It would be futile now to discuss what Tirey L. Ford should have done and should not have done; or to declare that no temptation should have led him to perform any other than legal work for the United Railroads.

"The Bee will say as little as it can say conscientiously under the circumstances. Human nature is human nature the world over. And The Bee men cannot forget the long, long years of intimate friendship with and faith in Tirey L. Ford. But every consideration of the eternal fitness of things demands that he should no longer remain a member of the State Board of Prison Directors."

one of the five governors, with power of parole in his hands. But it developed that Governor Johnson had power to set aside such parole. So Ruef could expect little from even the Board of Prison Directors.

Scarcely had Ruef been placed behind the bars, however, than a State-wide campaign was inaugurated to compel his pardon or parole. The public was treated daily by the newspapers with descriptions of the discomfitures [485] which Ruef was suffering. When he was found, for example, smuggling sweet chocolates into prison, and was punished for it, the Ruef-friendly press cried out at the cruelty and unreasonableness of such punishment.[486]

The suffering which his imprisonment has brought

---

[485] The following is a fair sample of the articles descriptive of Ruef's suffering in prison, which have been inflicted upon the California public ever since Ruef donned stripes; it appeared in The San Francisco Bulletin of December 21, 1912: "Ruef is an epicure. As discordant sounds do violence to the feelings of a musician gifted with an exquisite ear, so coarse, badly cooked or tasteless food does violence to the epicure who is gifted with exquisite nerves for inhaling, tasting and appreciating delicate flavors. The gastric juices of the epicure cannot become freely active on mere hunger as with men not so endowed. Digestion with the epicure must wait upon the fine dictates of the palate; and a stomach so guarded cannot wantonly change to an extreme opposite without material suffering. To eat merely to be filled, to overeat, to eat hurriedly, is for the epicure, as one epicure puts it, 'to commit moral sins.' Ruef since his imprisonment has been compelled to do all these things."

[486] To this complaint of cruelty to Ruef, The Fresno Republican made sharp answer: "A visitor," said The Republican, "smuggled articles to Ruef—nothing more dangerous than sweet chocolate and newspaper clippings, to be sure, but still a covert violation of a necessary rule—so Ruef is deprived of visitors and letters for two months, and the automatic application of a general rule postpones his application for parole for six months. Whereat there is wailing and woe, and the San Francisco Call says that Ruef's friends regard it as particularly unfortunate that he should be deprived of visitors just at the time when a movement for his parole is going on.

"To all: Let us be sympathetic. Only let us make it general. Ruef shall have his sweet chocolate. But all the other prisoners shall have it too. Ruef shall sneak things into prison, inside his blouse, by bribing the guards. But all the other prisoners shall have all the like privileges, though it is known that some of them would prefer dope, daggers and dynamite to sweet chocolate."

15

upon the members of his family is dwelt upon at length. Letters from them, pleading for assistance for their imprisoned relative have been received by many whose assistance it was thought might prove effective in securing his release. But when Ruef was brought back from San Quentin prison to San Francisco to testify at Schmitz's trial, the pathetic story was published broadcast that these letter-writing relatives had been kept in ignorance of his imprisonment, and thought him to be traveling in Europe.[487]

One of the most contemptible stories circulated to create public opinion for his release was that Ruef had been made scapegoat because of his religion. Ruef is a Jew, circulators of this story insisted that he is in prison because he is a Jew, while the gentile bribe-givers go free.

As a matter of fact, the gentiles associated with Ruef have gone free because of Ruef's treachery to the graft prosecution, but this does not prevent the circulation of the story.

A saner view, breathing of better citizenship, came

---

[487] Commenting upon this the Sacramento Bee, in its issue of February 9, 1912, said: "In an effort to create sympathy for Abraham Ruef, a story was originated at San Francisco, and has found wide publicity as news, that the aged mother of the felon has been kept in ignorance of his imprisonment, and does not even know of his conviction for bribery.

"Yet letters purporting to come from and to be signed by Ruef's mother, and pleading for his parole, have been received by The Bee and other newspapers for months past. Either these letters were forgeries and fabrications, or this tale of the mother's ignorance of Ruef's confinement is mere fiction.

"In either case a contemptible trick has been played by some agency both active and unscrupulous in seeking to promote Ruef's release. After this the public and the newspapers may well be suspicious of sympathetic stories respecting Ruef and his confinement. If he is personally responsible for the effort to exploit his mother in the manner here related, he is even a more despicable specimen of humanity than the known facts of his career would indicate."

from Rabbi Stephen S. Wise of the New York Free Synagogue. "Israel," said Rabbi Wise, "is not responsible for Ruef's crimes any more than the Roman or Protestant Church is responsible for the crimes of its communicants. But we of the House of Israel in America would be in part answerable for Ruef's misdeeds unless we made it clear, as we do, that Israel is unutterably pained by this blot upon its record of good citizenship in America."

By far the most astonishing support of the movement to free Ruef came from the San Francisco Bulletin and Fremont Older, its managing editor. Older was one of the strongest supporters of the graft prosecution, as was the paper under his management. But once the graft prosecution was concluded, Older and the Bulletin became the most persistent of the supporters of the movement to secure Ruef his freedom.[488]

---

[488] Older, in a letter to Dr. S. W. Hopkins, of Lodi, gives his reasons for working for Ruef's release as follows:

"San Francisco, September 25, 1911. Dr. S. W. Hopkins, President Board of Health, Lodi, Cal. Dear Sir: If you read my article in the Survey, I think there is much in it that you did not understand. Perhaps I did not make myself clear. I tried to. I wanted those who read the Survey article to believe that I at least no longer think we are going to better the world by punishing men individually. I do not feel that it is good for people or for the editor of the Pacific Christian to want vengeance administered to our brothers and sisters. I think vengeance, and by vengeance I mean punishment, makes us all worse rather than better. I have asked for mercy for Ruef because I felt that I, above all others, had done most to bring about his downfall. If you have followed the long fight the Bulletin has made during the past eight or nine years, you will recall that I was fighting Ruef long years before the city woke up. You will also recall that I attacked him bitterly with all the invectives that I could personally command, and all that I could hire. I cartooned him in stripes. I described him on his way to San Quentin; told how I thought he would act en route, and what his manner would be when the barber shaved his head, and how he would feel when locked up in a cell. I was vindictive, unscrupulous, savage. I went to Washington and enlisted Heney in the fight. Burns came, and Spreckels joined in the chase. Then I pursued with the same relentless spirit in the wake of these men. At last, after eight years of a man-hunting and man-hating debauch, Ruef crossed over and became what I had wanted him to

Largely through Older's influence, men of prominence throughout the country—with apparently no very clear knowledge of the situation—have been induced to express themselves as favorable to Ruef's release.

In the publicity campaign for Ruef's release which gives no indication of abatement, Ruef, and those who seek his release, are praised in the most extravagant terms, while those who will not enroll themselves in his interests are as extravagantly condemned.[489]

---

be, what I had longed and dreamed that he might be—a convict, stripped of his citizenship, stripped of everything society values except the remnant of an ill-gotten fortune. It was then I said to myself: 'I have got him. He is in stripes. He is in a cell. His head is shaved. He is in tears. He is helpless, beaten, chained—killed, so far as his old life is concerned. You have won. How do you like your victory? Do you enjoy the picture now that it is complete? You painted it. Every savage instinct in your nature is expressed on the canvas.'

"My soul revolted. I thought over my own life and the many unworthy things I had done to others, the injustice, the wrongs I had been guilty of, the human hearts I had wantonly hurt, the sorrow I had caused, the half-truths I had told, and the mitigating truths I had withheld, the lies I had allowed to go undenied. And then I saw myself also stripped, that is, stripped of all pretense, sham, self-righteousness, holding the key to another man's cell. I dropped the key. I never want to see it again. Let it be taken up and held by those who feel they are justified in holding it. I want no more jail keys. For the rest of my life I want to get a little nearer to the forgiving spirit that Christ expressed.

"Isn't what I am accusing myself of, true of all of us? Think it over. Think of your own life. Think of the lives of those around you, and see if you cannot discern that we are all guilty. And then think whether or not you believe that society will be benefited by denying Ruef a parole, which only gives him a half liberty and still holds him under the restrictions of the prison until his term is finished.

"I am surprised at the tone of the article you sent me, published in the Pacific Christian. It reads like a chapter out of the Old Testament rather than the New. But I fear that the world is being governed more upon the lines of the Old Testament than the New. I agree with the article about the young men who have been sent to prison for years. I would release them all if I could. But I can't. I can't even release Ruef, because society has not advanced far enough to make it possible. But I can at least be true to myself and express what I honestly feel.

"I wish as a favor to me that you would send a copy of this letter to the Pacific Christian, as I am leaving for the East and will not have time. I should like them to know what I am writing you. Sincerely yours,   Fremont Older."

489 The San Jose Mercury, controlled by Congressman E. A. Hayes, in its issue of September 22, 1911, published one of these Ruef campaign articles. The following description of Ruef occurs:
"Not many months have gone since Ruef found domicile in

But in spite of all that is being done to create public opinion favorable to Ruef's release, the sober expression of machine-free press and public is that Ruef should be treated both on the score of parole and confinement precisely the same as any other prisoner.[490] This attitude was clearly presented by the Fresno Republican at the time Ruef was found smuggling chocolate sweets into the prison.

In the attitude of prison officials toward Ruef, the Republican pointed out, there are two alternatives. "One," the Republican went on to say, "is the course of Warden Hoyle, in treating Ruef like any other prisoner, and disciplining him humanely but sternly, for any infraction of the necessary prison rules. The other is to let Ruef have privileges which the other prisoners do not and can not have. News travels nowhere faster or surer than in prison. If Ruef bribes guards, the officials may not know it, but the prisoners will. If Ruef

---

States prison. But what changes Time has wrought in that brief period. The little man sits in his cell, lonely and solemn, as he meditates on the singularities of mankind. With no bitterness in his soul, without a thought of revenge twisting his sense of peace and good will toward man, he passes the time planning the comforts of his fellow unfortunates and reading and rereading the letters that come so regularly from the loved ones whose burdens he so gladly carried and to whose joy he so gladly contributed. He is neither unhappy nor without hope."

The same article contains another word picture—of Francis J. Heney. It reads:

"But if Older has turned 'right about face,' Heney, the other member of the firm, has not. He remains the unforgiving, snarling, short-haired bulldog, with his hand against every man, and every man's hand against him."

Such is the character of the publicity campaign to release Ruef from prison.

490 When in 1914 Governor Johnson became candidate for re-election, extraordinary efforts were made to compel him to pardon, or to consent to the release of Ruef on parole. So persistent were Ruef advocates, that the Governor found it necessary to issue a statement of his position regarding Ruef. That statement will be found in full on page xxviii of the Appendix.

may have smuggled sweets, the other prisoner, whose every nerve-cell shrieks in agony for cocaine, but who knows he will be thrown in the dungeon if he smuggles it, will have no illusions about the smuggling privilege. If the very minions of justice do injustice, as between Abe Ruef and Convict No. 231,323, every man in that vast prison will be taught that he is the victim not of justice, but of force and favoritism. And if Ruef, at the expiration of a bare year, were to be paroled out, every other convict, whose very application can not be heard until he has served half his term, will know that he is suffering the penalty, not of his crime, but of his poverty and friendlessness. Shall Abe Ruef be suffered to teach that lesson? Shall he corrupt San Quentin prison as he did San Francisco? Or shall there be at last one place found where even Abe Ruef gets exact and equal justice?"

Ruef is getting equal justice at State prison, not because he corrupted San Francisco, not because a jury of twelve citizens found him guilty, not because seven out of eleven judges declared against him, but because the political machine, of which Ruef was one of the most powerful leaders, has been broken in California. Under the old order, to have kept Ruef jailed would have been impossible.

CHAPTER XXX.

Conclusion.

After the McCarthy-Fickert election there were rumors that the graft defense, flushed with its successes in the overthrow of the prosecution, would resort to reprisals, by singling out persons prominent in the movement to enforce the law, for trumped-up charges and possible indictment. But aside from an abortive attempt to make it appear that former Supervisor Gallagher had fled the State at the behest of William J. Burns, reprisals of this nature were not attempted.

The reprisals came in more subtle form. Members of the Oliver Grand Jury which had brought the indictments against Ruef and his associates, found themselves marked men in business, political and social circles. A member of the faculty of the State University who had been active in defending the cause of the prosecution, found his salary remaining practically stationary, while his associates received material advances. When the directorate of the Panama-Pacific International Exposition Company was formed, financiers who had supported the prosecution found themselves barred from directorships. It may be said, however, that the graft defense was well represented, one of the Exposition directors at least, Thornwall Mullally, having been one of those indicted in the graft cases.

When the suggestion was made that James D. Phelan be made Pacific Coast representative in President Wilson's cabinet, at once the graft defense pack was on his track, openly naming Mr. Phelan's assistance to the prosecution cause as reason sufficient why he should not be given the cabinet appointment.[491]

On the other hand, all danger of confinement in State prison being gone, the graft defense, through its various newspapers, urged incessantly that the past be forgotten, that San Francisco interests get together for the good of San Francisco. But this "getting together" meant the banishing from political, social, and, as far as practical, business circles, all who had sided with the prosecution, thereby giving control of all activities to sympathizers with the graft defense.

This is well recognized throughout the State, and the exclusive "get-together" movements are received with general ridicule.[492] The graft defense does not

---

491 The San Francisco Argonaut, one of the principal apologists for the Graft Defense, in its issue of November 23, 1912, said of the suggestion of Mr. Phelan's name for the cabinet: "Ex-Mayor Phelan, of San Francisco, would be in line for cabinet honors if our local war of the roses were not so recent and if its unfragrant memories and resentments could be set aside. But this is not yet."

492 The Fresno Republican in its issue of December 7, 1912, pays the following tribute to the graft defense's "get-together" plans:

"They are going to hold a 'burn the hammer' celebration in San Francisco on New Year's eve, for the cremation of knocking.

"It is a good idea, and one worth going the limit on. By all means, burn the hammers! But the only effectual way to get that done is for each fellow to burn his own. Unfortunately, when we begin knocking the knockers, the hammer we are after is usually the one with which the other fellow knocks us. There is no boosting way to dispose of the other fellow's hammer. If we go after it, we knock it, to the further multiplication of knocking. But if we begin at the other end, with our own hammer, that is real boosting. Besides, it gets the thing done. What we do to the other fellow's hammer may not succeed, and if it does, it is merely more knocking. But when we burn or bury our own, then we know that at least our part of the knocking is ended.

"The purpose of the 'burn the hammer,' or 'get-together,' is, of

stand well in California. The "vindication" that was heralded throughout the country when the indictments were dismissed has not been accepted in California as generally as those most immediately affected could have wished.

Then again, the corporations involved in the scandals, have a heritage from the graft defense which seems destined to bring confusion upon them at every turn of their development. Late in 1912, for example, a year and a half after the trolley-graft indictments were dismissed, the United Railroads attempted readjustment of its bonded indebtedness. This could be done only with the consent of the State Railroad Commission. The Commission, willing to allow any proper adjustment upon competent showing, asked that the corporation's books be produced. The books had, during the days of the prosecution, been sent out of the State. The United Railroads could not produce the books, and consent to its petition to readjust its financial affairs was withheld until the books should be

---

course, to bridge the breach left by the Graft Prosecutions. And to this end we suggest that——

"The higher-ups of the Pacific Union Club give a dinner at which Francis J. Heney and Rudolph Spreckels are the guests of honor.

"The directors of the Panama-Pacific Exposition elect James D. Phelan one of their number.

"William H. Crocker give a reception to such members of the Oliver grand jury as have survived the boycott.

"The San Francisco Post issue a congratulatory edition, commending the achievements of Governor Johnson's administration.

"Patrick Calhoun offer to take Abe Ruef's place in San Quentin for a year, and for alternate years hereafter, until they shall both be purged or pardoned of their joint guilt.

"These suggestions are all purposely addressed to the side which is most clamorous for 'getting together.' Since they shout the loudest for 'harmony,' presumably they are the ones who want it. The way to get it is first to put away their own implements of discord. And no better pledges of intent to do this could be conceived than are contained in the suggestions here offered."

forthcoming. Unofficial assurance was given officials
of the corporation that investigation would not be made
of its graft defense expenditures,[493] nor of any expenditures involved in the scandal of the alleged bribe-
giving. But apparently even this assurance did not
satisfy those connected with the United Railroads
whose reputations, at least, were at stake.[494] The com-

---

[493] The machine-free press of the State, however, openly insisted
that it would be a good thing if full publicity of the United Railroads expenditures could be had.

"What the missing books might contain of an interesting sort,"
said The Sacramento Bee in discussing the incident, "may be gathered from a 'list of expenses' submitted by Calhoun in lieu of the
books, including an item of $314,000 to Patrick Calhoun for 'services
rendered.'

"The character of these 'services' may be surmised by anybody
familiar with the history of the recent bribery and Graft Prosecutions in San Francisco. But surely the public and the stockholders
and creditors of the United Railroads are entitled to specifications.

"It is largely that corporations may not bribe in secure secrecy,
or otherwise commit criminal acts without detection, that the Progressive states are bringing them under strict regulation and inspection by proper authority."

[494] The Railroad Commission of California, in its Decision 1536,
made May 22, 1914, held "that the methods pursued by the former
officials of applicant in handling the funds in their care amounts to
nothing more than a fraud, not only upon the public forced to use
an inadequate and unserviceable system, but upon the bond and
note holders of such company."

Of one transaction, in which President Calhoun was permitted
to take $1,096,000 of the company's funds, which it was claimed he
had invested in a land project in Solano, in which Mr. Calhoun was
interested, the Commission said:

"No proof was made to this Commission that any part of this
money was actually invested in the so-called Solano project, but
we are confronted by the fact that Mr. Calhoun, under authority
of the board of directors, and ratified by the stockholders, took
from the treasury of applicant $1,096,000, and whether he invested
it in the Solano project or not is unimportant in the consideration
of this railroad company as a public utility.

"It seems that upon the taking of office by Mr. Jesse Lilienthal,
the present president of the railroad company, Mr. Calhoun was
forced to execute a promissory note for $1,096,000, payable one day
after date, in favor of the railroad company, secured by stock of
the Solano project; but the judgment of the value of this promissory note is perhaps best indicated by the fact that Mr. Lilienthal
immediately wrote this note down in the books of the company as
of a value of $1.00.

"We hesitate to put in words a proper characterization of this
transaction. In plain terms, Mr. Calhoun took from the funds of
this public utility corporation over $1,000,000, when every available
dollar was sorely needed properly to increase the facilities of this
company so as to serve the community of San Francisco, and at a

pany's books were not opened for the Commission's inspection.

By far the greatest sufferer from the graft defense was San Francisco. Here it was demonstrated that even with a District Attorney intent upon the discharge of his sworn duty, with upright trial judges on the bench, the machinery of the criminal law broke down when men with practically unlimited means were brought to bar. To accomplish this required a four years' contest, in which community resistance to political corruption was overcome, the people misled, their minds poisoned against that which is wholesome, and made tolerant of that which is base and bad.

The unhappy effects of this are just beginning to be understood. The evil of the graft defense will live long in San Francisco after the dismissal of the indictments. Four years after the defeat of the Graft Prosecution, Referendum petitions against State laws have been forged in San Francisco, and the laws, which had been passed by the State Legislature and signed by the Governor, have been delayed from going into effect for nearly two years, because of the forgeries. And yet, although the forgers are known, their prosecution, except in one instance, has not even been attempted. Governor Johnson has called the attention of the Attorney-General of the State to this condition, and has urged him to undertake the prosecution of these forgery cases.

---

time when this same company was urging upon this Commission the necessity of issuing further bonds to pay off maturing obligations, and also at a time when admittedly the outstanding obligations could not be paid at maturity by approximately $20,000,000."

This enormous sum had been taken in gold at various times, ranging in amounts from $250 to $85,000.

Tenderloin interests at San Francisco now indicate even greater power in the community than they exerted during the worst days of Ruef-Schmitz régime. The same is in a measure true of the public service corporations.

When District Attorney Langdon announced in 1906 that public-spirited citizens would assist in meeting the expenses of running to earth the corruptionists that had San Francisco by the throat, prospect of law-enforcement through the regular channels was welcomed, and ugly talk of lynch-law prevalent at the time, ceased. The success of the graft defense meant that the efforts to reach the corrupters of the municipal government through ˙ the courts had failed. San Francisco was beaten. In the community's present inability to protect itself against the encroachments of the public service corporations, and to correct vice conditions which are far worse than in the worst days of the Schmitz-Ruef regime, the effects of that beating are seen. San Francisco will be long in recovering from the effects of her defeat. Because of the results of it, she finds herself handicapped in her race for Pacific Coast supremacy with Los Angeles, Seattle and even Oakland. And the prospects are at the close of the year 1914, that the burden of this handicap will be increased before it is diminished. In the old days an invading army conquered a city and sacked it. The System conquered San Francisco and is exploiting it.

The defeat of the graft prosecution was a defeat for San Francisco alone. It was not a defeat for the State of California.

Conclusion

The evil influence of the graft defense did not reach beyond the metropolis. On the contrary, the success of the defense uncovered for the whole State the actual political conditions under which all California was laboring.

The registration of 47,945 Republicans at San Francisco to defeat Heney at the primaries, and the Republican vote of 13,766 at the final election, demonstrated the emptiness of partisan pretense. One of the immediate results was a uniting of all good citizens regardless of political affiliations for good government, and Hiram W. Johnson, Heney's associate in the graft trials, was in 1910, elected Governor of California. Four years later, James D. Phelan, Rudolph Spreckels's associate in financing the graft prosecution, was elected United States Senator from California, while Judge Lawlor was that year elected to the State Supreme Bench. Judge Dunne was in 1914 re-elected to the Superior Bench to serve until 1920.

Decisions from the higher courts—to the lay mind astonishing; to authorities on questions of law, vicious and unwarranted—which set free men who had been convicted of dangerous felonies; scandals which grew out of these decisions; the public's demonstrated helplessness against them, aroused the State. By overwhelming vote California added to her Constitution a provision under which The People may by direct vote remove a corrupt or incompetent judge from the bench.

The public had assumed that men trapped in bribe-giving would be measured by a fixed rule of the law, and their proper punishment in due course be meted out to them. That anything else could be had not occurred to the average citizen.

But the astonishing performances at the graft trials, the extraordinary anti-prosecution publicity campaign, and, finally, the amazing technical defense, and the failure of the graft defendants to take the stand and manfully deny under oath the charges brought against them, opened the eyes of the public to the fact that the methods of criminal procedure were sadly inadequate.

And the further fact was emphasized that while the weak points in the methods of bringing an offender to punishment could be used to advantage by the rich man, they were unavailable to the man without the means to employ a lawyer to present the technicalities governing his case.

Out of this conviction, came agitation for reform of the methods of criminal procedure. An elaborate plan for such reform was presented to the 1909 Legislature.[495] But the machine element controlled the committee organization of both houses, and the measures were defeated.

At the 1911 session of the Legislature, after Johnson had been elected Governor, measures for the reform of the criminal procedure similar to those defeated by indirection at the 1909 session, were introduced. Many of them became laws. But, unfortunately, certain labor leaders were made to believe that the measures

---

[495] These measures are described in "The Story of the California Legislature of 1909." The methods employed to defeat them were told in detail. See chapter "Defeat of the Commonwealth Club Bills."

were aimed at Labor. This led to opposition which resulted in the defeat of several of the proposed reforms.

One important constitutional amendment was, however, presented to the people that goes far toward correcting the abuses which attended the graft trials. This amendment provides that "no judgment shall be set aside, or new trial granted in any criminal case on the ground of misdirection of the jury or the improper admission or rejection of evidence, or for error as to any matter of pleading or procedure, unless, after an examination of the entire cause including the evidence, the court shall be of the opinion that the error complained of has resulted in a miscarriage of justice."

Not a vote was cast against this amendment in either house of the Legislature. The feeling against the use of trifling technicalities for the release of convicted criminals which the graft cases had displayed so glaringly, was shown in the popular vote on this amendment; 195,449 voted for the amendment, while only 53,958 voted against it.[496]

The San Francisco graft prosecution succeeded in sending but one of the corrupters of the municipal

---

[496] Under the provisions of measures which became laws at the 1911 session, it is held that it will be impossible hereafter to put grand jurors on trial as was done in the San Francisco graft cases. Hereafter, too, an indictment or information may be amended by the District Attorney without leave of the Court at any time before the defendant pleads; and at any time thereafter in the discretion of the Court where it can be done without prejudice to the substantial rights of the defendant.

Another measure takes from a witness his privilege of refusing to give testimony on the grounds that it may incriminate him. The witness is safeguarded, however, by a provision that he shall not be liable thereafter to prosecution nor punishment with respect to the offense regarding which such testimony is given.

government to State prison. He, too, would in all probability have escaped imprisonment but for the absence from the State of a single member of the Supreme Court at a critical moment.

But the graft prosecution did something infinitely more important than the sending of a few corruptionists to cell and stripes. It awakened a State to its helplessness against a corrupt system. The People arose in rebellion against the "System," and is laboring to throw the "System" off.

In 1910 and 1911 a political revolution was worked in California.

But the revolution had its beginning back in 1906, when Rudolph Spreckels guaranteed the expenses of the prosecution of the corrupters of the municipal government of San Francisco, and Francis J. Heney, as his share in the campaign, pledged his services.

Had there been no San Francisco graft prosecution, there would, in 1910, have been no successful political uprising in California. Hiram W. Johnson would not have been a candidate for Governor. The accomplished reforms which are the boast of the State, and the models which other States are adopting, would still be the unrealized dreams of "reformers." The "System" would still be in the saddle.

The graft defense has left its mark of ill upon San Francisco. That city has borne the brunt of the injury because of it.

The graft prosecution, by forcing the "System" out in the open, where all its power for evil can be seen, worked California inestimable good. And here, San Francisco, in common with the whole State, gains also.

APPENDIX

JUDGE LAWLOR'S RULING ON MOTION TO DISMISS GRAFT CASES, AUGUST 3, 1910.

On April 25th, 1910, an application was made by Patrick Calhoun, Tirey L. Ford, Thornwell Mullally and William M. Abbott to dismiss the indictments against them. The application is before the Court at this time for consideration.

When the defendants pleaded not guilty they exercised their statutory right and each demanded severance from each other and from their co-defendants, Abraham Ruef and Eugene E. Schmitz. (Sec. 1098 Penal Code.) There have been five trials—three of Tirey L. Ford and one each of Abraham Ruef and Patrick Calhoun.

The second trial of Patrick Calhoun was commenced on July 19th, 1909 (case No. 1437). Owing to the illness of one of his counsel the trial was suspended on August 16th, 1909, and resumed on September 30th, 1909. On the following day the trial was ordered continued until November 15th, 1909, on motion of the defendant, upon the ground of the pendency of a municipal campaign.

On January 8th, 1910, Mr. Charles M. Fickert assumed the office of District Attorney.

On February 7th, 1910, the District Attorney moved the Court to dismiss the remaining charges against these defendants (Sec. 1385 Penal Code), which motion was by the Court ordered denied. (Sec. 7, Art. I, and Sec. 19, Art. VI of the Constitution; Secs. 1041, 1042, 1126, 1385, 1386 and 1387 Penal Code.)

On February 14th, 1910, the parties announced that they were ready to resume the trial in case No. 1437 against Patrick Calhoun, but the Court continued the case for trial until February 17th, 1910. On the last named day the cause was ordered continued for trial until April 25th, 1910.

On April 25th, 1910, the four defendants interposed a motion to dismiss the remaining indictments against them. The further hearing of the motion was continued until July 29th, 1910. On the latter day the causes were continued until this time.

Two things are chiefly responsible for the Court's action in respect to the remaining indictments since the District Attorney moved to dismiss them on February 7th, 1910—first, the Court's apprehensions based on the declared attitude of the said District Attorney toward the remaining indictments, and, second, the absence from the State of

James L. Gallagher, a material and indispensable witness in the said causes. The second reason will now be considered.

It was the theory of the People in the five trials referred to that Abraham Ruef represented the defendants in the alleged bribery of the members of the Board of Supervisors, and that James L. Gallagher, one of its members, in turn represented Abraham Ruef in the transactions. In this way the Court is able to determine that the testimony of this witness is material, and now holds, as a matter of law, that unless additional testimony is produced, it is indispensable to the establishment of the res gestae.

In the early part of December, 1909, it became known that the witness had departed from the State. Up to the present time it has not been shown whether he had been formally subpoenaed or was otherwise under the authority of the Court to appear as a witness in the trials of the remaining indictments. If he is subject to the authority of the Court in any of these cases his absence would constitute a criminal contempt, and he could be extradited from any other State having provisions of law similar to those of this State. (Sub. 4, Sec. 166, and Sec. 1548 Penal Code.)

In this connection it may be proper to point out that practically ever since issue was joined on these indictments they have been on the calendar for trial, and that during the trials referred to the cases not actually on trial were from time to time called and the witnesses admonished by the Court to appear on the deferred date. But it has not been ascertained whether on this manner the missing witness has been so admonished to appear so far as the remaining indictments are concerned.

In the month of January, 1910, the Court directed that all persons who could give testimony concerning the absence of the witness be subpoenaed. On January 24th, 1910, the first hearing was had, and on several occasions thereafter witnesses have been orally examined on the subject. From this oral testimony it is difficult to determine the intentions of the witness concerning his departure from and his return to the State. It seems that in the latter part of November, 1909, he left for Europe, accompanied by his wife. Robert F. Gallagher, a brother of the witness, testified in effect that the witness never stated he intended to absent himself as a witness in the graft cases and made no suggestion of that nature; that he, Robert F. Gallagher, gained no such impression from anything he did say, except that it was a disagreeable situation for him to be a witness; and that their talk proceeded along the line that there was not going to be any future trial in the graft prosecution. This brother testified further:

"He did state on one occasion something to the effect that Burns had disappeared and that Heney had disappeared and that there wasn't any prosecution; that the incoming District Attorney would not certainly be in earnest in the prosecution."

Other witnesses testified to a variety of facts touching the departure of the witness from San Francisco and his declarations on the general subject. Dr. Alexander Warner gave testimony to the effect that he went to Europe on an Atlantic steamer with the witness and his wife. Thomas J. Gallagher, another brother, among other things quoted the witness to the effect that he was going to Europe, that he might settle in an eastern State, that he made no secret of his purpose, and that William J. Burns, special agent of the former administration in the District Attorney's office, knew of his intention to leave. Nothing definite appears in the oral showing concerning his intentions on the subject of his return, and so far as that showing is concerned the point is more or less involved in conjecture. But on July 29th, 1910, Frederick L. Berry, the Assistant District Attorney, assigned to this department of the Court, filed an affidavit embodying clippings from the local newspapers of the previous month, which state that the witness was, at the time the articles were written, in Vancouver, B. C. From these clippings it appears that the witness intended to permanently locate in Vancouver. The only tangible evidence from the witness himself, however, is found in his letter to Thomas J. Gallagher under date of June 29th, 1910, in which this excerpt appears:

"In reply to your inquiry I cannot state when I shall return to San Francisco, if at all. I may remain here."

In my judgment a review of the showing up to this time leads to the inference that the witness left this jurisdiction and is remaining away because of some form of understanding or agreement. The circumstances under which he left California clearly show that he was acting guardedly, notwithstanding the testimony, which there is no reason to doubt, that he informed several persons of his intention to take a trip. When the quoted statement of Robert F. Gallagher was first made I was disposed to assume that the witness left the State principally because he believed the prosecution was at an end, and that he made his plans quietly so that the step would not occasion comment. In other words, that he did not believe there would be any further attempt to prosecute the so-

called graft cases. But from a study of the entire showing I cannot adhere to that theory. I repeat that up to
the time his presence was discovered in Vancouver, the
showing was uncertain as to whether he really intended to
return to California, and if so, when he would return. It
was to be seen that the action of the Court would be influenced by this uncertainty, so when the exigencies of
the situation called for a definite showing as to the witness' intentions, he seems to suddenly appear in Vancouver, where, under the treaty conditions, he would be safe
from extradition, and is promptly discovered by the reporter of a New York paper. In the clippings his quoted
statements on the subject of his intentions are unequivocal.
He is to make his home in Vancouver. But his personal
communication to Thomas J. Gallagher, already referred
to, which he probably realized would be produced in Court,
is significant in tenor and he is apparently less certain of
his intentions. This would tend to make his future action
consistent should he hereafter return to California. From
the entire showing I do not entertain any serious doubt as
to what his real purpose is. I am inclined to believe that
when the necessity for his presence as a witness has passed
he will return. To entertain any other view, or be in
serious doubt on the point, is to ignore the inherent probabilities of the showing and to deny a fair consideration
to the known history of this litigation.

Now, it must follow that if the witness has left and is
remaining away from the State because of an arrangement
of some nature affecting these cases, the responsibility for
his absence should be placed where it belongs. On April
25th, 1910, the District Attorney stated to the Court:

". . . and it appearing also that James L. Gallagher
left with the consent and connivance of those who had
preceded me in office, I at this time do not wish to assume any responsibility for his disappearance. Whether
he shall return or not I cannot say. Some of the witnesses who were called here testified that he went away
with the intent and with the purpose of embarrassing my
administration and that he was supposed to keep away until
such time as certain persons would request his return. . ."

The foregoing fairly states the position of the District
Attorney on this point, as repeatedly expressed in Court
since he first moved the dismissal of these indictments. If
the charge that the former administration entered into a
bargain with the witness to default be true, there would
be no alternative but to dismiss the indictments without
delay. But I have found no evidence in the showing tending to support so grave a charge, and upon sound reason-

v

ing it would seem to be opposed to every reasonable probability. According to the showing, William J. Burns left the State about three weeks in advance of the witness, and, so far as the Court is advised, he has not since been in the State. That the former administration may have distrusted the official intentions of the District Attorney toward these indictments might be assumed from all the surrounding circumstances. But it does not seem probable that the former administration would induce a material and indispensable witness to leave the State and thereby make it easy for the District Attorney to secure a result which otherwise might entail serious embarrassment. So far as the showing is concerned there is no tangible proof tending to support the charge of the District Attorney, nor is there any proof which would justify such an inference.

Nor, on the other hand, do I find any formal evidence in the showing which tends to bring the responsibility for the disappearance of the witness home to these defendants. In the absence of tangible proof neither side should be charged with so grave an act. But if there has been complicity on the part of either of the parties, every effort should be made before disposing of these cases finally to establish the facts. It has been pointed out that if the former administration entered into a bargain with the witness looking to his absence, the application should be granted without delay. And clearly, if the defendants are responsible for the absence of the witness, under a familiar maxim of the law, the application should be promptly denied. (Sec. 3517 Civil Code.)

There being no tangible proof, therefore, before the Court, of the complicity of the parties, should the pending application be granted at this time?

A person accused of crime is entitled to a speedy trial. (Sec. 13, Art. I, Const.)

This fundamental right has been made the subject of statutory provision. The second subdivision of Section 1382 of the Penal Code provides that:

"**Unless good cause to the contrary is shown,** the court must order the prosecution to be dismissed if the indictment is not brought to trial within sixty days after the filing thereof."

More than sixty days have run in favor of this application, and the question presented at this time is whether the showing touching the absence of James L. Gallagher shall constitute "good cause" within the meaning of the law. This term must be construed and applied according to the peculiar circumstances of each case. It should be interpreted so that the rights of both parties shall be equally recognized. The absence of a material and indispensable witness for the People would, under proper circumstances, constitute good cause, provided that good faith and diligence are shown in the effort to produce the witness. In re Bergerow (133 Cal., 349) is a leading authority on this question and is almost invariably cited in support of applications of this character. It is proper to point out that in the prevailing opinion the Court studiously eliminates from the pertinency of the authority the absence or illness of a witness for the prosecution.

The conclusion I have reached is that under the law, and the surrounding circumstances, including the recent action of the witness, that another reasonable continuance should be directed in order, if possible, that the duty of the Court in the premises shall be rendered more clear. At this time the Court is not satisfied that the relief sought should be granted. On the other hand it is realized that a final decision should not much longer be delayed. In the determination of this matter the Court, while fully recognizing the rights of the defendants, is mindful of the rights of the People and its own sense of responsibility, and is anxious to avoid a decision which will serve as a mischievous precedent.

It is idle to attempt to ignore the inherent probabilities of the situation presented. A material and indispensable witness is absent from the State, and the Court is called upon to intervene because the District Attorney has at practically every turn followed the lead of these defendants. Through the influence of unusual agencies the law has broken down, so far as these cases are concerned. The crimes charged are of the most serious nature, because such criminal activity tends to sap the very foundations of government. The statute of limitations has run against these charges and if the application is granted, therefore, there can be no further prosecution, no matter what developments may follow. (Sec. 800 Penal Code.) In the trial of Patrick Calhoun the Court admitted evidence of a most extraordinary character on the theory of the People that it tended to show guilty consciousness on the part of the accused. This evidence was not contraverted. It included the dynamiting of the home of the witness under circumstances which threatened not only his life, but also the lives of several other persons. A certain other building, the property of the witness, was subsequently blown up by the use of dynamite. If the apparent design on the life of the witness had been successful, the Court would be less perplexed in deciding a question of this character. It is possible that these experiences and not the suggested arrangement with the witness are responsible for his absence. The evidence also included an effort to suppress testimony by an attempt to induce a witness to leave the jurisdiction of the Court, and other matters of a serious nature.

And, finally, while the Court is clear that it should not base any action at this time upon the assumption that either side is responsible for the absence of the witness, yet reason and the exercise of a sound discretion dictate that the Court should act with prudence. Before the indictments should be finally disposed of, every reasonable effort should be made to get at the truth of the situation. The disposition of grave charges other than on their merits is not to be encouraged and should not be allowed, except in the face of a strict legal necessity. Let the cases be continued until 10 a. m., Monday, August 29th, 1910. So ordered.

HOW THE SUPERVISORS WERE BRIBED.

Thomas F. Lonergan, when elected to the Schmitz-Ruef Board of Supervisors, was a driver of a bakery wagon. He recited at the trial of The People vs. Louis Glass, the manner in which he had been bribed by agents of the Pacific States Telephone and Telegraph Company. Lonergan's testimony was as follows:

"I reside in Sanchez street, San Francisco. I have lived in San Francisco since March, 1879. I have a family composed of a wife and three children. I was in the bakery business. I was in that business quite a number of years. I worked latterly for Mr. Foley. I worked in a bake shop quite a while and also drove a wagon for him. I do not hold any official position now. I did hold the position of Supervisor of the City and County of San Francisco. I was elected Supervisor in November, 1905, and took office on January 7th or 8th, 1906. I know John Kraus. I first met him some time after my election at my home. I did not invite him to come there.

"One morning, some time after my election, the doorbell rang, a gentleman was at the door and wanted to see me. I went downstairs. He asked me if I was Mr. Lonergan. I said yes. He says, 'The recently elected Supervisor?' or words to that effect. I said yes. He says, 'I don't think you are the man I wanted. I came out here from the

East a few years back with a Mr. Lonergan, and I thought
he was the one that might have been elected.' I said, 'No,
you are mistaken, it is the other one,' or something like
that. He then incidentally told me he was connected with
the Pacific States Telephone Company, and would be pleased
to take me around their works at any time that I would
find it convenient. I answered him as well as I recall now,
that I possibly would take it in some time. I subsequently
went to the telephone company's office. To the best of
my recollection I saw Mr. Kraus in the meantime before
going there, and made an appointment with him. I don't
well remember meeting him at the telephone company's
office. I think where I met him was on the corner of
Mason and Market or Powell and Market, one or the
other, around there. That was by appointment. Then I
went with him to the telephone company's plant on Bush
street, I think, out in the Western Addition at that time.
He took me through the works, showing me the works and
the arrangements in connection with it, and how they
treated their help, and stated to me they were installing
another new plant, I forget now whether it was one or
two or more. After we left there I had lunch with Mr.
Kraus. I don't well remember where. He spoke about an
opposition company in that talk. The opposition company
was spoken of, considering the appliances they had, and
the amount of work they were then doing, and the new
switchboards they would put in, that it didn't appear necessary to have an opposition company here. Mr. Kraus paid
for the lunch, I believe.

"I am acquainted with Mr. T. V. Halsey. I first met
him, I think, either on Pine or Bush street, to the best of
my recollection. I. N. Copus introduced me to him. To
the best of my recollection it was some time after meeting
Kraus and before I took office as Supervisor. That meeting
was by appointment. Mr. Copus made the appointment I
believe. To the best of my recollection that was my first
meeting with Mr. Halsey. I think I was introduced to him
by Mr. Copus at the time and place of the meeting. We
adjourned to lunch at a restaurant that we were standing
in front of. We went upstairs in the restaurant, had some
lunch. Nothing particular was spoken of there outside of
the current topics. The room we lunched in was not a
public dining room. It was a private room. Copus went
up to lunch with us. I believe Mr. Halsey paid for the
lunch. We were there possibly an hour or an hour and a
half. We had Sauterne wine to drink, as well as I remember. The next time I saw Halsey to the best of my recol-

lection was at his office on Bush street, in the telephone building there. It was some time between the 12th and 14th and the 20th of February, 1906, I should judge. I think I went there on that occasion on the invitation of Mr. Kraus, as well as I remember, that Mr. Halsey would like to see me. I found Halsey when I got there. I am not conversant with the building; I suppose the part of the building I met him in was his office. I don't remember whether there was any one else in the room. I had a talk with him in there. No one else was present while I was talking with him that I am aware of. Mr. Halsey, as well as I remember, spoke to me about the foolishness of having a second telephone system in San Francisco. He told me the same as Mr. Kraus had told me—all they had accomplished, and that they were going to accomplish, and that it would cost merchants twofold for the other telephone, and they wanted to know if I would not be friendly toward them. I told him I was deeply impressed with the workings as I had seen them, and that I felt that I could be friendly to them. I cannot remember the exact words he then said at the time. The substance of it was that it would be to my interest to be friendly, or rather, that they would make it to my interest to be friendly to them, and I was told—I think it was at that meeting—that there would be five thousand dollars in it for my friendship down, and $2,500 the following year, provided I did not accept a commission, or any such thing as that while I remained a member of the Board of Supervisors. To the best of my recollection at that time I received from him one thousand dollars in currency. I put it in my pocket and took it home. The next time I saw Mr. Halsey was some few days later. It was the Saturday previous to the passing to print of the ordinance relative to the Home Telephone Company. That meeting was held in a room in the Mills Building. I cannot well recollect whether I was telephoned for or not; I possibly must have been. The meeting was up in the building some few stories. To the best of my recollection it was on the side of the building that looked out on Bush street, and not very far from the corner of Montgomery street. I found Mr. Kraus there when I went in. There was no one else in the room where Kraus was. That room was furnished with a table and a couple of chairs. Well, he asked me if he could depend upon me as to my friendship in regard to the Pacific States Telephone Company, and I told him I saw no reason why he could not. I don't remember whether anything was said about the Home Telephone Company franchise. There may have been. I can't recollect just at this moment. He told me that he had a sufficiency of the members of the Board of Supervisors, to the best of my recollection, who were friendly towards the Pacific States, and that they did not particularly need Mr. Coffey, except that I had spoken well of him, and depending on my friendship, he gave me the four thousand dollars in currency. During our conversation I had mentioned Mr. Coffey as a friend of mine that I thought was particularly friendly towards them. I don't well remember whether he then said he would see Mr. Coffey, or not, or whether he made answer. I do remember that he said at the latter meeting that they did not particularly need him, that he had a sufficiency of the members. I took it home and gave it to my wife.

"To the best of my recollection I next saw Mr. Halsey at my home the latter end of the following week after I got the money. No one else was present when he talked with me. It was in the front room of my house."

Supervisor Michael W. Coffey was a hack driver. At the Glass trial he told the manner in which the bribe-givers approached him. He said:

"I have lived in San Francisco about forty years. I have been in the carriage business driving a hack. I own a hack of my own. My stand was on Fifth street, right opposite the Mint. I was elected a member of the Board of Supervisors in November, 1905, and took office early in January, 1906. I am a married man. My family consists of four girls and one boy. I am acquainted with T. V. Halsey. I first met him some time in the month of December at my hackstand. I am acquainted with John Kraus. I first met him about the same time. At the time that I met Halsey at the hackstand, Kraus was with him. I am not sure whether it was the first time, but probably the second time. I think Mr. Kraus came to see me first, and Mr. Halsey came with him afterwards. Well, he, Kraus, just came up merely to introduce himself to me, and asked me how business was. There was nothing said at the time that he brought Halsey to me. There was nothing said pertaining to telephone matters at that time, neither; it was simply merely to give me an introduction and ask me up to have a drink on the corner of Jessie and Fifth streets. Nothing was said about the telephone service at that time. I next met Halsey a few days afterwards. Both Halsey and Kraus were there together at that time, and we spoke— they spoke to me about my telephone service, both home and in the drugstore in front of which I had my hackstand, and asked me if the telephone service was satisfactory. I told them it certainly was, that I couldn't find any fault with either one. The drugstore 'phone I had nothing at all to do with, any more than I had the privilege of placing the number of the telephone upon my business cards so that my friends could know where to find me in case they wanted to telephone me. I paid for no service on that 'phone at all. My hackstand was right in front of the drugstore. I should judge Halsey and Kraus came around there to see me between three times and a half-a-dozen. I received telephone messages from Mr. Halsey several times. He called me by 'phone, he telephoned to the house, and to the stand, and wanted me to come down to see him. I went down to see him one time. He after that invited me around to the telephone company's offices, to view the system, but I never accepted his offer, I never went with him. The first occasion that I went down to the telephone company's office to see him he extended me an invitation to come around amongst the different branch offices there to see the system, how it was working, and show me the advantages of a one-system telephone. Kraus was there on one occasion. Somewhere around in the neighborhood of noon time, Mr. Kraus was there, and Mr. Halsey asked me if I had lunch. I told him no, not at that time, so he asked Mr. Kraus to take me out to lunch, excusing himself on the ground of a previous engagement, that he couldn't go to lunch, but he asked Mr. Kraus to take me out to lunch and Mr. Kraus did so.

"I had a talk with Halsey in the Mills Building. I can't exactly tell the date, but it was on a Saturday, in and around noon time. I can't exactly fix the date. It was some time, I think, in the month of February. We caucused on the Sunday night, and it was Saturday, either the week prior to the caucus or the day before the caucus. This caucus was the Sunday prior to the passing of the ordinance to print which was on a Monday. I went to the Mills Building by telephone invitation of Mr. Halsey. When I got down there I took the elevator and went up on, I think, the seventh floor at the extreme end of the building, on one of the rooms facing on Bush street, and the other on Montgomery street. I found Mr. Halsey there and no one else with him. To the best of my recollection there was either a box or a chair and a table, and a telephone in there, and no other furniture at all in the room. Mr. Halsey when I went in, said, 'Good day, Mr. Coffey.' Said I, 'How do you do, Mr. Halsey?' I says, 'Did you telephone for me?' He says, 'Yes, I want you to be friendly with the company,' and stepped into another room, the door leading into the Montgomery street entrance, and then came out with a parcel, a bundle, and handed it to me, and says, 'I would like to have your friendship for the company.' I did not open the package at that time. Nothing was said then about the Home Telephone Company's application for the franchise. I took this package that he handed me home and put it in a box in the room. I did not open it when I got home, not at that time. Subsequently I did. When I opened it I found in it five thousand dollars in United States currency. That was very shortly after I had been in the Mills Building on that occasion. I think it was a few days after that. After putting this money in the box I kept it there."

GALLAGHER'S ORDER REMOVING LANGDON FROM OFFICE OF DISTRICT ATTORNEY.

(October 25, 1906.)

"To the Board of Supervisors of the City and County of San Francisco:

"Gentlemen—Pursuant to the provisions of the Charter of the City and County of San Francisco, and especially in pursuance of Sections 18 and 19 of Article XVI thereof, I, James L. Gallagher, Mayor of the City and County of San Francisco, do hereby suspend William H. Langdon, District Attorney of the City and County of San Francisco, and an elected officer thereof, for cause, as hereinafter assigned and specified, and I hereby notify you of such suspension and the causes therefor, which are as hereinafter assigned and specified.

"Said cause is contained in the following specifications, which specifications I hereby also present to you as the written charges against said William H. Langdon, District Attorney as aforesaid, and I hereby present said specifications of causes of such suspension as written charges against said William H. Langdon, District Attorney, suspended by me as aforesaid.

"Specification 1:

"Neglect of Duty.

"In this, that for a period of about 30 days prior to the presentation of these charges the said William H. Langdon, District Attorney as aforesaid, has absented himself from the City and County of San Francisco, without leave, and has neglected his official duties, being during that time engaged in the canvass and campaign for the office of Governor of the State of California.

"That during said time, owing to the recent disaster, a large number of acts of violence have occurred at the hands of criminals congregated in said city, resulting in an excessive and unusual number of murders, maimings, assassinations, assaults and other crimes of violence, tending to render the city unsafe and to injure its reputation, yet the said District Attorney wilfully, without permission from any of the public authorities of said city and county, did absent himself a greater portion of said time from said city and county, and so negligently conducted and performed the duties of his said office as District Attorney as to render no active or efficient assistance to said city and county in the proper prosecution, detection or preventing of any of said crimes, and during the main portion of said period did leave his said office without the aid of his superintendence, direction or service, thereby being guilty of inefficiency in such public office and being negligent and inattentive in the performance of his public duties at a time when the unusual activity of those engaged in crimes of violence demanded and required his personal presence and greatest personal activity to aid in preventing or attempting to prevent, detecting or attempting to detect or punish the said crimes or the persons guilty thereof.

"Specification 2:

"Neglect and Dereliction of Duty.

"In this, that during the period of about 30 days last past, the newspapers of the City and County of San Francisco have published and proclaimed that the said William H. Langdon, as District Attorney, and others co-operating with him, were, and for months past had been, in the possession of evidence sufficient to convict certain officials of the city and county of serious crimes. These charges have been repeated daily and within the knowledge and cognizance of said District Attorney, and yet notwithstanding said knowledge and said purposes, the said District Attorney has failed to cause the arrest of any of said officials, and if the charges so publicly made are and were not true, the said District Attorney had knowledge of said falsity and untruth, and yet notwithstanding said knowledge has failed to cause the arrest of the publishers or editors of the newspapers for publishing said statements for criminal libel.

"Specification 3:

"Neglect and Violation of Duty.

"That under the provisions of the Charter of the City and County of San Francisco, it is part of the duty of the District Attorney, when required, to advise the Board of Police Commissioners, the Chief of Police, the Board of Health, or the Coroner as to the matters relating to the duties of their respective offices, yet notwithstanding said official duty, the said William H. Langdon, as such District Attorney, has entered into a combination and conspiracy for political purposes and effect to bring unmerited discredit upon said officials or some of them, and has failed to advise them relative to their duties, and has assumed a position and attitude inconsistent with his duty to the Police Commissioners and the Chief of Police, thereby tending to impair and demoralize the Police Department of said city at a serious and critical time.

"'Specification 4:

"Neglect and Violation of Duty.

"That the said William H. Langdon, being the District Attorney of said City and County of San Francisco, as aforesaid, during period above mentioned, in addition to neglecting his public duties, as above set forth, instead of aiding the authorities of said city and county, did on the contrary engage in and assist in a combination in the interest of certain insurance corporations and other persons to injure and defame the character of the Chief Executive of this city, Mayor Eugene E. Schmitz, in substance as follows:

"A large number of German insurance companies, having lost many millions of dollars by the conflagration of April 18, 1906, having denied their liability, Eugene E. Schmitz, Mayor of the City and County of San Francisco, deemed it advisable in the interest of the upbuilding and rehabilitating of the city, to visit the German Empire in his official capacity for the purpose of stating the true facts concerning said conflagration to the home officials of said companies and to use his personal influence wherever the same would be available in the German Empire, with a view to cause the said insurance companies to pay the said losses; and deeming said matter one of great public interest, the said Mayor did obtain from the Board of Supervisors a leave of absence from the City and County of San Francisco for a period of 60 days from October 1, 1906; and after he left on said mission, a combination, plot and plan was formed for the purpose of defaming and injuring and weakening the standing and reputation of said Eugene E.

Schmitz, in order that his said attempts might be discredited and to destroy whatever influence the Chief Executive of this city might have in dealing with the said insurance companies at their home offices and in obtaining influence abroad to compel said companies to properly recognize their obligations; and that as a part of said scheme, it was determined to print and publish in the newspapers of San Francisco charges against the said Mayor which were false, malicious and slanderous and known so to be by the parties engaged in said scheme, and among other things said persons so engaged did cause it to be published that the Chief Executive of this city was a fugitive from justice and had absconded from the City and County of San Francisco; and that the said William H. Langdon, as District Attorney of the City and County of San Francisco, and acting in his capacity as such, did aid, assist and abet and further the said scheme as aforesaid, and has become and is an active party thereto to the end that said Mayor should be induced to return to San Francisco to defend himself against such charges before he could have time to accomplish the said purpose for which he went to said German Empire.

"Specification 5:

"Violation of Duty and Use of Office for Ulterior Purposes.

"That during the fall of 1905, one Francis J. Heney, in a public speech in said city and county, aspersed the character and good name of a prominent citizen of this community, and stated that he knew him to be corrupt, and said citizen having instantly demanded that said Heney be compelled to make proof of said assertions and said Heney having been compelled to appear before the Grand Jury of said City and County of San Francisco with reference thereto, there admitted that he had made such statements without any personal knowledge regarding the same, which facts were widely published at the time, and brought said Heney into obloquy and contempt, from which time said Heney had been possessed of a purpose to effect a personal revenge both against the object of his false charges and against Eugene E. Schmitz, Mayor of San Francisco, and all of these facts were and are well known to said William H. Langdon, as District Attorney as aforesaid; yet notwithstanding said knowledge and within the month of October, 1906, the said William H. Langdon, in order to enable said Heney to use public office, position and power to gratify his spirit of revenge and malice, did appoint said Heney Assistant District Attorney of said city and county, and did turn over to him the powers of office of said District Attorney in order that he might gratify his private revenge and malice.

"Specification 6:

"That prior to such appointment as such Assistant District Attorney, said Francis J. Heney had publicly assailed the Judges of the Superior Court of the city and county as corrupt and crooked, and had denounced all or nearly all of them as dishonest and corrupt, and yet has failed at any time to make proof of such charges, which facts were all well known to said William H. Langdon, District Attorney as aforesaid, from the time of the utterance, which was long anterior to the time of said Heney's appointment by said Langdon, and said Langdon also knew that said Heney frequently, while intoxicated, made grave and serious charges involving the personal character of citizens of this city, yet notwithstanding such knowledge said William H. Langdon did appoint said Heney to such office, knowing that the said Heney in such office would be required to appear before the Judges whose character he had thus aspersed, and to practice in their courts, did appoint said Heney to said office, which appointment is not conducive to the proper co-operation which should exist between the Judges of the Superior Court and the office of District Attorney.

"Specification 7:

"That said Francis J. Heney at and prior to the time of his appointment as Assistant District Attorney was the representative of the corporation controlling the street car system of said city and county in a certain dispute between said corporation and its employes, That the appointment of said Heney to said office will, in regard to the enforcement of law against said corporation, be prejudicial and detrimental to the interests of said city and county.

"Specification 8:

"That prior to the turning over of said District Attorney's office and its powers to said Francis J. Heney, as hereinabove specified, the City and County of San Francisco had intended to procure its own water supply and thereby to prevent the exorbitant charges for water now exacted by the private corporation controlling the city's water supply, and that it was about to take proceedings to provide a safe and secure supply of water for said City and County of San Francisco for domestic use, extinction of conflagrations, etc., and that such purpose was greatly to

the interest of said City and County of San Francisco,
That said corporation now supplying water to said city and
county is bitterly opposed to the acquiring of a water supply to the City and County of San Francisco on account
of its present monopoly.

"Said Francis J. Heney has been and is attorney employed by said Water Company, and his attorneyship for
such company is inconsistent with the holding of a place
as Assistant District Attorney, and against the best interests of the people of San Francisco.

"Specification 9:

"That in the interest of the corporations and persons
before mentioned, or some or all of them, together with
persons unknown, large sums of money have been and are
being raised for the purpose of slandering, defaming and
injuring the reputation of said Mayor Eugene E. Schmitz,
and of suborning perjury against him, thereby injuring the
interests of said city and county and its residents and
inhabitants; and said William H. Langdon as such District
Attorney, knowing said facts, by the appointment of said
Heney, is knowingly aiding and abetting the said plot and
scheme.

"Specification 10:

"Violation of Duty and Ulterior Use of Office.

"That since the appointment of said F. J. Heney as an
Assistant District Attorney of the City and County of San
Francisco by said William H. Langdon, the said Langdon
and the said Heney have caused to be published or have
been parties to the publication of open and covert threats
against the Superior Judges of the City and County of San
Francisco for the purpose of influencing the judicial action
of said Judges.

"Specification 11:

"That the appointment of said Heney as such Assistant
District Attorney was made by said Langdon in furtherance
of the combination aforesaid, and at the dictation of certain newspaper influences and individuals, who have contributed many thousands of dollars to further the political
ambitions, and aspirations of said William H. Langdon and
other persons, and to secure through the appointment of
said Heney the consummation of a political plan and the
wreaking of their private revenges against Eugene E.
Schmitz, Mayor of San Francisco, and the Board of Supervisors and the Police Department of the City and County
of San Francisco and their political supporters, and to
generally disrupt the business and proper government of

this city, and also for the purpose of attempting to influence the ensuing election. And said combination is also in pursuance of a well-defined and organized plan for the purpose of controlling and subjugating the labor market and the wage-earners.

"And the said William H. Langdon turned over said office of District Attorney as aforesaid to said Francis J. Heney with the intent and purpose and with the understanding that said Francis J. Heney would and should abuse such position, and use his said position as a deputy in a substantial control of said office of District Attorney to gratify his own private and personal revenge, and also with the intent that said Francis J. Heney, through said office, should produce before the Grand Jury of said city and county illegal and hearsay evidence which by law said Grand Jury is forbidden to act upon, and procure such Grand Jury to return indictments against innocent citizens of said city and county upon such illegal and hearsay evidence for the purpose of gratifying the private revenge of said Francis J. Heney and the political ambitions of said William H. Langdon. And said William H. Langdon also further turned over said office and power to said Francis J. Heney with the intent and purpose that said Francis J. Heney in such position should advise such Grand Jury that matters and acts not constituting an offense at law were indictable offenses, and thus and thereby falsely and unlawfully procure indictments against innocent citizens of said city and county.

"Specification 12:

"That in addition to the purposes hereinabove specified as a foundation and reason for the acts set forth, that all the acts hereinabove charged and set forth as having been done, aided, abetted, procured or assisted by said William H. Langdon as said District Attorney, were so done and performed by said William H. Langdon as such District Attorney to promote his own political ambitions and upon and at the eve of an election about to occur in the State of California, at which said William H. Langdon is a candidate for Governor, all with intent to deceive and mislead electors and voters and to procure an increased vote for himself as such candidate for Governor.

"Inefficiency in the office of District Attorney, and neglect on the part of the District Attorney and his office to perform the duties of his office.

"Dated, San Francisco, October 25, 1906.
                    "JAMES L. GALLAGHER,
    "Mayor of the City and County of San Francisco."

THE RUEF "IMMUNITY CONTRACT."

The "immunity contract" given Ruef was as follows:

"Whereas, Abraham Ruef of the City and County of San Francisco has agreed to impart to the District Attorney of the City and County of San Francisco, State of California, a full and fair statement and disclosure, so far as known to him, of all crimes and offenses involved in the so-called 'graft' prosecutions or investigations now and heretofore conducted by said District Attorney by whomsoever such offenses or crimes may have been committed, and has agreed in making such disclosure and statement to state fully and wholly all the facts and circumstances known to him in, about, and surrounding the same, and in making such statement and disclosure to tell the truth, the whole truth and nothing but the truth;

"Now, Therefore, In consideration of the premises it is agreed by the undersigned that if said A. Ruef shall do said things and immediately make such full and fair disclosure of all such crimes and offenses involved in the so-called 'graft' prosecutions and investigations above referred to, and known to him, and shall state and disclose to the undersigned the truth, the whole truth, and nothing but the truth, and shall make full and fair disclosure of all said crimes and offenses known to him, and of all the facts and circumstances in, about and surrounding the same and known to him, and shall at all times whenever called upon, before any court, testify in regard thereto and to the whole thereof fully and fairly, together with all the facts and circumstances surrounding the same, so far as the same are known to him, and shall state, tell and testify on oath the truth, the whole truth, and nothing but the truth therein, then and in that event the undersigned, deeming it to be in the interests of public justice, and believing that said A. Ruef will thereby be equitably entitled to such consideration in accordance with the time-honored custom and practice of prosecuting officers in both State and Federal jurisdictions throughout this country, and in line with common law precedents.

"1. Will grant and obtain for said A. Ruef full and complete immunity from prosecution or punishment for all and any of said offenses and crimes involved in said so-called 'graft' prosecutions or investigations, and will not prosecute him for any thereof.

"2. Will cause said A. Ruef to be jointly and not otherwise indicted with all and any others against whom indictments have heretofore been or may hereafter be returned or found for or upon any crimes or offenses in which said

Ruef has participated or is alleged to have participated to this date; provided, however, that the undersigned shall not be bound to include any of the present members of the Board of Supervisors in any such indictments.

"3. Will, as any one of said joint indictments relating to a specific subject matter shall be taken up for trial, after the jury has been impaneled and sworn to try the same, dismiss the same and all other indictments and charges on the same general subject matter as against the said Ruef, under the provisions of section 1099 of the Penal Code of the State of California, and will at the same time dismiss all indictments relating to the same general subject matter, which are now pending against said Ruef singly.

"Any and all indictments or charges upon any general subject matter of which one shall not have been brought to trial before December 31st, 1907, shall be dismissed as to said Ruef and said Ruef discharged on or before December 31st, 1907, under the provisions of section 1099 of the Penal Code where applicable, or under provisions of other sections of said code in cases where said section 1099 shall not be applicable.

"It is however expressly agreed that in any event all indictments and charges now pending or hereafter to be brought against said Ruef (except action No. 305 which is herein otherwise provided for) shall be dismissed as against said Ruef under the provisions of section 1099 of the Penal Code where the same may be applicable and when said section is not applicable shall be dismissed under other provisions of the Code, all prior to December 31st, 1907; provided, the undersigned District Attorney shall not be re-elected as such District Attorney in November, 1907, and, in any event, prior to said District Attorney resigning or otherwise surrendering or giving up his office or terminating his tenure thereof, it being the understanding and agreement that each and every indictment and charge now pending or hereafter to be brought against said Ruef shall be absolutely dismissed.

"Provided, that said Ruef shall have fully performed so far as may have been in his power the spirit and letter of his agreement herein.

"4. All and any indictments or charges which are to be found or returned against said Ruef jointly or otherwise, shall be returned and found not later than October 1st, 1907, unless hereafter otherwise mutually agreed.

"5. In the event of the prosecution of said Ruef by any other officer or person on account of any of such crimes or offenses committed or participated in or alleged to have been committed or participated in by said Ruef to this date, the undersigned will employ every legitimate influence and power to secure a dismissal thereof, and in the event that a conviction shall be had in any thereof, the undersigned hereby agree to apply to the Governor of the State of California for the pardon of said Ruef therefor or therein and to use all legitimate influence and power to secure such pardon.

"6. It is understood and agreed that, notwithstanding the scope and effect of the language used throughout this agreement, it does not and shall not be construed to apply in any respect or particular to that certain indictment No. 305, or the offense charged therein, which is now pending against said Abraham Ruef jointly with Eugene E. Schmitz, in the Superior Court of the City and County of San Francisco, State of California, in Department No. 6 thereof.

"Dated, May 8th, 1907.

"WM. H. LANGDON,
"District Attorney of the City
and County of San Francisco.

"FRANCIS J. HENEY,
"Assistant District Attorney of the
City and County of San Francisco.

"Agreed to:
"A. RUEF."

"IMMUNITY CONTRACT" GIVEN SUPERVISORS.

"San Francisco, Cal., July 30, 1907.

"Whereas, James L. Gallagher, E. J. Walsh, F. P. Nicholas, C. J. Harrigan, Max Mamlock, J. J. Furey, Jennings Phillips, Thomas F. Lonergan, James F. Kelly, L. A. Rea, W. W. Sanderson, Daniel C. Coleman, Sam Davis, A. M. Wilson, M. F. Coffey, all of the City and County of San Francisco, State of California, have each made to me a disclosure of certain crimes and offenses committed by himself, and by himself jointly with others and by others, which he claims to be a full and fair disclosure thereof, so far as known to him.

"Now, therefore, in consideration of the premises, deeming it to be in the interest of public justice, and believing that each of the above-named parties will thereby become equitably entitled to such consideration, in accordance with the time-honored custom and practice of prosecuting officers, in both State and Federal jurisdictions throughout this country, and in line with common law precedence, it is agreed by me that if he has made a full and fair disclosure of all of such crimes and offenses and has stated to me the truth, the whole truth and nothing but the truth, and if he shall whenever called upon to do so by me, or by any other officer on behalf of the People of the State of California, to again make a full and fair disclosure of such crimes and offenses, together with the facts and circumstances surrounding the same and the persons therein involved, in any cause, action or proceeding whatever in regard thereto, fully and fairly, together with the facts and circumstances surrounding said crimes and offenses and the persons involved, and tell and testify the truth, the whole truth and nothing but the truth, then, and in that event, each one of them who so does shall not be prosecuted, complained against or indicted for any of said crimes or offenses, or his connection therewith.

"It is understood that the making or verifying of any affidavit or answer in the case of 'Langdon vs. Ruef, et al.,' heretofore brought in the Superior Court of this city and county, is included in this agreement; and it is further understood that Fred P. Nicholas shall not be further prosecuted in the case now pending against him in which he is under indictment in this city and county, upon the charge of accepting and agreeing to accept a bribe from one Holmes.

"Signed: W. H. Langdon, District Attorney; Francis J. Heney, Asst. Dist. Atty. Witness: James L. Gallagher."

The People vs. Ruef, page 1382.

DISTRICT ATTORNEY LANGDON'S PLAN FOR RE-ORGANIZING THE MUNICIPAL GOVERNMENT.
(See Chapter XVII.)

"San Francisco, July 9, 1907.—To the San Francisco Labor Council, the Merchants' Association, the Building Trades Council, the Chamber of Commerce, the Board of Trade, the Real Estate Board and the Merchants' Exchange: Gentlemen—We respectfully submit to your consideration and ask your co-operation in the carrying out of the following proposed plan for the selection of a Mayor of the City and County of San Francisco for the unexpired term of Eugene E. Schmitz, who, having been elected Mayor of the City and County of San Francisco in November, 1905, was on the 13th day of June, 1907, convicted of a felony; to wit, of the crime of extortion, by a jury in Department

No. 6 of the Superior Court of the City and County of San Francisco, State of California. Thereafter, upon the 8th day of July, 1907, judgment upon the conviction was duly pronounced and entered, by which a sentence was imposed of five years' imprisonment in the State Prison at San Quentin.

"The Political Code of this State, and the charter of the City and County of San Francisco, both provide that the office becomes vacant when the incumbent is convicted of a felony, and in several decisions our Supreme Court has held that the words 'convicted of a felony,' signify the verdict of a jury. That court has also held that this provision of the code and charter is self-acting, and that the vacancy is created 'eo instanti,' upon the happening of the event, and that all that is necessary is for the appointing power to fill the vacancy thus created. By virtue of the conviction of Eugene E. Schmitz, the office of Mayor of the City and County of San Francisco became vacant. Upon the 9th day of July, 1907, the Board of Supervisors, pursuant to the charter, elected as Mayor to fill the vacancy thus created Dr. Charles Boxton. This action was taken to avoid legal complications in the interim, before a permanent selection of Mayor could be made, and it is thoroughly well understood that the selection of Dr. Charles Boxton is merely temporary.

"The conditions surrounding the present Board of Supervisors have been so completely explained, through the public press, that it is unnecessary to go into further detail in that regard than to say that Dr. Boxton has offered to resign his office as Mayor, as soon as a suitable successor has been found. In the present unprecedented condition of the municipal government, circumstances have made it the duty of the District Attorney, in the interest of the public welfare, to take the initiative, in the endeavor to find such a successor.

"It is the desire of the District Attorney as speedily as possible to confine the operations of his office entirely to those duties ordinarily incumbent upon it. The next election for city officers takes place in November of this year, but the situation of the city government, and the material conditions obtaining in the city with regard to necessary public improvements, render it absolutely indispensable that we proceed with the utmost energy to obtain for the office of Mayor a man of unblemished integrity and great executive ability.

"The District Attorney and his associates, realizing that the selection of a Mayor to fill the unexpired term in question should be made by as representative a body of the people as possible, have deemed it wise to call together a convention that will be, as nearly as circumstances and the time at our disposal permit, fairly representative of the community at large. For that purpose they have decided to call together a convention composed of thirty delegates, fifteen of whom shall represent labor, and the remaining fifteen shall represent employers generally.

"It is, of course, impossible on account of the limited time at our disposal to accord representation to all the organized bodies in the city entitled to the same. All that we can reasonably be expected to do is to make a sincere and earnest effort to have the convention composed of delegates from such well-known organized bodies, large and varied in membership, that the people generally will be satisfied that the plan of selection is fair, reasonable and democratic.

"The prosecution in the graft cases feels that it is highly desirable to keep politics out of the organization of the city government as much as possible until the people, in the manner ordained by law, have an opportunity at the ballot-box again to express their will directly.

"We address this communication and invitation to the following bodies, to wit: The San Francisco Labor Council, the Merchants' Association, the Building Trades Council, the Chamber of Commerce, the Board of Trade, the Real Estate Board and the Merchants' Exchange. We respectfully request the foregoing associations to send delegates to the proposed convention on the following basis of apportionment, that is to say, that the two bodies representing labor shall select fifteen delegates, eight of whom shall be selected by the San Francisco Labor Council and seven by the Building Trades Council, and the remaining fifteen members of the convention shall be selected, three each, by the remaining five bodies above mentioned.

"It will be appreciated that it is necessary to impose a time limit within which the selection of delegates shall be made, and the subsequent nomination of a Mayor by the convention shall be accomplished. In that view we ask that a response to this invitation, containing the names of the delegates selected, be delivered to the District Attorney's office, 2181 Fillmore street, on or before Saturday, July 13, 1907, and that the Mayor be nominated within five days thereafter. The success of this plan, in our judgment, depends absolutely upon the harmonious co-operation of all sections of our people, who, we believe, are fairly represented by one or more of the foregoing associations. Consequently we deem it essential to prescribe as a condition for the assembling of the proposed convention that this invitation shall be accepted by all of these bodies.

"This plan for the selection of a Mayor is the result of most patient, thorough and anxious deliberation on the part of those associated in the graft prosecution, and its single purpose is to satisfy, so far as in our power, the desire of all good citizens to sink factional and political differences and choose for Mayor a man who will be generally recognized and accepted as representative of the whole people, who will bring to all industrial disputes a spirit of conciliation and harmony, and who will be possessed of the capacity, energy and honesty needed in the great work of rehabilitating our city and restoring it to normal conditions. We desire that perfect freedom and independence of action shall govern the convention from its inception to its close, and accordingly the District Attorney and his associates will wholly refrain from any participation after the convention has assembled. I have the honor to be,

"Yours very truly,

"W. H. LANGDON, District Attorney."

ROOSEVELT'S LETTER TO SPRECKELS ON THE GRAFT SITUATION.

"The White House, Washington, June 8, 1908.

"My Dear Mr. Spreckels—Now and then you and Mr. Heney and the others who are associated with you must feel down-hearted when you see men guilty of atrocious crimes who from some cause or other succeed in escaping punishment, and especially when you see men of wealth, of high business and, in a sense, of high social standing, banded together against you.

"My dear sir, I want you to feel that your experience is simply the experience of all of us who are engaged in this fight. There is no form of slander and wicked falsehood which will not as a matter of course be employed against all men engaged in such a struggle, and this not only on the part of men and papers representing the lowest type of demagogy, but, I am sorry to say, also on the part of men and papers representing the interests that call themselves pre-eminently conservative, pre-eminently cultured.

"In such a struggle it is too often true that the feeling against those engaged in it becomes peculiarly bitter, not merely in the business houses of the great financiers who directly profit by the wrongdoing, but also in the clubs, in certain newspaper offices where business interests exercise an unhealthy control and, I regret to add, in other newspaper offices which like to be considered as to a marked degree the representatives of the cultivation and high social standing of the country.

"Now, I do hope that you and your colleagues will treat all this bitterness with entire disregard. It is of small consequence to you, or to any of us who are engaged in this work, whether men think well or ill of us personally; but it is of very great consequence that we should do the work without flinching, on the one hand, and on the other hand, without losing our good-humored common sense, without becoming angered and irritated to a degree that will in any way cause us to lose our heads.

"Therefore, I hope that you and Heney and your associates will keep reasonably good-natured; but that above all things you will not lose heart. You must battle on valiantly, no matter what the biggest business men may say, no matter what the mob may say, no matter what may be said by that element which may be regarded as socially the highest element. You must steadfastly oppose those foolish or wicked men who would substitute class consciousness and loyalty to class interest, for loyalty to American citizenship as a whole, for loyalty to the immutable laws of righteousness, of just and fair dealing as between man and man.

"It is just as bad to be ruled by a plutocracy as by a mob. It is profoundly un-American and, in a social sense, profoundly immoral, to stand for or against a given man, not because he is or is not a brave, upright and able man, but because he does or does not belong to a labor union or does or does not represent the big business interests. In their essence, down at the foundation of things, the ties that are all-important are those that knit honest men, brave men, square-dealing men, together, and it is a mighty poor substitute if we replace these ties by those that bind men together, whether they are good or bad, simply because they follow a particular business, have a given social standing or belong to a particular organization. It is an evil and a dreadful thing for laboring men to endeavor to secure the political dominance of labor unions by conniving at crookedness or violence, by being 'loyal' to crooked labor leaders, for to be 'loyal' to the fancied interests of the unions when they are against the laws of morality and the interests of the whole people means ultimately the destruction of the unions themselves, as an incident to the destruction of all good citizenship.

"But it is, if anything, an even more evil and dreadful thing to have the merchants, the business men, the captains of industry accessories to crime and shielders and supporters of criminals; it is an even more dreadful thing to see the power of men high in State politics, high in finance, high in the social life of the rich and fashionable, united to stifle the prosecution of offenders against civic integrity if these offenders happen to be their friends and associates; and most evil of all is it when we see crooks of a labor party in offensive and defensive alliance with the crooks of a corporation party. Labor unions and corporations alike should be heartily supported when they do good work, and fearlessly opposed when they stand for what is evil. The best kind of wage worker, the best kind of laboring man, must stand shoulder to shoulder with the best kind of professional man, with the best kind of business man, in putting a stop to the undermining of civic decency, and this without any regard to whether it is a labor union or a corporation which is undermining it, without any regard to whether the offender is a rich man or a poor man.

"Indeed, if there can be any degrees in the contemptuous abhorrence with which right thinking citizens should regard corruption, it must be felt in its most extreme form for the so-called 'best citizens,' the men high in business and social life, who by backing up or by preventing the punishment of wealthy criminals set the seal of their approval on crime and give honor to rich felons. The most powerful ally of lawlessness and mob violence is the man, whoever he may be, politician or business man, judge or lawyer, capitalist or editor, who in any way or shape works so as to shield wealthy and powerful wrongdoers from the consequences of their misconduct.

"You have heart-breaking difficulties with which to contend. You have to fight not only the banded powers of evil, but, alas, that it should be said, the supineness and indifference of many good men upon whose zealous support you had a right to feel that you could rely. Do not be discouraged; do not flinch. You are in a fight for plain decency, for the plain democracy of the plain people, who believe in honesty and in fair dealing as between man and man. Do not become disheartened. Keep up the fight.

"Very sincerely yours,
"THEODORE ROOSEVELT.

"Rudolph Spreckels, Esq.,
"San Francisco, Cal."

GOVERNOR JOHNSON'S STATEMENT REGARDING RUEF'S IMPRISONMENT.

(See Chapter XXIX, page 453.)

Ever since Abraham Ruef was taken to San Quentin an organized and systematic agitation has been carried on to effect his release, and all that power, influence and money and favorable publicity could do to manufacture public sentiment for him has been done. His case has ever been before the people, and never since his confinement at San Quentin has he been permitted to be in the category of the ordinary prisoner.

Purposely have I heretofore refrained from any public utterance upon the subject, and this for reasons that may be obvious. Ruef's partisans now charge his failure to obtain his release to me.

In so far as I have expressed my views to certain members of the Prison Directors, and their views accord with mine, I accept the responsibility.

I do not believe that Ruef should be paroled at this time. I insist that he shall be treated just like any ordinary prisoner, neither more harshly nor more leniently.

As vigorously as I am able, I demand that there shall be no special privilege in the prisons of the State of California, and that when special privilege has been banished from every department of government, it shall not be permitted, no matter what the power or threats, to creep into our penitentiary.

The grossest injustice that could be committed against the other 3,300 men confined in our State prisons would be to single out the one rich, powerful and conspicuous offender and, because of his riches and his influence, grant him what is denied to the humble and friendless prisoner. If prisons are to be maintained, and the system in vogue continued, all prisoners must be treated exactly alike.

Since the parole law went into effect, the Prison Directors have continuously acted under a rule which required, save in exceptional cases, the service of half of the net sentence before an application can be heard. In the Roberts case, recently decided, the Supreme Court held this rule to be illegal, but also held that paroles rested in the absolute discretion of the Prison Directors, and that in determining whether or not parole shall be granted, it was the right and duty of the Board to take into account the length of sentence, the time served, etc.

As I understand the attitude of the Directors, they insist that in the matter of granting paroles, although applications may be made after one year, it is neither unjust nor unfair nor illegal that prisoners be required, save in exceptional cases, to serve half the net sentence.

This rule is applicable to 3,300 prisoners, most of them unknown and unheard of. It is demanded that another rule be made for Ruef.

Ruef's sentence was fourteen years. His net sentence will be eight years and ten months. Half of the net sentence will be four years and five months. He was received in San Quentin about March, 1911. If required to serve half his net sentence, presumably he will be paroled about August, 1915. Purposely, apparently, misapprehension has been created about the recent parole of Dalton. Dalton desired to be liberated before half his net sentence had been served, and was not. He was granted a parole at the last meeting of the Prison Directors, which takes effect some months after the completion of half of his net sentence.

The Recent Action of the Prison Board.

In behalf of the parole of Ruef it is insisted that any man is entitled as a matter of right to a parole after one year's imprisonment. I will not subscribe to this doctrine. It has been asserted that the Supreme Court has so decided. This is not true. The Supreme Court simply determined that after one year the prisoner had the right to make his application, but that his parole rested absolutely thereafter in the discretion of the Prison Board.

At the last meeting of the Prison Directors 78 men applied for parole, Ruef among them. None of these had served half his net time and this fact was known to all the members of the Prison Board. To four members of the Prison Board before that time every application had been presented with the history of the case, and with all the facts that had been filed concerning it. Every man, prison director or other, knows the facts of the Ruef case. The 78 were all denied parole. When the Ruef people assert he had no hearing, they mean he had no such hearing as Ruef desired. When they shout that his case was not considered, they mean not considered as Ruef demanded. If the hearing had been as Ruef and his partisans had staged it; if Ruef had delivered an oration, taken down by the shorthand reporter, brought for the purpose; if Ruef had dominated the entire situation, and the Directors had yielded to his power and his influence; if Ruef had been paroled, what a virtuous and glorious Prison Board it would have been! But the hearing being otherwise than had been staged, the determination being other than what the power of Ruef demanded, the Prison Board is abused and denounced; not denounced or abused because 77 other men were not paroled (they are unknown, poor, helpless, without friends), but abused and denounced because one man, Ruef, was not paroled; because one man, Ruef, was treated exactly as all others were treated.

The Charge of Bitterness and Vengeance.

I resent any imputation of bitterness or revenge on my part toward Ruef. I have neither. More than two years ago I expressed what I write to-day—that for the sake of society and the unfortunates confined in prison, Ruef must be treated like all others similarly situated. To yield because of fear to the persuasion, cajolery or the threats of a powerful prisoner, is to cause the iron to enter the soul of every obscure and friendless prisoner, and to make every other one of the 3,300 men in our jails know that even in prisons class distinctions prevail, and to add to the bitterness and the hopelessness of men confined.

The bitterness and revenge are on the other side of this controversy. It has become necessary to make this statement because of the unmerited abuse of the Prison Board, and because some individuals, while begging mercy for Ruef, have without mercy sought Ruef's release by threats of annihilation and destruction of all opposed.

The Plea That the Past Be Forgotten.

Often we hear that Ruef is the only one who has been punished of those guilty of the particular crimes of which he was a part, and that for this reason should be liberated.

If three men committed a murder, two escape and are never found, and the third is convicted, ought he to be released because he is the only one punished?

It is unnecessary, however, to discuss this phase of the case. After conviction and imprisonment, if clemency be asked, ordinarily the only question that can be considered is whether the prisoner is guilty or innocent. Does any person claim Ruef to be innocent? If guilty, then to him must apply the usual prison discipline and rules.

There is to-day in the same prison with Ruef a poor, uneducated, friendless Greek, the product of the graft prosecution just as Ruef is. Claudianes is serving a life sentence for dynamiting Gallagher's residence and almost murdering seven people. Claudianes was paid to do the dynamiting that Gallagher might be put out of the way. He was the ignorant, sodden instrument of men who would not stop even at murder; but he was only the miserable tool after all. No appeal has been made to me for Claudianes. No petitions have been presented in his behalf, no organized effort for his release, no threats of political annihilation unless clemency be extended to him. Why? Is it because Claudianes is unknown, ignorant, friendless, moneyless?

The Unjust Charge of Racial Prejudice.

Every cheap politician has been quick to seize upon the Ruef case and endeavor to make political capital for himself or create hostility to me out of it. Among the baseless and outrageous things that have been published is that Ruef is not granted special privileges and immunities because of racial prejudice. When Ruef was denied parole, denied with him were men of many races. No one has claimed that these were denied parole because of race prejudice.

In San Quentin to-day are thirty-one Jews. Thirteen of these, for one reason or another, have at times lost their privileges. Is it possible that Ruef is the only man to be considered? No complaint is made for the thirty-one, or for the thirteen. Since February 1, 1912, twenty-seven Jews have been paroled from San Quentin. Six of these have been returned for violations of parole. In relation to the twenty-seven or the six there has been neither outcry nor protest nor publicity nor effort of any sort. Why the astounding, organized effort and publicity campaign for Ruef alone?

The appointments that have been made by this administration include Rabbi Meyer, H. Weinstock, Paul Sinsheimer, Simon Lubin, Miss Steinhart, Julius Jacobs, E. Franklin, Louis Frankenheimer, A. Sapiro, Jacob Alexander, A. Bonnheim, Miss Peixotto, Judge Cerf and many others. No list of more able and patriotic men and women in the service of any State could be furnished than this.

Is Ruef the sole test of every question?

To two young men of Jewish faith lately have been granted pardons. No tremendous petitions loaded down with the names of politicians, no extraordinary publicity was presented in their behalf.

Is there no man in the list of appointees to whom in pride we may all yield our praise? Is there no man among the 3,300 prisoners in San Quentin and Folsom who justly can arouse efforts in his behalf? Or is the sole test of official action by the Prison Directors of California or the Chief Executive of the State to be the disregard of every other man's rights and the granting to Ruef alone of a privilege that none other enjoys?

California Prisons To-day.

In the discussion that has ensued from the Ruef case

and because of the Ruef case, the prisons have been said to be the one part of the present administration that is not progressive, and that they are yet a relic of the Herrin machine. Nothing could be further from the fact. I challenge contradiction of the following statements:

California is in the forefront of all the States in the management of her prisons. In matters of food, shelter, clothing, employment, recreation, medical attention, opportunities for education, general freedom consistent with discipline, encouragement of decent tendencies, and **in the number of paroles** (although these have been granted under the half term rule), no State has gone further.

Within the past three years the strait-jacket, the water-cure and the hooks, once so freely used, have not been tolerated. Every form of corporal punishment has been abolished. When prisoners are received the effort is made to get the history of the crime and possible cause of it, and then to apply corrective measures intelligently. As soon as received, every newcomer is given a thorough physical examination and his teeth are looked after by a dentist. It not infrequently happens that the first place a man is quartered in is the hospital. Special attention is given to tuberculars, alcoholics and dope fiends. Wassermann tests are made for the slightest indication of blood taint, and the best treatment afforded. After the physician and dentist conclude their examinations, the newcomer is turned over to the Director of Education, who endeavors to take the man's mental measurement and get at his moral status. There are now 200 pupils in the day school at San Quentin, and three rooms of thirty each in the night school. The educational facilities are being constantly increased. Two hundred and twenty-six are enrolled in the academic courses with the University of California and by correspondence are receiving their training from our great institutions of learning. The State Use system, which was enacted in 1911, furnishes work in industries for the State. In the matter of food the State purchases the best and the rations issued are abundant. Sanitary conditions are a model in the newly constructed portions of the prison and the best possible in the old construction.

In the last three years 1372 paroles have been granted by this harsh, cruel and outrageous Prison Board, as against 1132 granted in all the years from 1893 to 1910 inclusive. The paroles have been granted, however, justly. Because one was not granted unjustly and unfairly, the record of the Prison Board counts for naught.

I have purposely refrained from discussing the character

of Ruef's crimes or any matters extraneous to the one issue presented. I have tried to make clear that I believe Ruef should be treated just as the least known prisoner is treated. That his advocates wish him to be treated otherwise because he is Ruef will be clear to any who will reflect that had Ruef been paroled and the other 77 denied parole there would have been no agitation; if Ruef were granted what others were denied, there would be no fulminations against the Prison Board and petty politicians would not have seized upon recent events to bow and scrape and bend and crawl to the organized power of Ruef.

SCHMITZ'S ATTEMPT TO CONTROL SAN FRANCISCO RELIEF FUNDS.

In the early part of June, 1906, it was agreed that a committee consisting of Benjamin Ide Wheeler, Judge W. W. Morrow and James D. Phelan should go to Washington, in order to interest Congress in some project for financing the rebuilding of San Francisco.

Before their departure, Mayor Schmitz invited them and other members of the Committee of Fifty to his residence, where a luncheon was served. During the luncheon he stated that the Board of Supervisors were about to resume their public functions for which they were elected by the people, and the private persons who were administering the affairs of the city doubtless would employ their abilities for the rehabilitation of their own business, and he suggested that the relief fund be turned over to the Board of Supervisors for distribution. Judge Morrow, Mr. Phelan and others protested that it was not the function of the Supervisors to distribute relief, and that there was a trust relationship existing between the donors and the finance committee of the Relief and Red Cross Funds. After the luncheon, the Mayor handed Mr. Phelan his transportation, but later in the afternoon Mr. Phelan, suspicious of his purpose, sent word to the Mayor that he had decided to remain in the city. He remained behind to protect the funds.

As subsequently developed in the graft investigations, the Supervisors had accused the Mayor of abandoning the city government to his enemies, and insisted upon the enjoyment of all the rights and privileges of their office, and that the work of distributing relief at that time was the principal business of the city.

17

RECEIPTS AND DISBURSEMENTS OF PROSECUTION FROM JUNE, 1906, TO MAY 17, 1909.

(As shown by testimouy taken at trial of Patrick Calhoun.)
RECEIPTS.

Subscription account ....$ 73,384.75
Subscription account R. Spreckels................ 138,478.05
Cash received by W. J. Burns.................... 1,278.70
Refunded by the Bulletin account Older case..... 250.00

$213,391.50

DISBURSEMENTS.

W. J. BURNS ACCOUNT: W. J. Burns account, personal, $12,357.45; office expenses, $1,911.43; office furniture, $671.50; carriage hire, $27.25; auto hire, $2,700.75; auto expense, $4,162.36; traveling expense, $1,302.15; telegrams, $797.79; The Bulletin, $309.55; incidentals, $158.50; paid for account City and County of San Francisco, $223.52; detective services, $70,572.65; detective expenses, $27,277.35; extra salaries, $778.55. Total, $123,250.80.

F. J. HENEY ACCOUNT: Rent, $3,186.25; office expense, $1,522.02; private exchange and operator, $1,949.22; telegrams, $316.82; postage and messenger expense, $280.26; traveling expense, $118.45; office salaries, $8,684.67; office furniture, $433.50; auto and carriage hire, $957.05; stenographic and legal expense, $2,147.37; detective expense, $4,232.61. Total, $23,828.22.

SUNDRY DISBURSEMENTS: P. Dolman, $5,087.65; Hiram W. Johnson, $11,000.00; J. J. Dwyer, $13,400.00; C. W. Cobb, $10,000.00; legal expense, official count for judges, $191.50; George J. Cleary, $70.00; L. Kavanaugh, $506.20; D. M. Duffy, $1,878.85; W. J. Burns, $17,195.00; Jas. Foley, $1,010.00; Miler & Co., $40.00; automobiles, $5,100.00; auto expense, $815.98. Total, $66,295.18.

Total disbursements $213,374.20
Balance, cash 17.30

$213,391.50

ITEMS, W. J. BURNS ACCOUNT.

Personal: Salary, $8,548.80; subsistence, $2,081.75; rent, $1,726.90. Total, $12,357.45.
Office Expenses: Rent (R. L. Radke Co.), $935.00;

telephone, P. S. T. & T. Co., $398.93; light and heat—E. D.
Feil, $25.00; W. G. Stafford, $8.00; mantels, $0.95—$33.95;
towels (Star Towel Sup. Co.), $15.80; newspapers, $46.40;
P. O. Box, U. S. A., $12.00; stamps, U. S. A., $20.40; Purity
Water Co., $12.00; advertising—Call, $1.60; Examiner, $3.40
—$5.00; car fare, $3.20; stationary—Library Bureau, $7.40;
Mysell-Rollins, $3.00; Barry Co., $9.75; Brown & Power,
$59.90; E. H. Wobber and others, $76.70—$156.75; typewriter
expense—Vaughn, $56.30; Revalk, $77.10; Underwood, $5.50
—$138.90; stenographic, $43.80 (L. F. Hurlburt, et al.);
incidentals—pans, $0.40; opening Marchand's safe, $10.00;
safe dep. Crocker, $6.00; painting floor, $1.00; N. Y. Exchange, $0.95; express charges, $8.40; keys, $3.25; paint,
$1.00; tel. directory, $1.50; stars (spec.), $5.25; city directo-
ries, $9.00; elect. buzzer, $1.35; show cards (A. Unsworth),
$18.50; show card frames (Young & Rhodes), $2.00; whet-
stone, $0.70; hauling, $5.00; moving safe (Gorham & Thomas), $15.00—$89.30. Total office expenses, $1,911.43.

Office Furniture: Lamp, $3.55; two desk lamps, $7.80;
J. Breuner Co., $68.00; water heater, $19.20; Library Bureau,
$78.00; Ladd's Gun Store, $55.50; safe (Freeman, Brewster,
McCabe), $165.00; 2 gas heaters, $13.10; Spencer Desk Co.,
$37.50; Geo. Walcom (curtains) $3.35; E. Emerson (desk),
$10.00; Olympic Arms Co., $28.55; Library Bureau, $40.50;
L. & E. Emanuel, $12.00; Acme Furn. Co., $96.75; Hale's,
$23.20; C. P. Stanton, $9.50. Total, $671.50.

Carriage Hire: Kelly, $2.50, $4.00, $5.00, $3.00, $12.75.
Total, $27.25.

Auto Hire: Scott, $15.00, $5.00, $50.00, $65.00, $10.00;
H. M. Owens, $20.00; W. J. Burns, $90.00; March 30th,
$207.50; Ruef's arrest, $10.00; F. J. Heney, $10.00; W. J.
Burns, $5.00; April 27th, $32.50; L. Heidinger, $25.00; Auto
Livery Co., $73.50, $92.50; Kelly, $32.50; Otis Patkhill,
$45.00; Auto L. Co., $538.00; A. S. Lathaw, $105.00; Auto
Livery Co., $296.50, $60.00, $20.00; M. Mamlock, $17.50; auto
Livery, $78.00; Cal. & Coulter, $25.00; F. Coulter, $42.50;
Auto Livery Co., $25.00; Auto Livery Co., $288.00; Zim-
merline Bros., $5.75; Auto Livery Co., $132.50, $22.50,
$190.50, $35.00, $22.50; Broadway Garage, $8.00. Total,
$2,700.75.

Auto Expense: Goggles, $3.50; sundries, $9.35; Harris
Rubber Co., $120.98; Harris Rubber Co., $70.10; Geo. P.
Moore Co., $12.30; Geo. P. Moore Co., $9.35; Harris Rub-
ber Co., $48.58; Chanslor Lyon, $30.88; Harris Rubber Co.,
$24.39; Bauer Lamp, $1.50; Bauer Lamp, $4.50; Auto Livery,
$132.00; Auto Livery, $2.00; Chans. & Lyon, $12.75; Chans.
& Lyon, $14.05; G. P. Moore, $26.90; G. P. Moore, $6.12;
Arcade Garage, $51.20; towing auto, $5.00; Irvine Mch. Wks.,

$114.60; Harris Rubber Co., $6.00; Franklin Car, $59.12; Gillig & Son, $9.00; Gillig & Son, $5.00; Arcade Garage, $149.45; Arcade Garage, $134.25; G. P. Moore Co., $3.00; H. W. Bogen, $103.50; H. W. Bogen, $127.00; Pioneer Auto Co., $0.75; Pioneer Auto Co., $5.40; Gorham Rubber Co., $35.00; Berg Auto Supply Co., $1.50; Pioneer Garage, $6.00; Keenan Bros., $51.80; Keenan Bros., $23.05; Pioneer Garage, $186.70; Diamond Rubber Co., $222.50; Pioneer Auto Co., $2.50; Pioneer Auto Co., $24.00; Auto Livery Co., $166.00; G. P. Moore, $2.50; G. P. Moore, $4.50; Harris Rubber Co., $2.25; Arcade, $151.60; Arcade, $151.50; Bogan, $9.75; Bogan, $39.00; Pioneer, $3.00; Pioneer, $1.00; tire repair, $0.75; Pacific Gar., $12.85; Pacific Gar., $97.40; Arcade, $123.35; Keenan, $11.00; Keenan, $13.95; Chans. & L., $3.25; Chans. & L., $2.50; Bogen, $9.85; Bogen, $7.00; Osen & Hunter, $109.45; Pacific Gar., $5.25; Pacific Gar., $70.00; Irvington Garage, $71.50; Pioneer, $8.50; Pioneer, $6.00; J. E. Elkington & Sons, $55.50; Continental R. Co., $88.88; Schwartz & Gotlieb, $8.00; C. & L., $12.45; Pacific, $9.75; Pacific, $11.25; Spreckels Garage, $384.85; Sunset Garage, $14.50; Spreckels Garage, $82.65; Pioneer, $7.00; Letcher, S. Jose, $4.00; Keenan, $104.05; Pioneer Auto Co., $10.50; Pacific, $29.10; Halls Auto Rep., $32.30; Studebaker, $17.91; Arcade, $159.15; Spreckels Garage, $185.25; Jerome Garage, $2.25; Miller Bros., $8.75; Goodyear, $5.00; Cr. H. W. Bogen, $10.00. Net total, $4,162.36.

Traveling Expense: Kendall to Portland, $20.00; Ferry, $1.05; Halsey, $493.40; Geo. Burns, round trip home, $130.00; baggage transfer, $1.50; trip to Oakland, auto, etc., $7.10; trip to Oakland, auto, etc., $6.60; B. T. Block to San Jose, $2.15; ferryage auto, etc., $15.35; ferryage auto, etc., $6.60; F. A. Leach, $230.00; B. A. Libby, $100.00; ferryage, auto, etc., $1.90; ferryage auto, etc., $1.90; ferryage auto, etc., $1.00; W. J. Burns to Los Angeles, $57.40; W. J. Burns, $2.10; Slater witness Ford case, $168.90; trips Okd. Gallagher case, $13.20; Marie Ware McK. Port. S. F. Ret., $50.00; Cr. F. H. Leach, witness Ford case, $8.00. Net total, $1,302.15.

Telegrams: $797.79.

The Bulletin: 30,000 papers (10-31, 1908) $309.55.

Incidentals: Christmas turkeys, $37.85; 5 glove orders, $10.00; theater party, $6.00; C. P. Stanton (burglar alarm), $57.25; S. F. Call 1400 Jones, $2.25; expense account Blake case, $3.50; lunches, W. J. Burns et al., $41.65. Total, $158.50.

Paid for account City and County of San Francisco: Exchange on Washington, D. C., sent to F. A. Leach, witness, to cover expenses to S. F., $250.00; less amount refunded by City and County of San Francisco, $26.48—$223.52.

Detective Services and Expenses: D. F. Cecil, services $2,396.00, expenses $942.50; H. J. Woolman, services $476.00, expenses $328.00; R. J. Bergen, services $708.00, expenses $510.50; R. H. Perry, $3,095.00, expenses $1,318.05; I. H. Henderson, services $350.00, expenses $188.85; E. S. Spaulding, services $2,820.00, expenses $550.70; W. W. Farrell, services $704.00, expenses $196.50; L. G. Carpenter, services $225.00; expenses, $170.20; R. S. Spaulding, services $2,042.00, expenses $378.25; J. G. Lawlor, services $2,837.50, expenses $1,221.63; I. J. Scott, expenses $30.00; E. G. Borden, services $78.00; P. Hendirard, services $202.00, expenses $200.55; R. J. Burns, $2,810.00, expenses $2,076.47; S. S. Simon, services $206.00; B. Kohlman, services $248.00, expenses $18.75; G. E. Burns, services $2,510.00, expenses $4,369.62; C. F. Oliver, services $2,920.00, expenses $833.85; C. P. Fox, services $472.50, expenses $265.35; S. G. R. Ollsen, $40.00; G. W. Hess, $1,595.00, expenses $1,250.22; J. Mc-Carthy, services $1,313.00, expenses $227.35; J. C. Saulman, services $110.00, expenses $1.20; L. Pring, services $44.00; L. Cullen, services $60.00; M. C. Doyle, services $52.00; D. M. Duffy, services $150.00; Chas. Wyman, services $20.00; A. Steffens, $45.00; A. Greggains, services $780.00, expenses $665.85; J. H. Shiner, services $480.00, expenses $310.80; P. F. Roller, $290.00, expenses $349.20; P. E. Sowers, services $410.00, expenses $284.10; T. R. Sullivan, services $320.00, expenses $328.55; D. McCarthy, services $948.00, expenses $114.21; J. Compton, services $1,880.00, expenses $81.40; R. Ellis, services $246.00, expenses $6.00; P. Bergin, services $20.00, expenses $17.00; C. P. Stanton, services $2,645.00, expenses $4.20; H. Sullivan, services $95.00, expenses $1.70; J. S. Hensley, services $140.00; James Foley, services $2,335.00, expenses $134.10; J. F. Severney, services $285.00, expenses $15.55; A. Hornberg, services $44.00; E. W. Stow, services $342.00, expenses $216.60; G. M. Insley, $1,417.00, expenses $414.45; B. F. Daman, services $1,148.00, expenses $529.80; L. C. Caldwell, $896.00, expenses $360.25; R. N. Hamlin, services $1,902.00, expenses $50.00; F. Kingsberg, services $90.00; W. Bettiee, services $1,068.00, expenses $164.25; W. J. Dewer, services $160.00; J. F. Clark, services $1,072.00, expenses $501.29; W. J. Biggy, Jr., services $260.00, expenses $35.40; M. C. Perry, services $144.00, expenses $109.00; C. A. Spaulding, services $336.00, expenses $109.70; E. T. Newsome, services $364.00, expenses $58.85; F. J. Barry, services $32.00; J. H. Hamilton, services $26.00; R. C. Schindler, services $1,483.00, expenses $706.85; W. S. Schindler, services, $1,161.00, expenses $224.15; O. G. Schleicher, services $340.00, expenses $122.66; E. A. Platt, services $1,205.00, expenses $315.20; W. H. Russell, services $1,305.00, expenses $298.30; S. B. Priest, services $210.00, expenses $1.40; E. J. Whiskatchies, services $1,200.00, expenses $484.85; E. W. Madden, services $255.00, expenses $33.35; J. M. Creighton, services $1,494.00, expenses $667.60; G. E. Madden, services $30.00, expenses $1.70; J. Crawford, services $35.00; E. Graf, services $20.00; expenses $7.00; W. Duchion, services $100.00; J. V. Thompson, services $72.00, expenses $13.00; F. C. Boden, expenses $62.35; F. F. McGee, services $50.00; M. L. Doyle, services $286.00; E. M. Burgoyne, services $84.00, expenses $53.95; C. Bernstein, services $64.00; E. Goldstein, services $92.00, expenses $15.25; H. C. Willer, services $216.00; J. W. F. Jackson, services $384.00, expenses $178.50; D. L. Chiles, services $20.00; Mrs. May Schindler, services $154.50, expenses $3.50; L. Gold, services $805.00, expenses $58.65; J. M. Ullmache, services $40.00, expenses $93.20; C. P. Snell, services $12.00, expenses $0.65; W. C. Heney, services $1,939.00, expenses $20.05; E. C. Lange, services $42.00; expenses $2.60; E. Emerson, services $365.00, expenses $79.15; J. McKenzie, services $47.00; O. Hooper, services $85.00, expenses $12.45; Geo. Mane, services $15.00; Chas. Cook, services $40.00, expenses $0.80; C. T. Oliver, Jr., services $236.00, expenses $25.80; D. W. Armstrong, services $5.00; F. A. Neary, services $280.00, expenses $42.50; P. D. Code, services $280.00, expenses $35.65; Martin Judge, services $40.00; J. D. Silverthew, services $14.00, expenses $1.71; G. Hague, services $68.00; W. J. Kelly, services $199.00, expenses $3.75; S. G. Whitney, services $52.00, expenses $6.65; C. F. Schneider, services $148.00, expenses $9.30; L. R. Mower, services $34.00, expenses $26.50; G. L. Doolittle, services $26.00, expenses $7.10; W. A. Conneau, services $25.00, expenses $2.20; E. S. Newsome, services $125.00; J. M. Creighton, services $615.00, expenses $200.00; H. Beasly, services $175.00; L. J. Cass, services $155.00; L. Murphy, services $230.00; Ed. Hornback, services $71.00; E. M. ———, services $435.00, expenses $44.80; P. Berr, services $36.00; S. J. Rohan, services $70.00; Geo. Yearaner, services $237.50, expenses $11.60; E. Vetisarator, services $63.00; F. C. Boden, services $150.00; T. C. McGiff, services $12.00; H. J. Loventzen, services $680.00, expenses $471.25; A. H. Barr, services $748.00, expenses $2.00; P. M. McGee, expenses $100.50; N. Komgold, services $525.00, expenses $37.35; E. Gensler, services $15.00, W. J. Otts, services $510.00, expenses $423.85; J. H. Dewey, services $30.00, expenses $6.75; W. C. Knox, services $180.00; M. F. ———, services $1,162.50, expenses

$363.00; J. M. Kelly, services $35.00; R. H. Schouatt, services $161.00, expenses $2.25; D. S. Hutchins, services $80.00, expenses $40.45; Chas. Goff, services $127.15; C. P. Morey, Jr., services $10.00; S. F. ————, services $95; Jesse A. Gahans, services $30.00; A. Setrakian, services $12.00, expenses $14.50; E. E. Kam, services $10.00; J. Walsh, services $25.00. Total services, $70,572.65; expenses, $27,277.35.

Extra Salaries: O. F. Holmes, $25.00; S. S. Simon, $5.00; O. F. Holmes, $48.25; W. J. Flynn and 2 assts., $73.00; Wyman, $20.00; Steffen, $20.00; T. Lonergan, $50.00; T. Lonergan, $50.00; T. Lonergan, $50.00; Cullen-Watchman, $28.00; A. Fromberg, $8.00; G. H. Knox, $5.00; A. B. Lycaw, $48.80; W. J. Flynn, $50.00; securing information at Roys, $5.50; D. M. Duffy, $104.50; C. A. Sage, $30.20; B. Bergen, $20.80; P. Callender, $25.00; P. Callender, $2.00; J. C. Brown, $30.00; D. W. Armstrong, $10.00; D. W. Armstrong, $25.00; D. E. Scales, $5.00; Bob Ellis, $15.00; D. W. Armstrong, $1.00; S. Hitchcock, $1.00; D. Wilkie, $25.00. Total, $778.55.

ITEMS FRANCIS J. HENEY ACCOUNT.

—

Rent of Office: $3,186.25.

Office Expenses: Water, light, heat (repairs gas fixtures, $4.88; purity water, $22.75; Stafford & Co., $297.93; S. F. G. & E. Co., $209.59; gas regulator, $4.76; Gas Appliance Co., $18.00; gas mantels, $3.00; Bush & Lind, $17.00); stationery (E. H. Wobber & Co., et al., $314.90; numbering machine, $5.00; I. Upham Co., $97.23; Brown & Power, $1.00; Schmidt L. & L. Co., $6.00; Badescu Prtg. Co., $2.50); typewriter, rental and supplies (Remington T. W. Co., $139.80; Smith Premier, T. W., $8.00; Typewritorium, $7.50); newspapers, $126.15; janitor supplies (scavenger, $16.59; towels, $26.44; C. Brown & Sons, $19.80; J. H. Reardon, $2.40; W. E. Johnson, $3.35; Greenblatt & Co., $1.80; Newman & Levinson, $2.55; Brittain & Co., $19.00; O'Connor, Moffatt, $3.00; W. T. Wiley, $3.00; H. G. Root, $14.33; S. P. Co., $1.33; carpet-cleaning, $7.55; Hill & Co., $18.50); sundries, C. P. Stanton et al., $85.14; glazing, $11.25. Total, $1,522.02.

Private Exchange, Telephone and Operator: $1,949.22.

Telegrams: $316.82.

Postage and Messenger Service: $280.26.

Traveling Expenses: $118.45.

Office Salaries: J. H. Reardon, $1,050.00; W. E. Johnson, $1,650.00; Miss O. O. McShane, $1,934.66; Mrs. Smith, $806.25; Mrs. L. E. Russell, $2,085.00; C. H. Stanton, $377.51;

janitress, $156.25; voucher No. 1, Jany. 31, 1907; no detail, $625.00. Total, $8,684.67.

Office Furniture: J. Behrn & Co., $15.75; Fuller Desk Co., $27.00; Rucker Desk Co., $142.25; J. Breuner Co., $28.50; O'Connor, Moffatt, $91.65; Goodyear Rubber Co., $3.50; Sloane & Co., $52.37; G. Lipman, $7.50; Bush & Lind, $27.89; C. Brown & Sons, $6.05; shelving $10.00; Jewel Gas Appliance Co., $21.04. Total, $433.50.

Auto and Carriage Hire: United Carriage Co., $100.25; Pacific Garage, $100.00; Auto Livery, $70.00; Kelly's, $8.50; Arcade Garage, $5.00; Tom Sawyer, $17.50; J. W. Burke, $3.00; Max Mamlock, $15.00; T. White, $5.00; L. D. Crane, $632.80. Total, $957.05.

Stenographic and Legal Expense: L. Kavanaugh, $1,031.00; T. B. Elderkin, $83.40; G. W. Smith, $28.00; State of California, $3.50; H. Hernon, $18.10; County Clerk, $6.00; citation for Codes, $0.37; express on briefs, $2.65; F. L. Gauhey, $2.00; F. M. Handy, $1.50; R. B. Treat, $1.75; D. W. Burchard, $200.00; S. Potter, $15.00; notary fees, $2.00; H. Harper, $96.15; C. Bennett, $5.00; A. W. Reynolds, $13.20; W. C. Bristol, $77.15; H. C. Finkler, $6.40; Richards & Carrier, $258.20; Mrs. M. Moore, $10.00; Mr. Webb, $3.00; Mrs. C. Jellison, $5.80; D. Young, expert, $25.00; C. D. Stewart, expert, $189.00; G. W. Reynolds, expert, $63.00. Total, $2,147.37.

Detective Expense: W. J. Burns, $2,416.95; I. Rittenhouse et al., $1,815.66. Total, $4,232.61.